William Conant Church

Ulysses S. Grant and the Period of National Preservation and Reconstruction

William Conant Church

Ulysses S. Grant and the Period of National Preservation and Reconstruction

ISBN/EAN: 9783337214487

Printed in Europe, USA, Canada, Australia, Japan

Cover: Foto ©Suzi / pixelio.de

More available books at **www.hansebooks.com**

ULYSSES S. GRANT

ULYSSES S. GRANT
DURING HIS SECOND TERM AS PRESIDENT.

ULYSSES S. GRANT

AND

THE PERIOD OF NATIONAL PRESERVATION AND RECONSTRUCTION

By
WILLIAM CONANT CHURCH

BREVET LIEUTENANT COLONEL U. S. VOLS.; EDITOR "U. S. ARMY AND NAVY JOURNAL;" AUTHOR OF "THE LIFE OF JOHN ERICSSON," ETC.

GARDEN CITY   NEW YORK
GARDEN CITY PUBLISHING COMPANY
1926

COPYRIGHT, 1897, BY
G. P. PUTNAM'S SONS
Entered at Stationers' Hall, London

PRINTED IN THE UNITED STATES OF AMERICA

CONTENTS.

CHAPTER I.
INTRODUCTORY (1861–1865) 1

CHAPTER II.
BIRTH, ANCESTRY, AND EDUCATION (1822–1843) . 4

CHAPTER III.
FIRST EXPERIENCES AS A SOLDIER—THE WAR WITH MEXICO (1843–1848) 24

CHAPTER IV.
EXPERIENCES OF GARRISON LIFE—FAILURE AS A FARMER AND TRADER (1848–1861) . . 46

CHAPTER V.
FIRST EXPERIENCES AS AN OFFICER OF VOLUNTEERS (JULY AND AUGUST, 1861) . . . 65

CHAPTER VI.

SEIZURE OF PADUCAH—BATTLE OF BELMONT (SEPTEMBER–DECEMBER, 1861) 80

CHAPTER VII.

CAPTURE OF FORTS HENRY AND DONELSON (JANUARY AND FEBRUARY, 1862) 96

CHAPTER VIII.

BATTLE OF SHILOH, OR PITTSBURG LANDING (APRIL 6–7, 1862) 117

CHAPTER IX.

MISSISSIPPI CAMPAIGN—CORINTH AND IUKA (APRIL–OCTOBER, 1862) 137

CHAPTER X.

SIEGE AND SURRENDER OF VICKSBURG (OCTOBER, 1862—JULY, 1863) 152

CHAPTER XI.

INCIDENTS OF THE SIEGE OF VICKSBURG; MISFORTUNE FOLLOWS VICTORY (1863) . . . 177

CHAPTER XII.

RELIEF OF ROSECRANS—BATTLE OF CHATTANOOGA (AUGUST, 1863–FEBRUARY, 1864) . . . 194

CHAPTER XIII.

LIEUTENANT-GENERAL—GENERAL-IN-CHIEF—GENESIS OF A GREAT SOLDIER (MARCH, 1864) . 217

CHAPTER XIV.

CROSSING THE RAPIDAN; BATTLE OF THE WILDERNESS (MAY 4-7, 1864) 238

CHAPTER XV.

FROM THE RAPIDAN TO THE JAMES—CLOSING IN ON RICHMOND—THE SHENANDOAH VALLEY (MAY 4, 1864–MARCH, 1865) 259

CHAPTER XVI.

CAMPAIGNS OF SHERMAN AND THOMAS—OVERTURES FOR PEACE (MAY, 1864–FEBRUARY, 1865) . 284

CHAPTER XVII.

FINAL CAMPAIGN—SURRENDER OF LEE'S ARMY (MARCH–APRIL, 1865) 305

CHAPTER XVIII.

COLLAPSE OF THE CONFEDERACY—MUSTERING OUT (APRIL–MAY, 1865) 326

CHAPTER XIX.

CHIEF CITIZEN OF THE REPUBLIC—HIS PERPLEXITIES—SECRETARY OF WAR (1865–1868) . 341

CHAPTER XX.

PRESIDENT OF THE UNITED STATES—THE CABINET—REFORM IN THE CIVIL SERVICE—HOSTILITY OF SENATOR SUMNER (1868–1872) . . . 361

CHAPTER XXI.

FOREIGN RELATIONS—TREATY OF WASHINGTON—NEGRO ENFRANCHISEMENT—RE-ELECTION (1870–1873) 382

CHAPTER XXII.

SECOND TERM—FINANCIAL REFORM—RECONSTRUC-
TION COMPLETED—THIRD-TERM CONTROVERSY
—ELECTION OF HAYES (1873–1876) . . 402

CHAPTER XXIII.

TWO YEARS OF TRAVEL — HONOURS RECEIVED
ABROAD (MARCH, 1877–SEPTEMBER, 1879) . 423

CHAPTER XXIV.

"FORTUNE'S SHARPE ADVERSITE"—THE END (1880–
1885) 441

INDEX 457

ULYSSES S. GRANT.

CHAPTER I.

INTRODUCTORY.

1861–1865.

URING four years of civil strife, from 1861 to 1865, more than three millions of Americans—North and South—wore the uniform of the soldier, and in over twenty-two hundred and fifty recorded battles and skirmishes nearly half a million suffered wounds or death. Theories of peace, founded upon a government by the people, have not saved us from contributing our full share to the battle roll of the century.

For this loss we find compensation in the fact that these years of conflict, of suffering, and of death, formed an heroic period in American history. Individual selfishness was largely absorbed in the larger self-interest of State and Country. The young men of America (the average age of the soldier being twenty-five years) received in this experience a schooling in endurance and self-control such as a lifetime of routine could not have secured for them. The spirit of heroism and self-sacrifice was the transforming genius of the time. Under its influence, we, as a nation, put away childish things. Petulance, and nervous dread of foreign criticism, gave place to the calm confidence of strength, and with the applause of the world came comparative indifference to the world's approval. The United States, for the first time in its history, was universally recognised as something more than a geographical expression.

It is natural to seek as the hero of each historic movement some man who, more than any other, represents the spirit of his time. However opinions may differ as to the relative merits in a strictly military sense of the men who led our troops to battle, few will dispute the fact that the chief representative of the Union armies was Ulysses Simpson Grant. As was said by General Sherman, his principal competitor for the first place: " Each epoch creates its own agents, and General Grant more nearly than any other man impersonated the American character of 1861–65. He will stand, therefore, as the typical hero of the great Civil War of America of the nineteenth century."

To the success of Grant, and hence to his fame, so many contributed that it is impossible to assign to each his due measure of recognition, or to do more than present the result of their united efforts, as it appears in this story of the Great Leader. No man understood better than did General Grant his indebtedness to others; no one could be more ready to acknowledge it than was he. "If there is any quality for which General Grant is particularly characterised," said his comrade Burnside, "it is that of magnanimity. He is one of the most magnanimous men I ever knew. He is entirely unambitious and unselfish."

How it happened that a man so free from the passions supposed to dominate the soldier succeeded in the great game of war, where so many others failed, it is my purpose to show. If he could not have accomplished what he did without the help of many, it is equally true that their united efforts would have fallen short of a successful result except through his direction. His was the brain that so co-ordinated the action of the numberless organisations and individuals forming the great Armies of the Republic, that they advanced in triumph to the end.

CHAPTER II.

BIRTH, ANCESTRY, AND EDUCATION.

1822–1843.

THE Valley of the Ohio River early attracted the attention of the soldiers of the Revolution, and especially of Washington, whose youthful experiences as a surveyor had made him familiar with the beauty and the natural resources of that region. "If driven from the Atlantic seaboard," he once said to his officers, "we will retire to the Valley of the Ohio, and there we shall be free." Many discharged soldiers settled in Ohio after the War of Independence, and Lafayette, when he visited that State in 1825, said of these pioneers: "I know them well. I saw them fight the battles of their country at Long Island, Brandywine, Yorktown, and many other places. They were the bravest of the brave. Better men never lived."

One of the Revolutionary soldiers who moved to the Connecticut Reserve in Ohio in 1800 was Noah Grant. He was the father of Jesse Root Grant, and the eldest son of Jesse was Hiram Ulysses Grant, born at Point Pleasant, Clermont County, Ohio, April 27, 1822. Noah Grant was born in Tolland, Connecticut, June 20, 1748, and was the sixth in descent from Matthew Grant, the pioneer. Matthew is supposed to have been one of the "West Country" or "Dorchester Men" who came from England to Massachusetts with Winthrop in 1630. He first settled at Dorchester, Massachusetts, and removed to Windsor, Connecticut, in October, 1635, where he was one of the early members of what is now the oldest evangelical church in America, and, except the Southwark church, London, the oldest orthodox Congregational church in the world. Its orthodox influence descended through successive generations of Grants, in which Scriptural names abounded.

The surname of Grant is of great antiquity in Scotland and its earliest history is lost in traditionary uncertainty, but the speculations that associate Matthew Grant with the Scottish clan are much too vague to find a place in authentic history. General Grant could properly claim in his own right the motto borne by the clan Grant: "Stand fast—stand sure," but there is no proof that it pertained to him by the law of inheritance. There is a tradition in the family that they are of Scotch descent, but it is only a tradition.

The death in 1805 of Captain Noah Grant's second wife, the grandmother of Ulysses, left to the bereaved husband the care of seven children. He had not prospered in the world, and he abandoned the struggle to maintain a home for them, going with his two youngest children to live with his son Peter in Maysville, Kentucky. The other children were distributed among families in the neighbourhood of his old home at Deerfield, Ohio. Jesse Root Grant, who was born January 25, 1794, was at this time eleven years old. He was taken care of by George Tod, a native of Connecticut, who served with credit during the War of 1812, and was afterwards an Ohio judge. From Judge Tod and his wife, who lived at Youngstown, Ohio, some twenty miles from Deerfield, Jesse received all the tender care of parents, until he left them to learn a trade with his brother Peter, who owned a tannery in Maysville. He afterwards returned to Deerfield and lived with Owen Brown, the father of John Brown of Ossawatomie.

Jesse Grant's learning in the schools was limited to a year's instruction, but he was a constant reader and a close observer, and he educated himself sufficiently to obtain local reputation as a newspaper contributor and a poet, and also as a village debater and a very active man in politics. He was distinguished by great physical and mental activity, was somewhat eccentric, and had a fine presence, being only a little short of six feet in height. In June 24, 1821, he married Hannah, the daughter of John Simpson, a Pennsylvania farmer who, after her birth, moved to Clermont County, Ohio, from Montgomery County, Pennsylvania.

Mrs. Grant is described as comely, modest, and unselfish; full of good sense; a woman of strong religious convictions, and a devout Methodist. Her ancestors for several generations were Americans, chiefly "solicitous as to their standing in regard to integrity, veracity, and independence." Of Mrs. Grant her husband said: "Her steadiness, firmness, and strength of character have been the stay of the family through life. She was always careful, and most watchful over her children; but never austere, and not opposed to their free participation in innocent amusements." She was a devoted and consistent member of her church, and until the day of his death, Ulysses never ceased to reverence the religion of his mother. From her he derived some of his strongest traits of character: his reticence and self-control; his modesty and self-abnegation; his patience and equanimity. His capacity for expression came from the Grants. His grandfather, Noah, is described as a man of great conversational ability, and his father was much given to speech.

When the first man-child was born to Jesse and Hannah Grant, there was much speculation as to an appropriate name for him. The mother wished to honor her native State by calling him Albert Gallatin. Theodore and Hiram were also proposed, and Mrs. Grant's step-mother, who had been reading Telemachus, favored Ulysses. The character of the Greek warrior as pictured by Fénelon admirably fitted that of the coming hero; "his heart is an unfathomable depth; his secret lies beyond the line of subtlety and fraud; he is the friend of truth; saying nothing that is false, but, when it is necessary, conceding what is true; his wisdom is, as it were, a seal upon his lips, which is never broken but for an important purpose."

The question of a name was finally determined by the decision of the father.

Jesse Grant was an energetic man of business who prospered during most of his life and who was able to give to his family advantages of instruction which he had never himself enjoyed. When he married, at the age of twenty-five, he was considered the most successful man in Ravenna, Ohio, where he then resided. But the disease of new countries, fever and ague, prostrated him, reverses overtook him, and he moved to Point Pleasant, where his eldest son was born during this period of misfortune. The Grant home at that time was in a one-story wooden building with a sloping roof, having a large chimney on the outside, and a hut-like extension called a "lean to" in the rear. The house contained only two small rooms; in one the family slept; in the other they cooked, and ate, and entertained their friends. This cottage was removed to Columbus, Ohio, in 1886, and is there preserved as a relic.

The name of Point Pleasant suggests the character of the region. It was at that time a hamlet with pretensions to metropolitan possibilities because of its beautiful location on the Ohio. The Grant cottage stood at a bend in the river, giving a view up and down its broad stretches, and across to the Kentucky shore.

In 1824, when Ulysses was nearly two years old, his father moved to a more comfortable home in Georgetown, on White Oak Creek, a confluent of the Ohio, and seven miles back from that river in the adjoining county of Brown. Here there was an abundance of the bark required for the tannery he had established at Georgetown. He was once more on the road to prosperity and was able out of the profits of his first year's business to build a modest, two-story brick house, enlarging it as the needs of his family required. Five other children were added to his store: Simpson, Clara, Virginia, Orvil L., and Mary Frances.

In this Ohio hamlet, amid a rude and simple people, Ulysses remained for sixteen years; until he was appointed to West Point in 1839. He is described as being then an ordinary farmer's lad, with no marks of distinction other than those revealed to paternal eyes. He suffered from the malady of the locality—fever and ague—but was otherwise a sturdy youth. After receiving the rudiments of education at a dame's school, he was transferred to the charge of John D. White, a teacher of the old-fashion beech-switch variety—a kindly man but a strict disciplinarian, who compelled his pupils to gather each day, from a wood hard by, the switches consumed in their education. Young Grant was quick to learn but was not of a studious habit, and no doubt had his full share of experiences of the prevailing method of stimulating the brain by counter-irritation. In his fifteenth year, during the winter of 1836-37, he was sent for one term to the Academy at Maysville, Kentucky, across the Ohio, twenty miles from Georgetown. This school was kept by Mr. Richeson, who reports that Ulysses ranked high in his classes, and that his deportment was exceptionally good. In some reminiscences published by Mr.

Richeson in 1879, we are told that young Grant was a member of the Executive Committee of a school society, the "Philomathea," and took part in the school debates. His appreciation of "the importance of order, decision, and constancy" at that early age is supposed to be shown by these two resolutions which, according to the records of the school, were presented by Ulysses Grant in 1837:

"Resolved, That it be considered out of order for any member to speak on the opposite side to that to which he belongs.

"Resolved, That any member who leaves his seat during debate shall be fined not less than 6¼ cents."

It was the custom of the day to require the children even of well-to-do parents to occupy their time out of school in some useful employment. Ulysses had a boy's preference for play, but he was a dutiful lad. He protested, however, so vigorously against being compelled to serve in his father's tannery, that he was finally given the privilege of devoting himself to the farm. His passion for horses made any work in which they were employed a pleasure to him. "He hoed and mowed, and held the plow"; tended the cattle, assisted in sawing wood and hauling it, and occupied himself with the "chores" familiar to farmer lads. His parents, who were kindly and considerate, allowed him full opportunity to engage in boyish sports and the simple pastimes of country life: nutting, berrying, fishing, and hunting in the summer; sleigh-riding and coasting down the steep hills bordering the Ohio River during the winter. Rear Admiral Ammen, of the Navy, who was a boy in

Georgetown at that time, tells of saving Grant to the country by dragging him from the swift current of a swollen stream into which he had fallen, gorgeously arrayed in a Marseilles blouse with red stripes, which shared with its wearer in young Ammen's solicitude.

The precipitous banks of the limestone ledges through which the streams had cut their way in the vicinity of Georgetown, were covered with a dense growth of sugar maple, walnut, and ash; immense sycamores lined the borders of the large streams, and the level lands on the summit of the ridges were covered with superb beech, hickory, and walnut trees fading away into the interminable forests, broken only by little clearings, each surrounding a log house, the home of some pioneer who had hewn a place for himself in the heart of the woods. It was a primitive country, and its rustic influences long affected the character and habits of the tanner's son.

The boy's chief delight was in his father's horses. Numerous stories are told of his skill with them almost from his cradle. He rode upright standing on the horse's back when he was only five years old, and when he was nine would tear along the road at break-neck speed, standing on one foot and holding on by the reins. But he had his misadventures, as when he was landed in the middle of a stream by a vicious horse which objected to crossing it with a boy on his back.

The father's confidence in his son's skill was so complete that he would allow him, when a mere lad, to drive his horses seventy miles away to visit friends.

Returning one day from one of these long journeys, Ulysses traded one of his team for an unbroken colt whose first experience in harness nearly resulted in disaster. The plan of blindfolding the horse adopted by this youth of fifteen showed at once the daring of the coming soldier and his fertility in expedients. His tenacity of purpose was exhibited when he won the prize in the circus for riding the trick mule which had thrown every other boy. His fame as a trainer of horses was such that the farmers came from a long distance to get him to teach their horses to pace.

The father of young Grant found that it was useless to attempt to transform him into a dealer in hides or in any other commodity. He would work industriously, and earned so much money that his savings accumulated to several hundred dollars, but he was never keen at a bargain. It is told that on one occasion his father gave him fifty dollars, and with it permission to buy a horse which the boy coveted, saying at the same time the horse was worth only forty dollars, and should be bought for that price if possible. The ingenuous lad repeated his father's instructions to the horse dealer who promptly discovered that it was impossible to sell that horse at any less price than fifty dollars. Grant tells us in his *Memoirs* that he was eight years old at this time, and that he was so unmercifully ridiculed by his companions for his simplicity that life was made miserable for him. He was destined, later in life, to suffer still more severely from his inability to protect himself against the selfish arts of trade.

The new study of phrenology was attracting much attention in Grant's youth and parents carefully noted the phrenological development of their children for auguries of their future. A travelling phrenologist who examined the head of Ulysses at the age of ten said: "You need not be surprised if you see this boy fill the Presidential chair." No one who heard the prophecy, except the father, took it seriously, and it subjected the son to much raillery from his associates.

He was a self-reliant, honest lad, energetic and industrious, but gave no sign of future greatness. He was gentle and kindly, and popular, especially with young girls, who were secure from rudeness of speech or action when in his company. At sixteen years of age he gave his father notice that he would follow the tanner's business until his majority if it was required of him, but he would leave it as soon as he became his own master. Asked what he would like to do, he answered that he wished to be a planter or "a trader down the river," or to get an education. The Ohio flows into the Mississippi, and the Mississippi into the sea. Up and down the river passed the steamers that opened communication with the outer world, and beyond it lay that great mystery of life, filling the mind of the boy, with dreams of a possible future.

In the winter of 1838-39, when Ulysses was in his seventeenth year, his father wrote to his member of Congress at Washington, the Hon. Thomas L. Hamer, and obtained an appointment to the Military Academy for his son. Grant tells us that he went to West Point in accordance with his father's wishes, and against his own desire. He had a high idea of the requirements of the entrance examination and feared lest he be subjected to the shame of failure like his predecessor, whose father forbade him to return home when he learned the mortifying result of his experience at West Point. Aside from this fear, Ulysses was willing to go to West Point, if for no other reason than because it gave him an opportunity to add further to his reputation as "the best travelled boy in Georgetown." He does not appear to have had any dreams of soldierly ambition, and he shared the misconceptions current in an agricultural community as to the character of the soldier. He was more adventurous than ambitious; industrious, rather than enterprising, and of all careers, that of the warrior was the one for which he was seemingly fitted least. Gentle in speech and manner; without belligerent propensities; anxious to oblige, and unwilling to inflict pain, even on dumb animals; never at any time in his life able to bear with equanimity the sight of blood, or to listen unmoved to the cry of distress—who could believe that "Lys" Grant had in him the stuff to make

> " . . . A soldier fit to stand by Cæsar
> And give direction "?

In asking for young Grant's appointment to the Academy, Congressman Hamer had given his name as Ulysses S. Grant. Having been entered upon the records of the Academy by this name he could not get the War Department to change the record.

Thus Hiram Ulysses Grant became Ulysses Simpson Grant, known to his Academy associates as "Sam Grant." General Sherman tells of seeing, in 1839, when he was a first class man at West Point, "a list of new Cadets containing the name of U. S. Grant. A crowd of lookers-on read 'United States Grant,' 'Uncle Sam Grant,' 'Sam Grant'; and 'Sam Grant' he is to-day in the traditions of the corps and the Fourth U. S. Infantry."

A conscientious and industrious boy, Grant found no difficulty in obtaining a good standing at the Military Academy. His chief trouble was with the requirements as to exactitude in dress, for he was never a Beau Brummel. His studies during the four years' course included landscape drawing; topographical and figure drawing; higher mathematics; surveying and calculus; French; algebra; military and civil engineering; pyrotechny; artillery; infantry and cavalry drill; electricity; magnetism; optics; astronomy; chemistry; trigonometry; mineralogy; rhetoric; moral philosophy; and Kent's Commentaries.

Cadet Grant ranked well in most of these studies. In French, however, he dropped next to the foot in the first year, and was only number forty-four in a class of fifty-three the second year. Ethics also troubled him and his best record was twenty-eight in ethics in a class of thirty-nine. His standing in infantry drill was the same, and in artillery drill thirty-five. He was sixteen in engineering, and seventeen in mineralogy and geology. He stood sixteen in mathematics the first year and had risen to ten the second year; the classes in these two years numbering over fifty members.

The total number of cadets in the Academy varied between 270 and 233 in each of the four years, and Grant stood on the Conduct Roll for the several years at 147, 144, 157, 156. In the third year of his course he received one-half of the maximum number of demerits allowed, and a much smaller number in the other years. Demerits are incurred by the slightest departure from a system of artificial regulations, such as leaving a button loose, or shoes unlaced. They are no indication of scholarship, though they help to determine class standing. Grant appeared to the best advantage in the riding hall where he surpassed every other cadet in bold horsemanship. General James B. Fry, who visited the hall one day when he was a candidate for admission to the Academy, tells this story:

"When the regular services were completed, the class, still mounted, was formed in a line through the centre of the hall. The riding-master placed the leaping-bar higher than a man's head, and called out 'Cadet Grant!' A clean-faced, slender, blue-eyed young fellow, weighing about one hundred and twenty pounds, dashed from the ranks on a powerfully built chestnut-sorrel horse and galloped down the opposite side of the hall. As he turned at the farther end and came into the stretch across which the bar was placed, the horse increased his pace, and, measuring his strides for the great leap before him, bounded into the air and cleared the bar, carrying his rider as if man and beast had been welded together. The spectators were breathless.

"'Very well done, sir!' growled old Herschberger, the riding-master, and the class was dismissed and disappeared; but 'Cadet Grant' remained a living image in my memory.

"A few months before graduation one of Grant's classmates, James A. Hardie, said to his friend and instructor: 'Well, sir, if a great emergency arises in this country during our lifetime Sam Grant will be the man to meet it.' If I had heard Hardie's prediction I doubt not I should have believed it, for I thought the young man who could perform the feat of horsemanship, and who wore a sword could do anything."

A leap of five feet, six and one-half inches, made by Cadet Grant on Old York, a horse that no one else dared ride, still holds the record at West Point for high jumping. To a companion who said, "Sam, that horse will kill you some day," Ulysses replied: "Well, I can die but once."

Grant is described at this time as being cheerful, even-tempered, amiable, good-natured, and too tender-hearted to enjoy the rough fun of the Academy at the expense of the latest comers known as "plebes." He gave abundant evidence of ability, but he did not respond so readily as some others to the artificial standards of the cadet education, and he never enjoyed those advantages of deportment and aristocratic pretension that favoured other men of lesser capacity. According to his classmate Coppée, he was "a plain, common-sense, straightforward youth; quiet, rather of the old head on young shoulders order; shunning notoriety; quite contented, while others were grumbling; taking to his military duties in a very business-like manner; not a prominent man in the corps, but respected by all and very popular with his friends. He exhibited but little enthusiasm in anything." Though too good tempered to be easily betrayed into a quarrel, it is told of him that when an undersized cadet he was compelled to take a beating from some larger cadet. He went into training and tried it again with the same result. A third time he failed, but in his fourth fight with the same youth some months later he was the victor and gave his antagonist an illustration of the maxim that perseverance conquers all things.

Professor Mahan, his teacher in engineering, says:

"Grant is remembered at his alma mater as having a cheery, and at the same time firm aspect and a prompt, decided manner. His class-standing was among that grade which has given to the line of the army some of its most valuable officers, like Lyon, Reynolds, Sedgwick, etc. Unlike Lee, subsequently to graduating, he had none of the aids toward distinction which social position in private life and nearness to the commanding general in military life afford. He was what we termed a first section man in all his scientific studies; that is, one who accomplishes the full course. He always showed himself a clear thinker and a steady worker. He belonged to the class of compactly strong men who went at their task at once, and kept at it until they had finished; never being seen, like the slack-twisted class, yawning, lolling on their elbows over their work, and looking as if just ready to sink down from mental inanity. Grant's round, cheery, boyish face, though marked with character and quiet manner, gave no evidence of what he has since shown he possesses. His mental machine was of the powerful, low pressure class, which condenses its own steam and consumes its own smoke; and which pushes steadily forward and drives all obstacles before it."

Professor Davies is reported as saying the night after Grant's graduation: "I tell you that the smartest man in the class is little Grant." Early in the war, General Ewell of the Confederate Service, who was with Grant at the Academy, said: "There is one West Pointer, I mean in Missouri, whom I hope the Northern people will not find out. I mean Sam Grant. I knew him well at the Academy, and in Mexico. I should fear him more than any of their officers I have yet heard of. He is not a man of genius, but he is clear-headed, quick, and daring."

Among Cadet Grant's accomplishments were drawing and painting. Some very creditable illustrations of his work are still in existence. One picture is in the possession of the Borie family, of Philadelphia, and another belongs to Mr. W. E. Rothery, a merchant of Camden, N. J. A journey with the mother of Mr. Rothery (née Miss Low) was one of the romances of Grant's cadet days. The picture was given in return for a ring won by Grant in a wager that Miss Low would be married by the time he graduated.

Sitting over his camp-fire in front of Petersburg one night, General Grant told the writer of this biography that his cadet days were filled with dreams of a young lady he intended to marry as soon as he graduated, and his one thought at West Point was of her. The romance ended as do so many others, for the young woman did not become Mrs. Grant. In the recollection of Mrs. Rothery, Cadet Grant was a fine looking, smooth-faced young man, with clear eyes and good features; and in the eyes of an impressionable young woman, he was chiefly attractive on account of "his splendid carriage and soldierly bearing." Somewhat bashful and reserved, he was never awkward, lacking neither a subject of conversation nor readiness of speech. Polite literature was a fruitful theme of conversation between the young people, for Grant at this time was a great lover of good novels, devouring those of Bulwer, Cooper, Marryat, Scott, Lever, Irving, and others. "His most charming characteristic, however, was his extreme courtesy; he was full of delicate and kind attentions, not less to his aged grandmother, than to the most fascinating young woman." Another who knew him at that time says:

"I remember when he made his first visit home after a two years' stay at West Point. His cadet suit, white pants, blue jacket, gilt buttons and cloth cap, made quite an impression on the youth at that time. The impression his reception by the family made upon my mind has always been fresh. He came to my native town, which was the end of the stage route and the nearest point to his home. I drove him home, and expected to see, after so long an absence, a warm greeting; but it was simply, 'How are you, my son?' and 'How are you, brother?' Ulysses was entirely cool and without emotion, the same trait which characterized the General in his after life."

During his cadet days Grant and some of his chums, twelve in all, formed the T. I. O.—or twelve in one—Society, and each wore a ring having these mystic letters engraved upon it. This ring was to be kept until marriage and then given to the owner's wife.

During the last six months of his term at the Military Academy he suffered severely from a cough. This greatly alarmed his family, as two of his father's brothers had died of consumption. In spite of the fact that his preparations for the closing examination were made under discouraging circumstances, he acquitted himself with credit. He had had the honour of serving during his third year as one of the sergeants of the battalion into which the corps of cadets is organised. He was not able to hold this position, and in his final year at the Academy dropped back into the position of private.

Finally, came that greatest of all days to the graduate—when he doffs the cadet gray for the army blue, and assumes the full dignity of an officer in the Army of the United States. Cadet Grant's standing was twenty-one in a list of thirty-nine. Of those above him who served in the Civil War were Franklin and Raynolds of the Engineers; Quinby, Peck, Reynolds, Hardie, and Clarke of the Artillery, and Augur of the Infantry. One of his classmates, Deshon, became a Catholic Priest; three others joined the Confederate Army, and two were cashiered. Grant's ambition was to enter the cavalry, but as no one in his class was assigned to that corps in the Army, he had no cause to complain when on his graduation, July 1, 1843, he was promoted to Brevet Second Lieutenant in the 4th Infantry, a regiment organised in 1796.

When Grant left the Military Academy he was much better equipped for the struggle of life than are most American youths. He had received what was equivalent in mental training to a university education, and had had a physical discipline far beyond anything known to the college youth at that time. In addition to his military training he had acquired an excellent knowledge of the history of his own country; he had an unusual mastery of mathematical principles, he was a good English scholar, and had been carefully drilled into habits of order and systematic work. His experience at the Academy had not developed in him a taste for military life, and he was so anxious to keep out of the Army, if he honourably could, that he viewed with secret satisfaction the progress of a bill introduced into Congress at that time, to abolish the Military Academy.

In his *Memoirs*, Grant tells us of his experience one day when he was drawn up in line with the corps of cadets to be reviewed by the majestic General Scott, in showy uniform. He says: "I could never resemble him in appearance, but I believe I did have a presentiment for the moment that some day I should occupy his place on review—although I had no intention then of remaining in the Army."

How unlike he was to Scott was shown when this presentiment was fulfilled twenty-three years later, and as General of the Army (a grade beyond that held by Scott) he appeared in the section room of the Academy "leaning on the arm of the superintendent, shrinking and half drawing back, as with almost feminine timidity depicted on his face, he was led forward to be presented to his old professors."

At the time Grant was graduated from the Academy, he was in doubt whether he should be appointed to the Infantry or Dragoons, and delayed ordering his uniform; thus it happened that when he was temporarily assigned to duty with the Fourth Infantry, he was for several weeks deprived of the enjoyment of appearing in his full glory as an officer of the Army. No uniform ever shines so resplendently in the eyes of an officer and his friends as the one he first wears. Even the modest Grant felt the elation proper to the occasion, but he was awakened by the rude remarks of street urchins to the painful realisation of the fact that, even with the aid of a uniform, a rather undersized youth, weighing but one hundred and seventeen pounds, could not impress the imagination of the populace as did the magnificent proportions of the gigantic Scott.

CHAPTER III.

FIRST EXPERIENCES AS A SOLDIER—THE WAR WITH MEXICO.

1843-1848.

THE two years succeeding Grant's graduation from the Military Academy were occupied with the routine of life in garrison and camp. His regiment, the Fourth Infantry, was stationed at Jefferson Barracks, the largest military post in the West. It is situated on a high bluff on the west bank of the Mississippi River, ten miles below St. Louis.

At the conclusion of his graduation furlough, Brevet Second Lieutenant Grant joined his company, and entered upon his first experiences of regimental life, under the tutelage of that fine old soldier, Stephen W. Kearny, a veteran of the War of 1812. Colonel Kearny was a rigid disciplinarian, but he was also a liberal-minded gentleman; and he gave our young soldier a pleasant impression of army life, which his experiences at such an agreeable post were adapted to deepen. There were, however, other sentiments stirring in the heart of the youth than ambition for military distinction. Large army posts are social centres. The officers are usually good dancers: they understand the art of entertaining, and they and their families have leisure and taste for something besides the dull routine of life. Thus are presented all the conditions to create a charming social circle.

Jefferson Barracks was no exception to this rule. The entertainments there drew visitors from St. Louis and the country around. Among these visitors was a girl of sixteen, daughter of Colonel Dent, a business man of St. Louis, and one of the old style of Southern planters in the days of slavery. Colonel Dent was the father of Frederick T. Dent, Grant's room-mate at the Military Academy, and Julia was the eldest of Frederick's three sisters. Ulysses had frequent opportunities for meeting her at the garrison hops and balls, and, as the nearest friend of her brother, he was soon on a familiar footing. Acquaintance ripened into friendship, and friendship grew into a warmer sentiment, until the young woman was obliged to bear the teasing of the Army wits, who would inquire solicitously after her "little lieutenant with the big epaulets."

Both of the young people were excellent equestrians, and they soon found abundant excuse for long rides in the surrounding country. Miss Dent had a love of botany, and flowers must be sought in the loneliest paths of the woods. Still more to the point, the quick wit and prompt action of her lover had rescued her from following her horse when the treacherous earth on the bank of the flooded Mississippi River gave way under the animal and precipitated it into the river. Thus sentiment grew apace between Miss Dent and the Lieutenant.

Contest over the annexation of Texas was developing into war, and the crisis came in the affairs of love when orders were issued to send the Fourth Infantry to Fort Jessup, Louisiana. These orders were received at Jefferson Barracks while Grant was enjoying a twenty-days' leave on a visit to his family in Ohio, and was beyond the reach of commands. Returning, he found that his regiment would be detained at Fort Jessup and took advantage of a few days' extension of his leave to visit the Dent homestead,—an unpretentious country house pleasantly situated on the Gravois Road, a few miles from the barracks. The impetuous lover was nearly drowned in crossing a swollen stream, and had to urge his suit in ill-fitting garments, borrowed from his classmate Dent; but he was received with favour, and when he returned to his quarters, it was with the light heart of an accepted suitor. Another twenty-days' leave in May, 1845, gave him opportunity to secure the consent of the parents. Colonel Dent's business training did not dispose him to look with favour upon a subaltern with an income of $779 a year. The mother was kindlier disposed, and, with a woman's keener discernment of character, she declared that her daughter's lover had a noble heart, and would some day attain to greatness.

Grant's plans for the future contemplated an appointment as Assistant Professor of the Military

Academy; and a letter received from Professor Church, professor of mathematics, satisfied him that he would have received this appointment if war with Mexico had not changed his purpose. At the Academy he would have had an opportunity to indulge his taste for domestic life, which always had more charm for him than military service. As it was, more than four years were destined to elapse between the engagement and the marriage.

Previous to 1836, Texas was a part of the Republic of Mexico, and it was claimed by that country for ten years longer. The question of its annexation to the United States was during this period a disturbing element in our politics. The Southern States favoured annexation, as it increased their political importance by extending the area of slavery; and the growing anti-slavery sentiment in the North was opposed to it for this reason, and because annexation would involve a war with Mexico. In March, 1845, Texas was brought into the Union by a joint resolution of Congress. General Zachary Taylor was at that time in command of the First Military Department, which included Western Louisiana, with headquarters at Fort Jessup, Louisiana, twenty-five miles from the Texas boundary-line. Orders were given to concentrate in the vicinity of that post as many as possible of the troops belonging to our little army, which numbered altogether fourteen regiments, with only 5304 men actually on the rolls. The Third and Fourth Infantry and seven companies of Dragoons were soon on the move. The Fourth Infantry was ordered to Grand

Ecore, in the vicinity of Fort Jessup, where it arrived in July, 1844.

Instead of enjoying the summer in domestic felicity amid the cooling breezes of West Point, as he had hoped to do, Lieutenant Grant pitched his lonely tent with his regiment in Western Louisiana. The camp, known as "Camp Salubrity," was located on a high, sandy pine ridge midway between the Red River and the Sabine. The Fourth Infantry remained here for a year, or until July, 1845. There was little to do in camp; and much time was spent in social interchanges with the planters of the Red River country, and the residents of the old towns of Natchitoches and Grand Ecore near by. Young Grant passed most of his time out of doors and on horseback; and his health, which had suffered from his illness at West Point, was fully restored. His next orders took him with his regiment to New Orleans Barracks, in July, 1845. There he remained until September, when the regiment was transferred in sailing-vessels to Corpus Christi, Texas, at the junction of the Nueces River with tide water on the Gulf.

Corpus Christi Bay, on which were located the camps of Taylor's "Army of Occupation," is two hundred miles southwest of Galveston, on the Gulf coast. There was excellent salt-water bathing here, and fish and game abounded. With their usual readiness of resource, the officers were able to find abundant amusement while they were waiting three months for marching orders. They built a theatre, and gained sufficient from public performances to fit themselves out with costumes. Grant took part; and his smooth face, boyish figure, and pleasant voice led to his selection for the part of Desdemona in the play of *Othello*. Whatever his histrionic accomplishments, he did not succeed in exciting the proper emotions in the breast of Othello, Lieutenant Theodoric Porter, brother of David D. Porter who afterwards became admiral; and the Moor insisted that they should send to New Orleans for an actress, who brought with her inspiration for his love-making.

While at Corpus Christi, September 30, 1845, Grant received his promotion to Second Lieutenant, but escaped a transfer to the Seventh Infantry, to which his promotion carried him, by exchanging with an officer of that regiment. He was attached to the company of Captain George A. McCall, who afterwards served under him as a gallant major-general of volunteers.

Time at Corpus Christi was not altogether occupied with amusement. A level and extended plain in the vicinity of the camps enabled the troops to indulge in military exercises on a large scale, and afforded a rare occasion for drilling the various arms of the service together. The concentration of so many different commands gave opportunity for reviving old acquaintance, forming new ties, and bringing the troops into touch with one another preparatory to the serious work before them. It was a valuable experience for a young officer, and Grant took full advantage of it.

On the 8th of March, 1846, General Taylor broke

up his camp at Corpus Christi, and marched one hundred and twenty-five miles farther south, through a low and marshy country, to the mouth of the Rio Grande, locating at Point Isabel, near the north bank of the river opposite to Matamoras. Here he held a critical position in face of an enemy outnumbering him three to one. A movement against Matamoras led to a battle on May 8, 1846, on the spacious plain of Palo Alto. This was followed the next day by the engagement at Resaca de la Palma, or Resaca de Guerriero, four miles from the Rio Grande. These two battles decided the control of the Rio Grande; and May 18, 1846, Taylor crossed that river into Mexico, and occupied Matamoras. Here he remained until July, waiting for the arrival of steamers, and then moved one hundred and fifty miles up the river to Camargo, whence he proposed to operate against Monterey, the largest and most important town in Northern Mexico. The march from Camargo to Monterey was through a dreary desert and under a tropical sun, and was made by night as much as possible to escape the heat. Meanwhile re-enforcements arrived; and when Taylor finally captured Monterey, September 24, 1846, he had 6645 men, more than one-half of them being volunteers. After the surrender of Monterey, the Mexicans withdrew three hundred miles into the interior to San Luis Potosi; and as no attempt was made to follow them, operations were suspended for seven months.

In the marches and battles carrying the army from Corpus Christi, by a roundabout route of four hundred miles, into the enemy's country at Monterey, Grant bore an active and honourable part. He was not a mounted officer, but horses were so cheap at Corpus Christi that he was able to purchase three; and, as they lived off the country, their livery bills were not large. Unfortunately, his stud all ran away one day when they were being led to water; and when his company started on the march from the Rio Grande, he was obliged to trudge along on foot. A judicious expenditure of five dollars soon restored him to the dignity of a mounted officer. The country was new, the experiences were novel, the enemy were in front; and Grant enjoyed this life of adventure, his spirits rising higher as danger drew nearer.

At Palo Alto, Lieutenant Grant had his first experience of battle. He frankly admits that he did not enjoy it, for it is only the heroes of romance who delight in being made a target of. All accounts agree, however, in saying that he acquitted himself as a soldier should, the first time he was under fire. Palo Alto was mainly an artillery fight; but the Fourth Infantry had its full share of killed and wounded, and their hearts thrilled with more than the joy of victory when General Taylor said to them, " Gentlemen, you are veterans!"

At Resaca, Captain McCall was detailed to open the attack; and the command of his company fell to Grant, who led them into battle in face of the waiting army. It is a thrilling moment for the young soldier when he for the first time takes the initiative on the field of battle, and questions with himself whether he will prove equal to the great responsibility. These are moments of moral development that determine character. From the file-closer to the head of the company is the first step.

On the march to Monterey, Grant was detailed as Regimental Quartermaster and Commissary, and as such had charge of the waggons and pack-trains. He understood horses, but now had his first experience with the perversity of the army mule. Not even the annoyance which his mule-teams gave him would tempt him to depart from the rule he followed through life, never to use a profane expletive. If it be " that which cometh out of the man that defileth the man," then Grant was singularly blameless. Whatever his weaknesses, he was pure in thought and pure in speech, and never encouraged the impropriety of others with even tacit approval. It is told that on one occasion when he was in high command, an officer who introduced a doubtful story by saying, " I see there are no ladies present," was silenced by the cutting reply, " There are gentlemen here."

The position of staff officer relieved Grant from the necessity of appearing with his command in battle; but nothing could keep him out of a fight. As he said in a letter, his parents had taught him that the post of danger was the post of duty.

In the attack on Monterey, September 21, 1846, the Adjutant of the Fourth Infantry, Charles Haskins, was killed; and Grant was temporarily detailed to perform his duties, being always thought of when a reliable soldier for an emergency was needed.

By the 23d of September, 1846, Taylor's troops had secured possession of the east end of Monterey, but had still before them the heavy task of driving from the city the Mexicans, who were maintaining a galling fire from under protection of the houses. Ammunition grew scarce in Garland's Brigade; and the General asked if someone would volunteer to run the gauntlet of the sharpshooters, and carry word of his need to the division commander. He declined to give anyone orders to so expose himself.

"Sam" Grant was there, and, almost before the want was known, he was flying on his horse through the bullet-swept streets of Monterey, like Caius Cossus at Lake Regillus—

> "As the wolves of Apennine
> Were all upon his track."

Adjusting himself on his horse in Indian fashion, with one foot on the cantle, and holding to the horse's neck with his arms, he dropped on the side farthest from the enemy, and started the animal at full speed, reaching his destination without being injured, and delivering his orders.

General Wilcox, of the Confederate service, who was in Grant's mess at this time, describes him as " in manners quiet, plain and unobtrusive, of good common sense, with no pretension to genius, or, as I believed at that time, to a high order of talent, but much esteemed among his immediate assembled associates for kindly disposition and many excellent qualities."

But Grant at Monterey gave proof, as did Napoleon in the passage of the bridge of Lodi, that he possessed the genius for war. "The occasion," said Napoleon of Lodi, "furnished an opportunity for stamping, by some bold stroke, the character of my individual actions, and I did not let it escape." Quickness of decision, and resolution in action, with absolute disregard of personal risks, when the occasion calls for it, are essential qualities in war.

Monterey finally surrendered, and the troops remained there in camp for several months. The natives showed a disposition to be friendly; and time passed pleasantly until midwinter, when orders for the march came. Joseph Jefferson at that time belonged to a company of "barn stormers" who were trying to make an honest penny out of the war, and he appeared at Monterey as member of a travelling theatrical company. Grant was from his boyhood an enthusiastic lover of the drama, and especially of American plays. As he seldom missed an opportunity to attend theatrical performances, he was no doubt one of the motley crowd of "soldiers, settlers, gamblers, rag-tag and bob-tail," who, as Jefferson tells us in his autobiography, attended the old Spanish theatre at Monterey, where he played with his band of comedians.

General Winfield Scott, Taylor's senior officer, reached Point Isabel, at the mouth of the Rio Grande, towards the end of December, 1846, assumed command of the Army of Invasion, and withdrew from Taylor a portion of his troops. This led to the transfer of the Fourth Infantry from

Twiggs's division of Taylor's Army, to the division of General William Worth, assembled at the mouth of the Rio Grande for an advance on Vera Cruz.

At the time the Fourth Infantry received their return orders, they had advanced beyond Monterey to Saltillo in Mexico, and were on the eve of the battle of Buena Vista, which was fought just beyond that place. This was the only battle of the Mexican War in which Grant did not take part. Reaching Camargo, on the Rio Grande, after a hot and dusty march of ten days from Saltillo, he embarked with his command in steamboats, and descended the river to a point eighteen or twenty miles above its mouth. Here they went into camp, waiting for the vessels which finally took them to Lobos Island, near Vera Cruz, one hundred and fifty miles south of the Rio Grande. The voyage was a short one; but the men were cooped up for twenty days in a freight steamer before they could land, and their situation in that hot climate was almost unbearable. At Lobos Island they were sent ashore in surf-boats, packed like herrings, and subject to the risk of an assault in this defenceless position. Fortunately the enemy were not sufficiently enterprising to take advantage of their opportunity.

A blockade was established by the Navy, and the Army laid siege to the city, the Fourth Infantry holding one of the most exposed positions in the line of trenches. The siege began March 9th; and on the 28th Vera Cruz surrendered, just one year after Taylor appeared on the Rio Grande opposite Matamoras. It had been a year of stirring events and ripening experience for Grant, and the results of it followed him through life.

On the 13th of April, 1847, began that memorable march from Vera Cruz to the city of Mexico, over the road along which Cortes had led his conquering host more than three hundred years before. To the frost-bitten sons of the North the march was like one through fairyland. Leaving in their rear the stately castle of Vera Cruz and the grand mountains rising near the coast to the lordly height of noble Orizaba, they advanced step by step, until at Pueblo de los Angeles they stood in awe before the " solemn grandeur of the lofty volcanic peaks that bar the great highway north." In the rear of Pueblo appeared Orizaba, the " Mountain of the Stars," the topmost peak of Mexico, rising 18,314 feet above the sea; and in front were Popocatepetl, Ixtaccihuatl, and Malinche—a noble trio of snow-capped hills.

The march was a weary one, with the nipping air upon the heights, through clouds of alkali dust, and at times ankle-deep in mud and water, for this was the season of rain. But what compensation there was for trials and fatigue, in the grand scenery; in the flowers and fruits, excelling in richness and variety those of any other country of equal extent; in the picturesque costumes of the rancheros, and the beauty of the senoritas! Each hour was a delight: it was the romance of war.

At Cerro Gordo, a pass in the mountains sixty miles from Vera Cruz, on April 17-18, 1847, Scott had forced his way through the opposing Mexicans, and made his escape from the deadly *tierra caliente*, where they hoped to confine his army to waste away with disease. Now he was in the cooler and healthy table-lands at Pueblo; and here he remained for nearly three months, drilling his men on a broad plain where 100,000 could manœuvre. On the 9th of August the march was renewed, the men pressing forward in excellent spirits, and full of excitement at the prospect before them. The following day the beautiful valley of the city of Mexico was spread at their feet, and wonder succeeded wonder.

There was still fighting to be done before they could enter in and possess the land. The rocky hill of Chapultepec, with the castle crowning the summit, barred access to the two causeways leading into the city of Mexico through the Belan Gate and the San Cosme " Garita"; a *garita* being a covered post occupied by sentinels at an entrance to the city, and used for the collection of customs dues.

As Scott's little army of 7300 men closed around Mexico, the battle of Contreras was fought, August 19, 1847, the fortified hill with that name being carried in seventeen minutes. Churubusco followed the next day, succeeded three weeks later, on September 8th, by the battle of King's Mills, Molinos del Rey. The scene of this last battle was a large pile of stone buildings near Chapultepec (the hill of the grasshopper). These buildings were used for shelter by the Mexican troops, and the battle was fought under the guns of Chapultepec.

On the 13th of September, 1847, the heights of Chapultepec were carried by a bold assault after a bombardment lasting for many hours. Then came the advance along the causeways leading to the city gates, under a close fire from artillery and from infantry sheltered by breastworks. September 1st, Scott entered the city of Mexico in triumph.

In all of these notable scenes Grant bore an heroic part, and an unusually conspicuous one for so young a soldier. At Cerro Gordo he stood by the side of George B. McClellan, and with the aid of a field-glass directed the fire of a battery commanded by McClellan. At Molinos del Rey he won a brevet which officers most of all covet, that for gallant and meritorious conduct in battle, and he gained another at Chapultepec. The first brevet was that of First Lieutenant, the second that of Captain. Grant had received his promotion to full Lieutenant on the 8th of September, 1847, and he declined the brevet of First Lieutenant, partly for this reason, and partly because the same brevet had, as he thought, been unworthily bestowed on another. "If," he said, " he is entitled to a brevet, I am not."

Grant was with the advance at Molinos del Rey, and with General Worth in the attack on the suburb of San Cosme during the storming of Chapultepec on September 13, 1847. He showed unusual energy, enterprise, and sound military judgment at Chapultepec, where, by a skilful and daring reconnaissance he opened the way for an advance along the San Cosme road. He took possession of a church, and, dragging a howitzer up to the steeple with the aid of his men, created great confusion among the enemy by dropping shots among them from this elevation. This achievement secured from General Worth attention such as a general officer seldom gives to a subaltern. He sent Lieutenant John C. Pemberton of his staff, who became better acquainted with Grant at Vicksburg, to express to the young officer the great satisfaction he felt at the service rendered.

Grant was one of only two line officers mentioned by General Garland in his report upon the action of his brigade at Chapultepec. "I must not omit," he said, "to call attention to Lieutenant Grant, Fourth Infantry, who acquitted himself most nobly upon several occasions under my own observation."

Major Francis Lee, commanding the Fourth Infantry, reported that "Second Lieutenant Grant behaved with distinguished gallantry on the 13th and 14th." Captain Horace Brooks, Second Artillery, also spoke of the active part taken by Grant in carrying, "after an obstinate resistance, a strong field-work, turning the enemy's right." He was one of five officers in his regiment who participated in all the battles of the war except Buena Vista, and his regiment suffered a heavier loss than any other. He himself escaped without a scratch.

After the capture of Chapultepec, Grant had occasion to visit Colonel Howard, who was in command of the castle, and who occupied quarters in the corridors, reached by a long, steep flight of stone stairs. Finding no hitching-post outside, the lieutenant spurred his horse down these steps, and tied him in front of Howard's quarters. The apparition of the horse in such an unheard-of place was sufficiently astonishing; but the Colonel was still more astonished when he saw him climbing the steps, on his return, like a cat, with his venturesome rider on his back.

Grant indulges in some criticisms in his *Memoirs* upon the conduct of the war in Mexico; but he tells us at the same time what his large experience had taught him: first, "that things will seem plainer after events have occurred; second, that the most confident critics are those who know least about the matter criticised."

The Mexicans were badly commanded, and there was very little hard fighting during that war, at least nothing to be compared with what was seen afterwards in our Civil War. "I do not suppose," said Grant, "any war was ever fought with reference to which so many romances were invented as the war with Mexico."

Like most officers of our Army at that time, Grant was opposed to the annexation of Texas, and believed that the war with Mexico was political in its origin, and without proper justification. He thought that our desire for Mexican territory might have been satisfied by peaceable means; and that the Southern Rebellion, coming fourteen years later, was the direct result of the invasion of Mexico, and a just retribution for a war of spoliation. This opinion he held through life; and at a later period he was able to give effective expression to his interest in Mexico, and to show his appreciation of the wrong she had suffered at our hands in being made the victim of the desire which existed at that time for the extension of slave territory.

As the result of the war with Mexico, we secured undisturbed possession of a territory equal in extent to seventeen States of the size of New York. This territory includes California, New Mexico, Arizona, Western Colorado, Utah, and Nevada, with their immense stores of mineral and agricultural wealth.

The winter of 1847-48 was a quiet one for the Army; but the Quartermaster and Commissary of the Fourth Infantry had quite enough to do in clothing and feeding a regiment, looking after their regimental fund, and providing them with amusement. To respond with cheerfulness and alacrity to the daily and hourly demands of a garrison of idle men is a severe test of any one's ability and temper. Our young Quartermaster was faithful, industrious, and energetic; but he was not a man of method, and, as he tells us, never could find a place for a paper except in his pocket or in the hands of a clerk. Still, he was able to give such a good account of his service, that he largely increased the regimental fund, on which troops depend for their luxuries, having had the enterprise to hire a baker in Mexico, and to contract with the chief commissary of the Army, on behalf of his regiment, to furnish him with a large amount of hard bread.

He had made every effort to escape quartermaster's duty, for he wished to be always in the fighting line; and when he was told that his services could not be spared, he still insisted upon his right to go into battle with his company. In spite of the fact that he was compelled to do double duty, he made a record for himself as a regimental quartermaster second to that of no other officer. He met with a misfortune, however, for which he was in no way responsible, and which is explained in the following official statement:

CAMP NEAR JALAPA, MEXICO.

Statement.

About the 6th of June, at Tucabaya, Mexico, I took to Captain Gore's room the sum of $1000, quartermaster's funds, to be locked up in his trunk for safe keeping, my own chest having previously had the lock broken. I also deemed it safer to have public money in the room of some officer who did not disburse public funds, because they would be less likely to be suspected of having any considerable amount about them. On the night of the 16th of June, 1848, as shown by the accompanying affidavits, the trunk containing these funds was stolen from the tent of Captain Gore while he and Lieutenant De Russy, Fourth Infantry, were both sleeping in the tent.

(Signed) U. S. GRANT,
First Lieutenant, Fourth Infantry,
Regimental Quartermaster.

Sworn to before me this 27th day of June, 1848, at camp near Jalapa, Mexico.

(Signed) H. D. WALLEN,
First Lieutenant, Fourth Infantry.

Some years afterwards a bill was introduced into Congress to relieve Grant from the responsibility for the lost funds. A board appointed at the time, at his request, to inquire into the matter, completely exonerated him from all blame, declaring, after a thorough investigation, that he had taken every precaution in his power to protect the funds of the Government. Though he was not responsible for this loss, Grant, when he was able to do so, made it good to the Treasury.

While in the city of Mexico, after its capture, Grant joined with other officers in forming the Aztec Club. Its first President was Franklin Pierce; and of the one hundred and forty-nine original members, nearly all bore a distinguished part in the Civil War, including McClellan, Hooker, Porter, Kearny, Hatch, and Brannan on the one side, and Lee, Johnston, Beauregard, Hardee, Ewell, and Magruder on the other side.

In the spring of 1848 Grant visited Popocatepetl with a party of officers, and made the laborious ascent of that difficult peak until he could look into its rumbling bowels through the crater. He also attended a Spanish bull-fight; but he was too fond of horses and too tender-hearted to witness another such exhibition. When in Madrid many years later, he positively refused to take part in the Spanish national pastime. At Corpus Christi, Grant spent so much time in studying a map of Mexico he had obtained at New Orleans, and in gathering data concerning the topography of that country from an acquaintance who was thoroughly familiar with it, that he was constantly called upon by his superiors for information they had not been able to obtain. At Matamoras he secured a much more valuable map, which had been abandoned by a high officer of the Mexican Army in his flight, and reconstructed his other map from it, surrendering the original to General Scott after the capture of Vera Cruz. General Taylor, Captain Robert E. Lee, of the engineers, other staff officers, and the division and brigade commanders were also dependent upon this enterprising and studious second lieutenant for much valuable information concerning the country they were preparing to invade.

Major Hamer, who, when a member of Congress, had secured Grant's appointment to the Military Academy, in a letter from Camargo said:

"I have found in Lieutenant Grant a most remarkable and valuable young soldier. I anticipate for him a brilliant future, if he should have an opportunity to display his powers when they mature. Young as he is, he has been of great value and service to me. To-day, after being freed from the duty of wrestling with the problem of reducing a train of refractory mules and their drivers to submissive order, we rode into the country several miles, and, taking our position upon an elevated mound, he explained to me many army evolutions; and supposing ourselves to be generals commanding opposite armies, and a battle to be in progress, he explained supposititious manœuvres of the opposing forces in a most instructive way; and when I thought his imaginary force had my army routed, he suddenly suggested a strategic move for my forces which crowned them with triumphant victory, and himself with defeat, and he ended by gracefully offering to surrender his sword! Of course, Lieutenant Grant is too young for command, but his capacity for future military usefulness is undoubted."

For these facts and Major Hamer's letter, I am indebted to an interesting series of articles on "Grant's Life in the West and his Mississippi Valley Campaign," by Colonel John W. Emerson, appearing in the *Midland Monthly* while this volume is going through the press. Colonel Emerson also publishes this interesting correspondence:

"I respectfully protest against being assigned to a duty which removes me from sharing in the dangers and honors of service with my company at the front, and respectfully ask to be permitted to resume my place in line. Respectfully submitted,

"U. S. GRANT, 2d Lt. 4th Inft."

" Lt. Grant is respectfully informed that his protest cannot be considered.

" Lt. Grant was assigned to duty as Quartermaster and Commissary because of his observed ability, skill, and persistency in the line of duty. The commanding officer is confident that Lt. Grant can best serve his country in present emergencies under this assignment. Lt. Grant will continue to perform the assigned duties.

"LT.-COL. GARLAND, 4th Inft. Comdg. Brigade."

Later on Grant made another attempt to escape staff duty, and wrote this indorsement on the paper in which his request was denied:

"I should be permitted to resign the position of Quartermaster and Commissary. Why should I be required to resign my position in the Army in order to escape this duty? I *must* and *will* accompany my regiment in battle, and I am amenable to court-martial should any loss occur to the public property in my charge by reason of my absence while in action."

CHAPTER IV.

EXPERIENCES OF GARRISON LIFE—FAILURE AS A FARMER AND TRADER.

1848–1861.

THE war with Mexico was ended by the signing of the treaty of Guadalupe Hidalgo, February 2, 1848. News of the ratification of this treaty reached Mexico in June, and on the 12th of that month the Army of Occupation started on their return to the United States. Grant's regiment was sent to Pascagoula, Mississippi, to spend the summer. He promptly obtained a leave of absence, and went to St. Louis to see what Miss Dent had to say on the subject of marriage. The wedding was fixed for the 27th of August, 1848; and after a brief visit with his bride to his parents and relatives in Ohio, Grant joined his post at Sackett's Harbour, New York.* His rank at that time

---

* The following appears in a manuscript history of Sackett's Harbour, written by Colonel Edw. Vollum, M.D., U.S.A., and now on file at that post: "1st Lieut. U. S. Grant, 4th U. S. Inf., served at this place from some time in 1849 to 1852 as the Quartermaster of

was First Lieutenant, and his yearly pay about $1000, including rations and forage. He was a Captain by brevet only. In April, 1849, he was ordered to Fort Wayne, Detroit, Michigan, where he remained for two years.

The Fourth Infantry was scattered from Fort Howard, Green Bay, Wisconsin, to Plattsburg Barracks, New York. Grant was Regimental Quartermaster, and the fact that he still held this responsible position shows that his unfortunate loss of money in Mexico had left no stain upon his record. He was greatly respected and esteemed by all of his brother officers, especially by those who had served with him in the Mexican War, with a single exception: the Lieutenant-Colonel of the Fourth Infantry was not favourably inclined towards him. The Colonel being granted an indefinite leave of absence, the Lieutenant-Colonel assumed command, and made known his desire to select another quartermaster. He soon found, however, that the other officers of the regiment strongly objected to a change, and concluded that it was not wise to make Grant the victim of his hostility.

In May, 1852, the Fourth Infantry was ordered to rendezvous at Fort Columbus, Governor's Island,

---

his regiment. He is remembered by the citizens hereabouts as a diffident, plain-mannered gentleman, but little disposed to enter into conversation, but acute and sound when his spirit moved him that way. Some of his first appointments after his elevation to the Presidency of the U. S. were made among his old friends at this place. He was fond of good horses, and rather peculiar for his hatred of the garrison band music, from the sound of which he always escaped whenever he could."

New York Harbour, preparatory to embarking for the Pacific coast. Lieutenant Grant decided to leave his young wife with her parents in St. Louis until she could join him later. On the 5th of July he sailed with eight companies of the Fourth for Aspinwall on the steamship *Ohio*, commanded by Lieutenant-Commander, afterward Admiral, Schenck. Although it was well known that cholera was raging with great severity on the Isthmus, all the good berths on the ship had been taken by civilian passengers. The addition of seven hundred persons to the passenger list, including the families of officers and soldiers, greatly overcrowded the man-of-war, and the journey to the tropics in July was a very uncomfortable one. The regiment arrived at Aspinwall on the 16th of July, 1852, and Grant, who had been very seasick, welcomed the sight of shore. July 17th the regiment was carried by rail to the crossing of the Chagres River, thence by boat to Gorgona.

A difficult march from Gorgona, occupying three days during the uncomfortable rainy season, brought the troops to Panama, where they went aboard the steamship *Golden Gate*. Cholera broke out on board the ship the next day, and the vessel was detained at Panama for nearly three weeks; the regiment losing by death meanwhile one officer, many enlisted men, and some of the women and children.

This was a time that tried the soul of Quartermaster Grant. He had been left at Aspinwall with the baggage and stores of the regiment, one company being detailed as his escort. From Aspinwall he moved up the Chagres River to Cruces, a town somewhat nearer Panama than Gorgona. Then his troubles began. The contract of the steamship company included the transportation of the baggage and stores of the regiment. So many passengers had come on the steamer, that teams were in unusual demand, and the troops were neglected. Finding that he was to be detained at Aspinwall, Lieutenant Grant sent the company he had with him to Panama, and remained alone with the sick and the few soldiers who, having families, remained behind. Tiring at last of the steamship company's delays, he took matters into his own hands, hired men and mules, and transported everything to Panama over roads that were almost without bottom. This was a great responsibility for a quartermaster to take, with a treasury clerk sitting at Washington, watching to find flaws in his accounts when they were presented for payment.

Grant's services here were of the greatest importance, and were highly creditable to him and to the regiment. In the midst of cholera, with no physician, little or no shelter for his men, and dealing with incompetent contractors, his task was indeed a difficult and laborious one. His kindness and thoughtfulness were not confined to his own command, for he assisted many passengers of the *Ohio* in getting across the Isthmus. Among these were some Sisters of Charity, one of whom was taken with cholera at Cruces. When she had somewhat recovered, Grant hired bearers for her, and had her conveyed in a hammock to Panama. He finally succeeded in getting his stores on board the steamer *Golden Gate*, and the vessel was removed to Flamingo to rid her of the cholera. The disease soon abated, and the regiment sailed to San Francisco, arriving there in September, 1852, after a long and memorable voyage, during which the labours of Quartermaster Grant were unremitting, and his anxiety without relief. He never forgot this experience, and was accustomed to refer to it more frequently among his intimate friends than to his greater achievements as a soldier.

An officer who sailed with him on this voyage reports that one day some of the officers of the Fourth Infantry were engaged in a heated discussion on the main deck, while Grant was seated by himself at some distance from them. As the discussion grew warmer, and the prospect of agreement less and less, Adjutant McConnell broke in with: "I tell you, fellows, how we will settle this. Let's go across the deck and refer the whole matter to long-headed Sam, and whatever may be his decision we will abide by it." There were many disputes during this trying journey, and the services of "long-headed Sam" as umpire were in frequent request.

After spending a few weeks at Benecia Barracks, California, to recuperate, the headquarters and five companies of the Fourth embarked on the steamship *Columbia* for Columbia Barracks, now Vancouver Barracks, situated just across the river from Portland, Oregon. Here they arrived about the 22d of September. At Columbia Barracks Grant assumed the duties of Post Quartermaster. He and Captain Rufus Ingalls, better known later on as one of the ablest quartermasters our Civil War produced, Captain Thomas L. Brent, Depot Quartermaster, who died in 1858, and Colonel Henry L. Hodges, U. S. A., who was then a second lieutenant in Grant's company, and afterward Chief Quartermaster of the Army of the Cumberland, lived together for the winter in the Quartermaster's house under the hill. It was the era of high prices on the Pacific coast; and Grant and his mess concluded to raise their own potatoes, and sell any surplus they might have. The Quartermaster revived his early experiences as a farmer, bought a pair of worn-out horses that recuperated rapidly under his skilful management, and ploughed up the ground while his comrades planted the potatoes. The crop was immense; but so was the flood that overflowed the banks of the Columbia, and drowned it out before it was ready to be gathered. "This," said Grant in his *Memoirs*, " saved digging it up, for everybody on the Pacific Coast seemed to have come to the conclusion at the same time that agriculture would be profitable." A venture in ice, and another in cattle, were equally unfortunate. Business profits always flew away when Grant sought to lure them.

While stationed at Columbia Barracks, Grant took an active part in the occasional expeditions against the Indians. In September, 1853, he received notice of his promotion to the rank of Captain, dating from August 5, 1853, and his assignment to

Company F of the Fourth Infantry, then stationed at Humboldt Bay, California. To reach his new command, he was obliged to go to San Francisco, and thence in a lumber vessel up the coast. At Columbia Barracks he had met Brevet-Captain George B. McClellan, of the engineers, who visited that post to fit out an expedition for a survey of the passes of the Cascade range of mountains, for the purpose of determining a route for the Northern Pacific Railroad. While McClellan was at Columbia Barracks, Grant was guilty of an indiscretion not uncommon among young officers at that day, which gave McClellan an unfavourable impression of him, and influenced his judgment later on, when he was in command of the Armies of the United States, and Grant was an officer under orders.

Grant had one physical weakness, and that was an incapacity to take the smallest drink of spirituous liquor without being overcome by it. As a rule, he was extremely abstemious in both eating and drinking. At rare intervals, when a young officer, he would be betrayed into what was for him an over-indulgence. This led to a difficulty with his post commander, Major Robert C. Buchanan, who was a graduate of the Military Academy, an excellent officer, and something of a martinet. Life was dismal enough at that isolated post; the prospects of advancement were remote; and the separation from his family, to a man of Grant's domestic tastes, was unbearable. To these causes of discontent was now added the displeasure of his commanding officer; and he concluded to resign, though it was not in the power of his superior to compel him to do so against his will.

By the officers familiar with the circumstances, Major Buchanan was considered unnecessarily harsh in his dealings with Grant. Drinking in those days was much too common to be visited with severe penalties, except when it involved serious dereliction of duty; and Grant's reputation was that of a good, willing officer, always ready for duty, but extremely social and friendly with his fellows. There is a story told to the effect that when he resigned, and left his companions of the Fourth Infantry, Grant told them that within ten years they would hear from him in a way to compel their respect. The story may be true, though it is not in character, for Grant was never boastful. He had, however, a certain quiet confidence in his future that never forsook him. "I have seen some hard times in my life," he once said to the writer, "but I never saw the moment when I was not sure that I would come out ahead in the end."

In less than ten years from the date of his resignation, he was Lieutenant-General of the United States Army, in command as General-in-Chief of the Armies of the United States, and Buchanan was an officer under his orders. Grant was never prone to revenge, nor did he indulge it in this case, though his difficulty with Buchanan affected him injuriously through the whole of his military career. The Army is as prone to gossip as a New England sewing-society; and the story of his experiences at Fort Humboldt was spread abroad in an exaggerated form, subjecting him to unjust suspicions and false charges that discredited him with his superiors, and aroused popular clamour against him at critical periods in his history.

The pay of a captain in the Army, especially that of one who has a family to support, leaves no margin for contingencies, and the harsh judgment of his commanding officer had placed Captain Grant, late U. S. Army, in a most embarrassing position. When he reached San Francisco, on his way home, he had nothing in his pocket except an order for some forty dollars due for court-martial service, and on this he depended for the payment of his passage home.

There was some irregularity in the order; he could not get it cashed, and he slept that night in the office of the clerk of the Depot Quartermaster at San Francisco, who finally assumed the responsibility of cashing his draft, and secured such favours for Grant from the steamboat company that he was able to travel home in comfort. Captain Richard L. Ogden, the clerk in question, who records this episode in his diary, says:

"Having occasion to go to the steamer again to see some friends off, I met the Captain (Grant) again, and he showed me the nice stateroom that had fallen to his lot, and said : ' This is a great luxury and what I did not expect, and I am indebted to you for it. The prospect of ever being able to reciprocate is certainly remote, but strange things happen in this world, and there is no knowing.' With these prophetic words on his lips, Ulysses S. Grant sailed."

If he carried home with him little else, he did carry the respect and affection of those who knew him. "Sam Grant," said one of his acquaintances of that day (Colonel Henry C. Hodges, United States Army) to the writer, "Sam Grant was as honest a man as God ever made. He was not only an able officer, and one who was esteemed and loved by all, but he was one of the cleanest-mouthed men I ever knew, and in all my life I have never known a man so absolutely truthful as Grant."

This characteristic of absolute truthfulness explains many circumstances in Grant's subsequent career. Where he could not speak freely and frankly, he would not speak at all; for silence was with him the only possible refuge from a revelation of his thoughts.

Grant resigned from the Army, July 31, 1854, and the same year witnessed the resignation of a number of other officers who subsequently became distinguished: Generals Halleck, McClellan, Rosecrans, Slocum, Reynolds, Willcox, C. P. Stone, and William S. Smith, of the Union Army; and Bragg, Rains, Gustavus W. Smith, and Mansfield Lovell, of the Confederate service. To all of these, and to many others, Grant's story was known, and it created a prejudice against him that made his future career more difficult than it would otherwise have been, and more successful. To him were to come those lessons of hard experience which should teach him, as they did Lincoln, the virtue of self-examination, and save him from the dangers of self-conceit, without depriving him of confidence,—"that feeling on which the mind embarks on great and honourable courses with a sure hope and trust in itself;" which teaches the soul to say with Epictetus, in spirit if not in word, "Lead me where Thou wilt, clothe me in any dress Thou choosest."

Captain Grant was thirty-two years old when he retired from the Army, and he looked forward with cheerful anticipation to the possibility of accomplishing something in civil life. He was delighted, too, with the prospect of joining his family and enjoying the domestic comfort so difficult of attainment by an Army officer, in the days when frontier service and meagre pay were combined. When he reached his father-in-law's house in 1854, he was introduced to a son, Ulysses S. Grant, who was born July 22, 1852, while the father was struggling with his difficulties as quartermaster on the Isthmus of Panama. An elder son, Frederick Dent Grant, had been born two years earlier, May 30, 1850.

Mrs. Grant owned a tract of land hard by St. Louis on the Gravois Road, near her father's home. It was not stocked; there was no house on it; and the pay of $1200 or $1300, which this captain of infantry had enjoyed but a single year, furnished no surplus for investment. There was a hard and bitter struggle with fortune before him. He had to assist with his own hands in hewing the logs for a house with four rooms, which was to furnish in primitive fashion a shelter for his little family. The first winter was employed in clearing land, chopping wood, and hauling it to St. Louis for sale, Grant driving one team in person. In the spring he ploughed and planted; and when the crop was gathered, he was one of the foremost hands in the harvest field. He was an excellent farmer; he was industrious and energetic; but he was compelled to submit to the discomforts and restrictions inseparable from the life of a pioneer.

Coppée, in his *Life of Grant*, says:

"I visited St. Louis at this time, and remember with pleasure, that Grant, in his farmer rig, whip in hand, came to see me at the hotel, where were Joseph J. Reynolds, then professor, now Major-General, General (then Major) D. C. Buell, and Major Chapman of the Cavalry. If Grant had ever used spirits, as is not unlikely, I distinctly remember, that, upon the proposal being made to drink, Grant said: 'I will go in and look at you, for I never drink anything'; and the other officers, who saw him frequently, afterwards told me that he drank nothing but water."

The monotony of farming life was relieved by trips to St. Louis, and by occasional visits from old Army friends, who usually found the ex-captain busied with his farm work. One of his friends who followed him to the harvest field tells how he found him in shirt-sleeves, leading the mowers, and covered with the sweat of honest industry. He continued this work until 1858, when his old enemy of fever and ague again attacked him, and he resolved to seek a change of employment. Such leisure as he had on his farm was occupied in reading. General Sherman says:

"I recall an instance when I met him in St. Louis, in 1857, when he was a farmer in the country, and I too was out of military service. The only impression left on my memory is, that I then concluded that West Point and the Regular Army were not good schools for farmers, bankers, merchants, and mechanics. I did not meet him again until the Civil War had broken out, when chaos seemed let loose, and the gates of Hell wide open in every direction."

In the fall of 1858, Grant sold at auction his stock, crops, and farming utensils, and, leaving his family on his farm for the winter, went to St. Louis to seek employment. He formed a partnership in the real-estate business with a cousin of his wife, Harry Boggs. In the spring he leased his farm, and removed his family to St. Louis, occupying a little house on Barton Street. His venture in real estate did not prove a success. He never showed any ability as a solicitor or a tradesman, still less as a collector of rents; and his partner soon decided that the business did not yield enough to support more than one family. The *St. Louis Republican* says:

> "Some unfortunate tenant would appeal to him for time or help, and the time or help would always be given. His own noble and trustful soul made it impossible for him to question the word of a debtor who declared that he had no money, and he would trouble him no further. In a word, he was too tender-hearted and unselfish ever to make a success of business. The real-estate venture naturally did not thrive. The firm occupied an office on Pine Street, which is still standing; and many and vigorous were the scoldings given by the older partner to the younger, for his unbusiness-like habits and his many lapses from the path of commercial success. Grant was always good-natured. No one ever heard him complain of his lot. There were features which made the hardships harder: he had many mouths to find bread for, and there was little bread to be found."

If his farming life had not been profitable, it was at least congenial to his tastes. To the wife of a Congressman who knew him at this time, and who called on him when he was President at one of the White House receptions, General Grant said:

"Do you recollect when I used to supply your husband with wood, and pile it myself, and measure it too, and go to his office for my pay? Mrs. Blow, those were happy days; for I was doing the best I could to support my family."

Grant never forgot those who showed him kindness in the days of his humiliation. Those who befriended him were not always considerate in claiming the reward which his generosity prompted him to give them. On the files of the Treasury Department is a letter written by Grant just after the war, to the Secretary of the Treasury, introducing one of these friends of early days, and saying in substance: "Mr. —— was a friend to me when I was in sore need of friends. He is desirous of going South to buy cotton, and I shall be obliged if you will give him whatever facilities for doing so you give to any one." This letter was written just after the war ended, and before the restrictions placed upon free intercourse between the North and South were removed. Its recipient had it lithographed, and distributed copies among a number of agents. With such an introduction, these agents were permitted to pass the military lines, and, gathering large amounts of cotton on the Southern side, sold it at an immense profit in the North. Such a transaction simply illustrates Grant's unsuspicious generosity and kindness of heart; yet it was not unnaturally subject to misconception, and it gave those who were seeking for sinister motives abundant opportunity for criticism.

Once more out of employment after the failure of

his real-estate venture, Grant concluded that public office was his proper sphere, as is shown by the following document on file in the office of County Clerk of St. Louis County, labelled "Application of U. S. Grant for the office of County Engineer— Rejected." It is signed by several prominent citizens, and also by a number of persons who afterwards occupied positions in the Confederate service.

St. Louis, August 15, 1859.

Hon. County Commissioners, St. Louis County, Mo.:

Gentlemen,—I beg leave to submit myself as an applicant for the office of county engineer, should the office be rendered vacant, and at the same time to submit the names of a few citizens who have been kind enough to recommend me for the office. I have made no effort to get a large number of names, nor the names of persons with whom I am not personally acquainted. I enclose herewith also a statement from Professor J. J. Reynolds, who was a classmate of mine at West Point, as to qualifications.

Should your honorable body see proper to give me the appointment, I pledge myself to give the office my entire attention, and shall hope to give general satisfaction.

Very respectfully, your obedient servant,

U. S. Grant.

The years during which Captain Grant resided in St. Louis and its vicinity covered a period of great political excitement. The struggle between the forces of freedom and slavery for the possession of the new State of Kansas was exciting the country, and Missouri was the battle-ground of contending factions. The Republican party was forming, and entered upon its first great struggle for control in the Presidential campaign of 1856, when Buchanan and Fremont were the candidates. It was Grant's first opportunity to cast a vote, and he voted for

Buchanan; in part, as he tells us, because he knew Fremont too well to vote for him, and, further, because he believed that his election would precipitate secession and plunge the country into war. His political proclivities were in favour of the Whig party, which was moribund. As many of his neighbours, who sympathised with his views, had joined the Know-nothing or American party, which was afterwards absorbed in the Republican party, he was initiated in the local lodge of the Order, and attended one of its secret meetings, never entering another. The principle of secrecy was not congenial to his taste.

The party in Missouri opposed to the election of Buchanan was known at that time as the Free-Soil Democracy, and was marshalled under the leadership of the Hon. Frank P. Blair. He was a brother of Montgomery Blair, Mr. Lincoln's Postmaster-General, who was a graduate of the Military Academy of the class of 1835, and was then a Missouri lawyer and Solicitor of the United States in the Court of Claims. Frank Blair, who afterwards became a distinguished soldier, was a ready and forcible public speaker; and he tells of seeing on one occasion, when he was addressing an out-of-door audience, a little man, seated on the tail of a cart, who listened with great interest. At the close of the speech the little man was brought up and introduced as Captain Grant, late of the Army.

"Captain," said Mr. Blair, "I am going with my friends here to take some refreshment. Won't you join us?"

"I will go with you, Mr. Blair," was the answer, "but I am not going to vote for you." With this honest understanding, Mr. Blair's hospitality was accepted. In his *Memoirs*, Grant says, " Blair I knew very well by sight, and I heard him speak in the canvass in 1858, possibly several times, but I have never spoken to him." As this story was told by General Blair to the author of this biography, it would appear that General Grant was mistaken in his recollection.

Previous to his application for the office of County Engineer, Grant had for a short time held a position in the Custom-House at St. Louis, but was thrown out of office by the death of the Collector. He next turned to his father for assistance, and was offered a place as clerk, on a salary of $600 a year, in a store conducted by his younger brothers, at Galena, Ill. Thus by a series of misfortunes he was brought to the necessity of accepting his father's original proposition that he should become a purveyor of leather. The leather-store in Galena was founded in 1840 by E. A. Collins, who after a year formed a partnership with Jesse Grant, under the firm name of E. A. Collins & Co. The business prospered; and the invoiced value, when the firm dissolved in 1853, was $100,000. The dissolution was announced in some rhymes published by Jesse Grant in the *Galena Gazette*. They informed the public that

> "J. R. Grant, the old 'off wheel,'
> As firm and true as smitten steel,
> Does yet a strong desire feel

> To do some work.
> Expect, then, within the field,
> A brand-new store."

The business was put in charge of the two younger sons, who conducted the brand-new store as a branch of their father's business in Ohio. Some years afterwards the father divided his property equally among his children, reserving what he considered sufficient for himself, and the leather business was transferred to Grant's brothers. Ulysses refused to take his portion of the family estate, as he was prosperous at the time of the division, and did not think he had contributed anything towards its accumulation. He was faithful as a clerk, but was never at home in selling goods, and usually intrusted this delicate business of bartering to his shrewder brothers, while he sat in front of the store on a packing-box whittling. He bore a high reputation for honesty, truthfulness, and industry, and his small borrowings were always honourably returned, but he never had what is called " the nose for money."

The ex-soldier travelled occasionally through the Northwest to extend the business of his firm, and to attend to collections. On one of these journeys he found occasion to call upon a deputy-sheriff to serve a writ of replevin upon a delinquent creditor, who had locked himself in his store, and threatened violence against any one who entered. The timid deputy shrank from encountering the shot-gun with which the fighting creditor had armed himself. This was the soldier's opportunity. Grant asked that he be appointed a deputy to serve the process. In a few minutes the door was broken down, and the contumacious creditor was brought to terms. Had the business of dealing with warlike clients been sufficient to occupy his time, Grant would have been a brilliant success as a tanner's clerk.

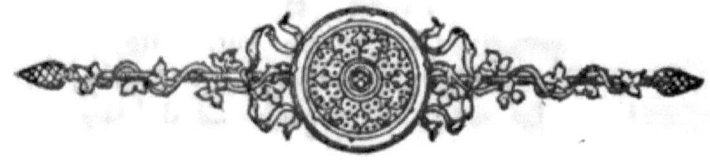

CHAPTER V.

FIRST EXPERIENCES AS AN OFFICER OF VOLUNTEERS.

JULY AND AUGUST, 1861.

DURING the winter of 1860-61, in the interval between the nomination and the inauguration of Abraham Lincoln as President of the United States, Grant spent much of the time in travelling on business in the Northwest. The question of war or of peace was then being discussed at every crossroad and in every country tavern. As an ex-captain of the Regular Army, who had served in Mexico, Grant was supposed to speak with authority on this subject; and in the towns where he stopped his opinion was eagerly sought by the residents who came to his tavern at night to question him. Captain Grant was fortunately well informed on public questions. His leisure had been largely occupied in reading. He was an eager devourer of newspapers, and was a close observer. He believed that war would result from the election of Mr. Lincoln; but he accepted the opinion current at the time, that it would be a ninety-days' affair. The storm that had been gathering for twenty-five years, since the agitation of the question of slavery became active in 1835, burst in full fury on the country when South Carolina defied the authority of the United States by firing on Fort Sumter in Charleston Harbour, April 12, 1861.

President Lincoln's proclamation calling for 75,000 militia for three months' service followed three days later. A second call was made May 3, 1861, and Illinois was preparing to furnish her quota. The dead walls of Galena were covered with posters, asking the citizens to meet at the Court-House in the evening; and men of every class, dropping their party distinctions, assembled to unite in demanding that this insult to the national flag should be promptly avenged. The modest ex-captain of infantry was dragged from his obscurity, and compelled to preside over the crowded meeting; though it was only with much embarrassment, and by the help of considerable prompting, that he was able to announce the purpose of the gathering, saying, in an almost inaudible voice:

"I thank you for honouring me with the position of Chairman of this meeting. You know the purpose for which we are assembled. We are needed to help preserve the Union. What is your pleasure?"

Two Democrats—one the Postmaster of the town, the other, John A. Rawlins, a young lawyer of Galena—were the principal speakers. E. B. Washburne, to whose friendship Grant was afterwards so much indebted, came in during the meeting, and also spoke. It would appear, from statements which he made afterward, that his confidence in Grant as a soldier was in inverse ratio to his respect for him as a presiding officer.

The meeting resulted in a resolution to support the Government, and in a call for volunteers for the two companies which Galena was expected to furnish. They were promptly raised, and the officers and non-commissioned officers elected. If he had consented, Grant would have received the appointment of Captain. He declined out of consideration for some one else who desired the command; but he promptly put his military experience at the service of the volunteers, and abandoned the leather business to devote his entire time to organising and drilling them. He directed the ladies of Galena in the patriotic work of preparing uniforms for the troops, and instructed the tailors in cutting the cloth, which the ladies made into military garments. Finally he accompanied the volunteers to Springfield, whither they went to be mustered into the service of the State.

A young merchant of Galena, who afterwards became a distinguished officer of our Army, was making an awkward attempt, one day in the early winter of 1861, to drill his company of militia. They were drawn up in a street of Galena in front of a leather-store. Hidden behind the soldiers was a little man seated on a packing-box. Some movement of the line brought him into view; and it suddenly occurred to the militia officer that this was Captain

Grant, whose service in the Regular Army should have taught him how to drill. The ex-regular was asked to take charge of the company, and a sword was handed to him. He buckled it on and took his position in front of the men. As he drew his blade from its scabbard, and it flashed in the sunlight, his whole nature seemed transformed, and to his fellow-townsmen was revealed the fact that here was a man who understood the business of war.

When the Governor of Illinois, Richard Yates, was suddenly called upon to officer and equip a large body of troops, he could find no one who understood even the simplest routine of military service. Colonels could not drill their regiments, and captains were ignorant of the simplest company movements. Asking a member of his staff, who had been appointed for the ornamental purposes of peace, whether he knew anything about organising troops, he was answered, " No." In response to a request for information concerning some one better instructed, the officer called attention to Captain Grant, formerly of the Regular Army, and a West Point graduate, whom he had known in Galena. As to his capacity he had no knowledge. He at least understood military drill, army regulations, and the routine of the service.

While stopping in a hotel at Springfield, the Governor, hearing a fellow-guest accosted by that name, introduced himself, and asked the Captain to call at the Executive office the following morning.

When Grant appeared at the Governor's office, he was engaged at a salary of three dollars a day to assist in the Adjutant-General's office at Camp Yates, where the troops were assembled. He had never distinguished himself as a clerk, but his familiarity with army papers and forms was of more importance than mere clerical ability. He had served in the field as adjutant of a regiment, as quartermaster and commissary, and thoroughly understood the details of his new duties. Matters at Camp Yates soon fell into order under his skilled direction. Governor Yates, in a speech in Congress, says of his first introduction to Grant:

"I did not then know that he had seen service in Mexico; that he had fought at Palo Alto, Resaca de la Palma, and at Monterey under Scott. In presenting himself to me, he made no reference to any merit, but simply said he had been a recipient of a military education at West Point, and, now that the country was assailed, he thought it was his duty to offer his services, and that he would esteem it a privilege to be assigned to any position where he could be useful."

After a short service with the Adjutant-General, Grant was sent to Southern Illinois to muster in three regiments assembled at Bellville. While there, he made a brief visit to St. Louis, and was present, as was also General Sherman, at the first encounter in Missouri between the armed adherents of the two sections.

In the latter part of May, Grant went to visit his parents at Covington, Kentucky, intending at the same time to visit Cincinnati, to see if he could obtain an appointment on the staff of McClellan, who was a major-general, and had his headquarters there. McClellan, in his *Own Story*, says:

"I think it was during my absence on this very trip to Indianapolis that Grant came to Cincinnati to ask me, as an old acquaintance, to give him employment, or a place on my staff. Marcy or Seth Williams saw him, and told him that if he would await my return doubtless I would do something for him; but before I got back he telegraphed that he could have a regiment in Illinois, and at once returned thither, so that I did not see him. This was his good luck; for had I been there, I would no doubt have given him a place on my staff, and he would probably have remained with me and shared my fate."

McClellan is mistaken as to his being absent at the time. In a conversation with Mr. Young during his journey around the world, Grant told the story thus:

"I knew McClellan, and had great confidence in him. I have, for that matter, never lost my respect for McClellan's character, nor my confidence in his loyalty and ability. I saw in him the man who was to pilot us through, and I wanted to be on his staff. I thought that if he would make me a major, or a lieutenant-colonel, I could be of use, and I wanted to be with him. So when I came to Cincinnati, I went to the headquarters. Several of the staff officers were friends I had known in the Army. I asked one of them if the general was in. I was told he had just gone out, and was asked to take a seat. Everybody was so busy that they could not say a word. I waited a couple of hours. I never saw such a busy crowd—so many men at an army headquarters with quills behind their ears. But I supposed it was all right, and was much encouraged by their industry.

"Finally, after a long wait, I told an officer that I would come in again next day, and requested him to tell McClellan that I had called. Next day I came in. The same story. The general had just gone out; might be in at any moment. Would I wait? I sat and waited for two hours, watching the officers with their quills, and left. This is the whole story. McClellan never acknowledged my call, and of course, after he knew I had been at his headquarters, I was bound to await his acknowledgment. I was older, had ranked him in the army, and could not hang around his headquarters watching the men with the quills behind their ears. I went over to make a visit to an old army friend, Reynolds, and while there learned that Governor Yates, of Illinois, had made me a colonel of volunteers. Still I should have liked to join McClellan. This pomp and ceremony was common at the beginning of the war. McClellan had three times as many men with quills behind their ears as I had ever found necessary at the headquarters of a much larger command."

From his home at Galena, Grant wrote to the War Department at Washington, offering his services as a soldier. He received no reply to his letter, and, as it is not on the files of the War Department, it was apparently overlooked in the confusion prevailing in Washington at this time. This is the letter:

GALENA, ILLINOIS, May 24, 1861.

Sir: Having served for fifteen years in the regular army, including four years at West Point, and feeling it the duty of everyone who has been educated at the government expense to offer their services for the support of that government, I have the honor very respectfully to tender my services until the close of the war, in such capacity as may be offered. I would say, in view of my present age and length of service, I feel myself competent to command a regiment, if the President, in his judgment should see fit to intrust one to me. Since the first call of the President, I have been serving on the staff of the Governor of this State, rendering such aid as I could in the organization of our State militia, and I am still engaged in that capacity. A letter addressed to me at Springfield, Illinois, will reach me.

I am, very respectfully, your obedient servant,

U. S. GRANT.

Among the regiments organised in Illinois at that time was the Twenty-first Illinois Infantry, composed of 1250 vigorous and intelligent young men from the " best families " of Coles, Cumberland,

Champaign, and Douglas Counties, all well disposed, but wholly unused to any restraint, and full of mischief. They had elected a colonel who did not command their respect, and who was controlled by the idea, so prevalent at that time, that good fellowship could be made a substitute for military discipline. He was soon satisfied of his own incapacity, and Governor Yates refused to commission him.

The Governor had found that Grant thoroughly understood the business of organising and drilling troops, and he had formed a high opinion of his force of character. He accordingly sent for him, and offered to appoint him Colonel of the Twenty-first, which was in a condition bordering upon mutiny. In answer to the question whether he thought he could control it, Grant promptly answered, "Yes."

Not having had time to procure a uniform, the new colonel, when he appeared to take command, wore a large bandanna tied around the waist of his sack coat for a sash, and was armed with a stick instead of a sword. His men soon discovered, however, that authority centred in the man, not in his sword or epaulets. The sons of the " best families " found that they had their master in the little gentleman from Galena, whose modest ways secured for him the title of " the quiet man." Major Wham, of the Army, who was then a lieutenant in the Twenty-first, says:

"We were in for thirty days at first, and had a colonel who wore two pistols in his belt and made speeches on dress parade. We refused to enlist unless we could have a new colonel, and the case was presented to Governor Dick Yates while the regiment was camped at Springfield. It was then that Colonel U. S. Grant was assigned to our regiment, and the Governor suggested that the boys be enthused with some speeches by Logan or one or two others. The programme was carried out; and the boys, who had been worked up to a three-cheers-and-a-tiger state of mind, and were accustomed to speeches from their old colonel, called for 'Grant, Colonel Grant,' with the accent on both words. There was a slight hesitation, and then Colonel Grant, who had been sitting down, arose and made an effective address without exhausting the English language. It could hardly be divided into the three parts required for rhetoricians, for it consisted of but four words: to wit, 'Go to your quarters!'"

On another occasion, before the regiment left Camp Yates, an Irish member who had been visiting Springfield, returned in a condition that made him entirely oblivious of authority. He so terrorised the camp, that the corporal and others ordered to arrest him shrank from the task. Without a moment's hesitation the Colonel knocked the Irishman down, bound him, and gagged him in the usual manner by tying a bayonet in his mouth.

A few such experiences of the regular army methods of enforcing discipline soon reduced the unruly regiment to order. But its ways were a sore trial to the patience of the new Colonel, who gave expression, however, to his discontent, in the mildest manner. When at drill his whole line was thrown into confusion by the inability of the men to understand a simple order, Colonel Grant sat on his horse in amazement and disgust. Without trying to extricate his men from their difficulty, he turned to the next in command, and exclaimed, "Confound that company, anyhow!" then, wheeling his horse quickly, he rode off without a word of criticism or explanation. The company officers extricated the men from the muddle in the best way they could; and they all marched to quarters, as the men said, " feeling a hundred times worse than if Grant had raised his voice and sworn till the air was blue."

The Twenty-first was ordered to Quincy, Illinois, on July 3, 1861, after the new Colonel had devoted three weeks of constant effort to their instruction. His ability was shown in the immediate improvement of the regiment in efficiency and discipline. He resolved to give them additional instruction in field duty by marching them across the country. At the Illinois River he was overtaken by a despatch ordering him to remain where he was until the coming of a steamer which was to take his command down the Illinois and Mississippi Rivers to St. Louis, *en route* to Ironton, Missouri. Before the boat was ready, orders came hastening them by rail to the relief of an Illinois regiment besieged near Palmyra, Missouri. They were too late, as the besieged regiment had concluded to run away without waiting for the re-enforcements.

Grant's next duty was to assist in building a railroad bridge across the Salt River. While at Salt River with his regiment, engaged in this work, he made an incursion twenty-five miles into the back country in search of Confederate troops reported there. This time it was the enemy who fled, and they were beyond reach before their pursuers arrived at their camp. This performance was repeated almost as regularly as if there had been an understanding, at that stage of the war, that when one side advanced, the other was to run away. It was Grant's quick appreciation of this peculiarity of untrained troops that enabled him to succeed when others failed.

He was next placed in command of a sub-district under General Pope, having three regiments of infantry and a section of artillery, with headquarters at Mexico, Missouri. His first order as a sub-district commander was to forbid entrance into private houses or interference with private property. Having some leisure, he brushed up his tactics, and drilled his regiment in battalion movements.

Nicolay and Hay, in their *Life of Lincoln*, tell this story:

"A short time afterwards, Fremont (then at St. Louis) made a preliminary order that Grant's regiment should be transferred to Quincy, preparatory to being sent against the bushwackers in northern Missouri. Pursuant thereto, the Adjutant-General directed the railroad agent to provide the necessary transportation. The agent went in person to Camp Yates to arrange the matter with Colonel Grant.

"'How many passenger and how many freight cars do you want?' asked the agent. 'I don't want any,' responded Grant bluffly and without explanation.

"The agent felt insulted, and reported as much to the Adjutant-General. The indignant Adjutant-General hurried to Camp Yates, and, confronting Colonel Grant, asked why his orders were disobeyed?

"'How much time have I in which to get to Quincy?' asked Grant unmoved.

"'I don't remember,' replied the Adjutant-General.

"'My written orders,' said Grant, drawing them from his pocket, 'give me ten days. What must I do when I get to Quincy?' 'Go to northern Missouri, I suppose,' replied the Adjutant-General.

"'Is there a railroad there from Quincy?' asked Grant. 'I believe not,' said the Adjutant-General.

"'Shall I wait there until one is built?' asked Grant. The Adjutant-General looked puzzled, and began to think he was dealing with a lunatic. Thereupon Grant continued:

"'As there is no railway to northern Missouri, and as I cannot wait to have one built, it is very clear that I shall have to march. Now, as it is generally understood that my regiment is in bad discipline, and as I have ten days' time, I have made up my mind that I will begin to work in earnest right at once by marching my men from here to Quincy. That was the reason for my answer. I don't want any railroad cars, but I do want equipments for a march.'

"This style of practical soldiering of course created a sensation both in camp and town. Grant adhered to his project, obtained his wagons, and personally superintended their being loaded with salt pork and regular army rations, and led the first regiment which ever left Springfield on foot, making some five miles the first day. That evening he issued an order that the regiment would march next morning at six. Six o'clock came, and many of the men were still asleep. It was seven before he got them off. The second evening he issued another order that on the following morning the regiment would march at six, ready or not ready. Morning and six o'clock came again; and the colonel formed his column promptly and peremptorily, many of the laggards being forced into the ranks barefoot, not having time even to put on their shoes, and being forbidden to carry them. After a march of two or three miles, the column was halted, and the shoes were sent for; and on the succeeding morning, the tap of the six o'clock drum found every man ready to fall in. Such is one of the local traditions."

Soon after Grant entered the volunteer service, the President asked the Illinois delegation in Congress to recommend seven citizens of their State for appointment as Brigadier-Generals of Volunteers. Colonel Grant's name was first on the list, and his appointment was dated from May 17, 1861, the time when he was still in the Adjutant-General's office, and the month before he became Colonel. This was a striking testimony to the impression which his modest merit had made upon public officials; and he was gratified to feel that he had attained so much more than he had possibly hoped for, without using influence of any kind to secure advancement. He chose for his aides Lieutenant C. B. Lagow of the regiment he commanded, and William J. Hillyer, a lawyer of his acquaintance. Neither of these displayed any capacity as a soldier. John A. Rawlins, another lawyer, and an able speaker, was appointed Adjutant. He was a much happier choice, and continued with his chief to the end, rising finally to the rank of Brigadier-General and Chief of Staff to the General of the Army.

The officers in high command had taken their pick of the best officers in the Regular Army for staff duty, and others were obliged to make such choice as they could from men who had not been instructed in staff duties, and whose abilities as soldiers were unknown quantities. Much of the time Grant had to serve as his own adjutant-general, quartermaster, commissary, and ordnance officer, and to instruct his officers in the details of making requisitions for rations and forage.

How well he understood the character of the volunteers he commanded, is illustrated by many anecdotes. His experience in civil life saved him from the mistakes made by men whose whole training had been in the Army, and who dealt with volunteers as they would with regular soldiers. He knew how to create a regimental public sentiment that favoured discipline, and he made effective use of the American sense of humour. An officer commanding his advanced guard, who ventured to assume the *rôle* of the commanding officer, was received with corresponding favour at a farmhouse where he stopped. When Grant passed by soon after, and asked for a meal at the same house, he was curtly told that there was nothing for him. General Grant had just been there and eaten up everything except one pie. A bargain was made for this pie on condition that it should be kept until sent for.

That evening when the brigade was in camp, a dress parade was ordered, a very unusual ceremony when troops are on the march, especially so in a camp commanded by General Grant. There was much excitement among the troops, and all sorts of rumours were afloat, until, after the usual ceremonies, the Adjutant stepped to the front and read the following special order:

"Lieutenant Wickfield, of the Indiana Cavalry, having on this day eaten everything in Mrs. Selvidge's house, at the crossing of the Trenton and Pocahontas and Black River and Cape Girardeau roads, except one pumpkin pie, Lieutenant Wickfield is hereby ordered to return with an escort of one hundred cavalry, and eat that pie also.
"U. S. GRANT, Brigadier-General Commanding."

The order was received with uproarious merriment at the expense of the Lieutenant, who was obliged to retrace his weary steps to the widow's house and eat his humble pie in the presence of his imposing escort of cavalry. He never forgot that pie; and the men of the command learned that their general was not to be trifled with, however forbearing he might be in administering the lesson of discipline.

General Rawlins, in a conversation shortly before his death in 1869, said, that, as a young lawyer in Galena, he had charge of the legal business of Grant's father, and lived next door to Mrs. Lee, a half-sister of Grant's mother. Her constant theme of conversation was "Ulysses," who was represented as the flower of the flock, though he had no business talent. When the war opened, Rawlins saw " new energies in Grant. A larger career had opened before him. . . . He dropped a stooped-shouldered way he had when walking, and set his hat forward on his forehead in a less careless fashion. Yet he never seemed to have an ambition above a regimental rank."

CHAPTER VI.

SEIZURE OF PADUCAH—BATTLE OF BELMONT.

SEPTEMBER–DECEMBER, 1861.

A MARKED feature of American topography is our system of navigable rivers. A struggle for the control of the Potomac, the Kanawha, and the James Rivers, in the East, the Mississippi, Tennessee, Cumberland, and the Ohio Rivers, in the West, determined lines of movement and the operations of strategy. It was easily seen that the power having possession of the navigable streams from their sources to their mouths, was master of the country. Armies and military divisions and departments took their names from them. We had the Army of the Potomac, the Armies of the Ohio, the Cumberland, the James, and the Mississippi.

The importance of securing the control of the Mississippi River was soon apparent to both parties. Early in the war John C. Fremont had been appointed Major-General of the Regular Army, and given command of the " Western Department," including within its boundaries Illinois and the States and Territories between the Mississippi and the Rocky Mountains. His field of operations was an extremely difficult one, as he was practically dealing with an armed population,—one of the most perplexing problems of war. General Grant was assigned to a command under Fremont, which gave him control of a full district with headquarters at Ironton, Missouri. At the time he took command, Fremont was threatened in all directions. A large Confederate force was on the frontier of Missouri; Pillow, with another body, threatened Cairo; Lyons was holding a superior force in check at Springfield; Thompson was threatening Cape Girardeau; and Hardee was advancing upon Ironton, where Grant was in command. Grant prepared immediately for action: but before he could move, General B. M. Prentiss arrived with orders to take command of the district; and General Grant, being the senior officer, and not subject to the control of his junior, started for St. Louis, where he was assigned to a more important command at Jefferson City, having been in command at Ironton only ten days.

At Jefferson City, where he arrived August 17, 1861, Grant found Colonel James A. Mulligan, an enthusiastic but untrained Irish soldier, in command of the 23d Illinois Volunteers, known as the "Irish Brigade." The city was in great confusion, and filled with fugitives, claiming to be sympathisers with the Government, fleeing from the attacks of the guerilla bands. It was a time when, in Missouri at least, a man's enemies were those of his own household; and friend was divided against friend, and neighbour against neighbour.

At this period of his career the military authorities appear to have been drilling their new brigadier-general in the art of rapid locomotion. He no sooner appeared in one place than he was ordered to another. Colonel Jefferson C. Davis presented himself on August 27th, with orders for Grant to yield possession to him, and report to Fremont at St. Louis for special instruction. Within an hour he had turned over his command, and was on his way to St. Louis with a single aide, to report for duty.

Fremont held at this time an important command; and he was fully conscious of the dignity of his own personality, assuming a state and a formality that were quite exceptional for American commanders. Grant found him as difficult of access as McClellan; and, as he was under orders now, he was obliged to wait upon Fremont's convenience, being much too modest a man to do as Sherman did on a similar occasion, and give the orderly in attendance peremptory orders to admit him at once to the presence of the General. After sitting for some hours upon a bench in the dark hall, he recognised General McKinstry, who was passing, and who had known him at West Point. Telling the story of this interview, General McKinstry says:

" Turning at the salutation, and seeing that it was General Grant, I said 'Sam, what are you doing here?' He replied that he had been ordered down by General Pope from Jefferson City to report to General Fremont, and had been seated there since early in the morning, endeavoring to comply with that order. I told him that was all right, and that I would see that he had an audience. I was called upon by General Fremont for my views as to the proper man. I replied that I had just the man, and that I had left him down stairs waiting an audience with the general. That man was General Grant, with whom I had served in Mexico, and whose gallantry I had witnessed on the battlefields surrounding the City of Mexico. I said that I knew him to be one of the most gallant of men, that in my judgment the country at that particular moment wished to fight, and the sooner we commenced, the sooner we should have a reliable army, and that Grant was the man to do that fighting and was a man on whom they could rely."

General Fremont says of this interview with Grant:

"He impressed me very strongly. I saw that he had the soldierly qualities of self-poise, modesty, decision, attention to details. I told him what I wanted for Cairo; we discussed all the points for two or three hours. I told him the purpose was to make Cairo, with Paducah opposite it, the base of important operations against Memphis and Nashville, assisted by Foote's fleet of gunboats running on the river between. During Grant's call I consulted other officers about him, and was warmly urged not to appoint him, for reasons that were well known. Grant's own presence was sufficient to counteract the influence of what they said, and before he left I offered him the command at Cairo, and he accepted it.

"Just before he left I said to him: 'General, I would like to have you wear your uniform.' He said that he had just given away his colonel's uniform, but as soon as his brigadier's uniform came, which he had ordered, he should of course wear it. I then explained that there were special reasons why officers in St. Louis should appear in their uniforms. Disloyal citizens had attempted to intimidate uniformed officers, and some of the latter had compromised with disloyalty so far as to leave off their uniforms whenever they could."

The special instructions received by Grant at St. Louis directed him to take command of the important district of southwestern Missouri, with headquarters at Cape Girardeau, where he arrived on August 30, 1861. His district was forthwith extended to include southern Illinois; and September 4th he made another move, establishing his headquarters at Cairo, Illinois.

The appearance of General Grant before the august Fremont without uniform was explained by the fact that his uniform as a brigadier-general had not yet arrived from New York, and he was compelled to wear citizen's dress for a month after he had received his appointment as a general officer. When the plain little man in " cits," as the West Point cadets call them, appeared at Cairo, sat down in the office of Colonel Richard Oglesby, and wrote an order relieving Oglesby from command of the post, the colonel did not at first know whether to obey the order or to put the writer under arrest. Rawlins, who was then a civilian, visited Grant at Cairo. Describing this visit, he said Grant " had an office in a great bank there, and I was amazed at the quick, prompt way in which he handled the multitude of letters, requisitions, and papers, sitting behind the cashier's window hole, with a waste basket under him, and orderlies to despatch business as he did." The official orders issued by Grant, even at this early stage of his career, showed the trained and experienced soldier.

Cairo was at this time an extremely important military position, as from it operations could be directed against the border States of Missouri, Kentucky, and Tennessee. The people of these States were opposed by large majorities to the doctrine of secession; but they did not favour the policy of coercing the seceding Southern States, with which they were allied by their common hostility to Northern interference with slavery. They endeavoured to maintain an impossible position of neutrality, and to act as buffer States, holding the belligerents apart. Both parties to the quarrel were warned by the border States to respect the neutrality of their territory, and, in the case of Kentucky especially, both made a show of doing so. It was impossible, however, for these States to escape the general conflagration, when the flames of war were lighted in every election district, and political prejudice and hostility were daily becoming more uncontrollably warlike.

By June, 1861, Tennessee had decided to cast its lot with the seceding States, and stringent measures were adopted by the State authorities to suppress the Union sentiment which still controlled the mountain district of East Tennessee. Kentucky, by heavy popular majorities, repeatedly refused to ally itself with the Confederacy; but it maintained its nominal neutrality until September, 1861, when its Union Legislature met, and passed resolutions directing the Governor to order the Confederate or Tennessee troops to withdraw unconditionally from Kentucky soil. They answered that they would withdraw if the Federal troops would withdraw also. Another resolution was promptly passed by the Legislature, declaring that this condition was an insult " to which Kentucky cannot listen without dishonour," and " that the invader must be expelled."

Up to this time both belligerents had treated Kentucky with great consideration, but each was eager to take advantage of some of the strong positions within her territory. On June 25, 1861, Leonidas Polk, a graduate of the Military Academy, and at that time the Episcopal bishop of the diocese of Louisiana, was commissioned Major-General in the " Provisional Army of the Confederate States," and assigned to a command intended to give him control of the Mississippi River, with headquarters at Memphis, Tennessee. Missouri was not included in his command; but he had authority to enter that State, if action on the part of the Federal Government compelled him to do so.

As the result of Lyon's vigorous action, Polk had turned a large force into Missouri, and was exerting himself to occupy the attention of the Union troops as much as possible, so that he might gain time to perfect his plans for defending the Mississippi. It was Polk's movement which had occupied the attention of General Grant while he was in Missouri. Though the Confederates had been successful with a superior force in overcoming Lyon at Wilson's Creek on August 10, 1861, no profitable result had followed their barren victory there, and by the end of August their plans for the relief of Missouri had been abandoned.

Fremont had ordered Grant to concentrate several detachments in Southwestern Missouri, to drive out the enemy, and to destroy a secession camp reported to be at Belmont. In this order General Fremont said, " It is intended to occupy

Columbus, Kentucky, as soon as possible." Columbus was immediately opposite Belmont on the Kentucky shore of the Mississippi. Columbus was Grant's real objective point in this movement against Belmont, and he had asked that he might be allowed to take that place. Before he reached Belmont he discovered, through a gunboat reconnaissance, that Polk was already advancing on Columbus in force, and that he himself was too late to secure that position, as he might have done if he had received the permission to take it at the time he asked for it. Polk's action relieved the situation, for it made it clear that there was no further occasion for respecting the neutrality of Kentucky.

With sound military judgment, Grant promptly decided that the time had come for action in Kentucky. He returned to Cairo with his little force of two regiments and one battalion, and hurriedly organised an expedition of two gunboats, with eighteen hundred men and sixteen field guns, the gunboats being under his orders. With this force he hastened to Paducah, forty-eight miles above Cairo on the opposite side of the Ohio, at the mouth of the Tennessee River. He also sent a detachment to occupy Smithland, just below the mouth of the Cumberland. He met with no opposition; but he was only a few hours ahead of the Confederates, who had contemplated the same movement. Grant had been informed of their plans for seizing Paducah, and his prompt action September 6, 1861, completely disconcerted them.

On September 13th the Confederate General,

Buckner, wrote to Richmond, saying, "Our possession at Columbus is already neutralized by that of Paducah." The occupation of Columbus and of Paducah was so nearly simultaneous, that each party had the privilege of abusing the other for its violation of neutral territory. The abandoned Missouri campaign had given General Polk the command of 6000 men under General Gideon J. Pillow; and it was with this force that he had occupied Columbus, moving Pillow's troops across the river from New Madrid on the Missouri shore, which had been in his possession since July 28, 1861. Grant had telegraphed to Department Headquarters for permission to make his movement against Paducah. Receiving no reply, he promptly acted on his own responsibility. He informed the Legislature of Kentucky of his action, and received the approval of the majority of that body. For this correspondence with the State Legislature he was reprimanded from Washington, and warned not to repeat the offence. Polk, whose action was equally a violation of the sacredness of Kentucky soil, received a despatch from Jefferson Davis at Richmond, saying, "The necessity justified the action." The same necessity would have led to the occupation of Paducah by the Confederates, if Grant had not been too quick for Polk, moving the very day after he assumed command at Cairo.

Active operations in Grant's department were now transferred to the soil of Kentucky, and his position at Cairo grew in importance. Considered as a place of residence, Cairo was scarcely an

"Eden," though Dickens has given it that name in his *Martin Chuzzlewit*, where it is described by Mr. Kettle as "an awfully lovely place—sure-ly, and frightfully wholesome." It is, as a matter of fact, a low, marshy, boot-shaped peninsula, protected from the Mississippi and Ohio Rivers by levees. Its jet-black soil was at that time full of the suggestions of disease, and pestiferous insects were numerous. Writing of Cairo, the Army humourist, John Phœnix, said, "The season is usually opened with great *éclat* by small-pox, continued spiritedly by cholera and closed up brilliantly with yellow fever."

These descriptions show that the disadvantages of Cairo as a residence could easily be exaggerated; but not so its advantages as a military position. The Ohio River, rising among the Pennsylvania Alleghanies, and running for one thousand miles along the line between the Northern and Southern States, empties into the Mississippi at Cairo, and there connects with the system of water navigation, extending for one thousand miles farther south, and another thousand miles northward to St. Paul, Minnesota. Cairo is in the southern extremity of Illinois, where the eastern and western boundaries of the State meet in a salient angle, interposed between the States of Kentucky and Missouri. Standing, as it does, at the junction of two great water courses, its strategic importance is apparent. It is the key to the Mississippi Valley, and, as the terminus of the Illinois Central Railroad, it is in communication with the railroad system of the North.

Governor Yates, of Illinois, had the foresight to garrison Cairo as early as April 23, 1861, with such feeble forces as he had at his command. It was threatened by an attack from New Madrid when Grant was ordered there, but his vigorous action soon changed the conditions of the problem in that region. Columbus was the headquarters of the forces of the enemy which were observing and threatening Cairo. Had they secured the control of Paducah, the position of Cairo would have been precarious. Its possession gave the Federal forces a great strategic advantage; and, until Columbus was secured, the Confederates had no defensible position on the Mississippi farther north than Fort Pillow, two hundred and fifteen miles below Cairo.

Of the few positions capable of effective defence found on the low banks of the Mississippi, Columbus was one of the best, and it had the advantage of being within eighteen miles of Cairo. It was on a high bluff commanding the river for five miles. Its works were of great strength, consisting of tier upon tier of batteries on the river front, and a strong parapet and ditch covered by thick abatis on the land side. Polk described this position as "the Gibraltar of the West," and declared that he could hold it against any force while the supplies he had for six months held out. The town of Columbus itself is described, at this time, as a straggling collection of brick blocks, frame houses, and whiskey saloons. As one of the means of defence against the advancing gunboats, Pillow, when in command, stretched a cable of seven-eighth-inch iron across the river, and gathered a large quantity of torpedoes, all of which proved worthless.

On November 5, 1861, Fremont telegraphed to Grant that the enemy were re-enforcing Price's army in Missouri from Columbus, and directed him to make a demonstration immediately against Columbus. Colonel Oglesby, who was in Grant's command, had just undertaken an expedition against the partisan leader, " Jeff " Thompson. Oglesby was telegraphed to change the direction of his column towards New Madrid; and on the evening of November 6, Grant started from Cairo with 3114 men of all arms of the service, in transports convoyed by two gunboats. He also telegraphed to General C. F. Smith, who had an independent command at Paducah, requesting him also to make a demonstration against Columbus. On the afternoon of November 7, Grant received information that the enemy had been sending troops across from Columbus to Belmont to cut off Oglesby; and he resolved to make an immediate and vigorous attack on Belmont, under the cover of his gunboats to which he could retreat in case of extremity. As Belmont was on low ground, and thoroughly commanded by guns on the opposite shore, he knew it would be impossible to hold the place after taking it.

That evening he landed at Hunter's Point, three miles above Belmont, and discovered the Confederate camp located in a large open field, where it was protected by the river on one side, and by a line of felled trees, or abatis, on the other. The single regiment of the enemy was found outside of the abatis, and after a sharp skirmish retreated behind it. Grant's men charged through this defence, and drove the enemy under the cover of the bank, where they received re-enforcements of five regiments from the opposite side of the river, and endeavoured to cut off Grant's retreat to his transports. They were driven back, and the Union troops were hurried aboard the boat. Grant, who was one of the last to embark, narrowly escaped capture. "In face of the advancing enemy, his horse slid down the river bank on its haunches and trotted on board a transport over a plank thrust out for him." The advance and retreat had been a running fight, and towards the end the Union troops were under the fire of heavy guns posted on the heights of the opposite shore.

In the quarters of the enemy deserted camp-fires were found burning, dinners cooking; half-written letters were scattered about, and there was every evidence of a hasty retreat. Tents, blankets, etc., were set on fire and destroyed, and two pieces of artillery were carried away. Four other guns, which it was found impossible to remove, were spiked, and left on the road to the landing. The purpose of the demonstration against Belmont was not understood at the time, and Grant rested under the stigma of having made an unsuccessful attempt to capture Columbus. The attack was one of the five serious engagements of the year 1861,—Bull Run (Virginia), Wilson's Creek (Missouri), Lexington (Missouri), and Ball's Bluff (Virginia) being the others,—and with it ended the serious operations of that year. It had not only accomplished its purpose of preventing the re-enforcement of Price, but it had inspired Grant's troops with confidence, which was of great service in the future. At the same time the Confederates, not improperly, claimed it as a victory, Grant having retired without accomplishing his purpose of driving them permanently from their camp, which was re-occupied as soon as he left.

The Federal movement against Columbus in West Kentucky was coincident with a similar movement in the eastern part of that State in the interest of the Confederacy. At the southwestern extremity of Virginia is the narrow pass through the Cumberland Mountains known as "Cumberland Gap." This pass was occupied September 5, 1861, by the enterprising Southern general, Zollicoffer; and he passed through it into Kentucky on September 10th with five regiments, and prepared for an attack on the Kentucky Home Guard assembled in Camp Robinson. The next day the Union Legislature of Kentucky adopted a resolution, which was subsequently passed a second time over the Governor's veto, ordering the Confederate forces from the soil of Kentucky. General Robert Anderson, a native of Kentucky, whose gallant defence at Fort Sumter had given him a national reputation, was requested to take military command in Kentucky, and to organise a force of volunteers.

This was the final declaration of Kentucky's hostility to the Confederacy; before the Legislature adjourned, enlistments for the Confederate Army had been declared to be a misdemeanour, and the invasion of the State by Confederate soldiers a felony. It was ordered that 40,000 volunteers be enlisted and mustered into the United States Service to repel invasion. The Confederate forces at this time were occupying the line along the boundary between Kentucky and North Tennessee. Zollicoffer was at Cumberland Gap, and Buckner at Bowling Green, which he had occupied on September 18, explaining to the Kentuckians that this was merely a measure of defence, while Polk occupied Columbus at the western extremity of the State. The Union line ran irregularly through the centre of Kentucky. Positions were occupied by the Union forces at Paducah and Port Holt on the Kentucky side of the Ohio River, and at Bride's Point, Cairo, Mound City, Evansville, and New Albany, on the northern side of the river. These were considered sufficient, with the gunboats, to guard the Ohio from Louisville to its mouth.

Nothing more than defensive action was expected. General Anderson, who had broken down physically, was relieved at Louisville, October 8, 1861, by General W. T. Sherman; and Sherman was oppressed by the dangers of his position, and a lack of sufficient troops to enable him to resist the aggressive movements of the enemy. He reported that with a front of over three hundred miles to guard, from Big Sandy to Paducah, he had fewer troops than either McClellan on his left, or Fremont on the right, each of whom had a front of less than one hundred miles. Men were abundant, but arms were scarce, and it was found impossible to equip troops properly with sufficient rapidity to meet the constant demands for re-enforcement that came from every direction.

Halleck, who relieved Fremont in command at St. Louis, November 9, 1861, two days after Belmont, changed the name of Grant's district from the District of Southeastern Missouri to the District of Cairo, and added to his command the district commanded by General C. F. Smith, embracing the mouths of the Tennessee and the Cumberland. Grant, whose voice was always for war, had twice asked permission to make a serious attack upon Columbus, believing that every day added to its strength, and that he was relatively better off than he would be later on. He could not obtain the necessary permission, and for the three following months there was a period of inaction all along the line. McClellan had accomplished nothing in the East beyond organising his troops; Buell, who was in command of the Department of the Ohio, was not acting in concert with Halleck; and the most persistent urging from President Lincoln secured from these two officers, and from McClellan, nothing but dilatory and unsatisfactory promises of future action. They asked for time to strengthen themselves, and to put their troops in better condition for action.

Grant's command suffered the same want of organisation, the same deficiency of arms, equipment, transportation, and supplies, which others complained of; but he always held, and acted upon, the belief that the time required to improve his own position would equally strengthen that of the enemy. He was like an eager hound, straining in the leash that he might get at his quarry.

CHAPTER VII.

CAPTURE OF FORTS HENRY AND DONELSON.

JANUARY AND FEBRUARY, 1862.

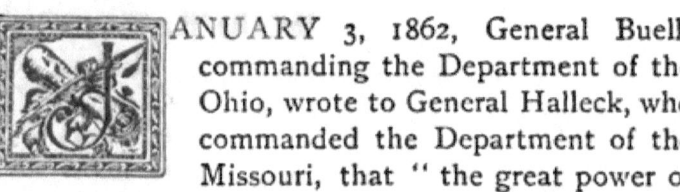ANUARY 3, 1862, General Buell, commanding the Department of the Ohio, wrote to General Halleck, who commanded the Department of the Missouri, that "the great power of the Rebellion in the West is arrayed" on a line from Columbus to Bowling Green. Bowling Green, Kentucky, was one hundred and sixty miles east of Columbus, Kentucky,—the town on the Mississippi River, which had been seized and fortified by Polk in September, 1861, as an outwork for the defence of Nashville against a movement from the North, and as a position giving opportunity for offensive returns. It is near the junction of two important railroads, one connecting Louisville with Nashville, and the other running from Louisville to Memphis, and at the head of navigation on the Barre River fork of the Green River, which runs north, and empties into the Ohio near Evansville, Indiana.

The line from Bowling Green westward to Colum-

bus was crossed by the Tennessee and Cumberland
Rivers. To prevent the use of these rivers as a
means of penetrating Tennessee, the Confederates
had erected forts near the points where they crossed
the boundary from Tennessee into Kentucky. One
of these works was Fort Henry, situated on the east
bank of the Tennessee; another was Fort Heiman,
a partially completed work on a bluff just across the
river from Fort Henry. Twelve miles east of Fort
Henry was Fort Donelson, a strong work on the
west bank of the Cumberland River. These three
forts were at the centre of the imaginary line running direct from Bowling Green to Columbus and
somewhat south of it. Their capture would turn
both of these important positions, and compel surrender or evacuation.

Learning that an attempt would be made to re-
enforce Buckner at Bowling Green, Halleck ordered
Grant, on January 6, 1862, to make such a demonstration against Fort Donelson as to convey the
impression that this movement was part of a concerted operation against Nashville, Tennessee. The
ever-ready Grant made immediate preparations to
obey, and arranged with Flag-Officer Foote of the
Navy to secure the co-operation of his gunboats.
He wrote to Halleck: "The continuous rains for
the last week or more have rendered the roads extremely bad, and will necessarily make our movements slow." This was not offered as an excuse for
inaction; and he added in the same despatch, "This,
however, will operate worse upon an enemy, if he
should come out to meet us, than upon us."

7

"My son," said an old Cossack general to McClellan, who asked him how the roads were in Napoleon's time, "the roads are always bad in war."

Grant's movement was delayed by Halleck's orders until January 12, 1862. Then, with various marchings and counter-matchings to mislead the enemy, he advanced one column of five thousand men under McClernand to Mayfield, Kentucky, twenty-six miles south of Paducah, midway between Fort Henry on the Tennessee, and Columbus on the Mississippi. This placed McClernand in a position to threaten both of these Confederate strongholds, and he pushed the reconnaissance nearly up to Columbus. General C. F. Smith, another officer under Grant's command, marched to Paducah, on a general line parallel to the Tennessee, until he was in the vicinity of Fort Henry. Grant went up the Tennessee with Flag-Officer Foote and his three gunboats as far as Fort Henry, where Foote drew the fire of the fort, and answered it with a few shells. No serious demonstration was intended, however, and, having diverted attention from the re-enforcement of Bowling Green, the troops returned. "The reconnaissance thus made," as McClernand reported, "completed a march of one hundred and forty miles by the cavalry, and seventy-five by infantry, over icy and miry roads during the most inclement season." It was excellent practice for the raw troops, and it demonstrated the possibility of a successful movement against Forts Donelson and Henry, which was destined to bear fruit ere long. On January 20, 1862, Halleck wrote to McClellan:

"This line of the Cumberland or Tennessee is the great central line of the western theatre of war, with the Ohio below the mouth of the Green River [that is, near Evansville, Indiana] as the base, and two good navigable rivers [the Cumberland and Tennessee] extending far into the Interior of the theatre of operations."

Recognising the importance of this line, neither Halleck nor Buell made any move to take advantage of his knowledge. On January 22, 1862, General Smith made another reconnaissance to within two and one half miles of Fort Henry, and reported that the river had risen fourteen feet since the last visit. He believed that two ironclads could capture the place. Grant and Foote accordingly decided that an attack was advisable, and Grant hastened to St. Louis to secure authority to make the movement. Halleck refused permission, and snubbed Grant so badly that he returned very much crestfallen. On January 28th, Foote joined his entreaties to those of Grant in a telegram to Halleck, and Grant at the same time again asked that he might be allowed to take "Fort Henry on the Tennessee and establish and hold a large camp there." Receiving no reply to this despatch, he telegraphed again the next day, and still more emphatically.

Meanwhile, news of an important victory by General Thomas over Zollicoffer, at Mill Springs, in Eastern Kentucky, gave courage to the halting Halleck. He also received a further stimulus to action in the information that Beauregard was on his way with fifteen regiments from Virginia to re-enforce Johnston in Kentucky. "I was not ready to move," Halleck said, "but deemed it best to anticipate the arrival of Beauregard's forces." It would appear that somebody was ready to move, if Halleck was not. His weakness was an unwillingness to assume responsibility. He was intellectually strong, and had a very unusual knowledge of war as a science, but when it came to action he hesitated, "letting I dare not wait upon I would." As Grant said, "He would never take a chance in battle. A general who will never take a chance in battle will never fight one."

On January 30, 1862, Halleck telegraphed to Grant: "Make your preparations to take and hold Fort Henry. I will send you written instructions by mail." These instructions were received February 1st. The next day Grant began to embark 15,000 men in transports, ready for his passage up the Tennessee from Paducah. Two days later, on February 4th, he started with one half of his force, accompanied by Flag-Officer Foote of the Navy, with seven gunboats, four of them lightly armoured. That afternoon, McClernand with his division was landed four miles below Fort Henry; and Grant hastened back to Paducah, sixty miles down the river, to bring up the rest of his command. Lacking transports, he was obliged to move his two divisions separately. February 5th there was a reconnaissance by the troops belonging to McClernand's division, and General Smith joined Grant with his division. The movement to invest the fort began February 6, 1862. The troops had eight miles to march, over roads heavy with mud, and across swollen streams that required bridging. The gunboats had only half that distance to move by steam power, and they arrived sufficiently in advance to open fire on the fort before the troops were in position to invest it.

General Tilghman, who commanded at Fort Henry, had that morning sent orders to his infantry—three thousand in all, who were manning the outworks two miles from the fort—to retreat to Fort Donelson, holding his single company of artillery to man his guns. Fourteen of these guns commanded the river, and were mounted in five bastions; five other guns commanded the approaches by land. The fort itself was an excellent piece of engineering work, and was solidly constructed of earth. During the bombardment by the fleet, which continued for one hour and a quarter, one gun in the fort burst, another was disabled by a broken priming wire, and five were disabled by the fire from the gunboats. Three others had been drowned out by the rise of the river before the attack. Having only four heavy guns left, Tilghman decided to surrender Fort Henry, which made the best record, in the promptness of its submission, of all posts seriously defended during the war. Fort Heiman was also surrendered.

On February 6, 1862, Grant telegraphed to Halleck, "Fort Henry is ours," adding, "I shall take and destroy Fort Donelson on the 8th and return to Fort Henry." The same day McClellan, who had not yet heard of the capture of Fort Henry, suggested to Halleck and Buell a rapid combined movement up the Tennessee and Cumberland. Buell replied that it would require from fifty thousand to sixty thousand men. Halleck thought that if he had ten thousand more men, he could take Fort Henry. Grant, with two divisions, and the valuable assistance of the gunboats, had frightened the Confederates out of Fort Henry, and captured the place without waiting for re-enforcements. If the gunboats had captured the fort, it was the advance of the troops which compelled the withdrawal of the garrison to Fort Donelson.

The fall of this fort, and the possession of the Tennessee River that resulted from it, cut off the Confederate Army at Bowling Green from communication with Polk's forces at Columbus. Orders to evacuate Bowling Green were immediately given on February 7th. The evacuation began on the 11th, and was completed on the 13th.

February 9th, Beauregard wrote, "The loss of Fort Donelson (God grant it may not fall) would be followed by consequences too lamentable to be now alluded to."

Could Grant have carried out his plan of attacking Fort Donelson on February 8th, he would have found but six thousand men to oppose him, but there was an enemy he had not reckoned with. "The floods came and the winds blew." He reported: "I contemplated taking Fort Donelson to-day with infantry and cavalry alone, but all my troops may be kept busily engaged in saving what we have from the rapidly rising waters." He was not able to move on Donelson until February 12th.

By that time the enemy had been able to gather twenty thousand men in the fort, with John B. Floyd as the senior officer, Pillow and Buckner being his immediate subordinates. They held a strong position, and exerted themselves to the utmost up to the last moment to make it still stronger.

Fort Donelson was a bastioned work, standing on a bluff one hundred feet above the Cumberland River, with flanks guarded by two creeks whose valleys were filled by the overflow from the river during this season of high water. In the rear of the fort was a series of irregular ridges surmounted by earthworks. A bend in the stream at this point gave the guns of the fort control of everything within range. On the slope of the bluff, between the fort and the river, water batteries were erected thirty feet above the level of the stream. It was a difficult place to assault; and ironclads were of less avail there than at Fort Henry, owing to the high elevation of the fort, and the fact that the boats were obliged to approach "head on," and could use only their three bow guns.

Grant decided to leave General Lew Wallace with 2500 men to hold Fort Henry, and to advance against Fort Donelson with his remaining 15,000 without waiting for the re-enforcements which Halleck was hurrying to him. With sublime faith in the virtue of audacity, he resolved to move against a superior force holding a fortified position. The whole country was afloat with freshets, and he was obliged to march from Fort Henry over muddy roads and through falling snow. He carried no transportation, and his only artillery was eight field batteries. For some reason no attempt was made to contest his march; and he met with no opposition until he encountered the pickets of the force immediately in front of Donelson, at about noon on February 12th. The remainder of that day was spent in "developing" the enemy's position, and acquiring an idea of the "lay" of the ground. That night was a dismal one for the men, who were without shelter, and had only what they carried in their knapsacks and haversacks.

Foote had sailed from Cairo with his boats, on February 11, 1862, and re-enforcements were on their way. On the 13th, as they had not yet arrived, orders were sent to Wallace to leave Fort Henry to care for itself, and hurry forward with his brigade. Meanwhile the work of closing in on Fort Donelson continued, and an assault was attempted against a salient position. It was not successful, but it misled the besieged as to the strength of the attacking force. One gunboat, the *Carondelet*, arrived on the morning of the 13th, and the others toward night. With the gunboats came transports bringing re-enforcements and supplies.

That night there was a heavy wind, with snow. The lines were too near together to permit fires to be lighted, and the troops suffered severely. Some of them had, with the improvidence of recruits, thrown away their blankets, and they sat up all night, hugging themselves to keep warm.

On the 14th, Wallace arrived from Fort Henry.

The day was occupied in skirmishing, and in readjusting the lines to make a place for the newcomers. Without waiting for Grant, the impetuous Foote, remembering his experiences at Fort Henry, resolved upon an attack with his fleet alone. The result was disastrous. In ninety minutes every vessel in the fleet was disabled, and was drifting down the river, wholly unmanageable. Ten men had been killed, and forty-four wounded, including the Flag-Officer. No damage had been done to the fort.

The failure of the gunboat attack prevented an assault from the land side that had been determined upon. On the night of Friday, February 14th, the thermometer fell to ten degrees below zero, and many men were frozen. The next morning the soldiers, stiffened with cold, moved reluctantly to their task, over the frozen snow and through the biting frost. But their work was nearly accomplished. The Confederate commander, General Floyd, had little confidence in himself, and, fearing lest he should be caught like a rat in a trap, he resolved to withdraw while he could, and made an attack to force an opening through Grant's lines. The attack began early in the day; Grant was absent at the time, having ridden down before dawn to the river, in response to a request from the disabled Foote that he would come to consult with him. It was decided that the gunboats be sent to Cairo for repairs, the troops holding a line of investment during their absence.

When Grant, on his return to his lines from his visit to Foote, discerned the situation of affairs, he despatched a message to the Commodore, asking that he would delay the departure of his vessels and make a show of attacking, if it was only by firing a few shells at long range. Pillow had turned McClernand's right by a bold assault, driving him back in confusion, and had opened a line of retreat for the besieged garrison. General Buckner, who attacked McClernand's left, was repulsed, and withdrew to his intrenchments. Grant arrived on the ground at one o'clock, and immediately ordered C. F. Smith, who held the left of his line, to prepare for an assault. He then hastened to the right of his line to arrange for a co-operative movement by the troops in position there.

Smith assaulted at two o'clock, and carried an important outwork after a gallant and spirited attack. Lew Wallace in the centre, and McClernand on the left, advanced at the same time, and regained the ground lost in the morning. This closed up the lines of investment, and deprived the enemy of their opportunity for escape. Pillow telegraphed to Richmond: "The day is ours. I have repulsed the enemy at all points, but I want re-enforcements." He met his officers in counsel that night, in a little tavern at Dover, a village within his lines, and decided that their case was hopeless.

Sunday morning, February 16th, a negro came into Grant's lines with a report that the enemy were debating about a surrender, and that Floyd was already leaving. The Confederate Commander, in addition to the weight of his own incapacity, carried the heavy burden of a guilty conscience. He had no idea of being carried North a prisoner, to answer for his treacherous management of the War Department in the closing days of his administration as Secretary of War under Buchanan. Floyd and Pillow distrusted each other, with good reason, and Buckner despised them both. Instead of remaining with his troops, Floyd turned the command over to Pillow, acknowledging that " personal reasons prevented him from taking part in a capitulation"; and that night he put 1500 of his command on steamers. Pillow and his staff joined him, and together they made their escape up the river. The cavalry general, Forrest, at the same time marched out by the river road with three hundred or four hundred of his command.

At dawn on February 16, 1862, General Buckner sent a flag of truce to Grant, asking for an armistice until noon, and for the appointment of commissioners to settle upon terms of capitulation. Grant replied:

" No terms except unconditional and immediate surrender can be accepted. I propose to move immediately upon your works."

With a sharp comment upon the want of chivalry in such conditions, Buckner accepted them, and surrendered the fort, with sixty-five cannon, about seventeen thousand small arms, and some fourteen thousand prisoners. The Confederates lost altogether, in killed, wounded, and missing, 2,331 men. The prisoners taken had suffered severely from cold, lack of food, and want of sleep. Their appearance gave pathetic proof of the poverty of the

South in equipment for war, and of its willingness to suffer and endure for its cause. In place of blankets, many of the men carried square pieces of carpet cut from the floors of their impoverished homes, home-made " comforters," and bed-covers. Some bore feather beds on their backs, and among their personal arms were knives beaten out of files and saw-plates by village blacksmiths.

Grant's men suffered with equal severity. They were better equipped, but were unaccustomed to campaigning; and they had not learned how to make themselves comfortable in the field, as older soldiers can do. To any army the march across the country from Fort Henry to Fort Donelson, in the fiercest storms of a severe winter, would have been a test of endurance. But victory compensated for it all, and this time the Navy had not wrested their honours from them. Without assistance from the disabled gunboats, they had captured this important outwork of the State Capital at Nashville, and the whole region of country of which that city was the centre lay open to their victorious arms.

General Halleck had not encouraged Grant with his approval of this bold attack on Fort Donelson; but when it was decided upon, he aided him to the best of his ability with re-enforcements, though Grant had not waited for them, believing that his force of 15,000 men would be more effective than three times that number a month later.

The plan was to hold the enemy within the lines while the gunboats attacked. The withdrawal of the fleet, and the assault of the enemy on the 15th, compelled a change, and threw the burden of the battle on the troops. Learning that the men attacking McClernand had come out with knapsacks and haversacks filled with rations, Grant quickly divined that the attack was to secure an opening for escape. Turning to Colonel J. D. Webster of his staff, he said: "Some of our men are pretty badly demoralized, but the enemy must be more so, for he has attempted to force his way out, but has fallen back; the one who attacks first will now be victorious, and the enemy will have to be in a hurry to get ahead of me." Grant reasoned that Floyd, being a civilian soldier, would accept the advice of Pillow. He had known Pillow in Mexico, and his own boldness was partly founded on a well-calculated knowledge of Pillow's incapacity.

General Jordan, in his life of the Confederate cavalry general, Forrest, who made his escape from Donelson, speaking of the operations against that stronghold and Fort Henry, says: "As it was, Grant, landing with the petty force of 15,000 in the very centre of a force of nearly 45,000, having interior lines for concentration and communication, by railway at that, was able to take two heavy fortifications in detail, and place *hors de combat* nearly 15,000 of his enemies." The biographer of General Albert Sidney Johnston, says:

"Mighty as was the disaster, its consequences on the minds of the parties to the civil strife were still more ominous to the Confederate cause. Where now were the impregnable fortifications said to be guarded by 100,000 desperate Southerners? Where now the boasted prowess of troops, who were to quail at no odds; where now the inexhaustible resources that were to defy all methods of approach? The screen was thrown down; the inherent weakness and poverty of the South were made manifest to all eyes: its vaunted valour was quelled, it was claimed, by inferior numbers and superior courage, and the prestige of the Confederate arms was transferred to their antagonists."

We are further told that Grant, by decision, force of will, and tenacity of purpose, had held up the sinking courage of a beaten army. If fortune helped him, his case was not different from that of many others who have thus become famous.

The fall of Donelson pierced the rebel centre, and uncovered the region beyond. It secured the whole of Kentucky and Tennessee; it opened up the Tennessee and Cumberland Rivers for hundreds of miles, and was accompanied by the evacuation of Bowling Green, and of Columbus, which gave the control of the Mississippi from St. Louis to Arkansas. These were blows, as Beauregard tells us, " that staggered the Confederacy; the demoralization of the army, the panic of the people, were complete."

In his congratulatory order following Donelson, Grant said: " The victory achieved is not only great in the effect it will have in breaking down a rebellion, but it has secured the greatest number of prisoners of war ever taken in battle on this continent." He declared his belief in after years that Donelson would have ended the war if all the troops in that section had been under one command, and the victory had been followed up. On the day of surrender, Grant telegraphed to Halleck: " We have taken Fort Donelson and from 12,000 to 15,000 prisoners, including Generals Buckner and Bushrod R. Johnson; also about 20,000 stands of arms, forty-eight pieces of artillery, seventeen heavy guns, from 2000 to 4000 horses, and large quantities of commissary stores."

Nicolay and Hay say:

"By this brilliant and important victory Grant's fame sprang suddenly into full and universal recognition. President Lincoln nominated him major-general of volunteers, and the Senate at once confirmed the appointment. The whole military service felt the inspiriting event. Many of the colonels in Grant's army were made brigadier-generals; and promotion ran, like a quickening leaven, through the whole organization. Halleck also reminded the Government of his desire for larger power. 'Make Buell, Grant, and Pope major-generals of volunteers,' he telegraphed the day after the surrender, 'and give me command of the West. I ask this in return for Forts Henry and Donelson.'"

As the result of Donelson, Grant, who had been known in his youth as "Uncle Sam Grant," received a new christening from the people as "Unconditional Surrender Grant."

On February 15, 1862, Grant was assigned to the new military district of Tennessee, with "limits not defined," and General W. T. Sherman to the district of Cairo. This was the beginning of a friendship between two great soldiers that lasted through life. On February 21st, C. F. Smith was ordered to Clarksville by Grant, and took possession of that place.

When they heard of the fall of Fort Henry, February 12th, the Confederates withdrew from Bowling Green, and went into camp ten miles from Nashville, across the river. When the news of the fall of Fort Donelson reached Johnston, he removed his troops to Nashville, and erected batteries below that city to delay Foote's gunboats, and would have obstructed the river with a raft but for the bitter opposition of the "river men." He had no intention of holding Nashville, but wished to remain there long enough to remove the public property, and this he succeeded in doing.

Nashville occupied in the West relatively the same position as Richmond in the East. Its surrender was regarded by the 50,000 or 60,000 people then having a temporary or permanent residence in that city, as equivalent to the surrender of the Confederacy itself; and in the wild excitement that followed Donelson, the bonds of civil control were so loosened that the disorderly elements had temporary control.

Johnston withdrew from Nashville to Murfreesboro, Tennessee, on the railroad connecting Nashville with the Memphis and Charleston Railroad, running from Memphis through northern Mississippi and northern Alabama to Chattanooga, and joining there the lines opening communication with all the principal towns of the Confederacy along the Atlantic seaboard. This was the new line of defence chosen by the Confederates. On the morning of Sunday, February 23, 1862, the advance column of Buell, who had been sent forward by Grant, appeared at Edgefield on the north bank of the Cumberland, opposite Nashville, and the next day he received the formal surrender of the place from its citizens.

During the operations against Fort Donelson,

Grant was cut off in part from communication with his superiors by the treason of the telegraph operator, who stole his despatches instead of forwarding them, and carried them South with him. This was not an unmixed misfortune, for it prevented Halleck from interfering with his plans. It resulted, however, in a misunderstanding with Halleck which deprived Grant for a time of the prestige of military authority, due to his ability and his remarkable success. Halleck had been promptly informed of the capture of Donelson, and that Grant, unless he received orders to the contrary, would proceed up the Cumberland River, and take Clarksville on February 21st, and Nashville about March 1st.

Receiving no reply from Halleck, owing to the interruption of communication, General Smith was sent to Clarksville at the time named, and found that it had been evacuated. The plan of sending Grant's troops to Nashville was abandoned for want of transportation. As Buell was known to be advancing on that place, the re-enforcements received from him after the fall of Donelson, were ordered to proceed to Nashville without disembarking. Acting under these orders from Grant, Nelson, who was in Buell's command, proceeded to Nashville, and took possession of that city. Grant telegraphed to Halleck that he should go to Nashville himself on February 28th, if he received no orders to the contrary. Hearing nothing in reply, he carried out his intentions, with the result which is told in McClellan's *Own Story.* In a conversation over the wires with McClellan on March 2, 1862, Halleck said:

8

> "I have had no communication from Grant all the week. He left his command without my authority and went to Nashville. . . . I can get no report, no information of any kind, from him. Satisfied with his victory, he sits down and enjoys it without any regard to the future. I am worn out and tired with this neglect and inefficiency. C. F. Smith is almost the only officer equal to the emergency."

McClellan replied by directing Halleck to arrest Grant " at once, if the good of the service requires it, and place C. F. Smith in command." Halleck responded: " I do not deem it advisable to arrest him at present, but have placed General Smith in command of the expedition up the Tennessee. I think Smith will restore order and discipline." On March 4th Halleck telegraphed Grant to place Smith in command of this expedition and remain himself at Fort Henry. He added: " Why do you not obey my orders to report strength and positions of your command?" This was the first intimation Grant had received that such orders had been sent to him.

On March 6, 1862, Halleck telegraphed to Grant, stating that his " neglect of repeated orders, etc., was a matter of serious complaint at Washington, so much so, that I am advised to arrest you on your return." Meanwhile the matter was satisfactorily explained and, in reply to an order from Washington, on March 10, directing that he report "as to Grant's unauthorized visit to Nashville, and as to his general conduct," Halleck stated that Grant had gone to Nashville to communicate with Buell, that his motives were proper, and advised that no further proceedings be taken in the case. The wording of the order which assigned him to his new command was sufficient answer to Halleck's complaint that in going to Nashville he had left his department.

Halleck informed Grant of his action in this matter, but discreetly refrained from telling him that he was himself the cause of the serious complaints reported as coming from Washington. This left Grant under the impression that his enemy was McClellan, and he was duly grateful to Halleck for his supposed interference in his behalf. It was not until after the war had closed that Grant learned the true state of the case from General McClellan, none of the correspondence being found upon the records of the War Department.

Halleck was a man of bitter prejudices. He did not believe in Grant, and distrusted him because of the stories of his drinking habits. He did believe strongly in C. F. Smith, who was indeed in every way worthy of his confidence. Smith was, from the point of view of the West Point officer, an ideal soldier, " whose shape was that of Apollo, and whose disposition in peace was that of a lamb; while in battle he was as fierce as a lion of the Jordan." In his *Memoirs*, Grant says:

> "It is probable that the general opinion was that Smith's long services in the Army, and distinguished deeds, rendered him the more proper person for command: indeed, I was rather inclined to this opinion myself at that time, and would have served as faithfully under Smith as he had done under me. But this did not justify the despatches which General Halleck sent to Washington, or his subsequent concealment of them from me when pretending to explain the action of my superiors."

General Smith was no party to this intrigue against General Grant, and he was unhesitating in his denunciation of Halleck's treatment of him. His death soon followed, on April 29, 1862, and the Army was deprived of one of its ablest soldiers.

On March 11, 1862, McClellan was relieved of the duties of General-in-Chief of all the Armies; and the three military departments west of Knoxville, Tennessee, were united under the command of Halleck.

CHAPTER VIII.

BATTLE OF SHILOH, OR PITTSBURG LANDING.

APRIL 6–7, 1862.

DURING Grant's campaign against Forts Henry and Donelson, General S. R. Curtis had been busy on the west of the Mississippi in driving Price and his men from southwestern Missouri, and had advanced in pursuit across the southern frontier of the State into Arkansas. General John Pope had also been very active in his "District of Central Missouri." On March 3d, Pope appeared with the Army of the Mississippi, 20,000 men, before the Confederate position at New Madrid on the Mississippi, and, after a vigorous siege, compelled its evacuation on March 13th. The Confederates still held a fortified position on an island in the Mississippi, known as Island No. 10, one hundred miles below Cairo, and just above New Madrid, whither they had removed the forces evacuating Columbus. Aided by Foote's gunboats, Pope succeeded in compelling the surrender of this place, with 7000 officers and men, April 8, 1862.

An order restoring Grant to full command was issued on March 13, 1862, and on the 17th he resumed his duties. The concentrated movement that he favoured was not undertaken, as neither Buell nor Halleck could be persuaded of its feasibility. " Of all the men whom I have encountered in high position," McClellan says, " Halleck was the most hopelessly stupid. It was more difficult to get an idea through his head than can be conceived by any one who never made the attempt. I do not think he ever had a correct military idea from beginning to end."

This is too strong a statement, and it does not accord with the opinion of Halleck entertained by both Grant and Sherman. He was an able officer; but his mind was too much occupied with the rules which he had formulated in a work on the strategy and logistics of war, to be always properly appreciative of the conditions of war as applied to the field actually under his command.

After a surrender of Fort Henry, Lieutenant-Commander Phelps, U. S. Navy, went with a gunboat up the Tennessee River, entirely across the State of Tennessee, to Florence, just over the boundary line in Alabama. The Confederates had taken up a new line of defence farther south; and the next objective point for the Union attack was Memphis, in the southwest corner of Tennessee, on the Mississippi River. To protect their railroad communication between Memphis and the East, the Confederates had established themselves in a strong defensive position at Corinth, Mississippi, where the two most important railroads in the Mississippi Valley cross each other. The gunboats could pass up and down the Tennessee; but to effect any permanent lodgment farther south, it was necessary to drive the enemy from Corinth.

Grant regarded Corinth as the " great strategic position between the Tennessee and the Mississippi Rivers, and between Nashville and Vicksburg." The Confederate general, Johnston, had determined to unite his whole army with that of Beauregard, and hazard a battle there. By the end of March the Confederates had been able to concentrate 50,000 men at Corinth. On March 28, 1862, Halleck telegraphed to Buell, who was at Nashville: " It seems from all accounts that the enemy is massing his forces in the vicinity of Corinth. You will concentrate all your available troops at Savannah or Pittsburg, twelve miles above. Large reinforcements being sent to General Grant. We must be ready to attack the enemy as soon as the roads are passable."

During the period of General Grant's suspension from command, his troops, under the command of C. F. Smith, had moved south up the Tennessee River above Fort Henry, to operate upon the communications of the enemy. Sherman, who was under the orders of Smith, had also been sent south by water to cut the Memphis and Charleston Railroad. This expedition was a failure, as an inundation made it impossible for Sherman to move his troops across the country from the transports. On the Tennessee River, twenty-two miles northeast of

Corinth, is Pittsburg Landing.* On his way up the river, Sherman had sent from this place a request that a division should occupy it to prevent the Confederates seizing it, and interfering with his expedition. Hurlbut's division was ordered there, and Sherman found it on board transports when he returned, on March 17th, from his unsuccessful movement inland. In a report to Grant at that date Sherman said that he was " strongly impressed with the importance of this place, both for its land advantages and its strategic position. The ground itself admits of easy defence by a small command, and yet affords admirable camping-ground for 100,000 men."

C. F. Smith agreed with Sherman in the opinion that Pittsburg Landing was the best base for the movement to occupy northern Mississippi and Alabama, control the railroad system of that region, and take Memphis in the rear while Halleck forced the Mississippi. Grant, to whom the direction of this movement had been assigned, wished to strike at once: he received positive orders from Halleck to act only on the defensive.

It was a season of high water on the Tennessee,

---

* The Tennessee River is so closely identified with the fortunes of General Grant, that its geography should be carefully studied. Its head waters are in southwestern Virginia, and it becomes a considerable stream at Knoxville, Tennessee, flowing thence southwest to Chattanooga, next west and southwest into Alabama, then through the northern part of that State for nearly two hundred miles, until it again enters Tennessee near Pittsburg Landing; then northerly across the States of Tennessee and Kentucky, and into the Ohio River at Paducah, Kentucky, not far from Cairo, Illinois.

and the banks of the river were flooded, except the bluffs, where steamboat landings had been established in the locality of Grant's operations at Savannah, Hamburgh, Crumps and Pittsburg Landings. The plan was to concentrate the forces of Buell and Grant, under the command of Halleck, for an advanced movement, and they were ordered to avoid an encounter with the enemy until Halleck arrived. The choice between Savannah and Pittsburg as a place of concentration had been very properly left by Halleck to the judgment of the officers on the ground.

Savannah, being on the side of the river away from the enemy, was the safer position: but concentration here involved the necessity for transporting across the water the large force gathering for an immediate advance; and the advantages of Pittsburg were so great in other respects, that Grant decided, when he arrived on the ground, to adhere to Sherman's and Smith's selection of this position. On March 17th he wrote to Sherman from Savannah, " I have just arrived, and, although sick for the last two weeks, begin to feel better at the thought of being again with the troops." He immediately gave orders to Smith's division to move to Pittsburg Landing, and placed Smith in command of the camp at Savannah. Hurlbut's division was already on the ground. On March 18th Sherman disembarked his division from the transports that carried them up the river. Prentiss arrived also, and organised a new division from unassigned regiments, camping with his green troops on the left of

Sherman. The divisions of McClernand and W. H. L. Wallace were farther up the river at Crumps Landing, guarding the road between Savannah and Bethel, on the Mississippi and Ohio Railroad.

Grant went into camp at Pittsburg, and began to get his troops into shape for the proposed advance on Corinth. The camps were located on wooded heights, hidden in most cases by a heavy second growth of timber, and approached across deep ravines or open fields. In the troughs of the ravines were brooks, swollen by heavy rains and having boggy places, hazardous for the passage of artillery, and difficult even for infantry. The country partakes of the general characteristics of southern Tennessee and northern Mississippi, where the level of the land is broken by a series of rounded and heavily timbered ridges, intersected by numerous streams running over miry bottoms, between banks of tenacious clay mud, and very difficult to cross under the most favourable circumstances. The river in the rear of the Union position flowed in the form of an S. Along it ran a line of bluffs, masking the stream from the view of the country beyond its banks. The roads leading to Pittsburg Landing were the common country roads,—bad for marching, at their best, and quickly made well-nigh impassable by heavy rains. The succession of ravines, ridges, and woods gave every opportunity for the selection of defensive positions.

General Beauregard says that the Union position gave the Confederates an opportunity for an almost fatal counter-stroke, such as has rarely been afforded to the one of two belligerents who was the weaker in the sinews and resources of war. It was in a narrow *cul-de-sac* formed by Snake Creek and Lick Creek, with the broad bank-full river as its bottom, —tactically as well as strategically a false position for an invading army. On the other hand, the biographer of General A. S. Johnston tells us that the Federal position here was

> "a formidable, natural fortification. With few and difficult approaches guarded on either flank by impassable streams and morasses, protected by a succession of ravines and acclivities, each commanded by eminences to the rear, this quadrilateral seemed a safe fastness against attack; hard to assail, easy to defend. Its selection was the dying gift of the soldierly C. F. Smith to his cause."

Sherman says, "At a later period of the war we could have rendered this position impregnable in one night, but at this time we did not do it."

It is easy to be wise after the event. At that time neither Army had learned the value of field intrenchments. Grant did propose to fortify, and sent General J. B. McPherson, who was an excellent engineer, to trace a line of works; but it was decided not to fortify, as the movement was intended to be an aggressive one, and the consensus of opinion was against intrenching. No one of the excellent soldiers present favoured it. The successes of Henry and Donelson had made officers and men over-confident. They had not yet learned the true measure of the task they had undertaken; and it was generally believed that a series of reverses had paralysed the Confederacy, in that section at least.

Two and one half miles from the landing at Pittsburg was a little one-story log meeting-house known as Shiloh Church, where Sherman had located his headquarters, on the advance line of Grant's forces. Southwest from Shiloh, across the boundary line of Tennessee at Corinth, Mississippi, the Confederates were gathering under Johnston, watching with eager anxiety the movement of concentration against them. Following the well-worn military rule of destroying your enemy in detail if you can, Johnston resolved to attack Grant before Buell arrived.

Though his troops had crossed the river, Grant continued his headquarters at Savannah, on the east bank, the point of rendezvous for the gathering army, his presence being required there to receive and organise the new troops which were constantly arriving, and to meet Buell, who was daily expected, so as to promptly arrange for carrying his troops across the river, and placing them in position. Buell's advance under Nelson arrived April 5th, and were ordered into position where they could be ferried over the river. Buell himself came that evening, but did not report to Grant. Johnston heard of his approach on April 2d, and resolved to strike at once.

Orders for the advance were given at one o'clock on the morning of April 3d, and by noon the whole Confederate Army was ready for the march. The intention was to attack on the morning of the 5th by columns of corps, to surprise Grant, and to crush him before Buell could re-enforce him. The difficulties of marching over the heavy narrow road from Corinth, and the interference of one corps with another, through want of concerted action between the corps commanders, delayed the movement of the Confederates so long, that it was fully believed that their enemy had been warned.

On Friday, April 4, 1862, Lew Wallace, five miles up the river from Pittsburg, reported that there was a heavy force in front of him, and he believed that this was a reconnaissance with a view to an attack upon him. On the same day, Colonel Buckland, commanding Sherman's Fourth Brigade, on visiting his picket lines, found the woods swarming with Confederate cavalry along his entire front, and the pickets reported that they had seen infantry and artillery.

The Confederates seen were Forrest's cavalry, pushed forward to obtain topographical information, but ordered not to undertake any aggressive movement that should warn the Union Army. Forrest captured an officer; and from him General Jordan, of Beauregard's staff, learned, by skilful cross-examination, that there were no earthworks to encounter, and that the commanders of the Union forces were wholly unaware of the proposed attack. This information was communicated to Generals Johnston and Beauregard. Sherman discovered no signs of infantry, though some of his men on picket asserted that they had seen them; and he decided that the troops on his front were merely a force of cavalry reconnoitring. Rabbits and squirrels running across the picket line indicated some movement beyond it, and the Union troops were ordered to be on their guard against an attack. The pickets were strengthened, and a line of sentries was established between the picket line and the camp.

Heavy showers fell during the night of April 4th; but these cleared off before morning, when the sun arose in a clear sky. On Saturday, April 5th, the forest in front of Grant's position was alive with the bustle of preparation for the coming struggle. At daybreak the advanced camps of the Union Army were so clearly in sight of the Confederate lines, that Johnston said to Beauregard, " Can it be possible that they are not aware of our position ?" Beauregard replied, " It is scarcely possible; they are trying to entrap us."

Sherman wrote to Grant on that day: " The enemy is saucy, but got the worst of it yesterday. . . . I do not apprehend anything like an attack on our position."

Grant wrote to Halleck: " Our outposts have been attacked in considerable force. I immediately went up and found all quiet. I have scarcely the faintest idea of any attack upon us." There was during the day unimportant but lively skirmishing with Forrest's cavalry on the further side of Lick Creek.

Johnston's troops had been ordered to attack at three o'clock on the morning of April 5th; but Polk's Corps did not arrive until two o'clock that afternoon, and it was nearly night before all the troops were in position. It was impossible to keep the green troops of the Confederate Army quiet; and the night was disturbed by the kindling of fires and the beating of drums, by cheering, and by a scattering fire of small arms as the men tested their ammunition to see if the rain had injured it. The wind appears to have swept the sound of the enemy's movements away from Grant's front; but the noise from the Federal camp was carried into the Rebel line, and they had the advantage of knowing what was on their front. The want of cavalry made it difficult to ascertain what was going on in front of the Federal position; and the troops were so near together, that the officers attributed the noises made by the enemy, and heard in their lines, to their own men. At a council of war, Beauregard advised that the Confederate Army return to Corinth, as the delay and noise had notified the Federals, and he believed that they would be found intrenched " to their eyes," awaiting an attack, and his troops were too raw to attack intrenchments.

On Sunday morning, April 6, 1862, the Confederates advanced to the attack on the Union lines, which were hidden by the morning mist lying low in the wooded valleys. Instead of moving in column of corps, three lines were formed. Hardee's Corps was in advance, his front extending for three miles; Bragg's Corps followed in the second line, Polk's in the third, and Breckinridge was in reserve. Forrest, with 4382 cavalry, guarded the Confederate flanks. In all, there were 40,000 Confederates in battle array, excluding all details. On the same basis of estimate, Grant had in the field 33,000 men. The first gun was fired at 5.14 A.M.

The Confederate reports show that on some points of the Union line they found no infantry picket in advance of the ordinary chain of sentinels, and no cavalry in front of Prentiss or of Sherman. It appears, however, that both of these officers were on the alert. Prentiss threw one regiment forward and attacked Hardee's skirmish line, thinking that it was an outpost. This regiment was repulsed, and followed into camp by the enemy.

Then the full crash of battle broke in all its fury without the ordinary prelude of a contest between skirmish lines, and the men in the Union advance had barely time to rally to meet the assault. Forrest reported that many of them were found in their blankets fast asleep, some were washing or dressing, some were cooking their morning meal, and the early ones were eating breakfast. Arms and accoutrements " were spread around in the orderless fashion of holiday soldiers."

It so happened that the most inexperienced soldiers had been placed on the front, and some of them hastened to the rear, two cowardly colonels carrying their entire regiments with them. The skulkers were speedily sifted from the fighting men, and those who remained vigorously contested the field. Confederate accounts report a desperate resistance and fearful loss.

Grant's flanks were protected by the swollen creeks, and the attack was delivered in front. As Johnston's first line pressed forward, the gaps made in it were filled from the second and third lines. General Lew Wallace, whose fame as a novelist should not obscure his reputation as a soldier, was not on the ground with his large division; and the Confederates were strongest at every point of contact except the left centre, where W. H. L. Wallace and Hurlbut held a strong position, to which the Confederates gave the name of " the Hornet's Nest."

" Here," says General Johnston's son and biographer,

"behind the dense thicket, on the crest of a hill, was posted as strong a force of hardy troops as ever fought; almost perfectly protected by the conformation of the ground, and by logs and other rude and hastily prepared defences. No figure of speech would be too strong to express the deadly peril of assault upon this natural fortress, whose inaccessible barriers blazed for six hours with sheets of flame, and whose infernal gates poured forth a murderous storm of shot and shell and musket fire, which no living thing could quell or even withstand."

The same writer says, " No Confederate who fought at Shiloh has ever said that he found any point on that bloody field easy to assail."

The Confederate forces were divided by the deep wooded ravines, and their attack was not continuous, but " in a series of disjointed assaults." These were sturdily met, and at some points of the Union lines were repulsed, and followed with counter-charges. The Yankee cheer and the Rebel yell mingled with the roar of artillery and the sharp whiz of the spiteful bullets. The Kentuckians in the Confederate line, as they advanced, sang their war-song, " Cheer, boys, cheer, we will march away to battle!" Firing from behind trees, within hearing distance, the Confederates would shout, " Bull Run!" awakening the Union retort, " Donelson!"

Thus the battle raged at half-past two in the afternoon when Johnston, who commanded the Confederate forces, was killed, and the command passed to Beauregard. This change occasioned a lull for over an hour, and then the contest was renewed. The Federal general, Prentiss, who had not been sufficiently prompt in withdrawing when the troops on his right and left were driven back, was enclosed on both flanks, and surrendered with 2200 of his officers and men. The Union troops had been driven from position to position, retreating step by step nearly to Pittsburg Landing, where their shortened line extended from the Tennessee River on their left, to the Snake Creek on the right. Thousands of Union soldiers—estimated by Grant to number 5000, and by Sherman, 10,000—had fled to the rear during the prolonged contest, until further progress was checked by the river, where they were crouching in a complete state of physical and moral collapse, on the water's edge, under the shelter of a high bluff.

Grant, who was at Savannah when the battle began, found them there, on his way to the field of battle, and not having other use for his cavalry, on account of the nature of the ground, sent them to the rear to stop further straggling, and to drive the skulkers to the front.

Grant had not forgotten his experience at Monterey and Fort Donelson; and he promptly organised an ammunition train to supply the men on the firing line, who speedily exhausted the cartidges they carried with them. The various commands had been badly broken up at the time of his arrival on the field, and there was great confusion for the want of proper directions. He rode to and fro along the front, smoking his cigar, giving few orders, but encouraging his officers everywhere, and bidding them to do their best.

The scenes of confusion and disorder in the rear of the Union lines were repeated in the rear of the Confederates. Johnston's men had been furnished with three days' cooked rations; but, with the improvidence of recruits, many had promptly devoured their supplies or thrown them away, and they went into battle hungry. When the Union troops fell back, their camps were left in possession of the enemy. The temptation they offered to luxurious indulgence was too much for the hungry and thirsty soldiers of the Confederacy. Many of them scattered to eat, drink, and pillage; so that the attacking force suffered nearly as much from demoralisation as Grant's men. Surgeon Carey, U. S. Volunteers, who was a prisoner in Beauregard's camp, says:

"I have often heard of demoralized armies, but the scene presented here beggars description. The woods were crowded with men running at full speed, with trunks filled with booty and with big bundles, some without packs or guns, divested of everything that offered an impediment to their running."

The time occupied in taking care of Prentiss's men also interfered with movements in the Confederate lines. Every man had been put into battle in the first attack, except two brigades of Breckinridge—in reserve; the battle had raged for ten hours;

and, in spite of their success, the Confederates had but little stomach for further fighting. They were badly disorganised in their encounter with an enemy who did not appear to know when he was whipped. Accordingly, Beauregard, who was in command, with his headquarters at Shiloh Church, where Sherman had been the night before, ordered a halt at five o'clock in the afternoon. He had not succeeded in his purpose of turning Grant's flanks, the left flank being protected in part by the gunboats *Tyler* and *Lexington*. General Jordan, Chief of Staff, describes Beauregard's Army on that night as "very much in the condition of a lump of sugar thoroughly soaked with water, but yet preserving its original shape, though ready to dissolve."

Lew Wallace, who had been ordered early in the day to join at Pittsburg Landing, owing to some misunderstanding or misdirection, did not arrive until too late to take part in the battle. The advance of Buell's troops joined from the other side of the river toward the end of the day, before the firing had ceased, and lost a few men.

On the night of the first day's battle, companies of the Union Army were commanded in many cases by sergeants, regiments by lieutenants, and brigades by majors. Both forces rested on their arms, getting what repose they could in a drenching rain. To enliven proceedings in the Confederate camps, the gunboats on the river dropped a shell every fifteen minutes among them.

On the day before the battle, General Grant had been severely bruised by his horse slipping on a log, and falling upon him, as he was returning in the dark from a visit to Sherman's picket line. On the night of the battle he sought shelter in a hut occupied by the surgeons as a field hospital; but the sight of the wounded drove him forth, and he obtained what rest he could for his bruised and aching body, lying on the ground under the trees in the rain with his soldiers. That night Forrest clothed some of his scouts in Federal overcoats, and sent them through Grant's lines to bring back information of the condition of things there. That they were able to get through, shows how ignorant the Union pickets were.

The morning of Monday, April 7, 1862, found Grant in position with his original commands, minus Prentiss's Brigade, and re-enforced by Wallace's division holding his right, and on the left Buell's Army of the Ohio, which during the night had completed the passage of the river. This was a day of victory for the Union forces. On the previous night Grant had said: " We must not give the enemy the moral advantage of attacking to-morrow morning. We must fire the first gun."

An assault was made all along the line at daybreak on April 7th, and the conditions of the previous day were reversed. In a series of charges and countercharges the Confederates were steadily driven back, and by three o'clock were in full retreat. " The attack of the Federal Army," says Johnston's biographer, " was well conducted, systematic, and spirited." " At four o'clock the flag of the Union floated again upon the line from which it had been driven the previous day, and General Grant's troops at once resumed their camp."

Lew Wallace had added 6500 men to Grant's Army; Buell brought 20,000 men; and there was a further re-enforcement by single regiments, numbering, in all, 1400. Wood arrived with his division before the close of the engagement, but too late to join in the battle. Thomas's division of Buell's Army did not reach the field until after the fight was over.

The Confederate retreat began at half-past two that afternoon. It was conducted in a cold and drizzling rainstorm, changing to blinding hail, and lasting for three hours. This subjected to great hardship the wounded and dying soldiers, who travelled through the storm in open waggons, without even a blanket to cover them. The retreat was made in good order, and there was no effective attempt at pursuit, owing to the conditions of the roads. The losses reported in the *Records of the Rebellion* (vol. X., Part I.) were as follows:

	Killed.	Wounded.	Missing.	Total.
Union	1754	8408	2885	13,047
Confederates	1723	8012	959	10,694

General Grant questioned the accuracy of Beauregard's statement of the number killed, stating that his men had kept count of 4000 Confederate dead buried by them. This would make the total of killed, wounded, and missing on both sides about equal, with a large preponderance of killed and wounded among the Confederates. Grant further says, that aside from the loss of Prentiss, with his 2200 officers and men, he took more prisoners on the second day than he lost on the first, and captured as many guns as had been taken from him the day before.

The list of casualties tells the story of stubborn fighting, and Shiloh or Pittsburg Landing—it is called indifferently by both names—was one of the most stubbornly contested battle-fields of the war. If there was surprise, it was shared by both parties. Grant encountered a force he was not looking for, and the Confederates met with a resistance they had not expected.

In answer to the criticism upon the position of the Union Army with a river in their rear, General Sherman says: " If there were any errors in putting that army on the west side of the Tennessee, exposed to the superior force of the enemy, also assembling at Corinth, the mistake was not General Grant's, but there was no mistake."

The stubborn resistance which the Confederates met with at the outset is shown by the fact that they were soon obliged to call upon their reserves. One regiment, the 16th Wisconsin, recruited in the lumber regions, had four hundred men good at a " turkey shoot." " Pretty busy, eh ? " said the Colonel to one of his men. " How many have you finished, Colonel ? " The Colonel answered, " I have fired thirty-seven cartridges, and I don't feel certain of six." Of the other thirty-one he was sure. The first panic sifted all the cowards out of Grant's

Army, and a large proportion of those who remained were cool-headed sportsmen, who took advantage of the defensive positions among the trees and fallen timber. The disorganisation of the battle extended only to the tactical formations.

CHAPTER IX.

MISSISSIPPI CAMPAIGN—CORINTH AND IUKA.

APRIL–OCTOBER, 1862.

T is difficult to formulate a strictly military criticism on the battle of Shiloh, and this fact may explain the endless disputes and discussions concerning it. We had no armies then, in the European sense, on either side. The combatants were citizens, full of zeal, full of energy, and fired with patriotic devotion; but they had few of the characteristics of unity and associated action which constitute the distinctive features of an army. To both sides may be applied Bragg's description of the Confederate force: " It was a heterogeneous mass, in which there was more enthusiasm than discipline, more capacity than knowledge, and more valour than instruction." In the *Life of A. S. Johnston*, the author quotes a friend who commanded a brigade in this battle as saying: "You know I was as ignorant of the military art at that time as it was possible for a civilian to be; I had never seen a man fire a musket; I had never heard a lecture or read a

line on the subject. We were all tyros—all the rawest of green recruits—generals, colonels, captains, soldiers."

An effective army is a vital organism, in which each part responds promptly to the demands of the whole, moving obediently to the suggestion of some single will. Such an organism is possible only to the extent in which each officer and man so thoroughly understands his duties that he does the correct thing in the moment of emergency, undisturbed by confusion and alarm, having full possession of his faculties in the hour of action, when every nerve and muscle is put upon the strain. Of the three thousand million thoughts the mind is said to be capable of containing, the dominant one in the mind of the new soldier going into battle is that of danger. Raw troops either promptly run away, or they stand well up to their work, as the majority of Grant's troops did at Shiloh. Inexperienced soldiers are not able to discriminate as to the nature of an attack; and if they fight at all, they will fight to the bitter end.

Those of Grant's soldiers who ran away at Shiloh were no doubt greatly surprised, as every untrained recruit is when he first realises by actual experience that there are men so reckless of his personal comfort as to willingly use him for a target. They carried with them, in their flight, stories of surprise and demoralisation that spread over the country faster than they could be followed by explanations. The Army of Shiloh suffered, too, from the ignorance of the science of outposts, which was common then. General officers seldom knew what was actually going on along their picket lines, as there was a great discrepancy between their orders and the execution of orders. Sherman wrote May 12, 1862: " I have been worried to death by the carelessness of officers and sentinels; have begged, importuned, and cursed, to little purpose. Sentinels fresh from home have as much idea of war as children."

Orders would leave the officers correctly enough, but they would never reach the front in the shape of a well-posted picket. The details that in their sum total make military efficiency were known to but few. Where the instructed ones were officers of rank, they found it difficult to understand the ignorance of their subordinates and to allow for it. Often it was the blind leading the blind, and they fell into the ditch together.

The security of an army depends upon its ability to obtain early information of any aggressive movement by its enemy. For this it depends on cavalry, scouting beyond its infantry lines, and on a cordon of infantry extended along its front, and keeping vigilant watch on suspicious movements. It is essential that the men forming this outermost line of an army should be sufficiently instructed to comprehend the significance of what they see. Otherwise they are worse than useless, for they awaken an undue sense of confidence. It is expected that an enemy approaching will be met by continually increasing resistance, and detained long enough to enable the main body of the assailed army to rally for the defence. When the ordinary precautions against attack fail in their purpose, in whole or in part, as they did at Shiloh, the result is confusion and too hasty preparation for battle. Sherman knew how ignorant his men were; and probably their reports of what was heard in his front did not sufficiently impress his mind, preoccupied with the conviction that no assault was intended. He knew, as Grant knew, that to men so ignorant as most of those whom they commanded, any suggestion of danger was demoralising. They needed the stimulus of motion, of action; the sense of doing something aggressive, to fire their spirits and give them confidence and courage. The confusion in commands on the battle-field is readily explained by the remark of General Beauregard, "that he had often seen new troops, when attempting to manœuvre, even on level ground, get so thoroughly mixed up in a few moments, that a long time was required to disentangle them." Cohesion, under the enormous strain of battle, is difficult with the best of troops; with raw troops it is impossible.

But these errors of ignorance were so evenly balanced, that it is difficult to say which side profited most by them at Shiloh. The best comment on the battle is, that both parties to it were engaged for many years afterwards in apologies and explanations as to what they did, and what they left undone. It was Halleck's purpose to concentrate his forces at Pittsburg Landing, and to advance on Corinth. Johnston checked this movement. It was Johnston's intention to destroy Grant's Army before Buell arrived; then to defeat Buell and carry the war across the Ohio River. He failed in the attempt. If Grant was misled as to the intentions of the enemy, he was only following an unbroken line of distinguished precedents furnished by great commanders since the beginning of war. "The prescience" and "intuitive divination" of an enemy's designs exist only in the imagination of historians. In but three days, in one of his campaigns, Napoleon made three erroneous calculations of the Prussian movements. Those who are disturbed by American ignorance of war may profitably recall the statement of Napoleon III., that the disasters of France in the war with Prussia were due to the general ignorance of his army.

The first aggressive campaign of the Confederates in the West was overthrown at Shiloh and at Murfreesboro, which followed it a few months later. But Shiloh won no honours for Grant, and he was again under a cloud. The host of newspaper writers in Halleck's Army could not resist the opportunity this battle gave them to display their superior knowledge of war, and to prove to their own satisfaction that Grant's career was a series of military blunders. According to them, he had been defeated at Shiloh, and nothing but luck had saved him at Donelson. The cowards who scattered to the rear in the fight of April 6th, in seeking excuse for their own delinquency, chose Grant for their scapegoat. Hostile feeling against him ran high, and active attempts were made to have him removed from command. Speaking of Shiloh, Sherman says: "Grant displayed the coolness, the personal courage, forethought, and deliberation which afterwards made him famous among men; yet he was traduced, slandered, and wronged, not only by the press universally, but by those who were in positions of authority over him."

A newspaper correspondent, Mr. Richardson, who was with Grant at this time, says of him: "He silently smoked and waited. The only protest I ever knew him to utter was to the correspondent of the journal which had denounced him with great severity. 'Your paper is very unjust to me, but time will make it all right. I want to be judged only by my acts.'"

Mr. Richardson further says:

"Hooker once boasted that he had the best army on the planet. One could have declared that Grant commanded the worst. There was little of that order, perfect drill, or pride, pomp, and circumstance seen among Buell's troops and in the Army of the Potomac. But Grant's rough, rugged soldiers would fight wonderfully, and were not easily demoralized. If their line became broken, every man from behind a tree, rock, or stump, blazed away at the enemy on his own account.

"Unlike Halleck, Grant did not pretend to familiarity with the details of military text-books. He would not move an army with that beautiful symmetry which McClellan displayed, but his pontoons were always up, and his ammunition trains were never missing. Though not occupied with details, he must have given close attention to them, for while other commanding generals had forty or fifty staff officers, brilliant with braid and button, Grant allowed himself but six or seven."

As Halleck had persistently ignored Grant, and had, in violation of military etiquette, received the reports of his subordinate officers and forwarded them direct to Washington, Grant made no official report of the battle of Shiloh. His opponent, Beauregard, was subjected to a similar experience from the Richmond War Office, and he also withheld his report.

The result of this sharp experience at Shiloh completed the change in Grant's views as to the struggle between the North and the South. He was fully satisfied, for the first time, that the contest was to be a long and bitter one, and he shaped his course accordingly. He abandoned his policy of protecting friend and foe alike, though he still extended protection to Southern sympathisers living quietly at home. He forbade pillage, but he took what he needed for public use, receipting to the owners for what was taken. Property he could not use, he destroyed, where he believed that otherwise it would be devoted to the uses of the Confederacy.

The movement to Pittsburg Landing had carried Grant and Buell across the State of Tennessee and nearly to the northern limit of Mississippi. Before leaving Nashville, Buell had sent General O. M. Mitchell, of astronomical fame, south with his command, across the boundary of Tennessee, into Alabama, with orders to operate against the Memphis and Charleston Railroad, connecting Corinth with the East. After the victory of Shiloh, Mitchell marched, April 10, 1862, from Fayetteville, Tennessee, to Huntsville, Alabama. From there he operated on the railroad as far east as Bridgeport, Alabama, and as far west as Tuscumbia, Alabama, destroying railroad bridges, capturing railroad stock and public property. He secured no lodgment in the country, and his movement was in accordance with the general policy of dispersion prevailing at that time.

Halleck's objective after Shiloh continued to be Corinth, but he was apparently in no haste to get there. His instructions had been to limit the movements beyond Pittsburg Landing to a day's journey, going and returning. Buell's explanation of his failure to follow the retreating enemy with his fresh troops was that he received no orders to do so. Grant, in his orders to his division commanders after the battle, said: " I have instructed Taylor's cavalry to push out on the road towards Corinth to ascertain if the enemy have retreated. Should they be retreating, I want all the cavalry to follow them." On April 8th, Sherman pursued the enemy, but only far enough to discover that they had withdrawn in good order. Halleck, who expected to arrive the next day, did not reach Pittsburg Landing, to assume command there, until April 11, 1862. Grant was then assigned to the position of second in command,—very honorary, but as unimportant as that of Vice-President, except that he had immediate control of the right wing and the reserve. His position was so embarrassing, indeed, that he made several applications to be relieved. He was not relieved, but he was allowed to move his headquarters, as Commander of the District of West Tennessee, to Memphis. He started for that city on June 23, 1862. As he travelled without escort, he narrowly escaped falling into the hands of a roaming force of Confederate cavalry.

Halleck had undertaken to capture the Confederate Army, which had retreated to Corinth after Shiloh, by a system of gradual approaches, fortifying as he moved. His attempt was as successful as the youthful expedient of capturing birds by the application of salt to their tails. After crawling painfully from position to position for nearly two months, he reached Corinth finally at the end of May, only to find that the bird had flown, and that there was nothing but an empty nest to compensate him for his labours. The humour-loving Confederates had found time before they left to inscribe on the empty buildings:

"These premises to let; inquire of G. T. Beauregard."

As the landlord was not present, the National troops took possession without the formality of a lease.

Pope, with his troops, had arrived at Pittsburg Landing on April 11th, fresh from the victories of New Madrid and Island No. 10; and by the end of April, Halleck had a force of nearly 100,000, including such officers as Grant, Sherman, Sheridan, Thomas, Buell, Rosecrans, Pope, and Logan. This force marched from Pittsburg Landing to the vicinity of Corinth, where they were drawn up in line of battle. On May 30th, Halleck announced in orders that he expected his left to be attacked that morning. The Confederate movement, which had excited his alarm, was not one of attack, but of retreat. On May 25th, Beauregard decided to withdraw from Corinth to Tupelo, Mississippi, forty-five miles southwest on the Mobile and Ohio Railroad, and had made elaborate and most successful preparations to deceive Halleck as to his intentions. On June 1st, Fort Pillow was also evacuated, under orders from Beauregard.

The Confederate troops withdrawn from Corinth, 10,000 in all, were halted behind the Tuscumbia River, six miles from Corinth, and again at Baldwin, thirty miles from Corinth, awaiting a pursuit by Halleck's forces, now numbering 120,000, but they were not disturbed. Instead of following up his advantages after the evacuation of Corinth and the capture of Memphis, Halleck scattered his army over such an extent of territory that it was powerless for offence. If Grant had been roughly handled at Shiloh, he had at least exposed the weakness of his enemy, and left them in a position to invite an attack from Halleck's superior forces. Instead of availing himself of this opportunity, " Old Brains," as Halleck was called, occupied two months in elaborate preparations to secure a strategic position that might have been secured by a prompt movement immediately after Donelson.

Spades were now trumps; and the applause, heretofore so easily won by spectacular generals, who ordered spades to the rear, was succeeded by an extravagant devotion to this humble instrument of war.

The idea of an unopposed march to the Gulf, that had preceded Shiloh, was definitely abandoned. General Grant believed that prompt action after the taking of Corinth would have resulted in a bloodless advance to Atlanta, Vicksburg, or some other desired point. He insisted that the dispersion of Halleck's forces after Corinth was a grievous mistake. Buell, who was ordered east towards Chattanooga, was compelled to delay his movement in order to repair the damage done to the Memphis and Charleston Railroad by Mitchell, acting under his orders. His slow movements gave Bragg, who had succeeded Beauregard in command, an opportunity to rest, reorganise, and recruit his Army. They also enabled Bragg to contest the control of Middle Tennessee and Kentucky, and prevented Buell from carrying out his plans with reference to Chattanooga and East Tennessee.

On June 27, 1862, Bragg began to transfer a large part of his Army to Chattanooga by rail, by way of Mobile, covering the movement by a cavalry raid into West Tennessee. On June 11th, Rosecrans took command at Corinth, and Thomas succeeded Pope, who had been ordered to the command of the Army of Virginia in the vain hope that he might be able to retrieve McClellan's disasters in that State. A week later the Confederate Army of the Mississippi was on its way from Tupelo, excepting 15,000 men left under the command of Price to watch Grant, and prevent him from sending further re-enforcements to Buell.

West Tennessee was now under full control of the National forces; Memphis had been secured by a naval attack on June 6th, and the Mississippi was held from that point northward to its source. Halleck was ordered East, July 11, 1862, to succeed McClellan as General-in-Chief. Before leaving, he assigned Grant to the command of all the troops west of the Tennessee River, including those at Columbus and Cairo, ordering him to send two of his divisions under Thomas to re-enforce Buell in Middle Tennessee, and to send Hovey to join Curtis at Helena, Arkansas. Buell at this time was in chase of Bragg, who was pushing north, and threatening Louisville and Cincinnati.

On taking this enlarged command, Grant returned to Corinth, and established his headquarters there. He was not, however, officially assigned to the command known as the Department of the Tennessee, until October 25, 1862. Halleck had recommended as his own successor, Colonel Robert Allen, a graduate of the Military Academy, who was then serving on his staff as an aide. This selection was overruled at Washington, and the command was given to Grant. The army of 120,000 belonging to his new department was so scattered, and the activity of the hostile population by which he was surrounded was so constant, that he was put on the defensive. His dislike of Halleck's engineering methods was shown by the immediate withdrawal from the lines of fortifications he established at Corinth with so much labour, to others more simple, and requiring a smaller force to man them. Grant tells us that the most anxious period of the war for him was when he was forced to abandon his natural *rôle* of the offensive to carry out the established policy of dispersion. He was required to hold as much territory as possible, and at the same time to keep his troops in readiness to re-enforce Buell.

During the period from July 17th, when Halleck went, to September 7, 1862, Grant was occupied with the routine duties of a department commander. There was constant fighting between his troops and those of the enemy, with losses equal to those during the heaviest battles of the war with Mexico, but with nothing rising to the dimensions of great war, as measured by the standards of our civil struggle. The chief event had been the surrender of the post of Clarksville, August 14th, by a weak-kneed commander. He was one of the two officers who led their regiments off of the field at the first fire at Shiloh, and had begged Grant with tears in his eyes to give him another opportunity. This was the result.

During the five months following Shiloh, McClellan had been busy at the East in unsuccessful attempts to capture the Confederate capital at Richmond. He had forced the evacuation of Yorktown, and had fought the battles of Williamsburgh, Seven Pines or Fair Oaks, and the series of battles known as " The Seven Days' Retreat." Pope, who had been ordered to Virginia to assist McClellan, had been defeated in the disastrous battle of the Second Bull Run, and Lee, who, in his eagerness to take advantage of this success, had marched north into Maryland, had been defeated in his turn by the forces under McClellan at Antietam.

Grant, during this time, was required to guard the long line from Memphis to Corinth, and to keep constant watch on Price and Van Dorn, who threatened to capture some of his insufficiently garrisoned posts. His own method was to keep his enemies too busy by constant attack to allow them time for brewing mischief, but he was not free to follow his own devices. Forrest and Morgan, with their bold riders, circulated in his rear, capturing Murfreesboro and other outlying positions occupied by weak detachments, destroying or helping themselves to the provisions and military stores they found insufficiently guarded, and securing numerous prisoners, including General Crittenden.

September 15, 1862, Price, in pursuance of his instructions to prevent Grant from re-enforcing Buell, united his forces with those of Van Dorn, and took possession of Iuka, twenty-two miles east of Corinth, on the Memphis and Charleston Railway. This post was garrisoned by a single regiment of Union troops, who withdrew when Price appeared. If he could have held this place, Price would have been free to re-enforce Bragg; but Grant promptly sent Rosecrans and Ord, with 17,000 men, to recover Iuka by a joint attack. This they did after a sharp battle, September 19 and 20, 1862. Grant lost 782 men. Price, who lost 1516, retired in good order, and was not pursued, the road he followed in retreat having been by some mistake left unoccupied. During the engagement, Grant directed operations from Burnsville, a position which placed him between the two wings of his command. When word was brought him that Iuka was recaptured, he ordered a pursuit by the whole of Rosecrans's command, accompanying it for a short distance to see that his commands were obeyed. When he turned back, the pursuit was discontinued by Rosecrans.

The various calls for troops had left Grant at this time with but 50,000 men, and further depletions of his forces to re-enforce Buell compelled him to abandon a portion of his own territory. By October 1, 1862, it became apparent that Van Dorn and Price had united their armies for a movement against Corinth. As a preliminary to it, Van Dorn had so stationed his forces as to prevent re-enforcements from reaching Corinth. An attack on that place was repulsed, with a heavy loss to the enemy, by Rosecrans, who held the works built under Grant's directions after Halleck's departure. Rosecrans had been ordered to follow up such a victory; but owing to delays, and mistakes in taking the wrong road, he did not overtake the fleeing enemy. He lost 2359 men in the battle of Corinth, and Van Dorn and Price lost 14,221. This battle finally relieved Grant from his anxiety as to the possession of the territory he commanded. After Corinth, he had 48,500 men, and the arrival of re-enforcements soon placed him in position for attack.

CHAPTER X.

SIEGE AND SURRENDER OF VICKSBURG.

OCTOBER, 1862—JULY, 1863.

Y November 2d, Grant was ready to assume offensive operations. Memphis was under his control, and Farragut had captured New Orleans; but the Mississippi did not yet run "unvexed to the sea." Between these two cities were the Confederate strongholds of Vicksburg and Port Hudson, standing on high bluffs, at sharp bends of the river, in excellent positions for defence, and very difficult to assault.

On October 8, 1862, Sherman was ordered to Memphis to take charge of a movement against Vicksburg, in co-operation with the fleet of Admiral Porter. November 2d, Grant commenced his own movement against Vicksburg, starting from Columbus as a base, and following the line of the Mississippi Central Railroad, Sherman's co-operating column moving soon after from Memphis down the Mississippi in transports. A depot of supplies had been established at Holly Springs, forty-three miles south-east of Memphis, on the Mississippi Central

Railroad. This place was in command of the Colonel of the 8th Wisconsin Regiment, who surrendered Iuka without a fight; and when Van Dorn appeared before Holly Springs, December 20, 1862, he repeated that performance, promptly yielding his important post garrisoned by fifteen hundred men. The seizure and destruction of the large quantity of stores gathered there completely disconcerted Grant's plan of proceeding against Vicksburg, with Columbus as a base and Holly Springs as a second base, and it was promptly abandoned. His plans were further disturbed by a cavalry raid by Forrest, which cut off all communication with the North for more than a week, and for two weeks he subsisted his army of 30,000 men on supplies obtained from the surrounding country. This experience satisfied him that it was impossible to maintain a long line of communication through an enemy's country, but that it was possible to subsist in a large part on the country itself.

Sherman marched into Memphis, December 12, 1862. Embarking his 32,000 men on transports, he reached the mouth of the Yazoo River, near Vicksburg, on Christmas Day, having increased his force on the way by the addition of 12,000 men from Helena, Arkansas. He expected co-operation from Grant, who was then at Oxford, Mississippi, twenty-eight miles beyond Holly Springs, and from Banks, who was at Port Hudson. Neither of them was able to assist him, Grant for the reason just given. After occupying several days in reconnoitring, and learning that the enemy were being heavily re-enforced, Sherman resolved to make an attack with the force he had, in order to get possession of the road which ran from the Yazoo River bottom to the Walnut Hills, six miles above the city of Vicksburg. There was no landing-place where he could secure solid footing, and he was compelled to conduct his fight in " an insular space of low, boggy ground, and with innumerable bayous, or deep sloughs." He met with determined opposition, and was compelled to reembark his command, after losing 1748 men in the battle of December 28 and 29, 1862, known as the battle of Chickasaw Bayou. The Confederate loss was 207. It was a season of unusually high water, and the region about Vicksburg was flooded; narrow strips of land offering the only foothold that was to be obtained along the Mississippi and the bayous running parallel to it.

The demands for the re-enforcement of Vicksburg, occasioned by Grant's movement against it, had so weakened Bragg, that Rosecrans was able to make an effective attack upon him at Stone River, or Murfreesboro, Tennessee, in an engagement lasting from December 31, 1862, to January 2, 1863, in which the Confederates were badly defeated. Bragg lost 25,560 men in this battle and Rosecrans, 11,578. This was a further illustration of the wisdom of Grant's policy of constantly maintaining the aggressive. After Stone River, Grant endeavoured, but in vain, to persuade Rosecrans, who was not then under his orders, to push Bragg vigorously, to prevent him from sending re-enforcements to Johnston in Mississippi.

General John B. McClernand, who was an officer of great political influence, had obtained permission from Mr. Lincoln to organise a special expedition under his command for a movement against Vicksburg. On January 3, 1863, he arrived at Milliken's Bend, thirty-five miles above Vicksburg on the opposite side of the river. The next day, in accordance with a suggestion from Sherman, he embarked 32,000 men in transports, and started, under the convoy of Porter's fleet, to capture Fort Hindman at Arkansas Post, fifty miles up the Arkansas River. He carried the place by storm, capturing 4791 prisoners; the total Confederate loss being 5500, and his own 977. The next day McClernand received orders from Grant to return to Milliken's Bend.

McClernand's success had cleared out a large force of Confederate troops, which, if left in the rear during the advance on Vicksburg, might have caused much perplexity. On January 10th, Grant established his headquarters at Memphis. On January 29th, he removed to Young's Point, some distance above Vicksburg on the opposite bank of the Mississippi, and took command of the combined forces of Sherman and McClernand. From this point dates the serious work of his campaign against Vicksburg.

This Confederate stronghold was located on the first high land coming to the edge of the river below Memphis. It stood two hundred feet above the river, amid a series of irregular hills. The Mississippi in its meanderings touches the line of bluffs at Vicksburg, and again at Warrenton, eight miles below Vicksburg, where it runs along the bluff for three miles. It again approaches high ground at Grand Gulf, just below the mouth of the Big Black River, and at Bruinsburg, ten miles below Grand Gulf, where there is a level bit of ground between the bluffs and the river. Access from the river, below Vicksburg, is cut off by swampy ground, except at the points named. The distance between Vicksburg and Bruinsburg, following the course of the stream, is thirty-five miles, the gigantic river sweeping through immense curves at this point. The bluff on which Vicksburg is situated extends from Haines's Bluff on the north, twenty miles to Grand Gulf on the south, and varies from fifty to two hundred feet in height.

In the spring of 1863 the Confederate Army, 30,000 men, under General Pemberton, held a strong line of works at Haines's Bluff above Vicksburg, at Vicksburg itself, and at Grand Gulf below it. Vicksburg was described by the President of the Confederacy as "the Gibraltar of America," the Confederates apparently having several of these Gibraltars for Grant to capture. To assault it he brought an effective force of 50,000 men; and he was aided by the Navy under Admiral D. D. Porter with seven armour-clads, protecting the large fleet of transports and barges, and ready to take part in offensive operations.

The batteries defending Vicksburg had been constructed by officers formerly belonging to the Engineer Corps of the United States Army, and were most perfectly adapted to resist attack from the water. The Mississippi here turns completely on itself. All along the bluffs cannon were mounted behind heavy parapets made of cotton bales covered with earth and having bomb-proofs and magazines. It was difficult to hit these almost invisible guns, and the curves of the shore gave opportunity for concentric fire on vessels struggling with the eddies and currents of the treacherous river.

The problem before Grant was much like that which confronted Archimedes. He sought a base for his fulcrum,—a sufficient footing of dry ground amid the flood of waters, on which to plant his troops and batteries. Having once resolved upon his task, he had determined to pursue it to the end, regardless of the difficulties he might encounter. It was a time of discouragement at the North. The war that was to have lasted only ninety days had dragged its slow length along for over two and a half years. Over seven hundred engagements, large and small, were on the records of battle, but no thoroughly decisive result had yet been obtained in any quarter. One demand for troops had succeeded another, until over thirteen hundred thousand men had been called into the National service for longer or shorter periods. The expenditure of treasure was sufficient to discourage even a power so rich in territory and resources as the United States. " There was nothing left to be done," says Grant, " but to go forward to a decisive victory."

In June, 1862, Farragut's fleet, which had captured New Orleans in the previous April, moved up to Vicksburg, and made an attempt to reduce the place by bombardment. After the trial of a month, during which our naval vessels had gallantly run the river batteries, this attempt was abandoned. An effort had been made about this time to get into the rear of Vicksburg by cutting a ditch or canal a mile in length across the peninsula formed by the sharp bend in the Mississippi. It was resolved to deepen and widen this canal; and much labour was wasted in the vain attempt to accomplish this, every effort being made meanwhile to discover some high ground to furnish foothold for a landing. Another attempt was made to cut a canal by making use of Lake Providence, a former bed of the Mississippi. This also proved a failure, as did other attempts to secure advantages by changing the customary course of the river. These various efforts to turn the forces of nature against Vicksburg occupied the season of high water, when troops could not move on land.

In March, 1863, Grant's quarters were at Milliken's Bend, fifteen miles from Vicksburg as the crow flies. His troops were stretched from Young's Point, ten miles nearer Vicksburg, to Lake Providence, farther up the river. Their camps were in low, swampy ground, and were frequently submerged. The levees between them and the river, holding back the waters of the Mississippi, were dotted for miles with the graves of their comrades killed in battle, or victims to the various diseases bred by unhealthy conditions, and who could find no other burial-place in that wet country. Toward the end of March orders were given to concentrate at Milliken's Bend.

The waters of the river were now receding, and, as it was becoming possible to move the troops by land, an attempt was to be made to take Vicksburg in reverse by conveying the troops down the river on the west bank, and crossing the river below. Through a region partially overflowed by water, sometimes marching, sometimes rowing through the woods in boats, and here and there waiting to bridge bayous, the troops advanced south from Milliken's Bend by way of Richmond to Perkins's Plantation, ten or twelve miles below New Carthage. It was found impracticable, however, to convey supplies to the Army from Milliken's Bend over the single narrow and almost impassable road through the flooded land. It was accordingly determined that Admiral Porter's vessels should run by the Vicksburg batteries, convoying vessels loaded with supplies. The first attempt was made on the night of April 15, 1863, when Porter ran the batteries with seven iron-clads, convoying three transports loaded with army supplies and ammunition, and protected by ten barges lashed alongside, and loaded with coal and forage.

General Sherman, in his *Memoirs*, says:

"I was out in the stream when the fleet passed Vicksburg, and the scene was truly sublime. As soon as the rebel gunners detected the *Benton* (Porter's flag-ship), which was in the lead, they opened on her, and on the others in succession, with shot and shell; houses on the Vicksburg side, and on the opposite shore, were set on fire, which lighted up the whole river; and the war of cannon, the bursting of shells, and finally the burning of the *Henry Clay*, drifting with the current, made up a picture of the terrible not often seen. Each gunboat returned the fire as she passed the town, while the transports hugged the opposite shore."

Every transport was struck, and one was sunk. On the night of April 26, 1863, six more transports, with barges loaded with army supplies, passed the batteries. One of these transports was sunk, one was burned, and five barges were disabled by the fire of the enemy. War-vessels had run by batteries before this; but it was a new experience for the Confederates to see unarmed river steamboats defying their guns, and the sight was not a comfortable one for them. As the hired crews of the transports and barges would not risk their lives before the Vicksburg batteries, volunteers from the Army were called for. They were so numerous and so zealous, that those who secured places on the boats were offered premiums for the privilege of taking their places, and one young soldier refused an offer of one hundred dollars for his chance of being killed. From a single regiment alone one hundred and sixteen men and sixteen commissioned officers volunteered as pilots, engineers, firemen, or deck-hands. It was found necessary to draw lots to select the number needed from the hundreds who wished to go.

An attempt was made to find a landing for the troops on the east bank of the Mississippi above Grand Gulf. This proving impracticable, they were moved farther down the west bank to a place called Hard Times; as many as possible being conveyed in the few transports available, the rest marching across the country, bridging three bayous as they went. From here it was necessary to pass the batteries at Grand Gulf in order to reach some point below that place. About 10,000 men, all the transports and barges could carry, were embarked ready to move as soon as Porter should have silenced the batteries; but, after a fierce bombardment of over five hours, he was obliged to withdraw his shattered fleet, without having been able to silence a single gun. It then became necessary to disembark the troops, and move across a point of land opposite Grand Gulf known as Coffee Point, using the levee for a road to De Shroon below Grand Gulf. The bombardment was renewed that night; and under the cover of Porter's guns, Grant boldly ran his transports, loaded with supplies, past the Grand Gulf batteries without losing one of them. It was a hazardous but successful venture.

At De Shroon, early on the morning of April 30th, McClernand's Corps and one division of McPherson's Corps were re-embarked on the transports, and moved down the river in search of a landing on the east bank, General Grant leading the way with Porter on the flag-ship *Benton*.

A landing was made at a dilapidated plantation known as Bruinsburg. Grant went ashore here, and obtained from a stray coloured man important information concerning the roads leading into the interior. The troops were then promptly landed, and the line of march was taken for Port Gibson, seven miles in the rear of Grand Gulf, and twelve from Bruinsburg. The enemy were encountered at two o'clock on the morning of May 1, 1863, and defeated after a sharp engagement lasting through the day.

The country through which operations must be conducted in the rear of Grand Gulf and Vicksburg was admirably adapted for defence. It was a series of rugged ridges, divided by deep ravines abounding in creeks and bayous, and covered with a tangle of vines and cane-brakes. Fifty miles to the east of Vicksburg was Jackson, the capital of Mississippi, where General Joseph E. Johnston was located with a heavy Confederate force. Grant's plan now was to interpose between Johnston and Pemberton, who was defending Vicksburg, and destroy the two in detail. He had landed in Mississippi, after crossing the river from the Louisiana shore, with a smaller force than the enemy he was seeking; but their 60,000 men were scattered for fifty miles, from Vicksburg to Grand Gulf, and he was stronger at the immediate point of contact.

To distract attention from his own movements, he had ordered Sherman to make, before joining him, a strong demonstration against Haines's Bluff, assisted by Admiral Porter with his fleet; and General Benjamin H. Grierson was started on a raid against the communications of the enemy, such as had upset Grant's own calculations at Holly Springs when undertaken by an enterprising Confederate cavalry leader. Grierson started from La Grange, Tennessee, April 18, 1863, with a force of 1700 mounted men, including a battery of artillery, made a clear sweep around the Confederate lines in the rear of Vicksburg, and finally brought up at Port Hudson, May 2d, after a march of 600 miles, or an average of $37\frac{1}{2}$ miles a day. He did much damage, and greatly demoralised the forces defending Vicksburg.

When Grant obtained a footing at Bruinsburg and

captured Port Gibson, the enemy retired before him
as his columns advanced. He took Grand Gulf in
the reverse, and secured possession of that place May
3, 1863, after some heavy skirmishing, but without
serious fighting. He had at this time about 20,000
men; and on May 7th Sherman joined him with two
divisions of the Fifteenth Corps, increasing his total
to 33,000. Re-enforcements subsequently received
added 10,000 men to his command.

Possessed of Grand Gulf, Grant decided on the
bold expedient of protecting himself against an
attack in his rear by leaving himself without any
rear. He determined to cut loose from any base,
carrying what supplies he could with him, gathering
others from the country as he went along. Nobody
believed in this venture but Grant himself; and
though Sherman was a subordinate, and a loyal
friend, he protested strongly against it in a letter
that Grant magnanimously withheld after his success
until Sherman made it public. The real danger was
from interference by the cautious and distrustful
Halleck. If the General-in-Chief had been on hand,
or had understood the situation and could have
reached Grant, the movement would have been cut
short at its inception. Grant counted upon advancing so far with his plan, that, before Halleck could be
heard from, his interference would come too late.
"I knew Halleck," he said, "and that he was too
learned a soldier to consent to a campaign in violation of all the principles of the art of war." Not
only did Sherman oppose the bold plan, but also
Logan, McPherson, and every prominent officer of the

Army. Never were Grant's self-reliance and determination shown so conspicuously as on this occasion.

When Grant arrived at Grand Gulf, he had been separated for a week from his baggage, and had nothing with him but a tooth-brush. He had had but little to eat, had been three days and nights in the saddle, without sleep, and was altogether in a condition most uncomfortable and very much out of keeping with the dignity of his position. So soon as he could do so, he visited the flag-ship of Porter's fleet, which had run the river batteries at Grand Gulf. Here he took a bath, borrowed some underclothing, and sat down to the first good meal which he had had for over a week. He had shared the fare of the common soldiers, and had slept with them upon the open ground, without so much as a blanket to cover him. His army had been without transportation; and the ammunition train was a curious assemblage of fine carriages, farm waggons, long coupled waggons with racks for carrying cotton bales,—every vehicle, indeed, that could be found on the plantations which had been used either for work or pleasure. These vehicles were a nondescript outfit, drawn by oxen and mules wearing plough harness, or straw collars and rope lines.

At Grand Gulf, Grant wrote letters to the General-in-Chief, prepared telegrams to be sent from Cairo, and gave his final orders to his corps commanders for the work before them. He started on his adventure, carrying only three days' rations for his troops, but an abundance of supplies was obtained by foraging on the country. His success in thus feeding his army made a complete convert of Sherman to his plans; and he made important use of the experience here acquired, when later on he cut loose from Atlanta and marched to the sea. The narrow ridge roads, which offered the only means of progress through the low country, compelled Grant to move his troops by detachments in parallel columns, keeping touch with each other by reconnoissances to determine lines of communication. He used his cavalry as he advanced to ascertain what was in front of him, and to open the way for the progress of the main body. The season had by this time so far advanced that the weather was intensely hot.

After a battle at Port Gibson, May 1, 1863, in which he lost 853 men, Grant encountered no serious opposition until he arrived at Raymond on May 12th. Here battle was again joined, and the enemy was driven back with a loss of 514 men, the Union loss being 442. This victory determined him to undertake the capture of Jackson by a bold stroke, and then turn upon Pemberton, who was on his left with nearly 50,000 men. Up to this time he had depended in some measure on rations brought up from Grand Gulf; but now he cut loose altogether from any base, in order that he might be able to bring into battle the troops that would be otherwise occupied in keeping open communications with the Mississippi River. He intended to protect his rear by keeping the enemy so well occupied that they would have no opportunity for detached movements.

So long as he was within reach of Grand Gulf, every restriction of red-tape routine was disregarded to secure the prompt forwarding of supplies from that point. His commissary there was ordered to load all teams presenting themselves for rations with promptness and despatch, regardless of requisitions or provision returns. Grant must have smiled to himself, when he remembered that, in swinging loose from his base on the Mississippi, he was shutting himself off from all communication with Washington, and that, whatever might be the result of his adventure, he would not be interfered with.

General Joseph E. Johnston had arrived at Jackson on May 13, 1863, and had taken command of the Confederate forces in Mississippi. With Pemberton in his rear at Vicksburg, and Johnston in front of him at Jackson, Grant's position was a critical one. He was between two formidable armies, and was without means of obtaining additional supplies except by foraging. He would be ruined if his enemies could combine their forces, or could prevent him from ultimately establishing a new base of supplies. Rapidity of movement and uniform success were essential to safety. An attack from Pemberton was fully expected and provided against, but it did not come. There were heavy rains on May 13th and 14th, and the roads were in some places a foot deep in water. Battle was opened by Sherman in front of Jackson by nine o'clock, May 14, 1863; and before night Grant had established his headquarters in the State House of the capital, having lost 294 men in the attack, and punished the enemy with a loss of 845.

Jackson was an important railroad centre, and

numerous factories for the manufacture of munitions of war had been established there by the Confederacy. It was fifty miles in the rear of Vicksburg, and controlled the railroads over which that post received supplies. Everything that could be of use to the enemy, including railroads and bridges, was destroyed at Jackson. Young women were found in the factories, undismayed by the sound of battle around them, hard at work manufacturing tent-cloth with the letters " C. S. A." woven into each bolt.

Meantime Pemberton had waked up, and was advancing from Vicksburg to assail his enemy in the rear. Withdrawing his troops from Jackson, Grant moved west towards Vicksburg, and encountered the enemy on May 6th at Champion's Hill,—a densely wooded ridge, some seventy feet in height, situated on Baker's Creek, a little stream running into the Big Black River, which empties into the Mississippi south of Vicksburg. He had received timely warning of Pemberton's movement from a captured despatch, and had concentrated his troops for the attack. After a hard-fought battle, the Confederates were defeated with a loss of 4300 men, the Union loss being 2457. After the battle, Pemberton retreated to Vicksburg, leaving behind him Loring's division, which was cut off from the main body, and withdrew to Jackson, making a long détour by way of Crystal Springs. Grant's total force for the line of battle was at this time but 35,000, with twenty field batteries.

The success at Champion's Hill had permanently divided the forces of Johnston and Pemberton, for a movement by Pemberton to join Johnston at Jackson would have surrendered Vicksburg. How very narrowly Grant escaped the chief danger he feared, was shown by the arrival of a staff officer from Banks on May 17th, bearing a letter from Halleck dated May 11th, and sent by way of New Orleans. This ordered Grant to return to Grand Gulf, and co-operate with Banks against Port Hudson, before laying siege to Vicksburg. Answer was returned that the order came too late, and that it never would have been given had Halleck understood the situation. That it was given at all was a striking illustration of the vicious system that prevailed under Halleck of directing men who knew more than he did, concerning matters which they understood far better than he possibly could, viewing them from the distance of Washington.

Pemberton made another and a final stand on May 17, 1863, at Big Black River, where he lost 18 guns and 1751 prisoners, besides his killed and wounded. Grant's loss was 279. The Confederates fled so precipitously that their chief loss was in prisoners, and in men drowned in undertaking to escape across the river in face of a pursuing enemy. The bridges across Big Black River had been destroyed, but three rude bridges were completed before the next morning; and on these Grant's whole force crossed, arriving on May 19, 1863, in the rear of Vicksburg.

Vicksburg was not yet captured; but after six months of infinite toil, patience, and hardship, Grant had accomplished his purpose of putting himself in a position to invest that stronghold. The campaign was a success thus far, however it might end. The methods adopted had placed Sherman in the position he had sought in vain to attain by more direct approach five months earlier. Grant was vindicated, and Sherman was satisfied. Halleck, if not content, could no longer complain.

By May 21st, the lines of investment drawn around Vicksburg were completed, six hundred yards from the Confederate works. The troops were made happy the same night by the arrival at Haines's Bluff of trains bearing the full army rations, including their much-desired coffee and hardtack. Living off the country was very well as a strategic necessity, and there was an abundance of food, but it was not of a kind to fully satisfy the army stomach. In his *Memoirs*, Grant says: " I remember that in passing around to the left of the line on the 21st, a soldier, recognising me, said in rather a low voice, but yet so that I heard him, ' Hard tack!' In a moment the cry was taken up all along the line, ' Hard tack! Hard tack!' I told the men nearest to me that we had been engaged ever since the arrival of troops in building a road over which to supply them with everything they needed. The cry was instantly changed to cheers."

On May 22d, 1863, Porter's war-vessels moved up before Vicksburg, and opened fire on the river front. The Army at the same time made three assaults in an attempt to carry the Confederate lines in the rear of the city. Though these assaults were unsuccessful, they are described by S. H. Locket, Chief Engineer of the Confederate defences, as " made with great determination and admirable courage." The losses on both sides were severe. It was an heroic attempt, and it satisfied the impatience of the Army for an immediate result. It was clear now that the only plan left was for a regular siege, and Grant was compelled to submit patiently to an application of engineering methods.

Within twenty days from the time he crossed the Mississippi at Bruinsburg, below Vicksburg, he had marched 180 miles, had gained five battles with a loss to the enemy of 88 cannon and 12,500 men, had captured the capital of Mississippi and destroyed it as a depot of supplies, and had finally accomplished his main object of drawing his lines of investment around Vicksburg. This result had occupied the supreme efforts of the force of 43,000 men he brought with him across the Mississippi. His successful movement had been made through a country excellently adapted for defence, and in face of the opposition of a scattered force of over 60,000 Confederates. He had divided and conquered. His own forces had been kept well together; and the largest number he had had to contend with in any one battle was 25,000, at Champion's Hill. His total loss up to this time was 4379 men, only 259 of whom were classed as missing.

The line of defence about Vicksburg was seven miles: the line of investment extended for fifteen miles,—from Haines's Bluff on the north, to Warrenton on the south. Grant's movement had interposed between Vicksburg and Haines's Bluff, and compelled the evacuation of the latter stronghold, which was now occupied as a base of supplies. Halleck had finally awakened to the situation, and concluded that Grant was more useful where he was than in undertaking to help Banks. He responded promptly to the call for re-enforcements; and by June 14th Grant's forces had been increased to 71,000 men, and new men were being forwarded with all possible despatch. The siege began with the field artillery of six thirty-two-pounders, and a battery of Navy guns borrowed from the fleet and manned by the sailors. Mortars were constructed for six- and twelve-pound shells by boring out logs of hard wood and strapping them with iron. The supply of ammunition was unlimited. With the assistance of negroes hired to do the work, two hundred and twenty guns had been placed in position by June 20, 1863.

The danger from Johnston in the rear continued, and it was feared that his force might be increased by re-enforcements sufficiently to raise the siege by a bold attack. To protect the rear, Haines's Bluff was still more strongly fortified, and batteries were located at all commanding points from there to the Big Black River, and these were connected by riflepits. Johnston finally moved; and news was received on June 22, 1863, that he had crossed the Big Black River, and was advancing to attack the besieging army. An intercepted despatch showed that the enemy in Vicksburg were so disheartened that they were not likely to assist Johnston by a cooperative movement; that Pemberton's soldiers were clamouring for a surrender; and that an attempt would be made to escape by crossing the river in the night. Every precaution was taken by Grant and Admiral Porter to prevent this escape.

Johnston's movement was not quick enough to be of any service to Pemberton. While he waited, Grant's engineers advanced their parallels and sap-rollers close up to one of the Confederate redans, and everything was now ready for the assault. This was ordered for July 6th. On July 1st a mine under one of the Vicksburg redans was exploded with one and a quarter tons of powder, destroying the redan, and making a breach of nearly twenty feet in the intrenchment across the gorge of the work. The men over the mine were blown into the air, and some of them descended alive within the Union lines, one negro coming down with the news that he had gone up " 'bout tree mile." The defence rallied, and poured so deadly a fire into the breach that the attempted assault was a failure.

By this time Pemberton had decided that a surrender was necessary. He was a Northern man, born in the State of Pennsylvania, and knew the sentiment concerning the Fourth of July. He reasoned that the eagerness of Grant to secure the celebration of that day by a great victory would secure for him better conditions. He raised the white flag on July 3d. Porter was notified, and hostilities by the Army and Navy were suspended. Says Grant in his *Memoirs*:

"It was a glorious sight to officers and soldiers on the line where those white flags were visible, and the news soon spread to all parts of the command. The troops felt that their long and weary marches, hard fighting, ceaseless watching by night and day in a hot climate, exposure to all sorts of weather, to diseases, and, worst of all, to gibes of many Northern papers that came to them saying all their suffering was in vain, that Vicksburg would never be taken, were at last at an end, and the Union sure to be saved."

Pemberton had asked for the appointment of three commissioners on each side, to arrange terms and "to save the further effusion of blood." Grant replied:

"The useless effusion of blood you propose stopping can be ended at any time you may choose by an unconditional surrender of the city and garrison. Men who have shown so much endurance and courage as those now in Vicksburg will always challenge the respect of an adversary, and, I can assure you, will be treated with all the respect due to prisoners of war. I do not favor the proposition of appointing commissioners to arrange the terms of capitulation, because I have no terms other than those indicated above."

If this communication had not been signed, its recipient could readily have supplied the omission by adding to it the words *Unconditional Surrender Grant.*

In answer to a verbal message from Pemberton, a personal interview was arranged for; and the two commanders, with their staff officers, met near a stunted oak-tree standing on a hillside just outside of the Confederate line. Pemberton and Grant had served in the same division during the Mexican War, and greeted each other as old acquaintances. Terms of "Unconditional Surrender" were repeated. Pemberton seemed disposed to reject them, and turned abruptly as if to leave. Confederate General

Bowen, who had known Grant at St. Louis, then proposed a conference between himself and one of Grant's generals, which resulted in a suggestion that the Confederates should be allowed to march out with the honours of war. This proposition was rejected without ceremony, and the interview ended with the promise that final terms would be sent by letter not later than ten o'clock that night.

Grant then called what he describes as the nearest approach to a council of war he ever had. He submitted the case to his corps and division commanders, inviting suggestions, but stating that he would reserve the right to finally determine the matter himself. His conclusion was in opposition to the almost unanimous judgment of the council. He wrote to Pemberton proposing to march a division to Vicksburg the next morning as a guard; to parole officers and men; and to allow officers to leave with their side-arms and clothing, men with their clothing, mounted officers taking one horse each. Thirty waggons were allowed for transportation, necessary rations and cooking utensils to be taken.

The Confederates had deciphered Grant's signal code, and read a communication to Porter concerning the disposition to be made of prisoners. In this way they learned that the Navy could not furnish transportation to the North for so many men, and that they would have to be paroled. It was this that encouraged Pemberton to insist upon his demands, and the necessity of taking care of so large a body of prisoners led Grant to modify his conditions of surrender to the extent which he did.

To Grant's letter Pemberton replied, proposing that he be allowed the additional favour of marching out with his colours and arms, and stacking arms in front of his lines; "officers to retain their side-arms and personal property, and the rights and property of citizens to be respected." This communication was received after midnight on July 3, 1863. In reply Grant declined to make any "stipulations with regard to the treatment of citizens and their private property." He said:

"While I do not propose to cause them any undue annoyance or loss, I cannot consent to leave myself under any restraint by stipulations. . . . If you mean by your proposition for each brigade to march to the front of the lines now occupied by it, and stack arms at 10 A.M. and then return to the inside, and there remain as prisoners until properly paroled, I will make no objection to it. Should no notification be received of your acceptance of my terms by 9 A.M., I shall regard them as having been rejected, and shall act accordingly. Should these terms be accepted, white flags should be displayed along your lines, to prevent such of my troops as may not have been notified from firing upon your men."

The white flags appeared, and the surrender of the fortress of Vicksburg was completed on the Fourth of July, 1863,—the day on which Lee's army had started on its return journey to Virginia, after three days' unsuccessful battle with Meade's forces at Gettysburg. Thirty-one thousand six hundred prisoners were surrendered, 60,000 muskets, 172 cannon, and large quantities of ammunition. The Confederate small-arms were so much superior to those borne by Grant's men, that an exchange was made wherever any advantage was found, and the inferior weapons were turned in as captured guns.

On the day of the surrender the Confederate general Holmes had made an attack on Helena, Arkansas, hoping to capture that place, preliminary to an attempt to raise the siege of Vicksburg. He was repulsed with heavy loss. As soon as the Confederates at Port Hudson heard of Pemberton's surrender, they concluded that further struggles were useless, and on July 9, 1863, unconditionally surrendered to General Banks, who obtained with Port Hudson 6000 prisoners, 500 muskets, 51 cannon, and a variety of stores.

The work of preparing the rolls of the Vicksburg garrison was completed on July 11th, and the Confederate prisoners marched out. During the week devoted to this work, they had been treated with the utmost consideration by their captors, and the men of the two armies had cordially fraternised. Grant's troops had been directed " to be orderly and quiet as the paroled prisoners passed," and " to make no offensive remarks." No cheers were heard from any of the victorious army on the day of surrender, except from some of the troops on the left of the line, who raised a hearty cheer for " the defenders of Vicksburg."

> " The truly brave,
> When they behold the brave oppressed with odds,
> Are touched with a desire to shield and save."

CHAPTER XI.

INCIDENTS OF THE SIEGE OF VICKSBURG; MISFORTUNE FOLLOWS VICTORY.

1863.

N the spot where Grant and Pemberton held the interview that resulted in the surrender of Vicksburg, is reared a monument with this legend:

"To the Memory of the Surrender of Vicksburg by Lieutenant J. G. Pemberton to Major-General U. S. Grant, U. S. A., on the 3d of July, 1863."

This stands as a memorial for all time of one of the most successful enterprises of our Civil War, and one of the most notable sieges in history. Fort Donelson ended the war in Kentucky; Pea Ridge ended the war in Missouri. Now the surrender of Vicksburg and of Port Hudson drove the Confederates from Mississippi, and restored to the nation its rightful control of that magnificent interior basin having a central watershed of more than twelve hundred thousand miles, and, with its tributaries twice that area. The territory included in the Mississippi basin exceeds that of the whole European continent, exclusive of Russia, Norway, and Sweden. Its river system includes 40,000 miles of steam navigation, and it is estimated that on its rich alluvial soil could be found homes for 200,000,000 people. Dispossessed of this magnificent realm, the Southern Confederacy's dream of a great semi-tropical slave empire was only a dream. No other river, except the Amazon, opens so wide an area of navigation: and not only the Mississippi itself, but its chief tributary streams north of Vicksburg, were in control of the National authority. As the National flag was unfolded to the breeze on the Court House at Vicksburg, the earth shook with the salvos of artillery, and the air rang with the huzzas of fifty thousand men. "Grant with placid smile raised his hat, turned to a drum-major behind him, and ere those joyous sounds could be repeated, every occupant of that plateau was listening to the swelling notes of that world-wide hymn of praise, 'Old Hundred.'"

The citizens of Vicksburg had equal occasion with the Union soldiers to join in this hymn and rejoice in the result. They had suffered great hardship and discomfort during the siege. Many of them had lived in caves, dug in the bluffs to protect them against artillery fire. The market price of even mule-meat had been a dollar a pound in Confederate currency; flour was a thousand dollars a barrel; meal, one hundred and fifty dollars a bushel; and those who sought for a stimulant to enable them to resist the depressing influences of danger and disease were obliged to pay one hundred dollars a gallon for rum.

Other stimulants were to be had outside the Confederate lines at least; for we are told that while his officers were celebrating the hundred and thirty-first birthday of Washington in champagne, General Grant pushed aside a glass of wine, and, taking up a glass of Mississippi water with the remark, "This suits the matter in hand," drank to the toast, "God gave us Lincoln and liberty, let us fight for both!"

Not a drop of intoxicating liquor of any sort was to be had on the steamboat where Grant had his headquarters; and an officer who spent a dry month with him there reports, that, while he was treated with the greatest hospitality in other respects, he was told that if he wanted anything to drink, he would have to go to another boat. General Grant led him to one of the staterooms on the boat, which was filled with cigars of varying degrees of excellence, all of which had been received with the compliments of the sender. The best brands were indicated, and he was told to help himself. The habit of smoking Grant acquired at West Point, partly, as he tells us, because it was forbidden there. Towards the close of his life he said: "Looking back at the comfort and refreshment which a cigar has given me through a pretty mixed career, mostly of hard knocks, I am free to say, that, even if I knew tobacco was shortening my life, it would take more than my personal desire to live, to induce me to throw away my good friend here forever."

The headquarters of the Commanding General were in the captain's cabin of the steamboat referred to, and there he transacted the business of his great army with singular absence of everything in the nature of formality and military display. He was accessible at all times to whomever chose to call on a legitimate errand, and his ears were always open to the suggestions that came from every quarter as to the way he should conduct the siege of Vicksburg. There was no negro so humble that he could not find a hearing if he sought it.

Grant listened and smoked, and smoked and listened. No one could divine anything of his intentions. His inscrutable "Scotch eye" inspired confidence, but it did not convey knowledge. The intelligence with which he received valuable information, and his readiness to act upon it, are shown by a story told by Col. E. P. Vollum, Medical Corps, U. S. A.

The total Union loss during the long siege of Vicksburg, and the subsidiary operations leading up to it, amounted to 10,842 killed, wounded, and missing. A very large number had died of disease, and the great ravages in the ranks of the Army were made more apparent because of the difficulty in finding a dry spot in which to bury the dead. The levees of Vicksburg were lined with graves, and they were in evidence alike to the soldiers and to the numerous visitors and camp followers.

The story of disease and death at Vicksburg was undoubtedly melancholy enough, but it grew in dimensions as it travelled North. The papers were filled with exaggerated statements, and again the clamour arose for Grant's removal. President Lincoln, when a heavy pressure was brought to bear upon him, nearly yielded. Finally, after thinking a moment, he said, "I rather like the man. I think I'll try him a little longer." The War Department decided to send a medical officer to make inspection, and Colonel Vollum, who was Medical Inspector of the Army of the Potomac, was chosen for the duty. He devoted a month to the most careful and critical examination of every detail of the medical and sanitary administration of Grant's command, and reported, that, while there was undoubtedly a great deal of disease and death, the percentage in the Army before Vicksburg was no higher than that of the Army of the Potomac.

When Colonel Vollum had finished his work and called upon General Grant to say good-by, he told him that he would furnish his Adjutant-General with a copy of the report he was about to make to the War Department.

"No matter about that," answered the General. "Sit down here, Doctor, and tell me the substance of your report." Colonel Vollum gave as concisely as possible the story of his investigations and their result. Grant listened in silence, and then said, "Now tell me, Doctor, what it is you recommend." When the Medical officer's account was finished, Grant said, "I will issue an order on that subject to-morrow." He drew a pad towards him, and, after writing in silence for a short time, he called a messenger, and said, "Take that to the printer!"

The next day a general order was issued, embodying the results of Colonel Vollum's month's investigation, stated in the most concise language, and with the nice adaptation of his recommendation to the possibilities of military administration. Most general officers would have asked the Doctor to draw the order himself, and Grant's action in this matter was characteristic of the readiness with which he absorbed information, and the quickness and intelligence with which he applied it. He was much less dependent than most officers of his rank upon his staff for the substance, or even the form, of his orders. He gave close attention to the administration of his great command, even in minute details. Finding that the officers and men who had permission to go North on leave or furlough were being overcharged by the steamboat men, he issued an order limiting the charge to seven dollars for officers, and five dollars for men. Learning that this order was being disregarded, he promptly arrested a steamboat captain who had charged from ten to twenty-five dollars, and compelled him to refund the excess. Aroused by this and other impositions of steamboat men, he said, " I will teach them, if they need the lesson, that the men who have perilled their lives to open the Mississippi River for their benefit cannot be imposed upon with impunity." When he was a colonel, Grant knew every man in his regiment by sight and by name; as a general officer, and until he became Commander-in-Chief, he knew all of his officers. He had, moreover, the thorough knowledge of army minutiæ, so essential to the success of the soldier.

The trait of character shown by Grant as a young officer, when in crossing the Isthmus he assumed a dangerous responsibility in order to relieve his suffering command, distinguished him throughout his military career. He never hesitated to depart from routine where the security or comfort of his soldiers required it. He was, like his father before him, "a good provider," ever ready to sacrifice himself for the benefit of those dependent upon him. When the incipient scurvy appeared in his hospitals, he sent North for vegetables and acids, saying, "Onions and potatoes are indispensable to the taking of Vicksburg." The ladies of the Sanitary Commission, who responded with enthusiasm to his call, also said, "Potatoes and onions captured Vicksburg."

One of the difficulties experienced during the siege was that common to the administration of military affairs,—the difficulty of bringing the consumer and the supplies promptly together in the event of an emergency. Some years after the close of the war, and when Grant was President of the United States, he was called upon at the White House in Washington by an officer who had served with him at Vicksburg as a quartermaster. This officer was asked, "What are you doing here?" "I am trying to get my accounts settled with the Treasury Department, General." "What is the trouble?" "They won't allow for some quartermaster's stores I issued to the hospitals at Vicksburg."

"I know all about that," said the President. "I gave you the order myself. Send for the auditor."

The auditor came, and reported that he could find

no law authorising the issue of the stores in question, which had been absolutely needed for the comfort of the sick and dying soldiers. " Very well," said Grant, " you will find the law, or I will find another auditor,"—a terse statement, more effective than a decision of the Supreme Court to guide that particular auditor through the labyrinth of legal complications.

It should be remembered that all public stores issued to a disbursing officer of the Army are charged against him; and, however legitimate or necessary the issue may have been, they remain a charge until the officer is able to satisfy various officials of the Treasury Department that it was made under proper authority. The officer understands the necessity; the Treasury official understands, or thinks he understands, the law; and there is often difficulty in reconciling the differing points of view.

As soon as an advanced position was obtained by the Army, the Government, greatly to the annoyance of the military officers, sought immediately to extend trade to the limits of the military line. General Grant was so greatly annoyed by this, that when at Holly Springs, in December, 1862, he got himself into trouble by an indiscreetly-worded order expelling from his department within twenty-four hours." the Jews, as a class, violating every regulation of trade established by the Treasury Department, and also department orders." This was revoked three weeks later by orders from Washington, and it was made the basis of unjust charges of religious prejudice. Grant declared that he had not found one honest man following the Army as a trader, and, be he Jew or Christian, he hated a thief. To a stranger who came with recommendations from members of Congress, and other politicians, he said:

"This is for a permit to buy cotton, is it not?" "Yes." "Well, you can take it and leave these headquarters at once. If I find you here again, I will have you arrested. Men of your class are doing more to corrupt this army than all other kinds of rascality put together."

Another distracting question, not strictly military, with which officers had to deal, was that concerning the negro slaves brought under their control by the extension of military lines. In the beginning the slaves were dealt with as private property, which can be taken, even in war, only for necessary purposes, and their master's rights over them were recognised. Finally, General Benjamin F. Butler conceived the ingenious plan of dealing with them as contraband of war, holding that their use in building fortifications and for other belligerent purposes brought them within this designation. They were henceforth known as "contrabands," and the master's right to his human chattels was no longer recognised.

August 9, 1863, President Lincoln wrote to Grant, asking for his co-operation in a plan for enlisting negroes for the Army, to which duty General Lorenzo Thomas, A.-G., had been assigned. The General cordially responded, saying:

> "I have given the subject of arming the negro my hearty support. . . . General Thomas is now with me, and you may rely upon it, I will give him all the aid in my power. . . . I would do this whether the arming the negro seemed to me a wise policy or not, because it is an order that I am bound to obey, and do not feel that in my position I have a right to question any policy of the Government. In this particular instance there is no objection, however, to my expressing an honest conviction; that is, by arming the negro we have added a powerful ally. They will make good soldiers, and taking them from the enemy weakens him in the same proportion they strengthen us. I am, therefore, most decidedly in favor of pushing this policy to the enlistment of a force sufficient to hold all the South falling into our hands, and to aid in capturing more."

Some captured negroes having been brutally hanged by the Confederates, Grant wrote to the Confederate commander, General Richard Taylor, son of Zachary Taylor, saying, "If it is the policy of any general intrusted with command of troops to show no quarter, or to punish with death prisoners taken in battle, I will accept the issue." He notified Taylor at the same time that he felt himself bound to give the same protection to negro troops that he did to any troops.

The storm of detraction that followed Grant through so much of his military career was quieted after Vicksburg. On July 13th, President Lincoln wrote:

> "My dear General: I do not remember that you and I ever met personally. I write this now as a grateful acknowledgment for the almost inestimable service you have done the country. I wish to say a word further. When you first reached the vicinity of Vicksburg, I thought you should do what you finally did—march the troops across the neck, run the batteries with the transports, and thus go below; and I never had any faith, except a general hope that you knew

better than I, that the Yazoo Pass expedition and the like could succeed. When you got below and took Port Gibson, Grand Gulf and vicinity, I thought you should go down the river and join General Banks; and when you turned northward, east of the Big Black, I feared it was a mistake. I now wish to make a personal acknowledgment that you were right and I was wrong."

Halleck's first message was one reproving Grant for paroling his prisoners, and was based upon an ignorance of facts. He followed later with a letter in which he said:

"Your narration of the campaign, like the operations themselves, is brief, soldierly, and in every respect creditable and satisfactory. In boldness of plan, rapidity of execution, and brilliancy of routes, these operations will compare most favorably with those of Napoleon about Ulm. You and your army have well deserved the gratitude of your country, and it will be the boast of your children that their fathers were of the heroic army which reopened the Mississippi river."

The Administration had given Grant generous support, according to their lights; but with the chief body of troops sent to him he had received what he regarded as a "thorn in the flesh,"—"a messenger of Satan to buffet" him, in the person of the political general, McClernand, who brought into the Army an element of criticism, self-assertion, and insubordination, that was a constant menace to the success of the plans adopted. McClernand even went so far as to raise the issue, which he proposed to refer to Washington, as to whether he or Grant should command.

Sherman had expressed the opinion that if Grant had adhered to his purpose in moving by way of

Holly Springs, he would have accomplished in January what he did not accomplish, as it was, until July. Grant himself declares that if he had then had the confidence in his ability to live off of the country that he afterwards acquired, he would have followed his original plan of getting into the rear of Vicksburg. Sherman hints that other considerations than purely military ones influenced the change of plan. These are explained by the fact that when Grant, who had assigned Sherman to the co-operative movement from Memphis, found that the general in whom he had full confidence was to be subordinated to McClernand, in whom he had little confidence, he felt compelled to take command himself of the forces on the Mississippi. When you go down into a well, you want to be sure as to who is holding the rope.

Reviewing his Vicksburg campaign in after years, Grant said:

"Some of our generals failed because they worked out everything by rule. They knew what Frederick did at one place, and Napoleon at another. They were always thinking about what Napoleon would do. Unfortunately for their plans, the rebels would be thinking about something else. I don't underrate the value of military knowledge, but if men make war in slavish observances of rules, they will fail. No rules will apply to conditions of war as different as those which exist in Europe and America. Consequently, while our generals were working out problems of an ideal character, problems that would have looked well on a blackboard, practical facts were neglected. To that extent I consider remembrances of old campaigns a disadvantage. Even Napoleon showed that, for my impression is that his first success came because he made war in his own way, and not in imitation of others. War is progressive, because all the instruments and elements of war are progressive. I do not believe in luck in war any more than luck in business. Luck is a small matter, may affect a battle or a movement, but not a campaign or a career. . . . War has responsibilities that are either fatal to a commander's position or very successful. I often go over our war campaigns and criticise what I did, and see where I made mistakes. Information now and then coming to light for the first time shows me frequently where I could have done better. I don't think there is any one of my campaigns with which I have not some fault to find, and which, as I see now, I could not have improved, except perhaps Vicksburg. To take Vicksburg according to the rules of war as laid down in the books, would have involved a new campaign, a withdrawal of my forces to Memphis, and the opening of a new line of attack. The North needed a victory. We had been unfortunate in Virginia, and we had not gained our success at Gettysburg. Such a withdrawal as would have been necessary—say to Memphis, would have had all the effects, in the North, of a defeat. This was an ever-present consideration with me; for, although I took no open part in politics, and was supposed to be as much of a Democrat as a Republican, I felt that the Union depended upon the Administration, and the Administration upon the victory."

The old controversy between Halleck and Grant was revived after Vicksburg. It had its origin partly in differences in temperament, and partly in differences of position. Halleck had practised as a lawyer, and perhaps he had acquired something of the lawyer's chronic disposition to " get an extension "; and then he was in Washington, where political and personal considerations were influential. Besides, he must wait until he could conduct a campaign according to the rules of war, and the opportunity never came. Grant, who was for immediate action, now proposed to strike at once for Mobile, capture that place, ascend the river extending from it north into the heart of Alabama, and thus open connection with the chain of posts stretching across

Tennessee to the northern limits of Alabama. This would have again divided the Confederacy, and practically limited the war to Virginia, Georgia, and the Carolinas.

This plan was entirely feasible, and its success would probably have soon ended the war. But Halleck always trembled before the grand operations of war involving risks, and, instead of embarking upon great ventures, preferred to paddle in the safer waters of secondary operations. Instead of keeping together the grand Army of Vicksburg, he ordered it scattered. One corps, the Thirteenth, was sent to Natchez to co-operate with Banks in his disastrous Red River campaign, organised for the purpose of securing a foothold in Texas, and incidentally opening the cotton regions of Louisiana. The purpose of this expedition was diplomatic rather than military, and Grant advised against it. Maximilian was endeavouring to secure a foothold in Mexico, with the aid of Napoleon III., and Confederate agents were making a desperate effort abroad to secure the interference of foreign governments on behalf of the South. It was thought that the possession, or partial possession, of Texas would thwart these movements. But Grant reasoned that if you strike at the heart you paralyse the limbs, and that secondary successes were valueless so long as the heart of the Rebellion was not pierced.

Another call was made upon Grant to succour Rosecrans at Chattanooga, and he was compelled to send to him all of his available forces remaining. These several drafts on the Army of the Mississippi reduced its activities to the suppression of guerilla bands in Mississippi and the adjacent borders. With the breaking-up of the Confederate armies at Vicksburg and Port Hudson, thousands of deserters and paroled prisoners had organised under two or three notable leaders, and were ravaging the country.

Once more the sun of Grant's prosperity was destined to a temporary eclipse. He was stripped of his troops, and physical infirmity for a time prevented him from assuming command of another department that offered opportunity for more active service. At the end of August, 1863, he visited New Orleans to confer with Banks, in obedience to orders he had received to co-operate with him in his movement beyond the Mississippi. While in the Creole city, he was offered the honour of a review by the Thirteenth Corps, which had just left his command. During the review he was thrown by his vicious horse shying at a locomotive, and was picked up in a condition of insensibility. Three ribs were broken, one side was paralysed, and he suffered excruciating pain. His brain was so affected by the concussion that it was for a time supposed that he could never again assume command. It was intended to assign him to the command of the troops moving in Tennessee toward northwestern Georgia, but the movement could not be delayed; and during his severe illness of over one month the command fell to Rosecrans.

Again Halleck was in a fever of impatience because he could not hear from Grant, ignorant of the fact that communication was interrupted by the carelessness or indifference of his own employees. Grant had established prompt communication between Memphis and New Orleans, and received within a day, from Memphis, despatches that had been from six to eleven days on their way from Washington to that city. In spite of his illness, there was no delay in action when the orders reached him.

Meanwhile Rosecrans was overthrown at Chickamauga, September 20, 1863, and the calls for Grant grew more urgent. While still lying helpless on his bed at New Orleans, unable even to turn himself, he received two telegrams urging him to hasten all available forces to the succour of the Army of the Cumberland. Helpless as he was, he resolved upon immediate action. He sent for a litter, and was carried on it to a steamer brought down the river as near as possible to the hotel. He was barely able to reach Vicksburg, and was then placed on his bed, unable to rise from it without assistance.

The situation of Rosecrans after Chickamauga was indeed alarming; for in one of the most destructive battles of the war he had lost the field, and his effective force had been reduced nearly one third. Re-enforcements were hastening to him from the East; and Grant was appealed to, to help him from the West. On October 3, 1863, a despatch was sent to Grant at Vicksburg, saying:

"It is the wish of the Secretary of War that as soon as General Grant is able to take the field, he will come to Cairo and report by telegraph."

Lame as he was, Grant started without delay, and from Columbus, on October 16th, reported by telegraph:

"Your despatch from Cairo of the 3d directing me to report from Cairo, was received at 11.30 on the 10th. Left the same day with staff and headquarters, and am here *en route* for Cairo."

CHAPTER XII.

RELIEF OF ROSECRANS—BATTLE OF CHATTANOOGA.

AUGUST, 1863–FEBRUARY, 1864.

RANT learned at Cairo that he was to have command of the Military Division of the Mississippi, controlling all the armies operating between the great river and the Alleghanies. The Army of the Cumberland, under Rosecrans, was the centre of a grand military cordon, of which the Army of the Potomac formed the left wing, and the Army of the Mississippi, until now commanded by Grant, the right wing. To prevent the enemy from concentrating against one of these wings, all must act together. That was Grant's policy, and the policy he intended to pursue, now that fortune had given him control.

Rosecrans's campaign from Murfreesboro to Tallahoma, Tennessee, had by the end of June restored middle Tennessee to the National troops, and he had driven the enemy south of the Tennessee River. The Confederate forces under Bragg were concentrated at Chattanooga, Tennessee, "the gateway of the Cumberland Mountains." In Bragg's rear were his depots of supplies, and by interior lines of railroad he was in touch with the other Confederate armies. In front of him were numerous spurs and ridges of the Cumberland Mountains, and a broad river, the Tennessee, protecting him from the advance of Rosecrans, whose assault must be conducted far from his base.

The Confederates abandoned Chattanooga, August 8, 1863, and were supposed to have retreated south, until one of Sheridan's scouts returned from within the enemy's lines, bringing a report that Longstreet from Lee's army was to join forces with Bragg, and that Bragg was so to manœuvre as to draw out Rosecrans and defeat him in detail. This news compelled the re-formation of Rosecrans's lines, which were too far advanced for security. On August 17th Bragg endeavoured to turn Rosecrans's flank and envelop his right, but he was driven back after sharp fighting. On the 18th, Rosecrans continued a movement for strengthening his left which he had previously begun. It was, as Sheridan tells us, "made by the flank, in the face of an exultant foe superior in number, and was a violation of the simple and fundamental military principle." Nothing but imperative necessity justified it.

Grant had been anxious to have Rosecrans coöperate with him during the Vicksburg campaign by a vigorous attack to prevent Bragg from sending reenforcements to the Mississippi; but Rosecrans remained idle during the whole of that time, and when he moved, he did so only in obedience to peremptory orders from Washington. By a brilliant strategic movement he secured possession of Chattanooga on September 19, 1863; and the battle of Chickamauga followed on September 20th and 21st, when Rosecrans's army was defeated, and he was only saved from destruction by the ability and stubborn determination of General George H. Thomas, whose conduct on that field secured for him the title of "The Rock of Chickamauga." Two weeks after Chickamauga, Rosecrans was re-enforced by the arrival of the Eleventh and Twelfth Corps, sent from the Army of the Potomac under the command of General Hooker. By a remarkable feat of railroad transportation, these 20,000 men, with their guns, munitions of war, and other equipments, had been transferred from Virginia to Rosecrans's army in Tennessee in eight days.

Though Rosecrans retained possession of Chattanooga, the Confederates had cut him off from the Tennessee River, his natural line of communication with his base, and had so hemmed him in that his army was gradually being reduced to starvation. His supplies had to be hauled for forty miles from Bridgeport, Alabama,—the terminus of the railroad running south from Nashville,—over a road lying back from the river; and this road was constantly raided by Confederate cavalry under the enterprising General Wheeler. Over 12,000 mules had been killed in transporting supplies. The distance was sixty miles, twenty-five miles of it through unfathomable mud, and across a mountain ridge where a misstep would precipitate a team over a frightful precipice. A thousand pounds was an unusual load for a waggon drawn by six half-starved and jaded mules.

Rosecrans's neglect to hold Lookout Mountain when he occupied Chattanooga transferred this strong position to Bragg, who succeeded in enclosing his enemy on his front and on both flanks. This was the situation when Grant, who had been promoted to Major-General in the Regular Army as a reward for Vicksburg, arrived at Chattanooga. He reached Cairo on October 16th, and there received telegraphic orders to proceed to Louisville for instructions. Within an hour or two after their receipt he was on his way. At Indianapolis, Grant was joined by the Secretary of War, Stanton, whom he here met for the first time. They proceeded together to Louisville, where a day was spent in conference. The Secretary was greatly troubled by despatches from Charles A. Dana, Assistant Secretary of War, then at Chattanooga, who described the situation of Rosecrans's army as desperate, with no outlook but starvation or disorderly retreat. The soldiers, he reported, were mutinous. On October 16th Mr. Dana wrote: " Nothing can prevent the retreat of the army from this place within a fortnight, and with a vast loss of public property and possibly of life, except the opening of the river."

October 18, 1863, Grant telegraphed from Louisville to Rosecrans assuming command of the Military Division of Missouri, and to Thomas assigning him to the command of the Army of the Cumberland, *vice* Rosecrans, and ordering him to hold Chattanooga at all hazards. To this the stouthearted Thomas replied, " We will hold the town until we starve." October 20th, Grant started from Louisville for the front, stopping over night at Nashville, and telegraphing from there to Burnside, who was in command of Knoxville.

General O. O. Howard, in a paper read before the Military Order of the Loyal Legion, of which Grant was a member, tells us that when Grant arrived at Chattanooga, Hooker sent a spring waggon and an officer of his staff to the depot for him, but did not go himself. The General was so quiet in his way, that subordinate officers did not always realise how ready he was on all proper occasions to assert his position and his authority. He replied, " If General Hooker wishes to see me, he will find me on this train." Hooker promptly appeared with offers of hospitality, which were declined. General Howard says:

" General Grant and I shared a common wall tent between us. He had a humorous expression which I noticed as his eye fell upon a liquor flask hanging against the tent wall.

" ' That flask is not mine,' I quickly said. ' It was left here by an officer, to be returned to Chattanooga. I never drink.' ' Neither do I,' was his prompt reply : and his answer was not in sport. He was at that time free from every appearance of drinking and I was happy, indeed, to find in his clear eye and clear face an unmistakable testimonial against the many falsehoods or exaggerations which envy and rivalry had set in motion, especially after the famous battle of Shiloh.

." The next morning, after a sunrise breakfast, General Rawlins lifted his general, then lame and suffering, as if he had been a child, into the saddle. The direct route across the Tennessee was held by

Confederate Bragg; and the river road by the way of Jasper on our side, was exposed to sharp shooters from the other bank, and to Confederate Wheeler's spasmodic raids.

"Yet almost without escort Grant risked the journey along the river, through Jasper, across swollen streams, through deep mud, and along roads that were already deemed too wretched and too dangerous for the wagon. This route was strewn with the wrecks of Army vehicles and dead mules. It would have been an awful journey for a well man—a journey of more than forty miles. At times it was necessary to take the General from his horse. The soldiers carried him in their arms across the roughest places. Yielding to no weakness or suffering, he pushed through to Chattanooga reaching General Thomas the evening of October 23d. It was this remarkable journey which put Grant *en rapport* with Thomas and Hooker; gave practicable shape to all good existing plans; and soon changed an army, on the very verge of starvation into an active, healthful, well-supplied conquering force."

During the journey Grant's horse had slipped with him on a mountain road, and still further injured his bruised limb. When he arrived after his hard journey of two days, he was lifted out of the saddle like a helpless child.

An officer of the Army reports that about this time he saw on the opposite side of a stream a sandy-bearded man on horseback, with a cigar between his teeth, who was endeavouring to force his unwilling horse to cross the stream on a narrow wooden bridge that was slippery with frost. The officer warned the stranger not to cross, and, as he persisted, he shouted in anger:

"Turn back, you darned fool! Do you want to get ducked or get drowned? Don't you see that the bridge is as slippery as glass?"

The stranger, who wore a blue army overcoat,

raised his cap, turned around, and galloped away. A few hours later this officer's command was ordered into line for review by the newly arrived commanding officer, who was recognised as the stranger at the bridge. At the close of the review General Grant sent for the officer, and said,—

"You are the person who prevented me from venturing on the bridge this morning, Colonel B——, are you not?"

Very unwillingly and with much perturbation the officer answered, "Yes, sir!" Grant replied, "I wish to tell you that I am very much obliged to you. You saved me from committing a very silly and foolhardy action, and probably also from an unpleasant drenching."

Among those from whom Grant received excellent suggestions, when he arrived at Chattanooga, was Rosecrans himself, who met him *en route* at Stevenson on the night of the 21st. "My only wonder," Grant says, "was that he had not carried them out." There was no officer in the Army more capable than Rosecrans of forming brilliant conceptions. What was needed was the vigorous will to carry them into effect, and this was furnished by the arrival of Grant. He took in the situation at a glance, and was prepared for immediate action.

Bragg's line ran from the Tennessee River, on the east of Chattanooga, southerly along the impregnable heights of Missionary Ridge, thence westerly across Chattanooga Valley; terminating in Lookout Mountain, whose precipitous cliffs nearly touched the Tennessee River west of Chattanooga. At

Chattanooga the river doubles on itself, forming a loop known as Moccason Point. Across Moccason Point, in possession of the Union troops, was a road running east and west, crossing the river at Brown's Ferry, and thence running south through Lookout Valley. From Chattanooga down to Bridgeport the river was controlled by Confederate sharpshooters. Had Bridgeport been in the possession of the Union Army, supplies could have been brought there, and sent up the river to Chattanooga by boat.

Chattanooga was surrounded by tumbling ridges and serpentine streams, and was situated at one angle of a triangle, Cleveland and Dalton occupying the other two angles. Railroads connecting these three places formed the sides of the triangle. The country is broken up in all directions by the East and West Chickamauga Creeks, and the more northern tributaries of the Tennessee; by Lookout Mountain, Missionary Ridge, Tunnel Hill, and numerous other colossal tumuli; and the railroads running through the passes among the hills mark the principal routes of communication, especially for large armies.

The strength of the Confederates' position was in their control of the two heights of Missionary Ridge and Lookout Mountain; limestone cliffs running a little west of south from the Chattanooga River, and nearly parallel with it, and enclosing between them the Chattanooga Valley. Above Chattanooga, North Chickamauga Creek flows into the Tennessee River from the north; and Chickamauga River, a stream one hundred and eighty feet wide, coming from the south, empties into the Tennessee River, four miles lower down. At the foot of the western slope of Lookout Mountain, Lookout Creek flows north-easterly through Lookout Valley, and empties into the Tennessee just below Chattanooga. Two miles farther east is Citico Creek.

It was for the control of this region that a struggle must be made if the Union Army were to continue in possession of Chattanooga. The President of the Confederacy, Jefferson Davis, visited Bragg's army at the time, and, from a lofty eminence commanding a view of five different States, observed with exultation Grant's army lying in the valley below. "I have them now!" he exclaimed, "in just the trap I set for them."

In Rosecrans's command was an engineer officer, Gen. W. F. Smith, who was in the Military Academy at the same time as Grant, and possessed his confidence. Smith proposed that Brown's Ferry should be seized, and that troops should be sent across the Tennessee at that point to take possession of Lookout Valley; Hooker advancing into the valley at the same time east from Bridgeport. This would open the Tennessee River to Kelly's Ferry, six or eight miles west, and that place was connected with Chattanooga by a good road. From Kelly's Ferry to Chattanooga the river ran through a chasm known as the "Suck," where the current was too strong for the steamboats.

The pontoons to transport Hooker's force across the river were already concentrated at Bridgeport, and, after a reconnaissance to satisfy himself as to facts, Grant ordered Hooker to move. First securing a foothold on the south bank of the Tennessee, Hooker was to march up the river to Brown's Ferry, while Smith was to march from Chattanooga down the right bank of the river to the ferry, and there lay a bridge as soon as he could secure a position on the stream at that point.

At three o'clock on the morning of October 27th, a portion of Smith's forces, 1800 men under Hazen, floated in the darkness of the night, on the swift current of the Tennessee, from Chattanooga, in fifty boats made of rude boards roughly put together. This required them to run the gauntlet of the enemy's pickets and batteries for nine miles, following the windings of the stream; but the movement was not discovered, thanks to a light mist and the darkness. Even the shrill cry of one soldier who had fallen into the river, and must be left to drown, did not attract the attention of the enemy to the flotilla.

Landing at Brown's Ferry at five in the morning, under a harmless fire of small-arms, Hazen hastened to secure his footing there. The axemen he had taken with him felled trees to protect his front with abatis; and under the cover of his advance the pontoon bridge was laid by Smith, and completed at ten o'clock. Meanwhile, Hooker crossed at Bridgeport, October 26th, found his advance practically unopposed, and on the 28th he entered Lookout Valley at Wauhatchie. On the night of October 29, 1863, Longstreet made an attack on Hooker's forces under Geary. It failed, as night attacks usually do; the Union mules taking an important part in it by rushing into the enemy's lines in their fright, and conveying the impression that their wild flight was a desperate cavalry charge.

The Army of the Cumberland had now joined forces at Brown's Ferry with their comrades of the Army of the Potomac under Hooker. Grant had secured possession of Lookout Valley; and free communication was established between Bridgeport and Chattanooga, by way of the Tennessee River, as far as Kelly's Ferry; thence to Chattanooga over a waggon road eight miles long, passing by Brown's Ferry.

As a counter-movement, Bragg resolved to send Longstreet to attack Burnside at Knoxville, acting in this matter under the inspiration of the Confederate President, Davis. To prevent this movement, which commenced November 4, 1863, Thomas was ordered to make an attack on Missionary Ridge, November 7th, with a wholly insufficient force. Fortunately the cool-headed Thomas protested against this order, and it was withdrawn.

To Burnside Grant telegraphed: "Hold on to Knoxville! If Longstreet moves his whole force along the Little Tennessee, cut his pontoons on the stream, even if it sacrifices half the cavalry of the Ohio Army."

Sherman had started from Memphis, October 2, 1863, to move with the Army of the Tennessee to the aid of Grant, four hundred miles by steam, and then four hundred miles more across a hostile country. On October 27th, as he was sitting on the

porch of a house in Iuka, he was approached by
"a dirty, black-haired individual, with a mixed dress
and strange demeanour," who looked like a hunter
or woodsman—anything but a soldier. It was the
bold Corporal Pike, who had floated down the Tennessee, under the enemy's fire, bringing this despatch:

"Drop all work on Memphis and Charleston Railroad, cross the Tennessee and hurry eastward with all possible despatch toward Bridgeport, till you meet further orders from me.
U. S. GRANT."

After overcoming great difficulties from bad roads and swollen rivers, Sherman reached Bridgeport on November 13th, and rode into Chattanooga on November 15, 1863, his troops following hard after. He found a cordial welcome. Everything awaited his coming. As he says, "All things had been pre-arranged with a foresight that elicited my admiration. From the hills we looked down on Chattanooga as on a map, and nothing remained but for me to put my troops in a desired position."

The whole philosophy of the battle was that Sherman should get by a dash a position on the extremity of Missionary Ridge, from which the enemy would be forced to drive him if he wished to secure his depot at Chickamauga Station. The other movements were to be subsidiary to this, but fate ordered it otherwise. Grant found that the valour and enthusiasm of the Army of the Cumberland were beyond what he expected after their bitter experiences under Rosecrans. The attack was planned for November 21st; but a furious rainstorm, continuing for two days, had made it impossible for Sherman to get into position as soon as was intended. Grant said at this time, "I have never felt such restlessness as I have at the fixed and immovable condition of the Army of the Cumberland." Fearful that Bragg would withdraw and throw himself at Burnside, he decided to attack at the earliest possible moment, without waiting for the complete disposition of his forces.

Deserters who had mistaken the meaning of Longstreet's movement against Burnside, arrived with the report that Bragg's army was falling back, leaving nothing on his front but a strong picket line. To determine the truth of this report, Grant ordered a reconnaissance in force by Thomas, who held the centre, his lines extending from Chattanooga Creek to Citico Creek, in Chattanooga Valley, and had strengthened his position by a series of redoubts, the most important of these being Fort Wood, mounting twenty-two guns.

An interval of a mile separated the Union and Confederate lines; the pickets of the two armies would draw water from opposite sides of the same stream, and were so near together that when on one occasion Grant approached his pickets along the river, and the call came, "Turn out the guard!— Commanding General," the Confederate sentinels on the other side took up the cry, and also presented arms to him. Friendly exchanges between the outposts were common in all the armies during the war; and among the many curious stories told of them is one by General Longstreet, who on one occasion found a Union soldier, *sans* uniform, *sans* everything, hiding in the bushes in front of his picket line. He had swum the river to have a chat with the Johnnies; and when Longstreet threatened to march him to Richmond as he was, the Confederate pickets interposed, and insisted that their honour should not be thus impeached.

The nature of the ground over which Thomas's reconnaissance was to be made was such that the enemy were able to observe the movements of the troops directed by Grant, who had taken his station at Fort Wood, with Thomas and other officers. Howard, who was present, tells us that Gordon Granger deployed in measured and precise movement one division of the Fourth Corps, and supported it by his other two. "This force, extended into line, presented a picture not often seen; the bayonets gleamed in the sunlight; the skirmishers sprang forward at proper intervals, and covered the entire front, as alert and active as children at play. The Fourteenth Corps supported the right, and the Eleventh, massed in close order, was ready in full view to follow up the left."

The Confederates stood on their breastworks to look at what they took to be review and drill, when, to their astonishment, the Union lines advanced with rapidity toward Orchard Knob. "Soon the enemy's pickets were driven back or taken; soon all those other defences for a mile ahead near the Knob were in our hands, but not without bloodshed. General Grant, at Fort Wood, kept looking steadily towards the troops engaged and beyond. He was slowly smoking a cigar."

At the close of the movement, Thomas was a mile in advance of the position occupied by the enemy in the morning. The positions gained were secured by a line of intrenchments, facing and parallel to Missionary Ridge, with Orchard Knob as a point of support.

When the night of November 23d closed down, the dispirited troops of Rosecrans could not be recognised in the exulting host surrounding Grant. In the five days following his arrival at Chattanooga the new commander had opened the way to Bridgeport, and the troops who had been living on quarter rations were, within a week of his appearance, receiving full rations. They had been re-clothed and were well fed, and hope and encouragement had taken the place of despondency. All were filled with the confidence of coming victory, and every man was resolved to show that Rosecrans's failure was not due to any lack of spirit or determination in the troops he had commanded.

That night the last of Sherman's divisions arrived, and were placed in position four miles above Chattanooga, opposite the mouth of the South Chickamauga. The local saw-mills had been running night and day to provide material for rude pontoons, built without the knowledge of the enemy, and concealed in the mouth of the North Chickamauga, five miles up that river. The main body of Sherman's command were gathered for a movement across the Tennessee at Brown's Ferry. The divisions above floated down with the current, thirty men in each boat, secured a footing east of the South Chickamauga, and established a *tête de pont*, under the protection of which a bridge was laid. Meanwhile a pontoon bridge thirteen hundred feet long had been thrown across the Tennessee, under the protection of forty pieces of artillery. To prevent communication with the enemy, the local residents were kept within doors, a sentinel being placed before each house.

Sherman's whole command was now in a position to advance against Missionary Ridge from the left. His movement against the enemy's right had been assisted by a feint from Howard against his left, and had been partially concealed by rain and fog. The right and left movements were intended to cover the main attack by Thomas to overwhelm the enemy's centre. Sherman rapidly advanced to the foot-hills, and soon secured two high points on Missionary Ridge, before the enemy were aware of what he intended.

On the morning of November 24, 1863, Hooker, taking advantage of the obscurity of the day, advanced against Lookout Mountain on the enemy's left, and by a bold and successful movement, which forms part of the romance of war, secured possession of its frowning crests, rising abruptly above the Tennessee River to the height of twenty-four hundred feet above the sea-level. The fog that had concealed Hooker's movement early in the day finally dispersed; and through the lifting haze, his comrades, who had watched his advance with strained and eager attention, discovered him in position on the rocky ledges in front of the Confederate works. Until then they could not tell whether this "Battle in the Clouds," of which they had caught but occasional glimpses through the rifts in the fog, presaged victory or defeat. When the curtain rose the scene had shifted, and Hooker was discovered in full possession of the enemy's works. With Lookout Mountain in his possession, he was able to establish communication with Chattanooga. Thomas, having secured the day before the position which he intended to occupy in the general line, took no part in the movement of November 24th.

That night Grant telegraphed to Washington:

"The fight to-day progressed favorably. Sherman carried the end of Missionary Ridge, and his right is now at the tunnel, and his left at Chickamauga Creek. Troops from the Lookout Valley carried the point of the mountain, and now hold the eastern slope and a point high up. Hooker reports two thousand prisoners taken, besides which a small number have fallen into our hands from Missionary Ridge."

The President replied:

"Your despatches as to fighting on Monday and Tuesday are here. Well done. Many thanks to all. Remember Burnside."

Halleck telegraphed:

"I congratulate you on the success, thus far, of your plans. I fear that General Burnside is hard pushed, and that any further delay may prove fatal. I know that you will do all in your power to relieve him."

During the night of November 24, 1863, Bragg

withdrew his troops on Lookout Mountain to concentrate on his right against Sherman at the north end of Missionary Ridge, and Hooker the next morning advanced across the Lookout Valley to take part in the combined movement ordered for the 25th. The different wings of Grant's army were now in close connection, and his lines had been shortened and strengthened; the left resting on Chickamauga Creek, and the right occupying the summit of Lookout Mountain. The fog that had filled the valleys had cleared away by the morning of November 25th, and the day was clear and cold. Sherman's maps had led him to suppose that Missionary Ridge was a single hill; but, after reaching the position he had aimed for on the 24th, he found that a valley separated him from the strong position of the enemy which was his objective. He had accordingly gone into camp for the night, fortifying himself.

At daylight on the morning of November 25th, Sherman advanced to the attack. Eagerly his troops pressed forward, down a hillside, across a gorge, and up a slope beyond, where a frowning line of breastworks barred further passage. After fighting for two hours, they secured a position threatening both flanks of the enemy, and compelling him to strengthen his right at the expense of other portions of his line.

The struggle continued until afternoon, and no sound was yet heard from the guns of Thomas. He was expected to open the attack along the centre early in the day; but his movements were to be timed by those of Hooker, and Hooker's advance against the flank of the enemy had been delayed four hours by the destruction of bridges in Chattanooga Valley. Three o'clock passed, and four o'clock drew near, before " a white line of musketry fire, in front of Orchard Knob, extending farther right and left, and on," showed that at last Thomas was moving on the centre to relieve Sherman.

When Thomas did move, he moved, as he always did, with great effect. The advance of his men was clearly seen by Bragg, who massed his troops against him. In spite of difficulties, Thomas's men soon gained a foothold on the southerly end of Missionary Ridge, and after a desperate struggle, and a wonderful display of resolute courage, secured its summit. The troops were obliged to climb the almost inaccessible heights like goats, and in face of a deadly hail of grape, canister, and musket-balls such as tries the courage of the most experienced veteran, even when the advantages are not, as they were here, three to one against him.

The men had no orders to take the summit of Missionary Ridge, but an uncontrollable fury seems to have seized them as they advanced; and they pressed forward in a series of rushes, stopping to take breath between them. The line was somewhat broken by the irregularities of the ground, but the movement was made with an irresistible impulse.

The enemy, though they had the advantage of a strong position, seemed to have been thoroughly demoralised by the fury of the assault. Sheridan, who was in advance, was naturally hugely delighted with the result. He told his men after the fight, that they all ought to be court-martialled for exceeding their orders. There was a twinkle in his eye and a tremour in his voice as he added, " If you will promise me to hold this position against everything that comes, I will say nothing about it." The day was cold, and so clear that the officers coming and going at Bragg's headquarters, and his columns moving against Sherman, could be seen distinctly from the elevated position on Cumberland Knob occupied by Grant. Speaking of the movement of Thomas in his official report, Grant says:

" These troops moved forward, drove the enemy from the rifle-pits at the base of the ridge like bees from a hive, stopped but a moment until the whole were in line, and commenced the ascent of the mountain from right to left, almost simultaneously, following closely the retreating enemy without further orders. They encountered a fearful volley of grape and canister, from nearly thirty pieces of artillery and musketry from well-filled rifle-pits on the summit of the ridge. Not a waver, however, was seen in the long line of brave men : their progress was steadily onward until the summit was in their possession."

On the night of November 26, 1863, Grant was able to announce complete victory over Bragg. The enemy were pursued November 26th and 27th up the Chickamauga River as far as Ringgold, Georgia, but the pursuit was not continued owing to the necessity of following the orders from Washington to re-enforce Burnside. Grant, who was in command of the advance, ordered Sherman to turn off at Greysville, just north of Ringgold, and march to the relief of Knoxville.

The Union loss in the series of attacks at Chatta-

nooga from November 23d to 25th inclusive was
5824. Sheridan lost in his charge on Missionary
Ridge, in one hour, twenty per cent. of his force of
6000 men. The loss in some of Grant's regiments
was over sixty per cent.; and the Confederate loss
8684, including 6142 prisoners. They also lost
forty-two pieces of artillery, and 7000 small-arms.
This was the greatest capture made in the open field
up to that time. Sixty thousand men had been
engaged on the Union side along the front of thirteen miles. The enemy had 45,000 men, and had
the advantage of holding strongly intrenched positions, but their front was too extended for successful
defence.

Grant had thus brought to a logical conclusion
the remarkable series of operations beginning with
the occupation of Chattanooga. In hotly contested
engagements he had succeeded in pushing back the
Confederate force step by step from their fortified
lines on the ridges fronting Chattanooga; he had at
the same time dealt them one of the most staggering blows they had yet received. The unfortunate
battle of Chickamauga prevented the realisation of
Rosecrans's admirable strategic plan; and his loss of
Lookout Mountain, when he drew back on Chattanooga, was a great military misfortune. Cooped up
in Chattanooga, the essential weakness of that point
revealed itself; and the confident assertions of the
Confederate press that the "Yankees" would be
either "driven out of Tennessee or captured," were
not altogether extravagant. Rosecrans's men had
been reduced to one third rations; his horses were

either dead, or so crippled by starvation that they were unable to draw his artillery into battle; and the artillery were dependent on Sherman's teams after he arrived. The Army of the Cumberland held the citadel; but the enemy were on the parapets (the mountain ridges facing Chattanooga), and only a wet ditch (the Tennessee River) was between them.

Longstreet promptly raised the siege of Knoxville after hearing from Chattanooga; and President Lincoln, in an executive recommendation of December 7, 1863, urged that all loyal people, in view of the withdrawal of the insurgents from East Tennessee, " under circumstances rendering it probable that the Union forces cannot hereafter be dislodged in that important position," should render thanksgiving for " this great advancement of the National cause."

The Confederate comment on the result was shown by the prompt removal of Bragg from his command. " The Southern people," wrote the *Richmond Examiner*, " never had greater reason to be serious and anxious than at this moment." Into an enemy's hands had passed the control of that great natural arsenal of East Tennessee whence the Confederates drew their lead, nitre, and coal,—that grand magazine containing their chief supplies of corn, and nine tenths of all their bacon.

In a letter to Grant, dated December 8, 1863, President Lincoln said:

" Understanding that your lodgment at Knoxville and at Chattanooga is now secure, I wish to tender to you, and all under your command, my more than thanks—my profoundest gratitude—for the skill, courage, for the perseverance with which you and they, over so great difficulty, have effected that important object. God bless you all!"

Congress tendered its thanks in a joint resolution, and directed that a gold medal be given to Grant for Vicksburg and Chattanooga; a diamond-hilted sword was sent by the citizens of Jo Daviess County, Illinois; and envy, jealousy, and detraction were silenced in the universal acclaim that followed the successful general. Even Halleck was finally convinced, and henceforth yielded to the judgment of Grant without discussion.

"After having broken the impediments which closed the passage of the Mississippi, it is again Grant," says the Comte de Paris, "who has just opened the doors of Georgia. The Federal armies have at last found the warrior worthy to lead them. The bold and skilful manœuvres which began in the valley of Lookout Mountain, and terminated a month later near the house whence Bragg and Davis had contemplated a Union Army besieged at their feet, enhance the glory of the conqueror of Vicksburg. He has proved that his mind, powerful to conceive, firm to execute, is fertile in resources at the critical time."

CHAPTER XIII.

LIEUTENANT-GENERAL—GENERAL-IN-CHIEF— GENESIS OF A GREAT SOLDIER.

MARCH, 1864.

DECEMBER 20, 1863, General Grant moved his headquarters to Nashville, leaving Thomas in command at Chattanooga. Seven days later General Joseph E. Johnston assumed command of the Confederate Army of the Tennessee with 43,000 men present for duty. At Nashville, Grant busied himself in preparing for a campaign against Atlanta, which was to be extended, if successful, to Savannah, or to Mobile if it was found that possession of that city could be obtained by an assault from the Gulf. When New Orleans fell, in April, 1862, the Confederates believed that Mobile would be the next point of attack. They did everything in their power to strengthen that place; and it continued in their possession until August, 1864, when it yielded to a spirited attack by the Navy under Admiral Farragut.

The winter of 1863–64 was a very severe one, and

was occupied on both sides chiefly in preparation for the campaign of the following spring. Grant was busied in strengthening his position and opening routes of transportation for his army. Having occasion to visit Knoxville, Tennessee, early in January, 1864, he chose a difficult line of travel, because it enabled him to ascertain for himself the possibilities of the country, and to determine upon a route for supplying a portion of his army, which was again short of supplies. On this journey, by the way of Cumberland Gap, Barboursville, Big Hill, Richmond, and Lexington, he encountered the coldest weather and the deepest snow known for a generation; and he and his staff had a bitter experience, being compelled to wade through the drifts, driving before them their half-frozen horses. A portion of the way was dangerous as well as difficult. It was by such attention to detail, at the expense of convenience and comfort, that Grant prospered. By the middle of January, railroad communication was established between Nashville and Chattanooga, and the Army of the Cumberland was no longer dependent upon muleteams, hauling supplies over roads barely passable under the best of conditions, and now at their worst.

Wherever he went during his journey, the hero of Vicksburg and Chattanooga was surrounded by crowds eager to see the man who had delivered them from the grasp of the enemy. He was then but forty-one years of age, and, as wisdom is associated with age, attention intended for him was directed to his venerable-appearing medical officer.

Grant was less impressive in appearance than

many of the leading soldiers who served under him. Sheridan was undersized; but Sherman, Meade, and Thomas were large men, as were most of the army and corps commanders. Their chief was a man of medium height, five feet eight inches, and slim in build, weighing at this time but one hundred and thirty-five pounds, though in later life he gained in weight and dignity of appearance. His frame was well-knit and compact; but he had a slight stoop, and his appearance was altogether unmilitary. In walking he made no attempt to keep step, his unmusical ear being so insensible to rhythm and cadence that the most emphatic tunes made no impression upon him.

His brow was straight and square, but his head gave no indication of unusual capacity. His full beard, cut close, partially concealed a square and heavy jaw and straight lips which gave indication of his strong will and inflexible purpose. Just above his beard, on the right cheek, was a wart. His hair, which was worn short, was chestnut-brown in colour. His eyes were dark gray, and when his purpose was to conceal his thought, they had an inscrutable look, though they could twinkle with laughter or melt with tenderness. A front view of his face showed that his left eye was a little lower than the right. His voice was musical, if his ear was not, and his utterance was usually clear and distinct. Horace Porter says that his voice " had a singular power of penetration, and sentences spoken by him in an ordinary tone in camp could be heard at a distance that was surprising. When not pressed by any matter of importance he was often slow in his movements, but when roused to activity he was quick in every motion, and worked with marvellous rapidity."

He was a remarkably good listener; and his mind was quick, receptive, and retentive. In speech he was usually slow, and sometimes embarrassed; but his thought was clearly expressed in well-chosen words, and when aroused he was fluent and forcible. When he did not thoroughly understand a subject discussed, he kept silence. His conclusions, once arrived at, were seldom reversed. As Badeau says:

> "The man was a marvel of simplicity, a powerful nature veiled in the plainest possible exterior, imposing on all but the acutest judges of character, or the constant companions of his unguarded hours. Not a sign about him suggested rank, or reputation, or power. He discussed the most ordinary themes with apparent interest, and turned from them in the same quiet tones, and without a shade of difference in his manner, to decisions that involved the fate of armies, his own fame, or the life of the republic; . . . enunciating opinions or declaring plans of the most important character, in the plainest words and commonest manner, as if great things and small were to him of equal moment; as if it cost him no more to command armies than to direct a farm, to capture cities than to drive a horse."

Even on occasions of great excitement Grant's manner was quiet, and had little of the magnetism that inspires the soldier,—a fact which he appreciated and regretted. His men did not bestow upon him the pet nicknames conferred upon other commanders, such as "Uncle Billy" (Sherman), "Pop Thomas," "Little Mac" (McClellan), and "Little Phil" (Sheridan).

The report of General Grant's success at Chattanooga reached Washington on the day that the Thirty-eighth Congress began its second session. Mr. Washburne, the representative from the Galena district of Illinois, at once introduced two bills,—one "to revive the grade of Lieutenant-General of the Army"; the other to provide that a medal be struck for General Grant, and that a vote of thanks be given to him and the officers of his Army. The act restoring the grade of Lieutenant-General was passed February 26, 1864, and signed by President Lincoln. This grade had been originally created for General Washington, and had been thus far held by no other officer of the Army. Scott's highest rank was that of Brevet Lieutenant-General. It was well understood that it had been revived for the purpose of honouring Grant, and on March 1, 1864, the President sent his name to the Senate. He was confirmed the next day; was ordered to Washington on the 3d; and on the 9th of March, 1864, received his commission from the hands of the President.

During the debate on the bill reviving the grade of Lieutenant-General, Mr. Washburne said:

"I am not here to speak for General Grant. No man with his consent has ever mentioned his name in connection with any position. I say what I know to be true when I allege that every promotion he has received since he first entered the Service to put down this rebellion was moved without his knowledge or consent; and in regard to this very matter of lieutenant-general, after the bill was introduced and his name mentioned in connection therewith, he wrote me and admonished me that he had been highly honored already by the Government, and did not ask or deserve anything more in the shape of honors or promotion; and that a success over the enemy was what he craved above everything else; that he only desired to hold such an influence over those under his command as to use them to the best advantage to secure that end."

Lieutenant-General Grant arrived at Washington on Tuesday, March 8th, accompanied by General Rawlins and Colonel Comstock of his staff, and by his son. His coming was so unostentatious that it was some time before his presence in the city was known. Then the modest soldier was subjected to what for him was the most trying of ordeals, that of public recognition. Cheers and serenades met him everywhere, and calls for the universal American speech. While he was taking his ease in his own inn, some enthusiastic member of Congress spoiled Grant's breakfast by calling attention to his presence, and compelling him to bear the ordeal of cheers and congratulations.

The commission of Lieutenant-General was presented at the White House in the presence of the entire Cabinet, the party accompanying General Grant, and a few others. The President thus addressed the General:

"GENERAL GRANT: The nation's appreciation of what you have done, and its reliance upon you for what remains to be done in the existing great struggle, are now presented with this commission constituting you Lieutenant-General in the Army of the United States. With this high honor devolves upon you also a corresponding responsibility. As the country herein trusts you, so, under God, it will sustain you. I scarcely need to add that with what I here speak for the nation goes my own hearty personal concurrence."

To which General Grant replied:

"MR. PRESIDENT: I accept the commission with gratitude for the high honor conferred. With the aid of the noble armies that have fought on so many fields for our common country, it will be my earnest endeavor not to disappoint your expectations. I feel the full weight of the responsibilities now devolving upon me, and I know that if they are met, it will be due to those armies; and above all to the favor of that Providence which leads both nations and men."

The Lieutenant-General was then introduced to the Cabinet, and some time was spent in conversation. The bill under which he was appointed provided for " a commander of the Army, to be selected during the war, from among those officers in the military service of the United States, not below the grade of major-general, most distinguished for courage, skill, and ability; and who being commissioned as lieutenant-general, shall be authorized, under the direction of the President, to command the armies of the United States." The control of military affairs now dropped finally from Lincoln's wearied hands into the strong hands of the Lieutenant-General, and he was left to form his plans without suggestion from the President or from his Secretary.

Grant had met President Lincoln for the first time at a reception at the White House on the evening of March 8th, where crowds had gathered in expectation of seeing the famous soldier. Lincoln's biographers tell us, that, after some conversation with Mr. Lincoln and Mr. Seward, Grant went " to the East Room, where his presence excited a feeling which burst the bonds of etiquette, and cheer after cheer rose from the assembled crowd. Hot and blushing with embarrassment, he was forced to mount a sofa, from which he could shake hands with the eager admirers who rushed upon him from all sides of the great room." In response to the President's announcement that he should deliver the commission the next day, " the General had hurriedly and almost illegibly written his speech on a half-sheet of note-paper in pencil. His embarrassment was evident in extreme," equal to that in which Washington delivered his inaugural address.

As soon as Grant learned that he was to be made Lieutenant-General, he wrote a private letter to Sherman from Nashville, Tennessee, March 4, 1864, saying:

DEAR SHERMAN : The bill reviving the grade of lieutenant-general in the army has become a law, and my name has been sent to the Senate for the place.

I now receive orders to report at Washington immediately, in person, which indicates either a confirmation or a likelihood of confirmation. I start in the morning to comply with the order, but I shall say very distinctly on my arrival there that I shall accept no appointment which will require me to make that city my headquarters. This, however, is not what I started out to write about.

While I have been eminently successful in this war, in at least getting the confidence of the public, no one feels more than I how much of this success is due to the energy and skill of those whom it has been my good fortune to have occupying subordinate positions under me.

There are many officers to whom these remarks are applicable to a greater or less degree, proportionate to their ability as soldiers ; but what I want is to express my thanks to you and McPherson, as the men to whom, above all others, I feel indebted for whatever I have had of success. How far your advice and suggestions have been of assistance, you know. How far your execution of whatever has been given you to do entitles you to the reward I am receiving, you cannot know as well as I do. I feel all the gratitude this letter would express ; giving it the most flattering construction.

The word *you* I use in the plural, intending it for McPherson also.

I should write to him, and will some day, but, starting in the morning, I do not know that I will find time just now. Your friend,

U. S. GRANT, Major-General.

Sherman, in a reply dated Memphis, March 10, 1864, and marked " private and confidential," said:

"You do yourself injustice and us too much honor in assigning to us so large a share of the merits which have led to your high advancement. I know you approve the friendship I have ever professed to you, and will permit me to continue as heretofore to manifest it on all proper occasions.

"You are now Washington's legitimate successor, and occupy a position of almost dangerous elevation ; but if you continue as heretofore to be yourself, simple, honest, and unpretending, you will enjoy through life the respect and love of friends, and the homage of millions of human beings who will award to you a large share for securing to them and their descendants a government of law and stability.

"I repeat, you do General McPherson and myself too much honor. At Belmont you manifested your traits, neither of us being near ; at Donelson also you illustrated your whole character. I was not near, and General McPherson in too subordinate a capacity to influence you. Until you had won Donelson, I confess I was almost cowed by the terrible array of anarchical elements that presented themselves at every point ; but that victory admitted the ray of light which I have followed ever since.

"I believe you are as brave, patriotic, and just as the great prototype Washington ; as unselfish, kind-hearted, and honest, as a man should be ; but the chief characteristic in your nature is the simple faith in success you have always manifested, which I can liken to nothing else than the faith a Christian has in his Saviour. The faith gave you victory at Shiloh and Vicksburg. Also, when you have completed your best preparations, you go into battle without hesitation, as at Chattanooga—no doubts, no reserves ; and I tell you that it was this that made us act with confidence. I knew wherever I was that you thought of me, and if I got in a tight place you would come—if alive. My only points of doubt were as to your knowledge of grand strategy, and of books of science and history ; but I confess your common-sense seems to have supplied all this."

Badeau, who was present, reports that when Sherman met Grant again, at Nashville, on March 17th, that officer said in his usual abrupt manner: "I cannot congratulate you on your promotion; the responsibility is too great." The other was silent and smoked his cigar. Sherman was urgent that Grant should remain at the West, saying:

"Here you are at home; you are acquainted with your ground; you have tested your subordinates; you know us, and we know you; here you are sure of success ; here, too, you will be untrammeled , at the East you must begin new campaigns in an unfamiliar field, with troops and officers whom you have not tried, whom you have never led to victory. They cannot feel towards you as we do. Near Washington, besides, you will be beset, and, it may be, fettered by scheming politicians ; stay here, where you have made your fame, and use the same means to consolidate it."

The generous disinterestedness of this advice is shown by the fact that Grant's withdrawal to Washington would put Sherman in control at the West.

The development of Grant into the dimensions of a great commander had been progressive, and there were no steps backward. Through victory and defeat alike he advanced in knowledge, in self-confidence, and in the mastery of the conditions of war. His early experience as a soldier had taught him useful lessons; but it had given him no undue confidence, nor was he hampered by the worship of precedents and the exaggerated respect for mere theories of war that paralysed others who had won the confidence of the country and of the authorities while he was still an obscure volunteer. His experience in the Army as a quartermaster had taught him the importance of looking after the means of transportation and supply for troops: and that memorable ride at Monterey had burnt into his memory, as no mere routine experience could have done, a knowledge of the necessity for keeping fighting men constantly supplied with ammunition. If he did not rank so high as some others as a student of the art of war as written, Grant was a close student of events. In his first movement against the enemy, as an officer of volunteers, he felt great concern; but the discovery that the Confederate commander, more frightened than he was, had left the field before he arrived, taught him a lesson he never forgot.

"From that event to the close of the war," he tells us, "I never experienced trepidation upon confronting an enemy. I never forgot that he had as much reason to fear my forces as I had his. The lesson was valuable."

Yet Grant was by no means ignorant of the historical records of war. Indeed, "in addition to his great common sense, he knew the lessons of war as completely as any general that ever lived." John Russell Young, who says this, illustrates it by a conversation he had with him during his voyage around the world.

"Walking up and down the deck, Grant went on to describe all of Napoleon's campaigns, from Marengo down to Leipsic, speaking of each battle in the most minute manner—the number of men engaged on either side, even the range of their guns and the tactics of both sides; why victory came and why defeat came—as thoroughly learned as a problem in mathematics. Then back to the battles of Frederick the Great ; Leuthen ; the campaigns of the Thirty Years' War ; back to the campaigns of Cæsar, and always illustrating as he talked the progress and change in the art of war, and how machinery, projectiles, and improvements in arms had made what would be a great victory for Napoleon almost impossible now. It simply meant this, that General Grant, with his marvellous memory, had not forgotten his West Point education. It is the only occasion on which I ever heard Grant speak of the art of war, because it was a subject to which he had an aversion. You might have known him for a year and never learned that he had fought a battle in his life."

Not only did General Grant remember his West Point education, but he had read much; and during the course of his garrison life in the Army, when he read everything that came to hand, even such abstruse works as those of Emanuel Swedenborg, he no doubt found opportunity to extend his knowledge of military literature beyond the recollections of his studies at the Military Academy.

At Paducah and Belmont, at Henry and Donelson, he had learned how great is the moral power of the initiative. Shiloh had convinced him, as well as it had convinced the enemy, that neither section could claim advantage in the superior pluck and prowess of the individual soldier; it had further taught the useful lesson of the value of field fortifications. At Holly Springs, where he was deprived of all communication with the North for more than a week, he had discovered how possible it was to disregard the usual means of communication, and feed upon the enemy's country.

Favouritism and prejudice are powerful factors with military men in determining professional reputations. It is difficult for a graduate of the Military

Academy to outlive the judgment passed upon him by his fellow-students there, however undiscriminating it may have been. It is still more difficult to overcome the harsh garrison determinations as to character and capacity, due oftentimes to incidents that are wholly inconclusive as to a soldier's actual quality. It was Grant's misfortune—or shall we not rather say, in the light of the result, that it was his extreme good fortune—to have incurred the distrust of officers of the old Army under whom it was his lot to serve when he re-entered the Army, and especially the hostility of Halleck. If this subjected him to sore humiliation and mortification, it also impressed upon him those lessons of patience, subordination, and self-abnegation, to which he was by nature most responsive. His trying experiences as an officer served as a check upon a too rapid advance, which might have subjected him to those perils of undue exaltation which wrecked so many promising military reputations.

Thus step by step, with steady progress, Grant advanced to the full height of his career, as the country gradually awakened to the realisation of the fact that they had in this modest soldier from Illinois a man who could be depended upon to do his duty to the fullest extremity, undisturbed by good or evil fortune, accepting both alike as the will of that Higher Power who sits in judgment on the purposes of men, and chooses His own instruments in His own time, without regard to the decisions of cabinets and councils.

The fortune of war had sifted from among the

officers high in rank those whose ability, experience, and disinterested devotion to duty, justified the fullest measure of confidence; and chief among these Congress and the President had rightly placed Ulysses Simpson Grant. While others were calling upon Hercules, Grant from the first put his shoulder squarely to the wheel. While other men demanded more of the troops and supplies needed by every army beyond the possibility of the Government to furnish, he was doing the best he could with what he had, and insisting that he could, if left to himself, do still more. He never made his failure to obtain all that he wanted, or what he needed, an excuse for inaction or delay; nor did he seek to throw upon the sorely harassed and perplexed civil authorities at Washington the responsibility for his own shortcomings. His correspondence with the Government will be searched in vain for the evidence that appears in the despatches of some general officers, of a desire to burden the records with proofs that others were responsible for their failures or partial successes.

Nicolay and Hay, who knew the mind of Lincoln, say:

"Grant's usefulness and superiority were evinced by the clearness and brevity of his correspondence, the correctness of routine reports and promptness of their transmission, the pertinence and practical quality of his suggestions, the readiness and fertility of expedient with which he executed orders. Any one reading over his letters of this first period of his military service is struck by the fact that through him something was always accomplished. There was absence of excuse, complaint, or delay; always the report of a task performed. If his means or supplies were imperfect, he found or improvised the best available substitute. If he could not execute the full requirement, he performed so much of it as was possible. He always had an opinion, and that opinion was positive, intelligible, practical. We find therefore that his allotted tasks from the first continually rose in importance. He gained in authority and usefulness not by solicitation or intrigue but by services rendered."

After the battle of Shiloh, President Lincoln was warned by devoted friends that his own fortunes depended upon his rejection of Grant. His only answer was:

" I can't spare this man; he fights."

" Generals," said Napoleon, " are rarely found eager to give battle; they choose their positions, consider their combinations, and their indecision begins. Nothing is so difficult as to decide."

To the question as to Grant's generalship, " Is he going to be the man ?" the President replied with great emphasis of tone and gesture:

" Grant is the first General I have had. You know how it has been with all the rest. As soon as I put a man in command of the Army, he 'd come to me with a plan of campaign and about as much as to say, ' Now, I don't believe I can do it, but if you say so, I 'll try it on,' and so put the responsibility of success or failure on me. They all wanted me to be the General. Now, it isn't so with Grant. He has n't told me what his plans are. I don't know and I don't want to know. I am glad to find a man that can go ahead without me. When any of the rest set out on a campaign, they would look over matters and pick out some one thing they were short of and they knew I could n't give 'em and tell me they could n't hope to win unless they had it ; and it was most generally cavalry. Now, when Grant took hold, I was waiting to see what his pet impossibility would be, and I reckoned it would be cavalry, of course, for we had n't horses enough to mount what men we had. There were fifteen thousand or thereabouts up near Harper's Ferry and no horses to put them on. Well, the other day, Grant sends to me about those very men just as I expected; but what he wanted to know was, whether he could make infantry of them or disband 'em. He does n't ask impossibilities of me and he 's the first general I have had that did n't."

To this testimony, reported by Murat Halstead, Frank B. Carpenter, the artist, adds, that Mr. Lincoln once said to him of Grant, " The great thing about him is his cool persistency of purpose. He is not easily excited, and has the grip of a bull-dog. When he once gets his teeth in, nothing will shake him off."

The adverse criticisms upon General Grant as a soldier by his contemporaries were largely the offspring of ignorance, jealousy, or malice,—ignorance of war itself, or of the conditions under which war must be waged in a country of vast distances and impassable roads; jealousy prompted by the ill success of those who were considered by themselves and by their friends more worthy than he; malice resulting from the inevitable antagonisms of military life, and due to its necessarily arbitrary action, its prompt and oftentimes harsh judgments.

Grant triumphed in spite of " the cliques and the underground intrigues of craving selfishness and unsatisfied ambitions," of the disturbing questions of seniority between officers of high rank, and of the disposition of the newspaper press not only to embarrass him with criticism, but also to deprive him of the advantages of the secrecy which is so essential to the success of military plans; in short, as a soldier, he met all the conditions of his time, and rose superior to them. It was not " luck," it was energy, zeal, and singleness of purpose, directed by exceptional military capacity, that explain his success.

What are the " rules of war " that General Grant violated ? They originate in the brains of civilian critics like Macaulay; for the best military authorities are agreed that it is impossible to formulate a code which can be so distinguished. The best generals are those who know when to disregard all rules. (" *La critique est facile, l'art est difficile* ".) The study of great campaigns may train the intelligence of the soldier, but it cannot guide his action on the field of battle into set forms. Cæsar's biographer tells us that he was " no deep calculator; his habit was to act for the immediate exigency."

General Grant not only conquered his enemy in the field, but he succeeded in so conquering the Administration at Washington as to make it the obedient servant of his will; if not wholly, at least to a greater extent than any commander who preceded him. He won its confidence because he showed the highest qualities of a general in his quick perception of the conditions of the military problem; not as it existed in Europe, not as it was in the time of Cæsar, or Hannibal, or Napoleon, but as it was right before him, on the Mississippi and the James, in Missouri, in Kentucky, in Tennessee and Virginia. He occupied himself less than others with the question as to how armies should be organised according to accepted maxims, but better than others he understood from the outset the art of making the most effective use of the material the American volunteer soldier offers to the commander.

Students of war criticised him, and doubtless will always criticise him; but they should not forget that if his method did not conform in every respect to their standards, it was always directed by a clearly defined purpose in his own mind as to the best way to accomplish the immediate object. In the face of storms of criticism he adhered to his purpose with a tenacity characteristic of the man, until results had vindicated the soundness of his judgment.

Rejecting at the beginning of his career the theories that hampered others, and that were only adapted to encounters between armies thoroughly organised and trained, Grant understood the importance of action, and continued action, to transform raw troops into veterans. Less fortunate than his critics, he was not able to review his plans in the light of accomplished facts; and in "the fog of war" were hidden from him circumstances that might have modified his action, or induced a change of programme. If he made mistakes, he showed how successive defeats, miscarriages, and disasters might be made the stepping-stones to final victory. The siege of Vicksburg, which brought clearly to view his characteristic tenacity, will challenge the admiration of men as a military feat, with Ciudad Rodriguez and Badajos, so long as history is read. It was clearly Grant's own work; and his complete success at Grand Gulf, when for the first time he was able to carry his methods to their final conclusion without interference from higher authority, throws a flood of light upon his previous career.

Grand Gulf was a brilliant military conception,—one of those audacities of genius, which, like Macdonald's crossing the Splugen, transcends all rules of military art.

The appointment of Grant to the office of General-in-Chief was designed to give to our armies the unity of direction essential to success, and heretofore lacking. The official reports of that period show how lamentably incoherent had been the exercise of the central military power. Operations were now under the control of the President and then of General Halleck; at one time directed by the Secretary of War, and at another time by the General in the field. It was intended to put an end to this confusion by the selection of an officer to whom should be intrusted the supreme control, and who should really " *command* the armies of the United States."

Grant's extensive experience in the field had given him a perfect appreciation of what a general-in-chief could do, and what he could not safely undertake. It had taught him how far the central authority should interfere in distant operations, and how much must necessarily be left to the commanders in the field. There was but little opposition to his new appointment, and even this opposition was due in large measure to a fear lest his duties as General-in-Chief might lessen his activity in the field.

The order of the Executive was designed to reconcile this double desire that Grant should have control of all the armies, and that he should be at the same time free for the immediate direction of troops so far as he considered this expedient. " The headquarters of the Army," it provided, " will be in Washington, and also with Lieutenant-General Grant in the field."

A man of Grant's martial spirit could not be confined to a bureau when great operations were on foot; again, as at Vicksburg, he resolved to disregard the advice of his most trusted friend, so far as related to his choice of a field of activity. Transferring to Sherman the immediate control of the principal army in the West, he decided to reserve for himself direction of the Army of the Potomac. That army, from its proximity to the Capital, was the one most subject to civilian interference, and it was best that he should meet this danger in person. In assuming command of the forces in Virginia, he possessed a supreme advantage over all who had preceded him there. To him had been granted a power hitherto unknown, except when sovereigns had been in the field as commanders. He was relieved from the necessity of applying to Washington for the control of the troops essential to his operations; he had full authority to call to his aid, from any part of the country, re-enforcements needed for success, where he in person should command. Moreover, his promotion to a rank one grade beyond that of all others served to elevate him above the jealousies, rivalries, and ambitions of those holding secondary commands, which had been the bane of the Army of the Potomac. To these may be traced the failure of more than one well-planned operation. It could not well be otherwise. Subordinate generals, holding the same rank as their chief, and hoping by adroit management to come into supreme command, were subject to the strongest temptations that assail the soldier. That they were not always proof against them the secret history of our armies would show.

CHAPTER XIV.

CROSSING THE RAPIDAN; BATTLE OF THE WILDERNESS.

MAY 4-7, 1864.

HE movements of the Army of the Potomac, and the Southern Army of Northern Virginia, during the two years preceding Grant's promotion to the rank of Lieutenant-General, had been a series of advances and retreats, without substantial gain to either side. McClellan had exhausted himself in the attempt to reach Richmond by way of the Yorktown Peninsula. Pope met his Waterloo at the battle of the Second Bull Run; Burnside, at Fredericksburg; and Hooker, at Chancellorsville. Lee, in his turn, had been overthrown at Antietam and Gettysburg, when he assumed the *rôle* of offence, and pushed his advance beyond the boundary of his own State. Neither side could claim any advantage. Altogether over a quarter of a million men had been killed, wounded, or yielded themselves prisoners, in the gigantic contest for supremacy in Virginia, this loss being nearly

equally divided between the contending forces. The movement of battle had swayed back and forth between the capital of Virginia and the capital of Pennsylvania; the high-water mark on the one side being Fair Oaks, and on the other Gettysburg. Meade alone, of all those who had commanded on either side, had no serious reverse to mar his record, and to his credit stood the decisive battle of Gettysburg, where the Confederates had suffered a larger loss than during any other single engagement of the war. He had given proof of his capacity for high command, and, if he had not succeeded in satisfying Northern craving for the possession of the Confederate Capital, he had shown that he was at all times a safe and reliable soldier.

If, then, there was any man who might reasonably object to the programme decided upon by General Grant when he resolved to assume the immediate direction of affairs in Virginia, it was Major-General George Gordon Meade, who during the preceding ten months had commanded the Army of the Potomac. But if Meade was a soldier, with a soldier's ambitions and a soldier's hopes, he was before all else a patriot who subordinated personal interest to his desire for the success of a great cause.

A part of the Lieutenant-General's preliminary work was to so re-adjust the various commands at the East and the West as to relieve as much as possible the friction between subordinate commanders originating in the previous experiences of ill success. There was in the Army of the Potomac a McClellan party and a Hooker party, if not a Burnside party, each representing the interests of officers who had preceded Meade in command. Rivalries of a corresponding nature disturbed the armies of the West. Numerous changes were required to establish the harmonious conditions essential to efficient action. This officer must be sent here, and another there, that old associations might be broken up, imbittered rivalries forgotten, and the stimulus of new ambitions presented to aspiring generals. Organisations of cavalry, artillery, and infantry must exchange stations between the East and the West for the same purpose. This difficult and delicate task was completed so quickly and quietly that few understood the work in progress. An effort was made to restore to active command officers like McClellan and Buell, whose abilities were recognised; but they were not disposed to serve without conditions, as others must do. Meade showed a different spirit. Says General Grant, in his *Memoirs*:

"He evidently thought that I might want to make still one more change not yet ordered. He said to me that I might want an officer who had served with me in the West, mentioning Sherman especially, to take his place. If so he begged me not to hesitate about making the change. He urged that the work before us was of such vast importance to the whole Nation that the feelings or wishes of no one person should stand in the way of selecting the right men for all positions. For himself he would serve to the best of his ability wherever placed. I assured him that I had no thought of substituting any one for him. As to Sherman he could not be spared from the West. This incident gave me even a more favorable opinion of Meade than did his great victory at Gettysburg the July before. It is men who wait to be selected and not those who seek, from whom we may always expect the most efficient service."

Sherman assumed command of the Military Division of the Mississippi, March 18, 1864, having control of all the troops west of the Alleghanies and north of Natchez, Mississippi. The force available for action under his immediate orders numbered about 100,000 men, and the Army of the Potomac about the same. West of the Mississippi River was Major-General N. P. Banks, who had had control of some 30,000 men during the short time he was in command before being relieved by General Canby. On the James River, in the vicinity of Richmond, was the Army of the James, commanded by Major-General Benjamin F. Butler, and acting in co-operation with the Army of the Potomac. In the Shenandoah Valley of Virginia was a force under Major-General Sigel, guarding the approaches to Washington from that direction. In addition to these large commands, there were numerous detachments holding positions along the southern coast, captured from the enemy at different times. The outlying garrisons were reduced to the minimum, so as to secure all available men for the movement against the enemy by the armies under Meade and Sherman.

Banks was expected to close up the ill-fated Red River campaign south-west of the Mississippi, which then occupied his attention, and with 25,000 men of his command, and 10,000 more to be sent by Sherman, to attempt to capture Mobile, Alabama, in co-operation with the Navy. Sherman was to advance upon Atlanta, and then to secure control of the country between that place and Mobile. The

Confederacy had been divided by the loss of the Mississippi River. The success of these joint operations was expected to bisect the country still under Confederate control east of that river. Butler, who had 23,000 men available for the field, was ordered to operate against Richmond from the south side of the James River.

General Joseph E. Johnston was in command of the Confederate troops opposed to Sherman; and Robert E. Lee commanded the Army of Northern Virginia, whose veteran soldiers barred the progress of the Army of the Potomac in its southward march. The main attacks were to be directed against the armies of Lee and Johnston; and the commanders of minor forces were expected to prevent the reenforcement of these armies by constant activity, so as to hold fast the enemy in front of them, if they could do no more. Speaking generally, the troops which the Confederacy had available for defence at the various points of attack, were about two thirds as numerous as those of their enemy; but this difference was neutralised, and more than neutralised, by the advantage that goes with the defence. The Confederacy stood on guard to meet the mighty assault behind its barriers of impassable roads, fordless streams, tangled woods, and abrupt hills, thrown out like buttresses to break the force of the attack.

The natural advantages of the defence were thus increased by the peculiar character and the wide extent of the terrain over which the tide of battle had swept back and forth during the three years of war. The great mountain system, which runs like a wedge into the heart of the Confederacy, has been aptly styled " the citadel of a large fortress of which the walls are formed by the parallel ridges, the ditches by the rapid streams in the valleys, and the doors by the gaps." Chattanooga is a natural bastion on the salient angle of the great line of the Confederate communications. The control of this position gave Sherman an advantage in the central zone which the Army of the Potomac did not possess.

Never in the history of warfare has the character of the country exerted more influence on campaigns than in the portion of Virginia between Washington and Richmond, which was the scene of the mighty struggles for mastery between the armies of the Union and of the Confederacy. On the right of the Army of the Potomac, under Grant's immediate direction, were chains of mountains admirably adapted for concealing flanking movements; while the valley of the numerous rivers carrying the waters from the heights south-easterly into Chesapeake Bay, afforded the Confederate forces the means for easy and uninterrupted passage above Washington, and almost entirely protected them from attacks in their rear. On the front of Lee's army were a succession of rivers presenting great natural obstacles to Grant's advance, and affording strong positions for defence. To ascend these rivers, for the purpose of turning the left flank of the enemy, was to open his rear to attacks from Fredericksburg; to cross below Lee's army was to leave the railroad connecting his rear with Washington open to cavalry attacks. The country, moreover, was masked in every direction by dense forests, rendering anything like a surprise in force impracticable. A few rebel scouts might at all times easily detect and thwart such a movement.

The Potomac River was under Union control, as was also the peninsula lying between the York and James Rivers, from Fort Monroe nearly up to Richmond. This enabled the Army of the Potomac, in moving against the Confederate capital, to concentrate its forces behind the screen of the Potomac, and advance either from the upper Potomac down the Shenandoah Valley; from Washington along the Orange Railroad to the Rappahannock River; from Acquia Creek on the Potomac, by the Fredericksburg and Richmond Railroad; up the Peninsula, between the York and James Rivers, adopting either stream as its base; or from the south side of the James River by way of Petersburg, Virginia. All but one of these lines had been used for advance movements previous to the time when Grant took command, and the choice between them was open to him. But his objective was not Richmond, but Lee's army; and his selection of a line of operations was determined, not by a desire to draw near to the Confederate capital, but to force the Confederate Army to meet him in the open field, and to there try the issue of battle.

To Sherman Grant had written: "You I propose to move against Johnston's army, to break it up, and to get into the interior of the enemy's country as far as you can, inflicting all the damage you can against their war resources." In his letter of instruction to Meade, he said:

> "Lee's Army will be your objective point; wherever Lee goes there you will go also. The only point upon which I am now in doubt, is whether it will be better to cross the Rapidan above or below him. Each plan presents great advantages over the other with corresponding objections; by crossing above, Lee is cut off from all chance of ignoring Richmond and going North on a raid. But if we take this route, all we do must be done whilst the rations we start with hold out. We separate from Butler so that he cannot be directed how to co-operate. By the other route Brandy Station can be used as a base of supplies until another is secured on the York or James River."

The final conclusion was that the movement should be by the left, against Lee's right flank. At this time (April, 1864) the Army of the Potomac was in its intrenchments between the Rapidan River and the Upper Rappahannock, in the fork formed by the junction of those two streams at a point ten or twelve miles above the city of Fredericksburg. The main body of Meade's infantry was half-way between the Union and Confederate capitals, in the vicinity of Culpeper Court-House, on the Orange and Alexandria Railroad, which connects Washington with Lynchburg, Virginia. The cavalry of the Army of the Potomac, observing Meade's front, was promptly re-organised by Grant, and placed under the efficient command of Sheridan, who had graduated from Grant's old regiment, the 4th United States Infantry.

Lee's army was intrenched on the opposite or southern side of the Rapidan, and occupied a front of eighteen to twenty miles, from Morton's Ford on the east, to Barnett's Ford on the west. Both armies were narrowly watching the fords of the Rapidan for tokens of hostile movement. Lee's headquarters were at Orange Court-House, sixty-five miles in the direct line from Richmond, and Meade's at Brandy Station, the same distance from Washington; an interval of twenty-five miles separating the two headquarters. On March 26th, General Grant had established his headquarters at Culpeper Court-House, eight miles nearer to Lee than those of General Meade.

On March 4, 1864, shortly before Grant took command, the five corps of the Army of the Potomac had been consolidated into three corps upon the recommendation of Meade. This was a measure of doubtful expediency. It destroyed corps traditions, wounded professional pride, and gave to the several corps commanders a force too large to be handled most efficiently in a broken country like Virginia. The total force of the three corps was 73,390 officers and men. To these were added the corps of Burnside, brought up from Annapolis to guard Meade's communication, and joining the Army of the Potomac May 6th, when Meade's advance relieved him from the duty of guarding the rear.

In spite of General Grant's intention to make Meade's position as nearly independent as possible, the division of responsibility between them was an embarrassment to both; and to some extent it diminished the efficiency of the troops over which they held what was, in effect, a joint command.

Routine and courtesy required that orders for the movement of the Army of the Potomac should go through Meade, and that he should be left to execute them; but orders sometimes passed direct from the Lieutenant-General to his troops, and his immediate presence could not fail to affect Meade's independence of action. There could be no finer body of troops in material, discipline, and military spirit, than those found in the Army of the Potomac, as at first organised; but the quality of the men composing it deteriorated somewhat when bounties took the place of patriotic zeal in stimulating enlistments.

Battle and disease had reduced many of the best regiments to battalions, and the companies to squads. In the new regiments the discipline of the hired soldier had superseded the zeal of the volunteer, and there was less of that cordiality of feeling between officer and men which constitutes the strength or the weakness of volunteers, according to the character of the officer. The bonds of discipline were strengthened when Grant came. When the note of preparation for battle was heard, " the enlisted men hurriedly discussed the military capacity of their new leader. Magazines, illustrated papers, and newspapers, which contained accounts of his military achievements, were sent for, and were eagerly and attentively read. The discussions were fruitless but combat-provoking, and frequently the wranglers adjourned to a secluded spot outside of the camp and fought it out with their fists."

Later on, when they had served under Grant for a few weeks, the general opinion among the enlisted men was: " Given Grant in command of the army of 1862, and the Rebellion would have been crushed that year." Asked how McClellan would have done with the army of 1864 under his command, they shrugged their shoulders, and said dryly, " Well, he would have ended the war in the Wilderness by establishing the Confederacy."

The determination of General Grant to make a direct march against Richmond, instead of repeating McClellan's movement of two years before by planting his men in front of its walls by way of the Yorktown Peninsula, as his critics would have had him do, was in accord with what the far-sighted Lincoln had from the first advised. In a letter of April 9, 1862, in answer to one of General McClellan's chronic complaints that he was not properly sustained, President Lincoln said:

"You will do me the justice to remember I always insisted that going down the Bay in search of a field, instead of fighting at or near Manassas, was only shifting and not surmounting a difficulty; that we should find the same enemy and the same or equal intrenchments at either place. The country will not fail to note, is now noting, that the present hesitation to move upon an intrenched enemy is but the story of Manassas repeated."

The Commander-in-Chief had at last found a soldier who was in full accord with his own conceptions of war, and his whole heart went out to him as it had to no other. Stanton complained in his impatient way because the Lieutenant-General had taken from the defences of Washington artillerymen that the Secretary thought were needed there, and he demanded an explanation.

"I think I rank you in this matter, Mr. Secretary," was the quiet answer.

"We shall have to see Mr. Lincoln about that," the Secretary replied.

"All right," said the Lieutenant-General. "Mr. Lincoln ranks us both."

They went to the White House. "Won't you state your case, General Grant?" said Stanton. Grant replied: "I have no case to state; I am satisfied as it is." Mr. Stanton stated his case. Then Lincoln answered:

"You and I, Mr. Stanton, have been trying to boss this job, and we have not succeeded very well with it. We have sent across the mountains for *Mr.* Grant, as Mrs. Grant calls him, to relieve us, and I think we had better leave him alone to do as he pleases."*

Left to himself, Grant had resolved to concentrate all his forces for a movement against Lee, and he meant to keep the Army of Virginia so busy that it would have no leisure nor opportunity for those side movements against the Capital which had so often disturbed well-laid plans for Confederate discomfiture. To reach Lee, and turn his right flank, which was the movement intended, it was necessary to cross the Rapidan. Such a movement, in the face of a resolute enemy, involved one of the most difficult operations of war; but Lee had decided to interpose no obstacle to the passage of the river, believing that in the impracticable country lying

---

* This story was told to the writer by Grant's chief of staff.

south of it he would have his enemy at a disadvantage more than sufficient to neutralise his superiority in numbers.

This region is what is known as the Wilderness, or the " Wild Place." It is an elevated pebbly plateau of about forty square miles, poor in soil, but rich in metallic ores, and the scene of mining operations dating from the earliest settlement. It is gullied by numerous small streams, and is covered with a second growth of timber following the destruction of the original forests by the miners. Besides two main highways, it is traversed by numerous paths winding in a perfect labyrinth through its almost impassable thickets of dwarfed oaks, scrubby pines, hazel and juniper trees, all tangled together by thorny plants and interlacing vines. It is a troublesome country for a stranger to pass through under any conditions, and it presents insurmountable obstacles to the rapid and connected movements of a great army.

The Wilderness was a name of horror to the Union soldiers. Its deep ravines, hidden by brush and trees, were full of mystery for them; while many of the Confederates, who had worked in the mines, knew the roads, could locate the streams and watercourses, were familiar with the natural lines of defence; and they were aided by the inhabitants, who were active spies on the movements of the invaders. It was the scene of the battle of Chancellorsville, fought one year before, on May 1 to 4, 1863. Officers of the Army of the Potomac who participated in that battle had obtained some acquaintance with it by bitter experience. Here it was impossible to use cavalry, and all but impossible to use artillery; and the contests between infantrymen recalled the experiences of Indian warfare, where each tree and tangled thicket hid an enemy, who could only be located by the flash of his deadly rifle. Directions were given by the points of the compass, and the troops were left to make their own battle, it being impossible for officers to see ten files away.

Promptly at midnight on May 3, 1864, Grant set his Army in motion to cross the Rapidan over five bridges, laid by the cavalry, and spanning its width of two hundred feet. Two bridges were laid at Germanna Ford on the right, two at Ely's Ford on the left, and one at Culpeper Mine Ford in the centre. The distance between the right and left fords was nearly six miles as the crow flies, eight miles following the windings of the river. The centre ford was devoted to the trains; the troops moving by the other fords, and concentrating south of the Rapidan on the two main roads through the Wilderness.

The movement of the troops, after crossing the river, was directed upon Chancellorsville and Wilderness Tavern; cavalry leading the march, and reconnoitring the Orange Pike and Plank Roads, the Catharpin Road and the Pamunkey Road, over which an enemy might approach. In a single day the Union Army crossed the river and advanced twenty miles beyond it. It was theoretically possible to advance ten miles farther in twenty-four hours, and thus escape an encounter with the enemy in this slough of despond. Burnside, who was ordered up from the rear, did make such a march with raw troops. A similar march by the main body, commenced at midnight, would have cleared the Wilderness before the enemy could have forced a general engagement; but the enormous *impedimenta* of an army of 100,000 men is as effectual a check upon celerity of movement as the brakes upon a railroad-train. Four thousand waggons, conveying supplies and ammunition, must be moved under the protection of the cavalry; and it was necessary that this movement, and that of the reserve artillery, should coincide with the march of the columns of infantry. Cavalry was delayed by infantry, and infantry by cavalry, and there were disputes as to which was at fault.

Concerning his initial movement, General Grant says: " This I regarded as a great success, and it removed from my mind the most serious apprehension I had entertained, that of crossing the river in the face of an active, large, well-appointed, and ably commanded army, and how so large a train was to be carried through an enemy's country and protected."

It was legitimate cause for congratulation, but Grant's trouble had not yet begun. He had no intention of giving battle to Lee's veterans in the Wilderness, hoping by a rapid movement to get beyond it, and interpose between the Confederates and their capital, so as to compel an encounter in a more open country. The passage of the river was substantially completed by the night of May 4,

1864, and the troops placed in position; but the rear trains were not clear of the Rapidan until the night of May 5th.

General Lee, from his signal-tower station on Clark's Mountain, had observed indications of Grant's movement as early as May 2d, and further observations on May 4th determined his plan of action. This was an attack in force on Grant's moving columns before he could clear himself of the Wilderness. The Union signal officers had interpreted Lee's signal, and Grant was prepared. Burnside was hurrying to join the Army by forced marches, and Lee was waiting for Longstreet's Corps before inviting a general engagement. Grant resolved to force the fight that he might anticipate the coming of Longstreet, but the difficulties of the ground greatly impeded his freedom of movement. His advance was over narrow roads, and these were closed in by thick woods and underbrush; formations in line of battle were slow and difficult; and the movement of some of his troops was greatly impeded by artillery occupying the road.

'The secret of success," says Marshal Saxe, " lies in the legs of the soldiers." The march of the Army of the Potomac, as a whole, had not been sufficiently rapid to secure the advantage hoped for. As many had done before him, and as the Prussian Guards did later on at St. Privat, Grant experienced the difficulty of handling in action, by orders given from headquarters, large bodies of troops which he could not see.

Skirmishing between the hostile armies began on

the morning of May 5th, and shortly before noon the issue was joined in what is known as the Battle of the Wilderness. The struggle continued with varying fortunes until night dropped its veil of darkness and silence over the scene of slaughter. Orders were given to renew the fight at five o'clock the next morning; but Longstreet arrived during the night, and a few minutes before the hour named he opened an attack against Grant's left, where Hancock "the superb" held the line with the Second Corps. Burnside, with his Ninth Corps, had arrived as well as Longstreet; and when it was found that the left, after a temporary success, was being too hard pressed, his Ninth Corps was ordered to relieve the strain upon Hancock by an immediate attack. This attack was delayed by the difficulty of penetrating the forest; and through some misunderstanding of orders, or a failure in their receipt, one division of Hancock's Second Corps was kept out of the fight. As a result his assaults, which, as General Lee wrote, were "heavy and desperate," met with a repulse; and Hancock's troops, after fighting fiercely from five o'clock in the morning, were compelled to withdraw behind the breastworks from which they had advanced to the attack early in the day.

The Confederates were prevented from taking full advantage of the temporary success by the wounding of Longstreet so severely that he was obliged to yield his command. "In this engagement," as the biographer of General Lee tells us, "the attack of General Meade was conducted with such vigor by Hancock, Warren, and Burnside, that under ordinary circumstances, with his superiority of force, it would have been successful; but here the difficulties of the country prevented his making systematic combinations, and failure was the consequence."

"Back in ceaseless flow from the line that marks this fierce struggle the wounded and maimed are borne on blankets, litters, telling by their numbers the deadly work going on in advance." Never was the mettle of troops more tried; never did they give better proof of quality. The battle recalls the stories of duels where the combatants are tied together and struggle to the death in a darkened room. The utmost that the much-enduring Army of the Potomac could accomplish was to force Lee to retire behind the intrenchments from which he had emerged to give battle. To the usual casualties was added the possibility of being burned alive; and this was the fate of two hundred wounded soldiers, the woods and the fallen timber taking fire from the flame of battle. The total killed and wounded of the Army of the Potomac and Burnside's Corps was 17,666, the missing numbering 2902. The enemy's loss in killed and wounded was about one third less. As little artillery was used, a large proportion of the wounds were slight, and many of the men speedily returned to duty. Grant's attacks were continuous, and were directed against intrenched troops with positions not defined. The counter attacks of the Confederates were against troops whose location was known, and who were not intrenched, with the exception of the action with Hancock in the second day's fight, where Lee lost more heavily than Grant. Elsewhere his losses were much less, though no exact estimate is possible. " The Wilderness," says Private Wilkeson, " was a privates' battle; the men fought as best they could, and fought staunchly; the generals could not see the ground, and if they were on the front line they could not have seen their troops. The possibilities of vision were limited to less than one hundred yards."

The Army of the Potomac, under the leaders preceding Grant, had never " fought to a finish." For what reasons it is not necessary to inquire here. Advances had been followed by retreats in dreary succession, and long periods of inaction divided between the trials of strength in the field. The manœuvres of strategy, designed to determine the theatre of war, and to place an army in the most favourable position in presence of the enemy, had been successful in a degree; but there had been no corresponding success in the department of tactics,— " the quick, orderly change of highly trained and flexible masses of men from one kind of formation to another, or their transference from point to point of a battle-field, for purposes which became suddenly possible in the changing course of action." How far Grant himself showed mastery in this department of war may be a question for argument, but he certainly had in high degree Marshal Blücher's quality of obstinacy; and no officer who preceded him in Virginia could say with equal effect, as Blücher said in 1815, " Criticisms and complaints upon the exhausted condition of the troops had rained upon me, but I have remained deaf to them all."

The Lieutenant-General had determined in his own mind that with the advance once begun there should be no steps backward, except in the face of such overwhelming disaster as he believed impossible. Assaults heretofore had nowhere been followed up as they should have been. Ten months of idleness, deliberately decided upon, had succeeded the staggering blows delivered at Vicksburg, Gettysburg, Lookout Mountain, and Knoxville. The reaction of success had shown itself as paralysing in its effect as the crushing force of defeat. McClellan's ultimate failure was ascribed by his Chief of Engineers, General Barnard, to the inaction of eight months, from August, 1861, to April, 1862.

Of the battle of the Wilderness, Wilkeson says, in his *Recollections of a Private Soldier in the Army of the Potomac:*

"Grant's military standing with the enlisted men this day hung on the direction we turned at the Chancellorsville House. If to the left, he was to be rated with Meade and Hooker and Burnside and Pope, the generals who preceded him. At the Chancellorsville House we turned to the right. Instantly all of us heard a sigh of relief. Our spirits rose. We marched free. The men began to sing. The enlisted men understood the flanking movement. That night we were happy."

General Horace Porter, in an article in the *Century Magazine*, reports, that as he rode with Grant by the troops that night, with horses' heads turned toward Richmond:

"Soldiers weary and sleepy after their long battle, with stiffened limbs and smarting wounds, sprang to their feet, forgetful of their pains, and rushed forward to the roadside. Wild cheers echoed through the forest, and glad shouts of triumph rent the air. Men swung their hats, tossed up their arms, and pressed forward to within touch of their chief, clapping their hands, and speaking to him with the familiarity of comrades. Pine knots and leaves were set on fire, and lighted the scene with their weird, flickering glare. The night march had become a triumphal procession for the new commander. The demonstration was the emphatic verdict pronounced by the troops upon his first battle in the East."

On that same night General Lee said to General James B. Gordon, "The report comes from all along our front that Grant is preparing to retreat." Then Lee sat in silence for a time, as if engaged in profound thought. "What do you think, General," said Gordon, "will Grant retreat?" "No, sir!" said General Lee, "Grant can't retreat, he won't retreat. There is but one thing for him to do as a good general (and, General Gordon, I rank him among the best); he will renew the fight in the morning at Spottsylvania Court-House, and you must move into position at once."

CHAPTER XV.

FROM THE RAPIDAN TO THE JAMES—CLOSING IN ON RICHMOND—THE SHENANDOAH VALLEY.

MAY 4, 1864–MARCH, 1865.

RANT'S movement across the Rapidan against Lee was substantially the same as the one undertaken in the Wilderness by Hooker, in the Chancellorsville campaign of May, 1863, and by Meade in the Mine Run operations of November, 1863. Hooker was disastrously defeated, and Meade was forced to withdraw across the river without accomplishing anything. For the first time in its history, the Army of the Potomac had obtained a good hold upon Lee's army, and Grant intended that they should keep it. Undiscouraged by his partial failure thus far, he resolved to continue his attempt to turn Lee's right flank.

The next movement was directed against Spottsylvania Court-House, the capital of Spottsylvania County, situated between the Po and Ny Rivers, and sixty-five miles north of Richmond. The desire to force Lee again to battle without delay was prompted in part by a fear lest he might by a rapid movement return to Richmond and crush Butler, who had taken City Point by surprise on May 5th. Lee's army had withdrawn behind their intrenchments in the Wilderness on the night of May 6th; and the following day was occupied by both armies in burying their dead, removing their wounded, and repairing so far as they could the damage received in battle. The desperate fighting of May 5th and 6th was succeeded by a lull in the storm, disturbed only by cavalry skirmishing.

Grant's orders for the movement against Spottsylvania Court-House were dated 6.30 A.M., May 7, 1864. The trains were set in motion at 3 P.M. on the 7th to clear the way for the troops, who began a night march at half-past eight that evening. General Sheridan with his cavalry guarded the right flank of the marching army, so disposing his troopers as to give timely notice of any movement of the enemy.

The race between Grant and Lee for Spottsylvania Court-House was a close one. Stuart's cavalry had reported the movement of the waggon trains of the Union Army on the afternoon of the 7th; and Lee, partially divining Grant's intentions, ordered Longstreet's Corps, then commanded by Gen. R. H. Anderson, to Spottsylvania. Anderson was ordered to move the next morning, but, without delaying, he pushed on that night.

Having a route shorter by three miles on an unobstructed road, Anderson was able to occupy Spottsylvania Court-House before the arrival of

Grant's advance—the Fifth Corps—under Warren. Warren had pressed forward with the utmost despatch; but his march was delayed by the movements of the Union cavalry, who occupied the road he had to follow, and were engaged with the Confederate cavalry intrenched on their front. The march of the Fifth Corps over the narrow roads of the Wilderness was a fatiguing one. The men were in no condition for battle when they arrived at their destination, in the middle of the forenoon of April 8th, and they had no opportunity to rest there; for Lee had succeeded in planting his army across Grant's line of advance, and was prepared to give battle, holding a strong position on a range of hills about a mile to the north and north-west of Spottsylvania.

The operations of Sunday, May 8th, developed Lee's position, and resulted in some loss of life in encounters with the enemy. May 9th was devoted to rest by the Army of the Potomac, and to the re-adjustment of its lines and the strengthening of its position with intrenchments. The Confederate skirmishers and sharpshooters continued at their work, and deprived General Meade of one of his most trusted lieutenants, Major-General John Sedgwick, commanding the Sixth Corps; that excellent soldier, Major-Gen. H. G. Wright, succeeding Sedgwick in command.

Further work was also done on the ninth in determining the character and position of the enemy's works. The Confederates were similarly occupied, and by the close of day the fronts of both armies were covered by continuous lines of formidable breastworks. The buzzing crowd of skirmishers and sharpshooters prevented too close familiarity with Lee's lines, but subsequent experience and investigation showed that they were very strong,— strong enough, indeed, to practically quadruple a force defending them against an attack.

On May 9th, Hancock's Second Corps was sent across the River Po, one of the four branches of the Mattapony River, with a view to attacking the enemy's left; but the operations were undertaken too late in the afternoon, and Hancock was ordered to return. His withdrawal across the river under the fire of an enemy—always a difficult operation— was in this case most skilfully and successfully conducted. In front was an aggressive foe; and in the rear, between the retreating force and the river, was a burning forest, where some of Hancock's wounded perished in the flames.

Tuesday, May 10th, was occupied by the Army of the Potomac in a series of front attacks upon the enemy's line. These were made with the most sublime courage, and resulted in heavy loss; but it was found impossible to break through Lee's intrenchments, which were defended with equal courage. Partial successes were gained at some points in the line, but night found the two armies in the positions they had occupied in the morning. Changes were made in these positions on May 11th, but no encounter resulted. In a letter to Halleck, dated that day, 8.30 A.M., General Grant expressed his unalterable determination to continue the movement that he had begun, saying:

"I am now sending back to Belle Plaine all my waggons for a fresh supply of provisions and ammunition, and I propose to fight it out on this line if it takes all summer."

On the afternoon of May 11th, Grant arranged for another vigorous assault on the enemy at four o'clock the succeeding morning. A salient on the right centre of the enemy's works had been discovered by a reconnaissance, and against this point the assault was directed.

The morning of May 12th was foggy, and the attack was delayed until 4.35 A.M. Then Hancock's corps advanced in quick time, reserving their fire, and with a bold rush carried the enemy's works, capturing 4000 of Ewell's corps, including a major-general and a brigadier-general, besides several colours, thirty-five pieces of artillery, and many small-arms. Hancock's attack was not vigorously supported at other points on Grant's front; yet repeated desperate assaults by Lee to regain his position were repulsed, and he did not succeed in retaking the important ground he had lost. Five times were his men urged to the attack, only to be hurled back each time with heavy loss.

This fight of Thursday, May 12th, is known as that of the "Bloody Angle." Well does it deserve its name. The corpses heaped up on its front, after the battle had ceased, bore testimony to the savage nature of the struggle, which has had few equals in the history of war. "The sight the next day," reported General Lewis A. Grant, commanding the Vermont Brigade, "was repulsive and sickening indeed. Behind their traverses and in the pits and holes they had dug for protection, the Rebel dead were found piled upon each other. Some of the wounded were almost entirely buried by the dead bodies of their companions who had fallen on them. Many of the dead men were horribly mangled, and the logs, trees, and brush exhibited unmistakable signs of a fearful conflict. The Rebel account of a tree over a foot in diameter (a hickory eighteen inches thick) being cut off by minie-balls is attested to by several Union officers." We are further told that " the brush and logs were cut to pieces and whipped into basket stuff."

The results thus far of the campaign against Lee had not disheartened Grant, if they had others. His line of policy had been determined on in advance after full reflection, and he showed no disposition to abandon it. Butler reports Grant as saying to him, in an interview at Fort Monroe, that the enemy should be conquered by continual attrition, and by inflicting loss in every way, and by wearing out their resources as fast as possible and at however great cost, relying upon our own more abundant money and men to bring out a successful result. He proposed to attack at all times and under all conditions, even at the risk of losing more men than Lee, for he knew he could afford to lose more. As the rate of death by disease and hardships incident to camp life was far greater than the loss of men by bullet and shell, he thought, upon the whole, that if the war could be pressed on, and ended shortly, the loss of life and the pecuniary expenditure would be less than if it were prolonged. The enemy occupying the interior lines of defence could hold their ground with fewer men, and, fighting behind intrenchments, their losses would be less; but, as they could not make their losses good, they would in the end fail from exhaustion, even if they were to escape serious disaster in battle.

The losses of General Grant on May 12th were 6020 men, besides 800 missing. Lee's total he places at between 4000 and 5000, including two general officers killed, four wounded, and two captured. On this day, in the matter of assaults, it was give and take. Three general officers of the Army of the Potomac were wounded, but none killed or captured. The Confederates had also suffered a severe loss in the death of their ablest cavalry leader, General Stuart, who was killed on May 10, 1864, in an encounter near Richmond with the cavalry of Sheridan, who was making a raid around that city. Stuart, as his biographer tells us, " could be ill spared at this critical moment, and General Lee was plunged into the deepest melancholy at the intelligence of his death."

From May 13, 1864, to May 17th there was a lull in the fighting. Grant was extending his lines to the left, and Lee was moving in the same direction to cover his menaced flank.

News was received during this period that Butler had captured the outer works of Drury's Bluff, that Sherman was driving Johnston before him in Georgia, and that Sheridan's raid had temporarily cut off all communication with Richmond except by courier.

To offset this cheering news, the report came that Sigel had been badly defeated at New Market, and was retreating down the Shenandoah Valley. He was promptly superseded by General Hunter, in accordance with telegraph orders sent by Grant to Halleck.

"All this news," General Grant says, "was very discouraging, but this was no time for repining. I immediately gave orders for a movement by the left flank on towards Richmond, to commence on the night of the 19th. I also asked Halleck to secure the co-operation of the Navy in changing our base of supplies from Fredericksburg to Port Royal on the Rappahannock." Thus did Grant always join issue with evil fortune.

The assault against the enemy's new line was opened May 18, 1864, but without result, except to add further to the casualties of both armies. At this time Grant received his first re-enforcements,— 6000 heavy artillery. They were raw troops, and were not in favour with the infantrymen, as they were supposed to have enlisted as artillery to secure the advantages of the shelter of the fortifications at Washington. They were accordingly received with the grim humours of the battle-field. "Wounded men would tauntingly point to a shattered arm or a wounded leg, or to bloody wounds on their faces, or to dead men lying in fence corners, and derisively shout, 'That is what you will catch up yonder in the woods!' and they would solemnly indicate the portion of the forest they meant by extending an arm from which blood trickled in drops."

The quality of these artillerymen was soon tested,

for they resisted an attack made upon them on May 19th, before they were in position, with the resolution of veterans, holding their ground until they were re-enforced; and Ewell, who had made the assault, " was whirled back speedily and with heavy loss." If he had the artillerymen, Grant got rid of the artillery, sending to the rear over one hundred pieces with horses and caissons, thus lessening the pressure upon the roads over which he was to march, and relieving him of what he regarded as so much useless lumber, under the conditions of the campaign.

This ended the series of battles around Spottsylvania Court-House. They had resulted in a loss, to the Army of the Potomac, of 16,141 killed and wounded, and 2258 missing. The Confederate loss was much less; " since," as General Humphreys says, " they remained on the defensive under the cover of intrenchments, entangled in their front in a manner unknown to European warfare, and, indeed, in a manner new to warfare in this country."

The two armies had been in such close contact from the time the Army of the Potomac crossed the Rapidan, that it was impossible to relax vigilance even during the intervals between the fighting. The strain upon the men had reached the limit of human endurance; for soldiers are not machines, as some critics of war would have us think, but flesh and blood and brains, that must always be calculated with by the successful commander. No one who has not had like experience can form any just conception of the enormous strain these heroic men had endured; and it is not strange that they should have suffered some loss of *élan*. Thirty-six thousand and sixty-five men had been added to the list of casualties during the campaign of sixteen days, but still the watchword of the Army of the Potomac was " By the left flank forward! "

The next movement was to the North Anna River, fifteen miles south of the Po. To conceal the march of the troops from the enemy, each corps was withdrawn in succession from the right, and marched in the rear of the other corps, taking its position on the left, thus gradually prolonging the line in that direction. Having the advantage of interior, and thus shorter lines, Lee was able to anticipate the movement, and Grant found him more strongly intrenched on the North Anna than he was on the bloody field of Spottsylvania.

May 19th, Hancock was ordered to move with his corps, with Torbert's cavalry, along the line of the railroad connecting Richmond and Fredericksburg, to Milford Station, twenty miles nearer Richmond. The purpose in detaching Hancock was to offer him as a bait to Lee, trusting, that, if the Confederates should be persuaded to come out to attack him, he could be re-enforced in time by the other corps following in his rear. But whether Lee saw the trap or not, he did not enter it. He again moved to interpose his army between Grant and Richmond, advancing toward Hanover Junction, where the Fredericksburg Railroad is crossed by the Virginia Central, running from the valley of the Shenandoah into Richmond.

Possession of Hanover Junction would cut Lee

off at one stroke from Richmond, and from his storehouses in the Shenandoah Valley. By the time the Army of the Potomac reached Hanover Junction, Lee had been re-enforced by a little over 9000 men from other commands, relieved from pressure by Confederate successes in the Shenandoah Valley, and by the inaction of General Butler at Bermuda Hundred.

On Sunday, May 22d, the Army received the encouraging news that Sherman was still in the ascendant; that he had crossed the Etowah River, and was advancing into the heart of Georgia. May 24, 1864, General Sheridan, with his cavalry corps, rejoined the Army, and a cautious advance on that day and the next showed that the Army of Virginia held a position too strong for direct attack. General Butler, having failed to accomplish with the Army of the James what was expected of him, was ordered to send one half of his force, 16,000 men, under W. F. Smith, to re-enforce the Army of the Potomac. This still left Butler with a force one half greater than that commanded by General Beauregard on his front.

On May 26th the Army of the Potomac again slipped away, making a third attempt to out-manœuvre Lee and get around his right flank. On that day General Grant wrote to General Halleck:

"Lee's army is really whipped. The prisoners we now take show it, and the action of his army shows it unmistakably. A battle with them outside of intrenchments cannot be had. Our men feel that they have gained *morale* over the enemy and attack him with confidence. I may be mistaken, but I feel that our success over Lee's army is already assured."

Grant's base of supplies was now changed to White House, at the head of navigation on Pamunkey River, twenty-five miles east of Richmond. The next objective of the Army of the Potomac was Hanover Town, thirty-two miles nearer Richmond, and fifteen miles north-west of that city. Hanover Town was occupied by Sheridan's cavalry May 27, 1864; and the infantry crossed the Pamunkey River and joined him the next day. A cavalry reconnaissance, pushed nearly up to Richmond, revealed Lee's army holding a strongly intrenched position on the Totopotomoy Creek, ten miles north of Richmond. From Hanover the two armies moved on parallel lines, Grant leading the movement, until the flanks of both armies rested upon the Chickahominy.

Lee's army was again in a position to invite, if not actually to compel, another assault upon strong intrenchments. Once more, and once too often, was the challenge accepted by the indomitable Grant. The attempt to turn Lee's flank, and to force him to fight in the open, had been in every case a failure. At no time in the campaign had he been brought to battle under conditions more advantageous to himself than now. His right flank was within six miles of the outer intrenchments of Richmond; and turning movements, whether they invited success or disaster, were no longer possible. The close proximity of the two armies led to numerous encounters from May 31 to June 2, 1864, with severe losses on both sides.

Lee was fated to try conclusions this time with

the Army of the Potomac in a region remembered as the scene of McClellan's unsuccessful ventures two years before.

Grant's order for the attack on Lee's intrenchments at Cold Harbor, as the locality was called, was issued June 2, 1864, and four o'clock the next morning was named as the hour of attack. A welcome rain came on that afternoon and continued through the night, laying the dust in which the moving trains had been enveloped. Two assaults were made on the intrenchments at Cold Harbor, and both met with a bloody repulse. Rank after rank of the Federal line went down before the deadly fire from the Confederate works.

Within an hour nearly 12,000 dead and wounded Union soldiers lay in front of the enemy's trenches. In addition to charging directly in face of a heavy fire from intrenched troops, they were subjected to an enfilading fire on both flanks. Lee's loss was scarcely a tithe of what he inflicted. The result is best told in Grant's own frank words. He says in his *Memoirs*:

"I have always regretted that the last assault at Cold Harbor was ever made. No advantage whatever was gained to compensate for the heavy losses sustained. Indeed, the advantages other than those of relative losses were on the Confederate side. Before that, the Army of Northern Virginia seemed to have acquired a wholesome regard for the courage, endurance and soldierly qualities of the Army of the Potomac. They no longer wanted to fight them, "one Confederate to five Yanks." Indeed, they seemed to have given up the idea of gaining any advantage of their antagonists in the open field. They had come to much prefer breast-works in their front to the Army of the Potomac. This charge seemed to have revived their hopes temporarily; but it was of short duration. The effect upon the Army of the Potomac was the reverse."

Cold Harbor was the least excusable of the series of desperate and unsuccessful attempts to carry Confederate intrenchments by direct attacks. The immense losses and the enormous fatigue involved in the campaign of the Army of the Potomac, commencing with the Wilderness, had somewhat shaken the courage of Meade's gallant army, but it had not correspondingly increased the spirits of his opponents. Lee realised that he had before him a soldier who would be satisfied with no half-way measures of victory or defeat, whose hold upon him could not be shaken off by anything short of such a crushing victory as it was beyond his power to inflict. On June 6th and 7th he did make two attacks on Grant's right flank, but they were without result.

Halleck now advised Grant to change his plan of campaign to a movement on his right against Lee's left flank, thus placing himself between the Army of Virginia and Washington; but Grant had not lost hope of accomplishing his purpose of cutting Lee off from his communications with the south, and he resolved to continue his movement by the left, and against the railroads over which Lee received his supplies. The Central and Fredericksburg roads had been already somewhat damaged, and Sheridan was sent with a strong cavalry force to continue the work of destroying them.

Unfortunately for Grant's plan, neither Hunter nor Butler was able to accomplish what was expected of him. Hunter had defeated the force on his front, and, forming a junction at Staunton with Crook and Averell, was threatening Lynchburg.

Hearing of this, Lee, June 13th, sent Early with his corps and Breckinridge's command on to attack Hunter's rear, and to follow up his advantage, if successful, by advancing upon Washington by way of Harper's Ferry. General Hunter's long march through a hostile country had left him short of ordnance stores; and when the enemy appeared in force in front of Lynchburg, he retired to Harper's Ferry by a circuitous route, that left the Shenandoah Valley open to Early's advance. This uncovered Washington, and by July 11th the Confederates were in a position to threaten that city from the north.

Then there was mounting in hot haste at the Capital, which was depending upon much too small a force for its protection, and was in more deadly peril than at any other time during the war. Partially disabled soldiers, organised as "Veteran Reserves," quartermaster's employees, government clerks, and all others who could be brought under military control, were forced to do duty. They were fortunately able to hold Early in check long enough to secure re-enforcements. The gallant Sixth Corps, under Wright, was sent from the Army of the Potomac; and so much of the Nineteenth Corps as had arrived at Washington from Banks's unsuccessful Red River expedition, on its way to join the Army of the Potomac, was detained for the defence of the imperilled city.

By an heroic defence, under conditions apparently hopeless, General Lew Wallace succeeded in delaying Early's assault for one day; and the day thus gained was just sufficient to secure the re-enforcements that made the Capital safe, and compelled Early's retreat before a pursuing army.

These mishaps were less injurious to Grant's projects than they might have been at another time, and they did not interfere with the plan he had resolved upon for moving his army south of the James River. Preliminary to this movement, on June 9th, Butler sent a force from the Army of the James to capture Petersburg, but it returned without accomplishing its purpose.

The movement of the Army of the Potomac to the James River commenced with the withdrawal of the Second Corps, on June 12, 1864, from in front of the enemy, and its passage of the river in boats on the 14th and 15th. It was intended that Hancock should advance directly upon Petersburg and capture that city, but various misunderstandings and mistakes delayed his advance until the opportunity to seize Petersburg by a *coup de main* was lost. Butler sent W. F. Smith, with a force of 16,200 men of all arms, to co-operate with this movement by an attack upon Petersburg from the north. Though the Confederate force in Petersburg at this time was very weak, it proved sufficient to delay a movement which lacked vigour and co-operation; and the Confederates were given opportunity to strongly intrench their lines at Petersburg, and to add to the strength of the force defending that city. Partial successes were gained in the attack by Smith, and some prisoners were taken, but no permanent lodgment was made within the enemy's works.

Want of bridge material delayed the movement of the main body of the Army of the Potomac across the James until June 16, 1864. The passage was then made without mishap, though it was very difficult, as the troops were obliged to cross the Chickahominy *en route* to the James, and to make exhausting forced marches of from twenty-five to fifty-five miles. By midnight of June 16th the entire Army, with its artillery and trains, had crossed this river, two thousand one hundred feet wide, seventy to ninety feet in depth in mid-channel, with a tide of four feet, and a strong tidal current. The transit was made in ferry-boats and across a pontoon bridge. One hundred and one pontoons were used for building the bridge, and these were anchored above and below the vessels moored in the river. The Navy assisted with its armoured ships and gunboats in covering the passage. The march of the troops was so directed as completely to deceive Lee with the idea that an attack upon Richmond was intended, and the crossing of the James was not interfered with by him. It was a masterly movement, and was made without the loss of a man or an animal, except a few in Warren's corps, which covered the advance of the main Army by a feint against Lee's right.

Movements intended to secure the possession of Petersburg having failed, much to the chagrin of Meade, that officer was resolved upon capturing the city at any cost; but an assault on the enemy's lines on June 18th satisfied him that it was impracticable to carry them by a front attack. This assault so far succeeded, however, as to compel the defenders of Petersburg to withdraw from their outer line to a new line; and a position was gained close against the enemy. The lines thus established remained substantially unchanged until the close of the war.

The lesson of the futility of front assaults on fortified lines had been learned at heavy cost by the Army of the Potomac, but it was thoroughly learned. In his *History of the Second Army Corps*, General Francis A. Walker, Assistant Adjutant-General of the corps, says:

"The terrible experiences of May and June in assaults on intrenched positions; assaults made, often, not at a carefully selected point, but 'all along the line'; assaults made as if it were a good thing to assault, and not a dire necessity; assaults made without an adequate concentration of troops, often without time for careful preparation, sometimes even without examination of the ground—these bitter experiences had naturally brought about a reaction, by which efforts to outflank the enemy were to become the order of the day, so that the months of July and August were largely to be occupied in rapid movements, now to the right and now to the left of a line thirty to forty miles in length, in the hope of somewhere, at some time, getting upon the flank of the unprepared enemy—the sentiment of headquarters, and perhaps the orders, being adverse to assaults.

"Unfortunately this change of purpose did not take place until the numbers and *morale* of the troops had been so far reduced that the flanking movements became, in the main, ineffectual from the want of vigor in attack, at the critical moments, when a little of the fire which had been exhibited in the great assaults of May would have sufficed to crown a well-conceived enterprise with a glorious victory. But that fire had for the time burned itself out; and on more than one occasion during the months of July and August, 1864, the troops of the Army of the Potomac, after an all-day or all-night march which had placed them in a position of advantage, failed to show a trace of that enthusiasm and *élan* which characterized the earlier days of the campaign. This result was not due to moral causes only,

Physically the troops were dead-beat, from the exertions and privations of the preceding two months. Men died of flesh wounds, which, at another time, would merely have afforded a welcome excuse for a thirty days' sick-leave. The limit of human endurance had been reached."

It was now determined to invest Petersburg, with a view to capturing it by regular approaches. The remainder of June and the month of July, 1864, were occupied in establishing the lines of envelopment, and in extending the flanks of the several corps so as to establish complete connection between them. An unsuccessful attempt was also made to so extend Grant's lines to the south and west as to secure possession of the Petersburg and Weldon Railroad running south, and the South Side Railroad running west to Lynchburg on the south side of the Appomattox River. In anticipation of the siege of Petersburg, Col. H. L. Abbot, an army engineer, then commanding a volunteer regiment of artillery, had been directed, on April 20th, to prepare a siege train. Two months later, on June 24, 1864, he reported with his train.

Toward the end of June, Sheridan returned from his cavalry raid on the enemy's communications. He had had various successful encounters with Hampton's and Fitzhugh Lee's cavalry, and destroyed large amounts of stores, and had done much damage in various ways. He had not, however, accomplished his main purpose by permanently destroying the Confederate lines of supply, and establishing connection with the Army in the valley of the Shenandoah. The railroads had been badly damaged, but the damage was speedily repaired, and the Confederates continued to control sufficient railroad communication for their necessary purposes. Sheridan's return had been hastened by the discovery of Early's successful movement up the valley.

June 22, 1864, the depot at White House was broken up, and a train of nine hundred waggons was sent to join the Army, under the escort of Sheridan's cavalry. A bold and successful attack by Hampton and Fitzhugh Lee's cavalry compelled the trains to move back to Douthard's Landing, farther down the river. They were ferried across the James River on June 25, 1864, the cavalry following them.

July 25th, the Second Corps and a force of cavalry were detached to make a bold dash against Richmond, to destroy the important railroads in its vicinity, and, if possible, to take the city itself by surprise. It was hoped, that, if not fully successful, this would at least compel a withdrawal of the force defending Petersburg, so as to cover an intended assault at a point where the opposing lines were only one hundred yards apart. From this advanced position a mine had been run under a Confederate redan, the work being completed July 23d by a detachment of experienced coal-miners belonging to a Pennsylvania regiment. Every precaution was taken to conceal this work; but the mine was discovered by the enemy, who, after failing in an attempt to countermine, established a new line of works to cover the threatened breach in their intrenchments.

The mine was fired early in the morning of July 30, 1864. A picturesque display of pyrotechnics resulted from the explosion; that was all. The assault that followed was a dismal failure. An immense crater was formed, and a wide breach was made in the enemy's lines; but, owing to the incapacity and cowardice of some of the officers leading the troops, the breach was not occupied. Instead of charging vigorously, the troops huddled together in a crowded mass around the edges of the crater, under the burning sun of a July day, but they made no attempt to go farther on. No order or enterprise was shown in the assault. Thus this second opportunity to capture Petersburg was lost. A large number of officers were captured in the crater, and, all together, 2098 officers and men were uselessly killed and wounded, and over 1500 taken prisoners. The Confederate loss was in the neighbourhood of 1000.

This affair of "Burnside's Mine," as it was called, was one of the most humiliating in the history of the Army of the Potomac. It led to a military Court of Inquiry, ordered at the request of General Meade, and, an investigation by the "Congressional Committee on the Conduct of the War." The conclusion was in effect that the assault had failed from mismanagement and misbehaviour on the part of several of those directing it, including the Corps Commander.

The natural result of the severe experiences of the Army of the Potomac since it crossed the Rapidan had been the loss of many of its most efficient and courageous officers, whose absence was sadly felt on this occasion.

The lines about Petersburg were now strengthened by the engineers with redoubts and return-works, so that they could be held with the smallest possible force, leaving the main body of the Army free for movement.

Everywhere, except in the Shenandoah Valley, the Lieutenant-General had succeeded in controlling the movements of troops without serious interference from Washington. But his orders were sent through Washington, which was a telegraphic centre; and at the capital presided Stanton and Halleck, who, like two nervous old women, were in a constant state of alarm lest something should be done to jeopardise the safety of the city.

President Lincoln thoroughly understood the situation, but was apparently unable to prevent the interference of the War Department with the orders Grant sent through it, directing movement of troops in the Valley. In a confidential cipher despatch to Grant, August 3, 1864, the President said that no one in Washington had any idea of following the enemy " to the *death* " in any direction. He added, " I repeat to you, it will neither be done nor attempted, unless you watch it every day and hour, and force it."

In two hours after the receipt of this despatch, Grant was on his way to General Hunter's army. He asked that general, when he arrived, where the enemy was. Hunter replied that he did not know. He was so embarrassed with orders from

Washington, moving him first to the right and then to the left, that he lost all trace of the enemy. He wished to be relieved from command; and Sheridan, who had already been decided upon as his successor, was telegraphed to come at once and take his place.

Under General Sheridan's vigorous administration the Confederates were defeated at Winchester, Virginia, on September 19, 1864, and again at Cedar Creek a month later. The losses in these two battles were nearly equal; but Cedar Creek substantially closed the Valley campaign, and the Sixth Corps was returned to the Army of the Potomac; Early, with his forces, rejoining the army of Lee. Sheridan made thorough work of destroying everything that could be used in supplying the enemy, and the rich valley of the Shenandoah was no longer a storehouse for Lee's army. As Sheridan reported, it was swept so bare that a bird could not fly over it without carrying his rations with him. It was this policy of unrelenting war that finally brought the Confederacy to terms.

While Sheridan was busied in "cleaning out" the Shenandoah Valley, Grant was conducting a series of operations in front of Petersburg, in part intended to prevent Lee from detaching troops to re-enforce the enemy in front of Sheridan. A movement to the north side of the James River, threatening Richmond, was undertaken for this purpose from August 13 to 20, 1864. The troops left about Petersburg were instructed to keep watch, meanwhile, to take advantage of any weakening in the enemy's line in that quarter. Not only was Lee prevented from sending re-enforcements to Early, but Warren, operating from the south side of the James, succeeded in securing lodgment on the Weldon Railroad; and it remained in Grant's possession from this time until the end of the war. The loss of his complete control over this road seriously embarrassed Lee, as it compelled him to draw his supplies from the south in waggons for a distance of thirty miles over a gap in the railroad.

On October 7th, Lee made a successful attack upon Grant's cavalry north of the James, but he was repulsed with severe loss in an attack which followed on the intrenched infantry line. Grant's operations around Richmond for the winter closed with an unsuccessful attempt made on October 27th to get possession of the South Side Railroad. The various operations during the autumn of 1864 had resulted in extending his intrenchments to the right and left, thus forcing Lee to attenuate his line of defence to cover a constantly elongating front. Lee warned the Confederate authorities at Richmond that it was getting so thin that it was in danger of breaking; but their resources were exhausted, and they could do nothing for him.

Another movement from Grant's right flank, on the north side of the James River, on September 28 and 29, 1864, and one in co-operation with it on the left of Grant's army, resulted in the capture of one of the enemy's forts, Fort Harrison, with a line of intrenchments, and the extension of Grant's lines on both flanks.

The winter of 1864-65 was a very hard one, and

both of the armies around Petersburg and Richmond suffered severely, especially the thinly clad and poorly fed Confederates. The successes of Sheridan in the valley of the Shenandoah, and Sherman's advance from the south, were constantly narrowing Lee's field of supply; and, with his railroad connections badly broken, he had difficulty in bringing within the reach of his men such scanty stores as were still available. The winter was occupied by his army in strengthening its intrenchments around Petersburg. In the spring they extended over a front of thirty-seven miles.

CHAPTER XVI.

CAMPAIGNS OF SHERMAN AND THOMAS—OVERTURES FOR PEACE.

MAY, 1864–FEBRUARY, 1865.

IN December, 1864, Butler had conceived the brilliant project of capturing Fort Fisher, on the North Carolina coast, by hauling a vessel loaded with three hundred tons of powder close under the works, and blowing them down by exploding the powder. It was supposed that the detonation of such a mass of explosives would not only injure the work, but demoralise the garrison so as to open the way for a successful assault.

The powder was duly exploded on December 23, 1864, but it did not disturb the enemy and the chief effect seems to have been to demoralise Butler himself. His movement was made in co-operation with the Navy under Admiral Porter, who insisted that, under the cover of a bombardment by his fleet, a successful assault was still possible. Butler did not think so. Withdrawing his troops from the position they occupied on the beach, he re-embarked them on transports, and returned to his position in front of Richmond.

Butler soon afterward visited the authorities at Washington; and while he was engaged in explaining to them that it was impossible to take Fort Fisher, he was interrupted by a newsboy crying an "extra" containing a report of the capture of the fort. General Alfred H. Terry, who had been sent to Fort Fisher on January 6th with 8000 troops, had made a successful assault on January 14th, aided by a force of sailors and marines. The Navy co-operated in this movement by a bombardment, and the fort passed under the control of General Terry.

Major-General William T. Sherman was the only officer commanding a subordinate army who had thus far fulfilled expectations. On May 5, 1864, the same day that Grant moved against Lee, Sherman entered upon his campaign in Georgia, having an effective force of about 100,000 men and 254 guns. Opposed to him was General Joseph E. Johnston, the ablest of the Confederate commanders, in the opinion of Grant, with about 60,000 men, to which an additional corps, under General Polk, was afterwards added. By a series of brilliant attacks and flanking movements, Sherman, in a campaign of four months, forced his antagonist over one hundred miles south, from near the northern boundary of Georgia down to Atlanta, Georgia. His line of operations was crossed by the Oostanaula, Etowah, and Chattahoochee Rivers, and by several mountain spurs, each of which afforded a strong line of defence. The movement was along the line of the Tennessee and Georgia Railroad, known as the Western Atlantic Road. As Sherman advanced and took possession of this road, it furnished him with the means of supplying his army; but it had to be guarded every step of the way by bomb-proof block-houses provisioned for a siege, and his fighting force was constantly depleted by the detachments required to guard the railroad carrying his supplies.

At the time the advance movement commenced, Johnston occupied an intrenched position across the railroad at Dalton, Georgia, and behind a mountain known as Rocky Face Ridge. Just north of Dalton is a gorge through Rocky Face Ridge, called Buzzard's Roost. The Confederates occupied this gorge, and an exceedingly strong and elaborately fortified position behind it, much too strong to invite a direct attack. They had neglected, however, to take possession of Snake Creek Gap, a wild and picturesque defile, five or six miles long, opening a way through the mountains in their rear. There was no road through the gap, only a trail worn by the country waggons in threading their way along the edges of the little creek passing through this cleft in the mountain. Thomas had discovered this possible but unpromising route to the rear of Johnston, and McPherson was sent with 23,000 troops to see if he could get through the pass, Sherman meantime occupying Johnston's attention by a front attack. McPherson moved May 9, 1864, passed through Snake Creek Gap without opposition, took Johnston in reverse, and compelled him to withdraw hastily from his position at Dalton on the night of May 15th. Then, after some skirmishing and fighting at Resaca, Johnston withdrew across the Oostenaula River.

Sherman occupied Resaca, and after waiting for a few days to rest his troops, repair the railroad, and provide supplies, advanced again. By a series of flanking movements and vigorous attacks, he gradually forced his enemy, during the month of May, 1864, to evacuate one after another the strong positions of Dalton, Resaca, and Allatoona. Johnston finally established himself near Marietta, where he occupied three fortified hills, known as Kenesaw Mountain, Pine Mountain, and Lost Mountain. The operations during the month of May resulted in the loss of about 9000 men to each army.

Sherman was now in possession of the railroad from Chattanooga south to Allatoona Station, which was occupied and fortified as a secondary base. Operations during the month of June were greatly interfered with by heavy rains, converting the country into a quagmire, and transforming streams usually dry into almost impassable obstructions. It was impossible to trace the roads through the wilderness of mire, and artillery and horses were frequently in danger of being ingulfed in quicksands. After a series of unsuccessful minor attacks, Sherman decided on a bold movement to break the enemy's line at Kenesaw Mountain. He lost 3000 men in an unsuccessful assault on June 21, 1864; but he accomplished his purpose of holding Johnston, so that it was impossible for him to detach any portion of his force to assist Lee in Virginia. This mutual co-operation and assistance is the key to the campaigns of Sherman and Grant.

Grant, having established himself in front of Petersburg, sent Sherman word on June 28, 1864, that he might leave the Army of the Potomac out of his calculations. Sherman at once resolved to resume his plan of flank operations; cutting loose temporarily from the railroad with ten days' supplies, and moving boldly by his right across the Chattahoochee, leaving Thomas strongly intrenched to guard his rear. This compelled Johnston to evacuate the works at Kenesaw on the night of July 2d and 3d, and to establish himself in a new position farther south, behind the Nickajack Creek, where an intrenched camp with a front of five miles had already been provided for him by Georgia militia, aided by negroes impressed into the service of the Confederate engineers.

Sherman was now in possession of the railroad from Chattanooga to the Chattahoochee. He proceeded to repair it, and his camps were soon within railroad communication with the North. From a hill near his headquarters at Vining Station the coveted city of Atlanta could be seen, and the movements of Johnston's troops noted. The movement southwards from the Etowah River had occupied but little more than a month, and had been made under the most trying circumstances of weather. From June 10th to July 3d, skirmishes alternated with occasional heavy engagements so closely as to almost constitute a continuous battle. Sharp experience had transformed the Union soldiers into an army of veterans; continued success had developed their confidence in themselves and in their commander, and there was nothing they were not ready to undertake. The casualties of the month of June had been 7500 men. The Confederate loss was about the same. With the exception of the attack on the Confederate lines, June 27th, the movement had been one of advance by skirmish lines and extension of flanks. Both armies had tried assaults, but these were not pushed to such extremities as in the Army of the Potomac.

After collecting fresh supplies, Sherman was prepared for another flanking movement. This was directed against Decatur, five miles east of Atlanta, on the railroad connecting Atlanta with Augusta and the seacoast. July 18th the commands of McPherson and Schofield were sent to destroy this road, and to sever Atlanta from the east while Sherman threatened it from the north.

Johnston was a skilled soldier; but his Fabian policy had not encouraged confidence in him at Richmond, and his removal from command was resolved upon. On July 17, 1864, he received telegraphic orders from Richmond to turn over his command to Lieut.-Gen. J. B. Hood, who commanded one of his army corps. This change while it pleased the Confederate Government, was equally satisfactory to Grant and Sherman. Hood determined upon a change of policy from the defensive to the aggressive, and this gave Sherman the advantage the Confederates had enjoyed up to this time. July 20, 1864, Hood made an attack on the Union Army, which resulted in his defeat at Peach Tree Creek; he losing 4796, and Sherman 1710. A still worse defeat resulted from Hood's attempt to overwhelm Sherman, on July 22d, by striking him on his moving left flank before he could get into position and fortify. Hood lost 8499, and Sherman but 3641; and this action, which was intended to seal the fate of the Union Army, was decisive as to the fate of Atlanta, enabling Sherman to draw his lines closely around the doomed city.

By July 25th, railroad communication with Chattanooga had been completed across the Chattahoochee, and Sherman was ready for a new flanking movement. The railroad connecting Atlanta with the Atlantic seaboard had been occupied by the Union troops, and thirty miles of it destroyed. This reduced Hood's means of supply to a road running south to East Point, Georgia, and branching thence into two roads,—one running south-west to Montgomery, Alabama; and the other south-east to Macon, Georgia. General Stoneman, having failed disastrously in an attempt to destroy these roads by a cavalry raid, an effort was made to prolong Sherman's right flank to East Point so as to cover them. The aggressive Hood attempted to defeat this movement by an attack on Sherman's right flank, July 28, 1864; but he was repulsed at Ezra Church with a loss of 4642, Sherman losing but 700. These experiences show what would have been the result in Virginia if Lee had followed Hood's policy of attack.

Attempts on both sides to destroy by cavalry raids the enemy's railroad communication led to but little result. Sherman's communications by rail and telegraph were interrupted nearly every night, but they were restored as fast as they were broken. In forty days, Gen. G. M. Dodge built more than one hundred miles of railroad in the rear of the advancing army, and one hundred and eighty bridges, using such material and tools as were to be gathered in the neighbourhood, meanwhile subsisting the 8000 men under his command by foraging on the country. The railroad corps organised by Sherman suggested to the Prussians the establishment of the similar corps used by them for the first time, and so effectively, in the Danish war of 1866, and on a larger scale in the Franco-Prussian war.

Taking advantage of the absence of a part of Hood's cavalry, Sherman, on August 19, 1864, sent his own cavalry, under Kilpatrick, on a raid against the Macon Railroad. They succeeded in doing some damage to the road about Jonesboro', and from there made a complete circuit around Atlanta before returning.

For over a month Sherman continued to extend his right in the direction of the Macon Railroad, fortifying step by step as he advanced. On August 25, 1864, he withdrew from the immediate front of Hood's army, and moved in force against the railroad from East Point to Red Oaks and Fairburn, and thoroughly destroyed it. By the 31st of the month he had made a permanent lodgment on the road from Rough and Ready to Jonesboro', the enemy being defeated in an attempt to dislodge him.

This closed Hood's last line of communication, and compelled the evacuation of Atlanta. On the night of September 1, 1864, Sherman was kept awake by the exploding shells with which Hood was destroying the public property, preparatory to his withdrawal. Early on the morning of September 2d, a note was received from General Slocum, stating that he was in possession of the city, which had been so stubbornly defended and so successfully assailed.

The news of the fall of Atlanta was received with great rejoicing by the Army, at Washington, and all over the North. It had an important influence upon the results of the National election, which, in November following, extended Mr. Lincoln's term as President for another four years. Lincoln telegraphed the National thanks " to Major-General W. T. Sherman and the gallant officers and soldiers of his command before Atlanta." General Grant informed them that he had " ordered a salute to be fired with *shotted* guns from every battery bearing upon the enemy."

During August and September, Sherman had lost 5139 men, and Hood 7143. Up to the fall of Atlanta, the total loss of the Union Army had been 31,687, and the Confederates 34,979. This does not include cavalry losses, which were about equal on the two sides. Sherman's total force had varied from 98,787 to 112,819, and he now had 81,158.

After lingering some time in the vicinity of Atlanta, Hood endeavoured to shake his adversary's hold upon that city by advancing north and attacking his line of communication. He did not succeed in accomplishing the intended result, though he did compel General Sherman to follow him with the main body of his army to protect his communication. Failing to reach Hood and bring him to battle, Sherman despatched General Thomas to Nashville, with two corps of his army, to defend the line of the Tennessee River while he himself made preparations for a further advance into the heart of Georgia. Meanwhile Hood rested at Florence, Alabama, and occupied a month there in gathering supplies and preparing for a further movement north.

On November 2d, Sherman's army lay stretched from Rome to Atlanta, Georgia, and he began his preparations for his famous march of three hundred miles from Atlanta east to the seaboard at Savannah. All detachments were ordered to concentrate at Atlanta; the railroad and telegraph communications in the rear were completely broken by November 12th; and Sherman, who had now with him 60,000 men, was completely isolated from all communication with the North, and in the heart of the enemy's country. Non-combatants, inefficient men, surplus baggage, and everything else not absolutely essential, had been sent away, and his force was stripped for the march and the battle.

On November 16, 1864, the Army finally turned its back upon Atlanta. It was a beautiful sunny day, with bracing air; and, full of confidence and expectation, the men started on their long tramp. All caught the inspiration of the occasion, and many a group called out to Sherman as he drove past them:

"Uncle Billy, I guess Grant is waiting for us at Richmond."

" The white people came out of their houses to behold the sight, in spite of their deep hatred of the invaders, and the negroes were simply frantic with joy." For them the "year of jubilee" had come. One poor negro girl was seen " in the very ecstasy of a Methodist shout, hugging the banner of one of the regiments, and jumping up to the ' feet of Jesus.' "

The various columns proceeding by different roads established communication with each other November 23d; the right being then at Gordon, and the left at Milledgeville, the capital of Georgia. They again communicated on December 3d, at Millen. From there the march was directed on Savannah by the four main roads, reaching the defences of that city on December 9 and 10, 1864. Here communication was opened with the fleet under the command of Admiral Dahlgren. Fort McAllister was carried by storm December 13th, and by the 21st of the month Savannah itself was in the possession of General Sherman, and he was able to send word to President Lincoln that he offered it as a Christmas gift to the country.

Meanwhile General Hood had not been idle. After some time spent at Florence, on the Tennessee River, in the north-west corner of Tennessee, preparing for battle, he crossed the boundary into Tennessee; and in the battles of Franklin (November 30th, 1864) and Nashville (December 15th and 16th) he dashed the Confederate Army of invasion into pieces against the invincible Thomas.

In these two engagements, so disastrous to the Confederacy, the fighting Hood had lost 21,252 men, and Thomas only 4466. Not only had Atlanta been captured, but the army defending it had been destroyed. With the exception of the rearguard, it was "a disheartened and disorganised rabble of half-armed and barefooted men, who sought every opportunity to fall out by the wayside and desert their cause to put an end to their sufferings." Hood's weakness had been his enemy's opportunity; his courage was that of a goaded bull, whose mad passion insures its own destruction. Failing to shake Sherman's hold upon Atlanta by threatening his communications, he had conceived wild dreams of marching to the defeat of Grant, and joining Lee in an attack on Washington. When he finally decided to strike at Nashville, he proposed, if victorious there, to move on to the Ohio River. His army, gathered together by great exertions, numbered from fifty to sixty thousand men, and included an excellent body of ten or twelve thousand cavalry under the redoubtable Forrest. Thomas had in the beginning scarcely more than half as many men; but at the time of the battle of Nashville he had gathered together about fifty-five thousand, and his force outnumbered the troops that Hood brought into battle. At Franklin the Confederates fought with desperate courage, but suffered a repulse involving a loss more than double that of the Union forces under General Schofield. At Nashville, as Hood himself tells us, his line " broke at all points," and he " beheld for the first and only time the Confederate Army abandoning the field in confusion." His rout was one of the most complete of the war; and it gave final and convincing proof of the consummate ability of Thomas.

Hood's movement northward naturally gave great anxiety to Grant and to the Administration. The situation up to the battle of Nashville was a serious one, and Thomas's deliberate movements seemed to Grant's impatience to portend disaster. He had the highest respect for Thomas's character and ability, but he never seemed to come in touch with him as he did with Sherman and Sheridan. When he was a cavalry instructor at the Military Academy, Thomas had acquired the sobriquet of " Slow Trot Thomas," because in cavalry drill he would never permit the cadets to go beyond the slow trot, and Sherman records the single and only instance in which he ever saw him urge his horse beyond that gait. Thomas's slowness was physical, not mental. He was sufficiently prompt to act when the occasion called for it, though nothing could hurry him in advance of his judgment. Hood certainly had no occasion to consider him too slow.

The battle of Nashville relieved the tension upon

Grant, which had become almost unbearable. While Hood had been threatening the States along the Ohio River in his movement north, Sherman had been lost in the wilds of Georgia, and the air was filled with prophecies of disaster to him. Grant himself had not succeeded in taking Richmond, and, as his army was farther away from it than it had been six months before, his critics had full course in encouraging the popular opinion that his campaign was a failure.

Nor had he succeeded according to his own expectations; for the army of Lee, which he set out to destroy, was still defiant; but if defiant, its ardour for aggressive action had sensibly cooled. Lee had made no serious attempt to reverse the *rôles* of offence and defence since the Battle of the Wilderness. He was only too happy if he could maintain his position behind his formidable line, and retain at least a sufficient hold upon lines of communication to save his troops from actual starvation.

If he had not succeeded in destroying Lee, Grant had succeeded in holding him in so tight a grip that Sherman was able to accomplish his purposes without being molested. To use Lincoln's homely simile, Grant proposed to hold the leg while Sherman took off the skin. The movement across Georgia was practically unopposed; indeed, it had been a sort of a holiday picnic. The air was filled with flying bulletins issued by the Confederate and State authorities to fire the Southern heart; but the actual record of opposition is shown in the list of only 531 killed and wounded, and 1616 captured and missing. Sherman was fortunately favoured by good weather in his march across Georgia; and when he arrived in sight of the Atlantic, after a tramp of four weeks, his waggons were still loaded with supplies, and his men and animals were in much better condition than when they left Atlanta.

As the result of Grant's supreme command of the Union forces for eight months, the year 1864 closed with joyful auguries. Despair had settled upon the Confederacy; hope and confident expectation filled the heart of every man who desired the perpetuation of the union of the States. The re-election of Abraham Lincoln, in November, 1864, made it clear that there was to be no change of policy in the conduct of the Government. On the theory that the Confederate authorities were sufficiently discouraged, movements looking to negotiations for peace were started both North and South. As the authorities at Richmond still continued to demand independence, and Mr. Lincoln insisted without qualification upon the complete restoration of Federal authority over all places within the States of the Confederacy, no result followed beyond conferences under a flag of truce.

The Confederate commissioners came through Grant's lines January 29, 1865, and met him at his headquarters. One of them, Alexander Stephens, in his *War Between the States* (vol. ii., page 597), records his surprise at the great simplicity and perfect naturalness of the General-in-Chief, and the entire absence of anything like affectation, or even the usual air of authority customary to men in his position. Mr. Stephens says:

"He was plainly attired, sitting in a log cabin busily writing on a small table by a kerosene lamp. It was night when we arrived; there was nothing in his appearance or surroundings that indicated his official rank. There were neither guards nor aides about him. . . . The more I became acquainted with him, the more I became thoroughly impressed with the very extraordinary combination of rare elements of character which he exhibited."

The commissioners had good reason for their impression of Grant's character, for they had found the simplicity of the soldier too much for the arts of the politician. Hoping to escape the humiliation of unconditional submission to civil authorities, they sought to persuade Grant to open negotiations with Lee on his own account, thus putting the Confederate authorities at Richmond in a position to treat with the Government at Washington on the footing of independent States. The suggestion to this effect was received by the General-in-Chief in silence, "not feeling at liberty," as he informed Mr. Stanton, "to give them any hint of his opinion on the subject of peace." This was wise reticence, as the event showed.

The failure of peace negotiations compelled the Confederates to choose between surrender and the hopeless task of staying the further march of the Union Army; but their humiliation had not yet reached the point of surrender. Davis, the President of the Confederacy, who forgot nothing and learned nothing, in a speech at Richmond, defiantly announced that they would yet " compel the Yankee to petition us for peace on our own terms."

This was the defiance of despair. Doubt and despondency were already sapping the foundations of Southern persistency; and the purchase of a thousand dollars in Confederate promises to pay, with a single barrel of flour, was a better test of Confederate prospects than the assertions of the Confederate President. As General Grant expressed it, " the cradle and the grave had been robbed " by a sweeping conscription to secure recruits for the Southern Army. Desertion was becoming more and more common, and the criminations and recriminations that hasten the fate of a failing cause were already disturbing the councils of the Richmond Government.

On learning the news of Sherman's arrival at the coast with his army, Grant had sent him orders to embark his troops on transports, and to bring them north to join him in the movement against Lee. On January 2, 1865, General Barnard, Grant's Chief Engineer, arrived at Savannah, bringing despatches for Sherman, and among them a revocation of the order to bring his troops north by sea. This left Sherman free to carry out his own plan, which was to march across the country in the direction of Richmond. This movement was a bold one, and involved far greater risks than his " march to the sea," which had set the country wild with enthusiasm at his success, and admiration of his daring.

After detaching a garrison to hold Savannah,

Georgia, Sherman had some sixty thousand men under his command. These he proposed to move north in two columns,—one following the line of the Savannah River in the direction of Augusta, Georgia; the other moving farther to the east, threatening Charleston. Starting his movement on January 2, 1865, the General set his columns in motion as speedily as possible; and by the middle of the month he had secured a foothold on the soil of South Carolina, between Pocotaligo and Coosawhatchie. Here he was delayed until February 1st by bad weather, and by the difficulty of safely transporting his troops across the swamps and streams that here indent the Atlantic coast.

The first move was directed against Branchville, South Carolina. There Sherman destroyed the railroad connecting Augusta with Charleston. He continued his work of railroad destruction to Orangeburg, which cut off Charleston from Columbia, the capital of the State, and isolated it from the interior. These movements were practically unopposed. There were troops at Augusta and Charleston on Sherman's flanks, as he marched, but they were so busy in preparing for the defence of those cities, both of which expected an attack, that they did not venture upon aggression. The remnants of Hood's broken army were gathering in front, and there were other forces scattered through the State, —sufficient, in combination with Hood's troops, to make a very respectable army. The chief danger feared was that Lee might break away from Grant and join the forces opposing Sherman.

Preparations for such a contingency had been made by sending supplies to the various points on the Atlantic held by the Union troops, and notifying the Navy to be in readiness to co-operate if the opportunity should offer. In addition to the supplies he carried with him in waggons, Sherman calculated that his animals could be slaughtered in an emergency, and they would furnish him with sustenance for two or three months. As he advanced, he learned of the fall of Fort Fisher on January 15th; and later on, that Schofield, who had been sent to capture Wilmington, had succeeded in taking possession of that place on February 22d. These were strong diversions in his favour, and greatly increased his confidence of success.

On February 17, 1865, Sherman entered Columbia; and on the day following, Hardee, who was in command of Charleston, evacuated that city, and it was occupied by Union troops from Morris Island.

From Columbia, Sherman directed his march by Cheraw on Fayetteville, where he arrived on March 11th. At Fayetteville he succeeded in opening communication with the fleet by the way of the Cape Fear River. Crossing that river on March 15th with his troops, he reached Goldsboro', where he joined forces with Schofield, in command of the Twenty-third Corps. The march from Columbia to Goldsboro' was vigorously opposed by the Confederate army under the command of Hardee. There was constant skirmishing, and active engagements at Averysboro', where Sherman lost 554 men killed and wounded, and at Bentonsville, where the loss was 1604. Summarising the result in his *Memoirs*, Sherman says:

"Thus was concluded one of the longest and most important marches ever made by an organized army in a civilized country. The distance from Savannah to Goldsboro' is 425 miles, and the route traversed embraced five large navigable rivers, viz.: the Edisto, Broad, Catawba, Peedee and Cape Fear, at any of which a comparatively small force well-handled, should have made the passage most difficult, if not impossible. The country generally was in the state of nature with innumerable swamps with simply mud roads, nearly every mile of which had to be corduroyed. In our route we had captured Columbia, Cheraw, and Fayetteville, important cities and depots of supplies; had compelled the evacuation of Charleston City and harbor; had broken up all the railroads of South Carolina, and had consumed a vast amount of food and forage, essential to the enemy for the support of his own armies. We had in mid-winter accomplished the whole journey of 425 miles in fifty days, averaging ten miles per day, allowing ten lay days, and had reached Goldsboro' with the army in superb order, and the trains almost as fresh as when we started from Atlanta."

Lee had not disturbed Sherman during his march, and he was assisted by the success of the operations of Generals Schofield and Terry against Wilmington. Together they had a force of about thirty thousand men; and, besides capturing Wilmington, they had fully occupied the attention of troops that might otherwise have concentrated against him.

The opportunity now offered for the concentration against Lee. In preparation for it, it was proposed to cut Richmond off from all communication north of the James River. Most of the Confederate troops in the valley of the Shenandoah had been sent south, or withdrawn to Richmond to replace troops taken from that vicinity. Sheridan was accordingly directed to move against Lynchburg, and from there to destroy the railroad and canal so completely that it would be of no further use to the enemy. Thence he was to push on to join Sherman. He had partially completed the work of destruction, but was not able to capture Lynchburg, 115 miles west of Richmond, and, instead of going south, was compelled to turn off to join the Army of the Potomac by the way of White House, reaching its lines March 27, 1865.

CHAPTER XVII.

FINAL CAMPAIGN—SURRENDER OF LEE'S ARMY.

MARCH–APRIL, 1865.

HEN the spring campaign in Virginia opened in March, 1865, Grant was holding Lee's army as in a vice in front of Richmond and Petersburg; Sherman had reached Goldsboro' without serious loss, and had there re-enforced his armies by the addition of the Army of the Ohio under Schofield, this giving him an effective strength of 88,948 men. Canby was moving against Mobile, which was defended by the Confederate Army under General Dick Taylor; Thomas had sent out two large cavalry expeditions, one under Stoneman against Lynchburg, and another under Wilson to Alabama, and was preparing for offensive operations from East Tennessee; Pope was preparing for a campaign against Kirby Smith and Price west of the Mississippi; and Hancock was gathering a force in the vicinity of Winchester, Virginia, to use as necessity might require.

At the end of March, 1865, Grant had under his

immediate orders 124,700 men of all arms, and Lee 57,000.* Of nine lines of communication centring at Richmond and Petersburg, only two remained under Confederate control: the Southside road, running west and southwest across Virginia and into the State of Tennessee, and the Richmond and Danville Railroad, running southwest to the boundary of North Carolina. These two railways crossed each other at Burkesville Junction, sixty miles from Richmond and fifty miles west from Petersburg. Grant's plan of operations was to extend his lines south of Petersburg far enough to the left to secure control of these railroads, for this meant the destruction of Lee's army. His extreme left was already within a few miles of the Southside road, and when he was joined by Sheridan and his cavalry he resolved to make a final attempt to cut Lee off from further communication with the outside world. The fate of the Army of Northern Virginia was practically sealed; the matter of immediate concern was to prevent Lee from breaking away, joining Johnston, and with him attacking Sherman. Grant tells us that he " spent days of anxiety lest each morning should bring a report that the enemy had

---

* The muster rolls nearest to this date show the following comparisons:

	Grant, April 30, '65.	Lee, Feb. 20, '65.
Present for duty	116,742	59,588
Aggregate present	149,889	79,124
Present and absent	251,737	169,867

Included in Grant's forces are the Department of Virginia (Ord.) and Sheridan's cavalry. Lee's aggregate includes the Department of Richmond (Ewell) from 4,013 to 9,456 men.

retreated the night before." Sherman was confident of his ability to withstand the forces of Johnston and Lee combined, but even a victory over their united armies would not necessarily prevent a movement to the south which might indefinitely prolong the war.

Orders were given on March 24, 1865, for a general movement around Lee's right flank, so to threaten his communications as to compel him to come out from behind his intrenchments. Learning of his danger, Lee resolved on a counter-movement. The point of nearest approach between the two lines was at Fort Stedman, a strong work two miles east of Petersburg, captured by Grant on June 16, 1864. Lee's position suggested the possibility of an assault there, and special preparations had been made to guard against it. In spite of these precautions, Longstreet succeeded in surprising and capturing the fort on the night of March 25th, and with it a part of the lines to the right and left, turning the guns of Fort Stedman on its defenders. The assaulting party were mistaken for deserters, who were constantly coming in at this point, bringing their arms with them.

The Confederates' success was short-lived. As soon as daylight permitted, the fort was retaken and a portion of the intrenched picket-line of the enemy secured. Thus defeat was turned into victory, and an important advantage was gained by securing a position from which Wright was able to assault and carry the inner line of Confederate works a week later. In the contest over Fort Stedman, Lee lost 3515 and Grant 2587. The Confederate retreat had already been decided upon, but it was hoped by this attack to delay Grant's movements long enough to give the roads time to dry for the march of Lee's army, and to secure re-enforcements for it. This purpose failed, for preparations for the attack ordered on March 24th were continued and completed by March 29th.

At that time the Army of the Potomac, Meade commanding, was stretched in a semicircle around Petersburg. The Ninth Corps under General Parke held the lines on the east of the town, from the James River to Fort Howard. Next following, and south of Petersburg, were the Sixth Corps, Wright; Second Corps, Humphreys; and the Fifth Corps, Warren. Sheridan's cavalry, armed with deadly repeating-rifles, held the extreme left. Ord had been called from the north side of the James with three divisions, leaving twenty thousand men under Weitzel, to hold the lines of the Army of the James. Ord was placed in position near Hatcher's Run, in the rear of the Sixth Corps.

Parke and Wright were to hold the lines in front of Petersburg, leaving the rest of the army free for an advanced movement, to be led by Sheridan with his cavalry. Rain delayed action until March 31st. Then Sheridan moved from Dinwiddie Court-House to Five Forks, where he found the enemy in force, and fell back slowly before them, making all possible resistance and holding ground with great skill and tenacity until Dinwiddie Court-House was reached. His orders were to draw the enemy out of his intrenchments, if possible, and this he succeeded in doing. At Dinwiddie, Sheridan was re-enforced by Warren's corps, and on April 1, 1865, the cavalry and infantry advanced to Five Forks and captured that place with its artillery and five or six thousand prisoners after a series of attacks and counter-attacks, giving hope first to one side and then to the other. Five Forks, as this battle is called, was one of the most brilliant actions of the war and one of the most decisive. It shattered Lee's right and broke his attenuated line. "With the advantage here gained by the Federal Army," says Lee's biographer, "Lee's position at Petersburg became untenable, and nothing remained but a retreat, either to the fortifications about Richmond or to the mountain regions to the west." Grant did not at first realise the full measure of the advantage gained, and, in his anxiety to prevent a concentration on Sheridan, ordered a bombardment that night all along his front, and an advance against the enemy's works at four o'clock the next morning.

Sunday, April 2d, opened bright and beautiful, but the glories of the lovely spring day brought no solace to Lee's beleaguered veterans.

"Our noble beasts," says Longstreet, speaking for the Confederates, "peered through the loaded air and sniffed the coming battle; night birds fluttered from their startled cover, and the solid pounding upon Mahone's defensive walls drove the foxes from their lairs. A hundred guns or more added their lightning and thunder to the storm of war that carried consternation to thousands of long-apprehensive people. The cause was lost, but the end was not yet. The noble Army of Northern Virginia, once, twice conqueror of Empire, must bite the dust before its formidable adversaries."

Advancing to the assault, inspired by the confidence of victory, Grant's columns broke through all along the line of the outer works guarding Petersburg. Their losses were heavy, but the reward was sure. At eleven that morning Lee telegraphed to Richmond, " I see no prospect of doing more than hold our position until night. I am not certain that I can do that."

Grant telegraphed, " The whole captures since the army started out will not amount to less than twelve thousand men."

The victory of Five Forks had violently wrenched Lee's right from his centre, and his troops were fleeing west in disorder instead of falling back on the main body. They were followed sharply and threatened on both flanks by Sheridan's cavalry, and attacked in front, when they made a stand, by a division of infantry sent from Petersburg. After a brief battle they broke in confusion, continuing their retreat westward along the Appomattox River.

No sound of the battle that finally broke the Confederate line had reached Richmond. The usual Sunday observances were occupying the attention of the population, and at St. Paul's Church Jefferson Davis sat stiff and alone in the " President's pew."

As the worshipping congregation rose in response to the clergyman's invocation, " The Lord is in His Holy Temple, let all the earth keep silence before Him," the quiet was disturbed by the heavy step of an armed courier, who advanced up the aisle to Mr. Davis's pew and handed him a despatch. It told the story of ruin and despair. Leaving the church, the Confederate President took prompt measures for evacuating Richmond. The city was given over to scenes of the wildest panic as the news spread. Maddened men, despairing women and children, crowded the various avenues of escape, while the more self-contained residents of the doomed city composed themselves to meet with becoming fortitude the fate from which there was no escape.

Richmond and Petersburg were evacuated on the night of April 2, 1865. Early on the morning of the 3d, heavy explosions heard from the direction of the Confederate Capitol, and the flames lighting the sky in that direction told the Union Army of the destruction of public and private property following the retreat from the city. Weitzel's advancing columns speedily occupied Richmond, and were received as deliverers, for the flight of the Confederate Army and the Confederate authorities had left the people without protection. Mr. Davis and his cabinet had taken the train for Danville; the Legislature and Governor of Virginia had fled to Lynchburg in a canal boat on the James River Canal; and citizens who had not been able to find a place on the crowded cars, or in the vehicles pouring in steady streams over the country roads, leading from the city, were in a state of helpless fright. Established organisations, military and political, had collapsed, and society was resolved into its original elements.

In accordance with previous orders, fire had been set by the fleeing Confederates to the public ware houses, and from these the flames had extended to private buildings. Nine naval vessels lying in the James River were blown up; the arsenal was fired, and the air was filled with the sound of exploding shells. In all, seven hundred buildings disappeared before the advancing flames. Unhappy Richmond was given over to riot and drunkenness. An eye-witness describes the appearance of a crowd of leaping, shouting demons in parti-coloured clothes, with heads half-shaved; they were the convicts from the penitentiary, who overcame their guards, set fire to the prison, and made their escape into the streets. Plunder was so abundant that the mob was for the moment satisfied, and scattered in various directions with its spoils. Through streets filled with rejoicing negroes, General Weitzel's troops marched into Richmond, restoring order and saving the people from the starvation that threatened them, by a generous distribution of army rations. All were destitute, and among those receiving the relief a few days later was Gen. Robert E. Lee and his staff.

Meanwhile Grant's troops were following the wild flight of Lee's army toward Danville, and following it without rest or refreshment by day and by night. Lee hoped to join Johnston at Danville with what was left of his broken army. The movement was first to Amelia Court-House, thence to Burkesville Junction, where the railroads from Richmond and Petersburg unite. At Amelia Court-House Lee expected to find supplies, but they were not there, and he was detained twenty-four hours in gathering food for his famishing men from the farms near by.

This gave Sheridan an opportunity to head off the fleeing enemy at Burkesville. The pursuing army was divided into three parts, Sheridan leading the advance, Meade following him, and Ord bringing up the rear. On the evening of April 4th two soldiers in rebel uniform were brought in as prisoners and taken to Grant, who was then with Ord's command. One of them took from his mouth a quid of tobacco, and from that a small pellet of tinfoil, containing a tissue note from Sheridan to Grant, asking him to come at once to his headquarters. The men bringing the note had come straight through the enemy's line to save distance. Grant was obliged to make a detour of thirty miles; and did not reach Sheridan until about midnight. Then he was informed that Meade had given orders to move on Lee's right flank and cover Richmond. This movement, Sheridan thought, would enable Lee to escape toward Johnston; he wished to move on the left flank, interposing between Lee and the road south, leaving Richmond to take care of itself, and pressing Lee on his left. Grant coincided with this view, and wrote out an order directing the whole force to move on the left flank the next morning at four o'clock.

On April 5th, Grant wrote Sherman:

"Sheridan is up with Lee and reports all that is left, horse, foot, and dragoons, at twenty thousand men, much demoralized. We hope to reduce this number one-half. I shall push on to Burkesville; and if a stand is made at Danville, will in a few days go there. If you can do so, push on from where you are, and let us see if we cannot finish the job of Lee and Johnston's armies."

After a running fight of fourteen miles with the whole Army of the Potomac in pursuit, Lee was brought to bay at Sailor's Creek. Here followed a series of battles, with a loss to the Confederates of 8000 more prisoners and a large part of their precious trains. Ewell's whole force surrendered. Despatches were exchanged with Washington:

Sheridan: " If the thing is pressed, I think Lee will surrender."

Lincoln: " Let the thing be pressed."

During April 6th and 7th, the pursuit was continued with unabated vigour. Immense quantities of property were abandoned and destroyed by Lee as he fled.

"The scene," wrote General Mahone, "beggars description,— hurrying teamsters with their teams and dangling traces (no wagons), retreating infantry without guns, many without hats; a harmless mob, with the massive columns of the enemy moving orderly on. At this spectacle General Lee straightened himself in his saddle, and looking more the soldier than ever, exclaimed as if talking to himself, ' My God! has the army dissolved?' "

The Confederate losses during the week numbered 19,735 men, and Grant had lost in that time 7292. The Army of Northern Virginia had not only been defeated, but destroyed, and General Grant resolved that it was his duty to relieve himself from the responsibility for a further and useless loss of life. He arrived at Farmville a few miles west of Sailor's Creek, Virginia, on April 7th, and established his headquarters on the broad piazza of a village tavern. As he sat there, the Sixth Corps marched past, hastening to re-enforce a hard-pressed detachment of cavalry across the Appomattox. The air was filled with the notes of victory. Bands played, men shouted as they marched, flung their muskets into the air, catching them as they fell, improvised torches and lighted them at the bonfires lining their path. In every possible way they sought to testify to their joy that their struggles and trials had not been in vain; that their confidence in their leader had not been misplaced.

Grim and silent sat the conqueror; in the hour of victory his thought was not of himself but of his country; not how he might win honours the soldier covets, but how he might so gather the fruits of success as to unite in the bonds of brotherhood the States now " dissevered, discordant, belligerent."

A little after nightfall a flag of truce appeared under torchlight in front of Mahone's line, bearing this note to General Lee:

HEADQUARTERS ARMIES OF THE UNITED STATES,
5 P.M. April 7, 1865.

GENERAL R. E. LEE, Commanding Confederate States Army.

GENERAL: The results of the last week must convince you of the hopelessness of further resistance on the part of the Army of Northern Virginia in this struggle. I feel that it is so, and regard it as my duty to shift from myself the responsibility of any further effusion of blood, by asking of you the surrender of that portion of the Confederate States Army known as the Army of Northern Virginia.

Very respectfully, your obedient servant,
U. S. GRANT,
Lieutenant-General Commanding Armies of the United States.

Lee had already been informed by a number of his principal officers that further resistance was hopeless, and that negotiations should be opened for surrender. But he wrote in reply on the night of the 7th:

"GENERAL: I received your note of this day. Though not entertaining the opinion you express on the hopelessness of further resistance, on the part of the Army of Northern Virginia, I reciprocate your desire to avoid useless effusion of blood and, therefore, before considering your proposition, ask the terms you will offer on condition of its surrender."

Grant was still at Farmville, when this note was handed to him early on the morning of April 8th. He had slept the night before in the room just vacated by Lee. In reply to Lee he wrote a note, in which he said:

"*Peace* being my great desire, there is but one condition I would insist upon, namely, that the men and officers surrendered shall be disqualified for taking up arms again against the Government of the United States until properly exchanged."

In this letter Grant proposed a meeting to arrange terms. Meanwhile the pursuit was resumed; the rear-guard of the enemy was skirmished with; twenty-five pieces of artillery and a hospital train were captured, and four trains of cars, loaded with supplies for Lee's army, were taken on the railroad at Appomattox Station.

It is a curious fact that both Lee and Grant were suffering from illness at the time of the negotiation; Lee from an attack of rheumatism and Grant from a severe sick headache brought on by fatigue and want of sleep and nourishment. Though accustomed to ride from breakfast until two o'clock the next morning without food, and subjected much of the time to violent exertions, in this case his efforts had proved too much for him. He bathed his face in hot water, applied mustard plasters, and was lying on a sofa trying to get some rest, when he received a further note, dated April 8th, in which Lee said:

"I received at a late hour your note of to-day. In mine of yesterday I did not propose to surrender the Army of Northern Virginia, but asked the terms of your proposition. To be frank, I do not think the emergency has arisen to call for the surrender of this army, but as the restoration of peace should be the sole object of all, I desire to know whether your proposals would lead to that end. I cannot, therefore, meet you with a view to the surrender of the Army of Northern Virginia; but, as far as your proposal may affect the Confederate States' forces under my command and tend to the restoration of peace, I should be pleased to meet you at 10 A.M. to-morrow on the old stage road to Richmond, between the picket lines of the two armies."

Early the next morning General Grant replied:

"I have no authority to treat on the subject of peace; the meeting proposed for 10 A.M. to-day could lead to no good. I will state, however, General, that I am equally anxious for peace with yourself, and the whole North entertains the same feeling. The terms upon which peace can be had are well understood. By the South laying down their arms they will hasten that most desirable event, save thousands of human lives, and hundreds of millions of property not yet destroyed. Seriously hoping that all our difficulties may be settled without the loss of another life, I subscribe myself," etc.

Lee still had hopes. Supposing that there was nothing but cavalry in his rear, he endeavoured to break through, but found the cavalry supported by the infantry of Ord and Griffin, who had marched thirty miles during the day and night. General Gordon sent word: "Tell General Lee I have fought my corps to a frazzle, and I fear I can do nothing unless I am heavily supported by Longstreet's corps."

"When I bore the message back to General Lee," reports General Venable, of his staff, "he said, 'Then there is nothing left me but to go and see General Grant, and I would rather die a thousand deaths.'" General Grant was on his way to join Sheridan at Appomattox when he received the following from Lee, dated April 8th:

"GENERAL: I received your note of this morning on the picket line, whither I had come to meet you and ascertain definitely what terms were embraced in your proposal of yesterday with reference to the surrender of this army. I now ask an interview, in accordance with the offer contained in your letter of yesterday, for that purpose."

Sitting by the wayside, Grant immediately wrote in reply:

"Your note of this date is but this moment (11.50 A.M.) received, in consequence of my having passed from the Richmond and Lynchburg roads to the Farmville and Lynchburg roads. I am at this writing about four miles west of Walker's Church, and will push forward to the front for the purpose of meeting you. Notice sent to me on this road where you wish the interview to take place, will meet me."

The interview was held at Appomattox Court-House; the result is set forth in the following correspondence:

APPOMATTOX COURT-HOUSE, VIRGINIA,
April 9, 1865.

GENERAL: In accordance with the substance of my letter to you of the 8th instant, I propose to receive the surrender of the Army of Northern Virginia on the following terms, to wit: Rolls of all the officers and men to be made in duplicate, one copy to be given to an officer to be designated by me, the other to be retained by such officer or officers as you may designate. The officers to give their individual paroles not to take up arms against the government of the United States until properly exchanged; and each company or regimental commander to sign a like parole for the men of their commands. The arms, artillery, and public property to be parked and stacked, and turned over to the officers appointed by me to receive them. This will not embrace the side-arms of the officers, nor their private horses or baggage. This done, each officer and man will be allowed to return to his home, not to be disturbed by the United States authority so long as they observe their paroles and the laws in force where they may reside.

U. S. GRANT, *Lieutenant-General.*

General R. E. LEE.

HEADQUARTERS ARMY OF NORTHERN VIRGINIA,
April 9, 1865.

GENERAL: I have received your letter of this date containing the terms of the surrender of the Army of Northern Virginia as proposed by you. As they are substantially the same as those expressed in your letter of the 8th instant, they are accepted. I will proceed to designate the proper officers to carry the stipulation into effect.

R. E. LEE, *General.*

Lieutenant-General U. S. GRANT.

The scene of the actual surrender was a two-story brick house on the outskirts of the little village of Appomattox, occupied by Wilmer McLean. Lee was accompanied thither by General Babcock, of Grant's staff, who carried to him his General's letter consenting to an interview. Grant on his arrival entered the house, where he found Lee, who had the shorter road to travel, waiting for him. He was sitting in a little room on the left of the broad hall running through the middle of the house, in company with Colonel Marshall of his staff, and Sheridan and Ord were waiting in the yard in front of the house. Grant entered into pleasant conversation with Lee concerning his recollections of the Mexican War, and the prospects of peace. Finally, the object of their meeting was suggested by Lee, who seemed anxious to confine himself as much as possible to the purpose of the interview.

Calling for his manifold order-book, General Grant wrote out the terms of surrender. As he wrote his eye fell on the handsome sword worn by General Lee, and he added the clause excluding the side-arms of the officers, and their private horses or baggage from the property to be surrendered. Wiping and adjusting his spectacles, General Lee carefully read the draft of the letter until he came to the clause concerning the property of officers, when his countenance lighted up, and, finishing the letter, he said with some warmth: "This will have a very happy effect upon my army."

Asked whether he had any suggestions to make, Lee called attention to the fact that his cavalrymen and artillerymen owned their own horses, and inquired whether they would be permitted to retain them. Grant responded that the terms of surrender did not admit of this, to which General Lee, after examining the paper again, assented. Then, without waiting for a direct request, General Grant said that he would not change the terms as written, but would instruct the officers appointed to receive the paroles to let all the men, who claimed to own a horse or a mule, take the animals home with them to work their little farms.

General Lee responded: "This will have the best possible effect upon the men. It will be very gratifying, and will do much towards conciliating our people."

Copies of the letters of surrender were then made by Colonel Marshall, who was a grandson of the chief justice of that name, and by Col. Ely S. Parker, of General Grant's staff, who was a full-blooded Indian, a descendant of Red Jacket, and through him the inheritor of the position of Chief of the Six Nations. Lee next asked that he should be supplied with rations for his famishing men, who for several days had had nothing to eat but a little parched corn. This request, which had been made in a whispered conversation between the two chiefs, was promptly granted.

Calling his officers about him, General Grant said, as Gen. George H. Sharpe of his staff reports, " You go on to the Twenty-fourth, and you to the Fifth," and so on, naming the corps, " and ask every man who has three rations to turn over two of them. Go to the commissaries, go to the quartermasters; General Lee's army is on the point of starvation!" And thus twenty-five thousand rations were carried to the Army of Northern Virginia.

The Army of the Potomac had, at this time, so nearly exhausted its own supplies that it could not have followed Lee another day, but would have been compelled to fall back on Danville to open communication with its rear, if the surrender had been further delayed.

During the interview, the Union officers were presented to Lee, who had known some of them in former days. They sought to be as conversational and pleasant as possible, but their advances were received with cold formality, General Lee shaking hands and conversing with only one of them, General Williams, who was his adjutant when Lee was Superintendent at West Point before the war. Who could fail to be gracious to gentle-hearted Seth Williams?

The contrast between the two chief actors in this historical scene at Appomattox was striking and significant. Lee was Grant's senior by thirteen years, and was graduated from the Military Academy fourteen years before him. His entire training had been in the military service, and he represented the exclusive element of the old army, who considered that deportment was as essential to a military character as a uniform. His dignity and reserve well became his handsome presence, and he looked every inch the soldier.

Grant, who was thoroughly democratic in all his ideas and ways, was dressed on this occasion in a plain and well-worn uniform, and wore an enlisted man's overcoat covered with the dust of travel. Having no sword, he felt it necessary to explain that he seldom wore one. He had found, like many other officers, that it was a useless weapon and a serious encumbrance in riding long distances by day and night. The triple stars shining upon his shoulders were all that indicated his rank, and he looked more like a Missouri farmer than the general-in-chief of a great army, and the ablest and most successful of living soldiers.

Grant represented the principles of equality and human brotherhood that make America what she is; Lee was the type of a departing era, destined henceforth to take its place with the expiring traditions of royal and aristocratic pretension. But no Bayard of romance could have borne himself with more knightly consideration for a fallen foe than did the plain man, whose action, not his dress, so well became him on an occasion giving such opportunity for the display of the littleness and self-assertion of a small mind, or the greatness and self-forgetfulness of a noble soul.

The thought uppermost with General Grant seemed to be sympathy for the hard fortune of his fellow-soldier. So far as concerned General Lee, everything was forgotten except that he was an alumnus of the same institution; a comrade of the same battlefields in distant Mexico. Most fortunate for the country was it that this spirit of comradeship was the controlling influence in this scene so full of the possibilities of bitterness. How different might have been the result, had Lee's surrender been received by some spectacular general, playing to the galleries, and anxious to add the sting of humiliation to the pangs of defeat!

The spirit that controlled General Grant determined the action of those about him. Finding that his soldiers were preparing to celebrate their victory, he gave orders that no salutes should be fired, and as soon as the surrender was completed the two armies were mingling together in friendly intercourse. Among the officers old comrades exchanged recollections of their experiences together before the war, or discussed the battles in which they had borne a gallant part as foes seeking each others' destruction.

H. J. Hunt, Grant's Chief of Artillery, who had at West Point instructed in artillery Colonel Alexander of the Confederate service, sought him out, and, in the course of their conversation pleasantly chaffed him because he had not followed the maxims of his preceptor in handling his guns at Gettysburg. Among the enlisted men the "Yanks" and the "Johnny Rebs," who, in spite of war, had been accustomed to friendly interchanges between the picket lines, came together in still closer fellowship as fellow-countrymen once more.

Everybody was happy; even the surrendered Confederates, who were receiving the first full meal they had had in many days, were in a measure consoled for the bitterness of their defeat by the reflection that their struggles were over, and that they could now return in peace to their homes and families.

The wave of rejoicing that swept over the country when the news of Lee's surrender was carried with the swiftness of the lightning's flash to every city and hamlet, will never be forgotten by those who witnessed it. Bells were pealing, bonfires blazing, orators declaiming, and from many a quiet fireside that night went up the prayer of thanksgiving that the days of strife and bloodshed were at last at an end; and that Rachel would be called upon no more to mourn for her children.

Apparently the least moved of all the actors in that scene was the General-in-Chief. Gen. Horace Porter, of his staff, to whose description of the surrender in the *Battles and Leaders of the Civil War* I am much indebted, tells us that when Grant returned to his camp that night, his first words were addressed to Gen. Rufus Ingalls, to whose genius as a quartermaster he owed so much:

> "'Ingalls, do you remember that old white mule that so-and-so used to ride when we were in the City of Mexico?' 'Why perfectly,' said Ingalls, who was just then in a mood to remember the exact number of hairs in the mule's tail if it would have helped to make matters agreeable. And then the General-in-Chief went on to recall the antics played by that animal during an excursion to Popocatapetl. It was not until after supper that he said much about the surrender, when he talked freely of his entire belief that the rest of the rebel commanders would follow Lee's example, and that we should have but a little more fighting even of a partisan nature. He then surprised us by announcing his intention of starting to Washington early the next morning."

The proposed visit to Washington was delayed until the succeeding day. Grant and Lee had another interview with reference to the details of the surrender, and Grant was visited by Gen. Cadmus M. Wilcox, who had been his groomsman when he was married, by Longstreet, who had been at his wedding, and by scores of his late antagonists who had called to pay their respects, and were received with great cordiality.

CHAPTER XVIII.

COLLAPSE OF THE CONFEDERACY—MUSTERING OUT.

APRIL–MAY, 1865.

T Appomattox ended what must be admitted to be one of the most remarkable campaigns in history, when we consider the magnitude of the forces engaged, the skill with which they were handled for offence and defence, and the topographical difficulties to be overcome. To move 150,000 men in such a country, in constant contact with an enemy, was in itself no small feat of arms. Advancing from base to base, with flanks exposed, and extending his line of communication with each advance, Grant had kept his enemy on the move from one strongly intrenched position to another, holding him in place until he was himself ready to attack, and never giving him the advantage of the initiative. He had defended Washington, and succoured Sherman and Sheridan, not by weakening his own army, but by keeping that of Lee so constantly occupied that, in spite of its interior lines

and intrenched positions, it finally fell exhausted—
"fought to a frazzle."

"More scientific methods might have accomplished the same result, with less loss of life," do I hear some one say? Had not every method been tried in the same field without any result, except to temporarily change the relative positions of the two armies? From the time he crossed the Rapidan, May 4, 1864, to the surrender of Appomattox, April 9, 1865, Grant had lost 124,390 men in killed, wounded, and missing. These losses, with the exception of about one thousand men, were incurred in eight months of active campaigning, nothing being attempted during the three winter months of 1864-65. From the time McClellan opened the siege of Yorktown, April 5, 1862, until Grant assumed command in Virginia two years later, the same period of time had been devoted to active field work, long intervals of inaction occurring between the several campaigns. McClellan, Pope, Burnside, Hooker, and Meade had each essayed in the same field the work Grant carried to a triumphant conclusion, and together they had lost 139,751 men without accomplishing it.

The following figures are given on the authority of the Board of Publication of the Official Records of the Rebellion:

McClellan, April 5–August 8, 1862	24,448
Pope, June 26–September 2, 1862	16,955
McClellan, September 3–November 14, 1862	28,577
Burnside, November 15, 1862–January 25, 1863	13,214
Hooker, January 26–June 27, 1863	25,027
Meade, June 28, 1863–May 4, 1864	31,530
Grand aggregate	139,751

*Grant's combined armies (Potomac and James) May 5,
1864–April 9, 1865:*

May 5–June 24—Army of the Potomac, Rapidan to James,	54,926
May 5–June 14—Army of the James, south of James River,	6,215
June 15–July 31—Army Potomac and Army James.......	22,936
August 1–December 31—Army Potomac and Army James..	24,621
January 1–April 9—Army of the Potomac, Army of the James and Sheridan's Cavalry............................	15,692
Grand aggregate............................	124,390

These figures will appear less formidable, if we recall the fact that in the single battle of Königgrätz, or Sadowa, the Austrians, in July, 1866, lost 40,000 out of a total force of 220,000, and in the campaign of two months, 84,051, of which total, 10,994 were killed and 29,300 wounded. During the Franco-German war, the Germans lost 17,000 of the 60,000 men they carried into battle at Vionville, or Mars la Tour—a larger relative loss than that experienced by Grant in any one of his Virginia battles, and nearly equalling, in the actual total, his loss in the bloody battle of the Wilderness.

The victories of Antietam and Gettysburg, important as they were, had been gained by armies in retreat and acting on the defensive on Northern soil. Aside from their grand results in staying the progress of Confederate invasion, they brought the Union no nearer to final victory. When Grant took command, the Army of the Potomac was within thirty miles of the original battlefield of Bull Run, and had been resting there for five months after unsucccessfully attempting at Mine Run substantially the same movement as the one that led to the battle of the Wilderness. There was nothing to indicate that the contest might not continue indefinitely; Richmond had not been captured, and the Army of Northern Virginia was relatively stronger than it was when McClellan advanced against it on the Yorktown Peninsula. Grant, with a smaller loss in battle, had pulverised the Confederacy.

When other losses are taken into account, the contrast between Grant's campaign in Virginia and those preceding it becomes still more striking. The statistics of the war show that for every man killed by the missiles of the enemy, two died of disease; and the discharges from various causes, the resignations and desertions, taken together, exceed by one-half the total of wounded and missing.*

Grant understood perfectly the significance of these facts. He knew that where he lost two men in action within a given time he lost three from other casualties, and that a campaign of rapidly succeeding engagements that hastened the end, was economical in men as well as in treasure. No criticism upon Grant is more unjust than the one that accused him of being a " butcher." Not only did he accomplish great results, but, taking everything into the account, he was far more saving of his men than were those who had preceded him in the same field, and who expended men in double ratio, without bringing the war one step nearer to its end.

* These are figures reported in *Phisterer's Statistical Record*. Killed in battle and died of wounds, 93,443; died of disease, 186,216; wounded in action, 280,040; missing and captured, 184,791; discharged for disability, 285, 245; honourably discharged 174, 578; dishonourably discharged, 5,398; resigned, 22,281; deserted, 189,045.

When Grant was promoted to the supreme command, the Confederates held 800,000 square miles of territory, and they had 400,000 men on their muster rolls. Even the territory previously secured by the Union troops in the Southern States was held by no certain tenure; a large force was constantly occupied in guarding it and protecting the communications of the armies in the field from the attack of enterprising guerillas and raiding cavalry.

Within one year all of this immense territory, thanks to General Grant's policy of concentration and persistent fighting, had come under the control of the Government at Washington. The last Confederate soldier had passed through the Caudine Forks as a prisoner of war. Thus was accomplished the result which foreign observers had from the first said was impossible.

The chief actor in these events had been Lieut.-Gen. Ulysses S. Grant, and the important part he had played in bringing about the grand result was universally recognised. In the North he was almost worshipped as the saviour of the Union, and in the South he was remembered as the generous conqueror, who, in the hour of triumph, had not forgotten that the vanquished were his fellow-countrymen. To him, more than to any other man, was due the fact that immediately upon the close of the war, a spirit of affiliation sprang up between the two armies which has no parallel in the world's history.

Following the surrender at Appomattox, events moved swiftly to the end. After leaving Richmond on April 3, 1865, Jefferson Davis proceeded to Danville with the principal officers and archives of his government, and made a show of re-establishing his capital there. On April 5th he issued a proclamation to the Southern people, declaring that Virginia would " be held and defended, and no peace ever made with the infamous invaders of her soil." The news of Lee's surrender immediately followed, and the broken remains of the Richmond government were again in full flight to Greensboro', North Carolina.

There was no certainty at this time that General Johnston would surrender. Before leaving City Point, Grant had sent Sherman information of the surrender of Lee, and authorised him to give the same terms to Johnston. During Sherman's visit to Grant at City Point, on March 29th, arrangements had been made for a movement from Goldsboro' northwards, on April 10th. Receiving news on April 6th that Lee was retreating southwards and was expecting to make a stand at Danville, Virginia, Sherman set his troops in motion as speedily as possible on the march for that place. At Smithfield, North Carolina, half-way between Goldsboro' and Raleigh, where he arrived on April 11, 1865, he learned that Johnston, whom he had expected to find there, had retreated to Raleigh, and that Lee's army had surrendered. Pushing on to Raleigh, twenty-seven miles away, he arrived there Thursday, April 13th, and the next day received a letter from Johnston opening negotiations for surrender. These negotiations resulted in a written agreement on April 18, 1865, General Johnston availing himself of the opportunity meanwhile to consult with Jefferson Davis and his Cabinet.

President Lincoln had visited City Point three weeks before; reviewed, amid wild enthusiasm, the troops marching in pursuit of Lee's army; visited the captured cities of Petersburg and Richmond, and consulted with Grant and Sherman as to terms of surrender. Sherman had reason to suppose that he understood the policy of the Administration, and he endeavoured to carry it out in good faith. But, when his agreement with Johnston reached the capital, Lincoln was no longer there to receive it. He had fallen a victim to the assassin on April 14th, and Andrew Johnson was President, with Secretary Stanton as his viceregent. Sherman's agreement with Johnston was sharply disapproved of, and he was placed before the country in a most unwelcome light.

Anxious to settle the difficulty with the least friction, and with a considerate regard for the feelings of his friend and subordinate, Grant resolved to carry the Government's disapproval of Sherman's convention to Raleigh in person. He arrived at Raleigh on the evening of April 24th, and instructed Sherman to give Johnston the forty-eight hours' notice, required by the terms of the truce agreed upon with him, and then to proceed to attack or follow him without delay. Johnston was notified of the termination of the truce, and at the same time his surrender was demanded on the terms granted to General Lee. This resulted in another interview with General Johnston, and the surrender of his army on April 26, 1865, upon the terms and conditions previously granted to Lee. Grant's nice regard for the feelings of Sherman was further shown in his despatch to Washington, saying, " Johnston has surrendered to Sherman," ignoring his own agency in the matter.

Jefferson Davis had not waited to learn the result of Johnston's negotiations with Sherman. With a few followers belonging to the civil government at Richmond, and a small escort of troops, he pursued his flight southward, intending to continue it beyond the Mississippi River, and gather there the scattered wrecks of the Confederacy to make another stand for freedom—and slavery. But the soldiers had had quite enough of fighting, if the civilians had not. Gradually Davis's military escort fell away from him, and with them the faithful few who had determined to follow his fortunes. He now changed his plans, and decided to fly to Florida, and there take a sailing-vessel for Texas. But the new Administration at Washington had resolved to treat him as a felon, and the "hue and cry" was out. On May 10, 1865, he was surprised by Union cavalry, in the grey of the morning, in his camp in the depths of a pine forest near Irwinsville, Georgia, taken to Fort Monroe, and held a prisoner there for two years.

Thus disappeared the hope of the Confederacy; its last flickering flame dying out when its chief yielded to the inevitable demand of fate. The result was hastened by the vigorous action of the cavalry forces under Gen. J. H. Wilson, who, as he swept in a masterly march across the States of Alabama and Florida, with twelve thousand mounted men, closed in finally on the fleeing representatives of the Richmond government, and made impossible Davis's plan of renewing the contest beyond the Mississippi River.

On May 4, 1865, Gen. Richard Taylor surrendered to General Canby all the Confederate forces east of the Mississippi. Those west of the Mississippi were surrendered, May 26th, by Gen. Kirby Smith. There was, then, a general " round up " of all the Confederate forces, including the detached commands of " Sam Jones," " Jeff Thompson," and others. General Canby completed his operations at Mobile previous to the surrender, and secured possession of that city on the morning of April 3d. The war was over, though there were encounters at different points up to May 13th, when some troops in distant Texas had a small engagement.

Without waiting to visit Richmond or to celebrate his great triumph, General Grant, on the second day after Lee's surrender, had hastened to Washington, to consult with the authorities there, and to arrange for the cessation of recruiting, and the reduction of the expenses of the Government, amounting at that time to four millions of dollars a day. He arrived in Washington on April 12, 1865, and immediately opened communication with his subordinate commanders in regard to the change of situation resulting from the surrender of Lee.

By the 14th of the month, the General was sufficiently at leisure to plan a visit, with Mrs. Grant, to their children who were attending school at Burlington, New Jersey. That day he attended the regular Cabinet meeting at the Executive mansion, where the subject of governing the Southern States was discussed.

The President and Mrs. Lincoln had accepted an invitation to attend Ford's Theatre that night, and General and Mrs. Grant were invited to accompany them, but declined the invitation, and started by the evening train for Burlington. At the Broad Street Ferry in Philadelphia General Grant was handed despatches informing him of the assassination of the President, and requesting his immediate presence in Washington. He returned without delay by special train, and found the city, which had been illuminated thirty-six hours before in honour of his victory, now shrouded in mourning. His own heart was filled with grief, for he knew that President Lincoln's disposition was in accord with his own generous purposes towards the South, and he distrusted his successor in office, Mr. Johnson, who had shown much bitterness of feeling towards the Southern people in speeches and conversation. "I felt," he said, "that reconstruction had been set back, no telling how far." Booth's plot included the assassination of Grant, as the General learned from an anonymous letter sent by a repentant conspirator, who followed him to Philadelphia, but could not reach him because the door of his private car was locked.

The promptness and completeness of Grant's work

in closing up the war was shown by a reduction of 93 per cent. in the military budget during a single year; or, from $516,240,131 to $33,814,461. The Union Army, at the time of Lee's surrender, numbered one million men, including all on the rolls, with 602,598 present for duty. This force was distributed through twenty-six armies and departments, from Maine to California. Four days after the surrender of Lee, notice was given that all drafting and recruiting and the purchase of supplies would be stopped. Within less than six months from that time most of the officers and men had received their discharge and were on the way to their homes.

Bearing with them the record of honourable service, and having had the advantage of military training, with its ideas of discipline and order, the discharged veterans were speedily absorbed into the great mass of population, and gave to industrial, commercial, and professional enterprises in all parts of the country a new impetus by their zeal and energy. If they were fond of recalling the days when they fought under Grant, they never forgot that they were now citizens devoted to the pursuits of peace. Their conduct completely answered the fears of those at home and abroad, who had prophesied evil to the Republic because of the transformation of so large a proportion of its citizens into soldiers for the time being. They furnished the nation with presidents, with cabinet officers, with judges of the Supreme Court, and other judicial officers. The present Chief Magistrate of the Republic, McKinley, is one who as a youth bore a musket in the ranks. In all departments of public administration, in the Federal and State governments, in Congress and State legislatures, the discharged soldiers were found performing their duty in loyal recognition of the supremacy of the civil over the military authority. In the spirit of their great leader they banished all bitterness from their hearts, and received their old antagonists, wherever they met them, with fraternity and good-will, and with the respect which the true soldier never fails to accord to those who have had a like experience of the trials and dangers, the comradeship and good-fellowship of the field and the camp.

The experience of the Southern soldiers was not unlike this. They, too, rapidly dispersed to their homes, carrying with them the story of generous treatment. Those who were held as prisoners of war (98,802) were furnished with transportation at the expense of the Federal Government. All but a few thousand of these were captured after General Grant took command as Lieutenant-General. In addition, 174,223 Confederate officers and men surrendered, and were paroled in the closing days of the war. One thousand six hundred and eighty-six cannon and nearly one hundred thousand small arms were part of the spoils of victory.

Before the curtain finally fell upon the great drama of the war the armies of Grant and Sherman, who had conquered a glorious peace, passed in review at Washington before the President of the United States, and the Lieutenant-General, in front of the executive mansion, May 23 and 24, 1865.

Fine weather favoured this spectacle, and as the veterans, two hundred thousand strong, marched down Pennsylvania Avenue from the Capitol to the White House, to the sound of martial music, and carrying their battle-rent flags, spectators, who had gathered at Washington from all parts of the Union, filled the windows and occupied the streets along the line of the march, rending the air with their joyous shouts.

The roads were good; the troops, under the prospect of release from hard toil and the restraints of service, were in high spirits; the columns marched well; the streets were gay with colours and animated with life, and the children of the schools, in blue and white, greeted the returned heroes of the procession with inspiring songs and pretty ceremonies. Banners and mottoes of praise decorated the houses. Flowers were flung from every direction upon the column; they decorated the torn flags, the bayonets which had so often been hurried to the murderous charge; and the rumbling field-pieces from whose black muzzles death had so often hurtled. Bands flooded the avenue with music, the horses pranced, ambulances rattled, the artillery rumbled and clanged on heavy wheels, the drums ruffled salutes, and the sabres and bayonets flashed in the sunlight.

It was a wonderful display of martial strength; grand as a spectacle; solemn in its significance; telling the story of peace conquered through war; of a new union of the States, cemented with the blood of patriotism and self-sacrifice. The bronzed faces testified to the exposure and hardships of the campaign; the thinned ranks and the tattered ensigns were eloquent with their story of battles lost and victories won. Yet in the hour of triumph and rejoicing many hearts grew heavy as they thought of those who would no more march with the Grand Army of the Republic; whose glorious youth had been offered as a willing sacrifice to the cause of their country.

The soldiers reviewed at Washington had marched to the Capital from their camps in Virginia and North Carolina; the men of Sherman's army having made a circuit of nearly a thousand miles. All had been mustered out of the service before the review, and after it they were distributed to fifty depots throughout the country, where they received their final pay, and scattered to their homes. Thus, within two months, 800,963 men in arms were released from military restraint and returned to civil life, without any one of them committing an act of lawlessness to disgrace his uniform.

General Sheridan was not present at the grand review, having been sent with one hundred thousand men into Texas to prevent the possibility of the smouldering embers of the Rebellion flaming up there, and more especially to act as an army of observation along the Rio Grande frontier. Taking advantage of our preoccupation with war, the Austrian Grand Duke, Maximilian, aided by the Emperor Napoleon III., had endeavoured to transform Mexico into a foreign empire. This was regarded as a menace to the United States, and General Grant held that the advent of Maximilian to the pretended throne of Mexico, was a part of the Rebellion; and that his immediate expulsion should be a part of its history.

Re-enforced by this display of strength on the frontier, our Department of State succeeded in securing an agreement for the withdrawal of the French troops under Marshal Bazaine. Deprived of their support, the empire of Maximilian fell into ruins, and the amiable but misguided young Archduke answered with his life for his error in defying the traditions of American independence of European control. In August, 1865, the order was given to muster out the troops under Sheridan, and they, too, were returned to their homes; greatly to their satisfaction, for there had been much complaint because of the prolongation of the service of those who enlisted for the war only.

CHAPTER XIX.

CHIEF CITIZEN OF THE REPUBLIC—HIS PERPLEXI-
TIES—SECRETARY OF WAR.

1865-1868.

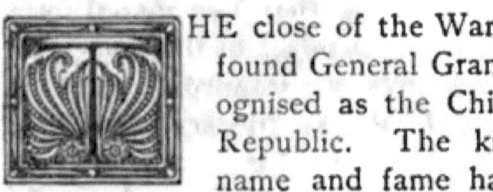THE close of the War of the Rebellion found General Grant universally recognised as the Chief Citizen of the Republic. The knowledge of his name and fame had reached every household, North and South, and his voice was more potent in public affairs than that of any living American. It was a dangerous eminence; subjecting him to the jealousies of some, to the intrigue and flattery of others, who sought to use his great reputation to promote political or personal ends.

Among the chief conspirators against his peace was Andrew Johnson, who had succeeded to the Presidency on the death of Lincoln. Commencing his life at the South as a tailor's ignorant apprentice, who had not even learned to read and write until he was nearly of age, Johnson was held in contempt by the leaders of public opinion in his own section.

Their hostility to him as a "poor white" was intensified by the fact that he had taken an active part in sustaining the Government during the war. He displayed an equal bitterness of spirit in return, saying, while Vice-President, in a speech denouncing the Southern Rebellion, "Show me who have been engaged in these conspiracies, and, were I President of the United States, by the Eternal God, I would execute them."

The liberality of General Grant's terms at Appomattox did not meet with universal approval. Mr. Johnson lodged a formal protest against them with President Lincoln, declaring that Lee should have been seized and confined, pending instructions from Washington. There was an influential party in Congress and throughout the country, who held with the Vice-President that "treason should be made odious." They reasoned that at least the leaders of the South should be subjected to punishment.

An attempt was made to try Jefferson Davis for treason. Mrs. Davis appealed to Grant, who could not interfere if he wished to do so, as Davis was not included in the surrender at Appomattox. He did, however, use his influence to mitigate the hardships of his imprisonment. But when Gen. Robert E. Lee applied to him for protection against civil prosecution, his soldierly sense of honour was touched. He flamed up with an indignation he rarely displayed, declaring that if the terms he had given Lee and his army were not respected, he would resign his commission and appeal to the country. Scores of other Southern officers, who were included in the terms of his surrender, were also protected.

"When can these men be tried?" asked the President.

"Never," was the answer, "unless they violate their paroles."

And they never were tried; for the stubborn President had encountered a will even stronger than his own, an influence paramount to that of the Chief Magistrate. Many civilians, as well as many soldiers, were saved from imprisonment and confiscation by the interposition of Grant. His generosity awakened a very warm feeling for him in the South, as was shown when in November, 1865, he visited Virginia, North and South Carolina, Georgia, and Tennessee, and reported on the condition of those States, and the feeling of the Southern people.

He declared that the mass of thinking men at the South accepted the situation at that time in good faith, but advised that a military force should be retained there until society was reorganized and a stable civil government secured.

The policy of President Johnson, so far as it revealed itself, seemed to be to strike terror into the hearts of the South by punishing its conspicuous leaders, or at least to compel them to appeal to him for the exercise, on their behalf, of his prerogative of pardon. He proposed to treat the South as a whole with the utmost liberality; at once admitting the States lately in rebellion to a complete control of their own affairs; permitting them to be represented in Congress, and making them in every way as independent of Federal authority as the States which had loyally sustained the Government during the four years of war. He held, moreover, that the work of reconstruction was under the exclusive control of the Executive, and that it was his province to determine who should, and who should not, be suffered to participate in it.

This brought the President into disagreement with the law-makers, who were not willing to concede this extent of authority to the Chief Magistrate; fearing to restore the Southern States to their full right as independent communities, without a guaranty as to their acceptance of the results of the war, and as to their future good behaviour. Various theories concerning the status of the South prevailed, the most extreme being that held by Mr. Sumner and by Mr. Thaddeus Stevens, who urged the doctrine of State suicide, and contended that all that was left of the States lately in insurrection was "men and dirt."

There were differences of opinion in Congress, but the ruling sentiment was in favour of taking entire control of the government of the late Confederated States, where the machinery of civil administration was in a state of collapse and society in chaos. The negroes had ceased to be slaves, but they had not yet become free men, and there was no guaranty that they might not be subjected to some new form of oppression. The South was filled with disbanded soldiers, who were without occupation; universal poverty had followed the long and exhausting war; doubt and distrust prevailed; and the very foundations of co-operation and control in organised society had been shaken. Communities without a recognised leadership, except that which had arrayed the South in hostility to Federal authority, were called upon to settle most perplexing problems as to the new relations between whites and blacks; between the rich whites and the poor whites; between the landowners and the landless; between those who had obtained favour at Washington by their claim of sympathy with Union sentiment, and those who had staked everything upon the destruction of the Union.

The struggle to maintain the Union had been inaugurated on the theory that it was a war to suppress an insurrection against Federal authority; not a war between independent States, which left the vanquished at the mercy of the victor. It logically followed from this theory that when the contest ended, the Southern States were as free to take part in the affairs of the Government that was to judge their default, as if they had never questioned its authority. Mr. Johnson pushed this theory so far as to encourage hopes that the Confederates might regain by the ballot what they had lost by their rash appeal to arms, and with the help of Northern allies secure control of the Government. This, it was believed, involved the repudiation of the debt incurred in the prosecution of the war, or, at least, the recognition of the debt of the Confederacy, as equally binding; the recognition of the Confederate soldiers as having equal rights with the Union soldiers in the payment of pensions, and the payment of the

Southerners for their negroes set free by emancipation. It was further feared that the theory of negro inequality would be pushed to such an extent as to re-establish slavery in some form. As a matter of fact, one Southern State after another passed laws designed to perpetuate the scheme of enforced labour by establishing a system of apprenticeship, more heartless and cruel than slavery had ever been, and lacking the ameliorating features of the " patriarchal institution."

Congress took the alarm, and differences of opinion in the Republican party, which controlled that body by a large majority, were reconciled by a common sentiment of hostility to the Presidential scheme of reconstruction. Southern States had taken advantage of the liberty granted them to elect senators and representatives, and the feeling against the President was heightened by the appearance at the doors of Congress of what were known as " unreconstructed rebels," arrogantly demanding to be admitted, not as a matter of favour, but as a constitutional right.

This resulted in the passage of a series of enactments designed to restrict the power of the President to an extent that was not, in his opinion, and in the opinion of his supporters, justified by the Constitution. These laws were one after another vetoed by the President, and passed over his veto by the necessary two-thirds majority. To secure its own ascendancy, Congress determined not only to hold the Southern States under probation, but to exclude the President practically from all share in the making of laws, and to compel him under his oath of office to execute enactments against which he solemnly protested, as not only inexpedient but unconstitutional.

In spite of himself, Grant was drawn into the controversy between the President and Congress. With the purely political questions he had nothing to do, but he was forced to decide whether he would obey laws imposing upon him specific duties, or suspend them at the behest of the President, who, as the constitutional Commander-in-Chief, was his superior officer. The President made the situation more difficult by seeking to persuade Grant to assume the responsibility for acts he was not willing to order in writing when requested to do so. An ambitious and intriguing politician, Johnson was much more than a match for the single-minded soldier in artfulness and craft. By various subtle methods he sought to entangle the General in his controversies with Congress, to make use of his popularity to aid him in carrying out policies obnoxious to public sentiment, and to protect the President from the consequences of the opposition he had aroused.

To add still further to his embarrassment, Johnson compelled General Grant, by the pressure of earnest personal solicitation, to accompany him on a journey through the Northern States, during which he indulged in the most unseemly assaults upon Congress. Wherever the President went, enthusiastic crowds demanded to see and hear the great soldier who was in his company. Grant presented himself in answer to the calls for him that greeted the Presidential train wherever it stopped, but he refused to speak, partly because he could not, and partly because he wished to keep in seclusion as much as possible. His situation was very uncomfortable; and when a fortunate indisposition enabled him to plead the excuse of illness, he left the uncongenial society of Johnson and his supporters.

Nor was Grant wholly in sympathy with Congress, for they enacted or proposed measures to which he could not give unqualified approval. His report upon the condition of the South had been denounced by the impetuous Senator Sumner as a "white-washing" document, and it excited sharp criticism from others of the dominant party in Congress.

President Johnson, who continued to make a display of good-will toward Grant, was continually seeking to bend him to his purposes. He was not satisfied with the General's policy in dealing with the Southern States through the military arm, for the logic of the situation compelled the soldier to temper his generosity and kindness with discretion, and to maintain a firm control over those disposed to turbulence and discontent, who were described in his annual report for 1866 as a class who "will acknowledge no law but force."

In the midst of partisan and sectional strife, Grant was able to exert an important influence in reconciling differences and softening asperities, for his house in Washington was a Mecca to which pilgrims journeyed from every State in the Union; some to gratify curiosity, and others to pay homage of sincere respect; some to tender advice, and others to ask for it. Republicans and Democrats, the party of the President and the party of Congress, South and North, all took counsel with him. More strictly within the line of his official duty were the difficult questions of military policy or practice referred to him by army officers in the South, and their appeals for support in carrying out measures essential to the preservation of order, in the enforcement of the acts of Congress, and in the protection of their soldiers and the freedmen and Union men from local hostility and violence. "Left in the breach," as Sherman said, "to catch all the kicks and cuffs of a war of races, without the privilege of advising or being consulted beforehand," the lot of the military commander was not a happy one. Like most men disposed to moderation, and incapable of unreasoning partisanship, Grant himself at first failed to secure the full confidence of either party to the bitter controversy which distracted the country, and increased the difficulties of the sufficiently perplexing problem of maintaining order at the South.

Lacking the support of the executive head of the Government, and tied hand and foot by restrictions they could not disregard, our soldiers were compelled to witness scenes peculiarly galling to military ideas of government. Neither life nor property was secure in the States lately in rebellion, where fierce antipathies menaced a war of races; the South was convulsed with dissensions, and those who loved order and peace favoured military control. But to this American traditions and American prejudices were alike opposed, and the conflicts of jurisdiction were constant and vexatious.

In Texas, Union soldiers were shot by citizens, and no grand jury would indict. Negroes were killed in large numbers throughout the South without even an attempt to hold any one responsible for their murder. Citizens who had served faithfully and honourably in the Union Army, and who were living in the South, were prosecuted in the courts for acts done by them under military authority, and judgments were awarded against them by partisan courts and judges. As the President, by a proclamation dated April 2, 1866, had formally declared that "the insurrection" was ended, the military were powerless to help these men, and as they were unable to carry their cases to the United States courts for lack of means, they were despoiled of their property.

All of this was very irritating to the dominant sentiment of the North, which held that negroes and Union men were entitled to special favour, and especially the soldiers of the Army of the Union. The natural disposition of the South to defend the cause of secession and to glorify its heroes was another cause of irritation.

As the measures of reconstruction for the South adopted by Congress were in direct opposition to the wishes of the President, and had been passed over his veto, he refused to be bound by them. It was accordingly determined to limit his control over the Army to an extent which was believed by him and his supporters to trench upon his prerogative as Commander-in-Chief. An Act was passed establishing the grade of general, and on July 25, 1866, Grant received the appointment of this new rank. The unfortunate contest between the President and Congress continued, and in a confidential letter to Sheridan, dated October 12, 1866, Grant said:

> "The former becomes more violent with the opposition he meets with, until now but few people who were loyal to the Government during the Rebellion seem to have any influence with him. None have unless they join in a crusade against Congress and declare their acts, the principal ones, illegal, and, indeed, I much fear that we are fast approaching the time when he will want to declare the body itself illegal, unconstitutional and revolutionary. Commanders in Southern states will have to take great care to see, if the crisis does come, that no armed headway can be made against the Union."

Finding it impossible to mould General Grant to his purposes, the President endeavoured to get rid of him by sending him on a mission to Mexico, and substituting Sherman in command at Washington. Both Grant and Sherman protested against this action. Grant wrote the President, declining to leave the country.

> "Nevertheless, in a day or two he was summoned to a full Cabinet meeting, when his detailed instructions were read to him by the Secretary of State, exactly as if objections and refusals had not been offered; but Grant was now aroused; and before the whole Cabinet he declared his unwillingness to accept the mission. The President also became angered. Turning to the Attorney-General he inquired: 'Mr. Attorney-General, is there any reason why General Grant should not obey my orders? Is he in any way ineligible to this position?' Grant started to his feet at once, and exclaimed: I can

answer that question, Mr. President, without referring to the Attorney-General. I am an American citizen, and eligible to any office to which any American is eligible. I am an officer of the Army, and bound to obey your military orders, but this is a civil office, a purely diplomatic duty which you offer me, and I cannot be compelled to undertake it. Any legal military order you give me I will obey, but this is civil not military; and I decline the duty. No power on earth can compel me to it.' He said not another word. No one replied; and he left the Cabinet Chamber."*

The President still insisted, until Sherman assured him that Grant would not go to Mexico, and told him very plainly that he could not afford to quarrel with Grant at that time. It was finally decided that Sherman should go himself, to cover the President's defeat. The papers were filled with rumours as to the purpose of Sherman's visit to Mexico, but all conjecture was at fault. At this time General Sherman said, in a letter to the author of this biography: " No one will probably ever know why I went along, and no journalist thus far has guessed within a mile." It was long before the secret was revealed.

Congress continued its efforts to curb the Executive, passing, in March, 1867, by large majorities over the President's veto, an act dividing the South into five military districts, and declaring that military rule should be supreme there. The civil courts were superseded by military tribunals, and all civil authorities and State governments were declared provisional and subject to the paramount authority of the United States. This immediately resulted in friction between the President and the military officers who endeavoured to carry out the law, and cre-

* Badeau's *Grant in Peace*, page 53.

ated difficult situations. In dealing with them, Grant showed his usual sound judgment and good sense. As the controversy grew, he found himself more and more in sympathy with the majority in Congress, which returned his confidence.

In the Army Appropriation Bill for 1867-68, passed in February, 1867, Congress further provided that all military orders issued by the President or the Secretary of War should go through the General of the Army, and that he should not be removed, suspended, or relieved from command without the consent of the Senate; orders issued contrary to this provision were declared void; the person issuing them was declared guilty of a misdemeanour, and the officer obeying them was subject to imprisonment from two to twenty years. This was followed by an act increasing the powers of the district commanders, subjecting their acts to the approval of the General of the Army, and to this extent transferring the work of supervising the reconstruction of the Union from the hands of the President, where it belonged, to those of the General-in-Chief. Congress would have gone still further, making Grant even more independent of the President, and substantially a dictator over the Southern States, had not he himself advised against it in the most urgent manner. He had more power than he cared to exercise; much more than he would have exercised had not circumstances compelled, and the law required it.

This situation naturally increased the friction with the President, who did his best to prevent the operation of the law; yet, under the wise administration of Grant, it resulted in greatly improving the condition of the South, in repressing disorder, and securing in greater measure just and impartial rule.

The Secretary of War, Mr. Stanton, who was opposed to the policy of the President, was asked to resign, his removal being subject, under the Tenure of Office Act, to the approval of the Senate. As he declined to yield his office, he was suspended, and Grant was appointed Secretary *pro tem.* He accepted the office under protest, and by agreement with Mr. Stanton, to prevent a less desirable appointment. He entered upon his new duties August 12, 1867, and five days later he was directed by the President to remove Sheridan from his command at New Orleans. His vigorous protest failing to change the purpose of Johnson, he was compelled to issue the order. He took occasion, however, to assure Sheridan of his unalterable confidence in him, and that he had sustained his course publicly, privately, and officially, not from personal feeling or partiality, but because he was right. Other district commanders were suspended under like circumstances, but the changes made no practical difference, as the new appointees were in sympathy with Grant, with the single exception of General Hancock, who soon asked to be relieved, finding that he was powerless to carry out his own views of policy.

Grant remained in the Cabinet of Mr. Johnson until January 13, 1868. He made an excellent Secretary of War, despatching business with great promptness, and with an intelligent knowledge of the necessities of the Army only to be acquired by experience in contact with troops. Decisions were arrived at promptly; papers were not allowed to accumulate; and his thorough knowledge of the routine of the Service enabled him to make important reductions in the Quartermaster's Department and the clerical force; efficiency being the only thing considered, and not favour to individuals. An order was issued, however, directing that where necessary appointments were made, preference should be given, first, to soldiers wounded in the service; second, to honourably discharged soldiers; third, to civilians having families to support.

The new *régime* in the War Office was typified by the substitution of a small bell for the one of ferocious sound, in which Mr. Stanton delighted. "There goes Stanton's bell!" officers were accustomed to exclaim, as its clang sounded through the halls of the War building. Every one was in a tremble of anticipation and alarm; for each vibration told of an irascible bell-ringer, wrought up to the highest pitch of ferocious impatience, and greedy to pounce on some careless or incompetent underling for faults committed or suspected.

Under the new management of the War Office there was courtesy everywhere; in transacting his business there, an officer of the Army received the treatment to which, as a gentleman, he was entitled. When summoned by the Secretary, he knew he was not to be catechised or subjected to suspicious cross-questioning, but that his aid was sought in the transaction of business of the War Bureau. He responded with alacrity and pleasure, and left the presence of the Secretary with his self-respect unimpaired.

General Grant's quiet, undemonstrative, and practical methods resulted in economy as well as despatch. His routine duties as Secretary of War were congenial to him, but his position as a member of President Johnson's Cabinet was very irksome. At Cabinet meetings, he was obliged to listen to political discussions in which he could not properly take part, because of his position as an Army officer, and which often involved action which he considered unwise. He asked that he might be relieved from political duties as a member of the Administration. As no notice was taken of frequent requests of this nature, he finally limited his participation at Cabinet meetings to the transaction of business relating to his department, retiring from them as soon as this business was completed. As this did not altogether relieve him from a seeming participation in partisan politics, he shared in some measure in the indignation directed against the Administration of Mr. Johnson.

Receiving official notice on January 13, 1868, that the Senate had declined to concur in the suspension of Stanton, Grant immediately vacated the War Office, resuming his duties as commanding general. Soon after this, Secretary Stanton asserted his authority by sending a messenger to Army Headquarters to say in the phraseology of a superior officer that: "The Secretary desires to see General Grant." This unnecessary display of authority was not altogether agreeable to the General, and did not in his judgment accord with the courtesy he had himself shown to Mr. Stanton when he succeeded him in the preceding August. But it was Mr. Stanton's way arbitrarily to assert his prerogative as the representative of the President in his dealings with Army officers.

More than once had Grant been made the victim of this disposition of the imperious Secretary to stretch his authority to its limits. He was an extremely sensitive man, in spite of his appearance of stolidity, and though he submitted in silence to orders rudely expressed, and so framed as to imply a rebuke, his relations with the Secretary were never cordial or familiar. Stanton's apparent purpose was to keep the Army constantly in mind of its subordination to the civil branch of the Government, interpreting in his own favour all doubtful questions as to the limitations of authority. This went so far that Grant on one occasion wrote an appeal to the President, but decided to withhold it for the sake of peace.

The prompt surrender of the office of Secretary of War had convinced Congress and the country that Grant was free from any complicity in the plans of the President, but it involved him in further difficulties with Johnson. The differences between the two men reached an acute stage. The President, who had in some way conceived the idea that Grant had agreed to hold the War Office subject to his disposal, accused him of bad faith in surrendering it so promptly. This was the culmination of a long series of exasperations which Grant had borne with his usual good temper. He was slow to anger, but when once thoroughly aroused, he was implacable. The President's implication upon his honour touched the old soldier in his tenderest susceptibilities. An embittered discussion arose, in which several Cabinet Ministers joined in defence of the President. From that hour Grant refused to have any personal or social intercourse with the men who had joined with the President in impeaching his veracity. In one of a series of letters growing out of the dispute, he said:

" The course you would have it understood I agreed to pursue was in violation of law and without orders from you, while the course I did pursue, and which I never doubted you fully understood, was in accordance with law, and not in disobedience of any orders of my superior. And now, Mr. President, where my honor as a soldier and integrity as a man have been so violently assailed, pardon me for saying that I can but regard the whole matter, from the beginning to the end, as an attempt to involve me in the resistance of law for which you hesitated to assume the responsibility in orders, and thus to destroy my character before the country. I am, in a measure, confirmed in this conclusion by your recent orders directing me to disobey orders from the Secretary of War—my superior and your subordinate—without having countermanded his authority to issue the orders I am to disobey. With assurance, Mr. President, that nothing less than a vindication of my personal honor and character could have induced this correspondence on my part, I have the honor to be, very respectfully, your obedient servant,

" U. S. GRANT, *General.*"

This controversy was important in a historical sense, and its results were far-reaching. The termination of Grant's career as a soldier soon followed, and he was introduced on the world's stage as an administrator of civil affairs on a large scale. The question of the succession to President Johnson was approaching determination, and political parties were manœuvring to obtain the advantage of position in the coming contest. Grant was still recognised as the most influential citizen. Democrats and Republicans were each in hopes of obtaining his support, as his political position was undetermined. Though it was known that his sympathies previous to the war had been with the Union Democrats represented by Stephen A. Douglas, times had changed and he had changed with them. Still, as the fundamental article of his very simple political creed was faith in the people, and a disposition to submit to the will of the majority when declared by constitutional methods, he had never been in harmony with what he regarded as Mr. Johnson's revolutionary methods. The breach with the President was irreconcilable, and it was apparent that if Grant assumed any political position, it must be with the party who sustained Congress. The impeachment of Andrew Johnson followed; Grant, who was summoned as a witness, was absolutely impartial in his testimony, showing no feeling, and confined himself simply to a statement of facts. He refused " to exaggerate either the language or the acts of the President, or his own impressions of them; though he was certain that this very moderation would be an argument in Johnson's favour." Yet he strongly approved of the President's impeachment, and did not hesitate to use his influence to bring about his removal from office as a dangerous conspirator against the peace of the country.

The impeachment proceedings failed for the lack of a single vote to make the necessary two-thirds. Benjamin F. Wade, the President of the Senate, would have succeeded Johnson had he been removed. On May 15, 1868, the day before the decision was reached in the Senate, Mr. Wade called upon Grant to consult him about his Cabinet, saying that as he, Grant, would be the candidate of the Republican party, and the next President, he wished to make his temporary appointments satisfactory to him. The next day Johnson was acquitted, and Mr. Wade never became President. A year previous to this, Senator Wade made a visit to the home of General Grant's parents in Covington, Kentucky, and satisfied himself by personal inquiries that Grant's views were in harmony with the action of Congress. Grant expressed his opinions freely enough in his own home, but he considered that it was unbecoming in a military officer to give public expression to political opinions.

CHAPTER XX.

PRESIDENT OF THE UNITED STATES—THE CABINET—REFORM IN THE CIVIL SERVICE—HOSTILITY OF SENATOR SUMNER.

1868-1872.

THE availability of General Grant as a Presidential candidate was so apparent, and the question as to his political proclivities so much in doubt, that each of the great political parties had hopes that they might secure him as their standard-bearer for 1868. He had refused to permit the use of his name for the Presidential campaign of 1864. In March, 1866, the Republicans of Rochester nominated him by acclamation as their candidate for the coming Presidential election, and leading Democrats sounded him on the subject of accepting a nomination from their party. Suggestions that he should enter upon a political career were distasteful to him, and he completely discomfited those who approached him on the subject by the exercise of his remarkable gift of silence. Even disclaimers might have given some clue to his feelings, but no conclusion could be drawn from absolute silence, and from a face void of expression. Grant never dissembled, but no one could enter into his secret thought who was not welcome there. He knew too well the difficulties attending the office of Chief Magistrate to have any illusions on the subject; he was not actively ambitious, nor was he disposed to relinquish an office for which he was fitted, and which gave him congenial occupation to enter upon an uncertain career. There was but one consideration that could move him; that was in appeal to his sense of duty.

Events so shaped themselves as to convince him that he must cast his great reputation into the scale to determine the approaching political contest. Then his personal enemies and the enemies of the Republican party, to whose fortunes he had finally committed himself, joined forces in the attempt to destroy that reputation. Some of these, who had been loudest in praise, blinded by partisanship, now decried his career and his abilities. He was a "wooden man," a drunkard, and a dolt; the favourite of fortune and the pet of Lincoln, who had advanced him at the expense of better men. But, in the midst of this clamour of detraction, the listless auditors heard, out of the distance of years, the roll of the drums, the peal of the bells, and saw in fancy the waving of the banners that told of victories in war,—of a country saved. Even among his political opponents were found men honourable enough to say, with the Democratic candidate for Governor of Massachusetts, John Quincy Adams,—

"I have seen General Grant stigmatized as a bad general, an incompetent man, and a confirmed drunkard. I have not the honor of his acquaintance, but when I am told he is no soldier, I can only say 'Donelson'; when you say he is a dolt, my heart responds, 'Vicksburg'; and when I hear of his intemperance, I can only quote Mr. Lincoln, and wish he had more generals in the war who knew where to get the same brand of whiskey. No, gentlemen, he finished the war, and that is enough to entitle him to my respect and admiration." *

On May 19, 1868, a Soldiers' and Sailors' Convention at Chicago declared their "deliberate conviction" that Ulysses S. Grant is the choice of the soldiers and sailors of the Union," and the next day the National Republican Convention, held in the same city, unanimously nominated him for the Presidency on the first ballot; Schuyler Colfax being nominated for the Vice-Presidency on the sixth ballot.

When the news of the nomination arrived in Washington, Secretary Stanton hurried to the Army Headquarters, arriving out of breath in his eagerness to be the first to announce it. Grant himself received the news without a sign of agitation or exultation. Whatever satisfaction he felt was tempered by regret that this ended his career as a soldier. He refused to take part in the canvass, and hid himself away in Galena, Illinois, directing that no letters should be sent to him. This gave offence to the party managers, but he had resolved that he would keep clear of entanglements and pledges of all kinds, that he might maintain his

* It is to be borne in mind that Mr. Adams was not quoting facts concerning Grant, but simply charges for which, as appeared later, there was but trifling foundation.

freedom of action. He refused to attend a political meeting at Galena, and, during a visit to intimate friends at St. Louis and Chicago, avoided political demonstration. He read the newspapers closely, however, and was not unwilling to discuss the chances of election with his intimate friends.

The Democrats nominated for President Horatio Seymour of New York, and for Vice-President, F. P. Blair of Missouri. Their platform demanded the overthrow of the reconstruction acts of Congress, " as usurpations, unconstitutional, revolutionary, and void." The Republicans resolved that the debt incurred for the war should be held as a sacred obligation; the Democrats demanded that it should be paid in " lawful money "; that is to say, unredeemable paper money, except where made payable in coin by the express term of the contract. It was the first election since the war, and the canvass was fought substantially on the lines which had divided the North during the period of civil strife.

In a letter accepting the nomination, Grant said:

"If elected to the office of President of the United States, it will be my endeavor to administer all the laws in good faith, with economy, and with the view of giving peace, quiet, and protection everywhere. In times like the present it is impossible, or at least eminently improper, to lay down a policy to be adhered to, right or wrong. Through an administration of four years, new political issues, not foreseen, are constantly arising, the views of the public on old ones are constantly changing, and a purely administrative officer should always be left free to execute the will of the people. I always have respected that will, and always shall. Peace and universal prosperity, its sequence, with economy of administration, will lighten the burden of taxation, while it constantly reduces the national debt. Let us have peace."

Wearied of war, and the constant distractions that followed during the period of reconstruction, the country longed for rest, and seized with avidity upon the concluding sentence of Grant's letter of acceptance.

"Let us have peace!" was the refrain of the campaign.

The election held November 3, 1868, resulted in the choice of General Grant by the vote of twenty-six States, having two hundred and fourteen electoral votes, Seymour receiving eighty. The popular majority for Grant and Colfax was 308,584; Virginia, Mississippi, and Texas not voting. The report of the result was received by the successful candidate, as he had received the announcement of his nomination, without a sign of gratification or elation. In a little speech to his fellow-citizens of Galena, gathered around his house on the night of his election, he said:

"The responsibilities of the position I feel, but accept them without fear."

He returned to Washington soon after the election, being followed there by the usual stream of applications for office, all of which were turned over to an aide-de-camp, who opened them, but none were ever answered. The President-elect had very high ideas on the subject of appointments, holding that a man's fitness for office was in inverse ratio to his eagerness to obtain office. In all matters concerning appointments, he observed the reticence customary with him while in command of the Army. Not even his closest confidants were admitted to the secret of his intentions concerning the choice of his Cabinet. To the Committee of Congress, who came to announce his election, he said:

> "I have always felt that it would be rather indelicate to announce or even consult with the gentlemen whom I thought of inviting to positions in my Cabinet before the official declaration of the results of the election was made, although I presumed there was no doubt what that declaration would be, . . . If announced in advance, efforts would be made to change my determination; and, therefore, I have come to the conclusion not to announce whom I am going to invite to seats in the Cabinet until I send in their names to the Senate for confirmation."

The inauguration of Ulysses S. Grant as the eighteenth President of the United States, serving in the twenty-first Presidential term, took place at the Capitol at Washington on March 4, 1869. It was the occasion for a grand display of popular enthusiasm; the contest at the polls was over, the bitterness of partisan strife had passed for a time, and men of all parties united in doing honour to America's greatest citizen—the hero of war, the promoter of peace, who had won his high distinction at an earlier age than any other President. He entered upon the duties of his office at a time when political and sectional animosities were at white heat. The controversies between the retiring Chief Magistrate and Congress had fanned into a flame the expiring embers of the Rebellion, and had encouraged deceptive hopes of mastery in the breasts of those, who, at the close of the war were content to be treated as a conquered people. The South was distracted by controversies and bloody conflicts between the champions of reaction and the friends of reconstruction; the North was divided in opinion between those who sympathised with the old order and those who were struggling through much doubt and difficulty to establish the new upon the solid basis of National legislation and popular approval. Grant understood that he was not the leader of a faction, but the spontaneous choice of the People, and he felt that it was his duty to establish an administration independent of party control. He did not fully appreciate, however, all the difficulties before him, nor had his previous experience, in all respects, been such as to enable him to deal with them successfully. By his personal character, by his lofty spirit of patriotism, by his high sense of public duty, he was admirably fitted for his new office. No man better understood the condition of the country, or was more thoroughly imbued with the spirit of true Americanism. He had been brought into close relations with men of all sections of the divided country, and was more familiar than any one else with the sentiments of the people, North and South, upon whose vigorous manhood its future depended. He was, moreover, thoroughly informed as to the geographical and industrial characteristics of the United States, and realised fully what was essential to secure its commanding position as an imperial State.

The weakness of Grant was in his lack of experience in civil administration; in his inability fully to understand and to circumvent the intrigues of partisans and place-hunters; in his ignorance of the art of bending other men to his purposes, by consulting their wishes and their prejudices in lesser matters, that he might control them in the greater. In short, he was a soldier, and not a politician. He was a statesman in his large views of public and national interests, but he lacked the experience that had once led Lincoln to make the extreme statement that " honest statesmanship is the employment of individual meannesses for the public good."

The new President's inaugural address was moderate, conciliatory, and patriotic in tone, and his declaration that he would have a policy to recommend but none to enforce against the will of the people gave great encouragement to the country, harassed by the long controversy between Congress and the President under the previous Administration. Equally encouraging was the declaration that " no repudiator of one farthing of the public debt " would be " trusted in public place." This meant much, for Grant was no mouther of smooth phrases. With him speech and action were one.

The announcement of the Cabinet which followed the inauguration was a disappointment, not only to the party leaders, but to all who wished well to the new Administration. In departing from the usual custom of consulting political leaders as to his appointments and making them known to those he was to favour, the President had carried reserve too far, as the result soon showed. He found himself somewhat in the position of the certain man in Scripture who " made a great supper and bade many . . . and they all with one consent began to make excuse." Mr. A. T. Stewart, the dry-goods merchant of New York, who was selected for the Secretary of the Treasury, had been notified so that he might have time to arrange his private affairs, but it does not seem to have occurred to the President that the business of others, if not so complex, was quite as important to them. After Mr. Stewart had been confirmed by the Senate, it was discovered that he was ineligible under an old act of Congress forbidding the appointing as Secretary of the Treasury of any person " concerned or interested in carrying on the business or trade of commerce. George H. Boutwell, of Massachusetts, was hurriedly chosen to fill the vacancy, but he was from the same State as E. Rockwood Hoar, who had been appointed Attorney-General, and this violated the unwritten law forbidding the selection of two Cabinet officers from the same State. Mr. Hoar was taken by surprise; hesitated to surrender his private business so abruptly, and resigned the following year, as did Jacob D. Cox, of Ohio, Secretary of the Interior, and for the same reasons. Adolph E. Borie, of Philadelphia, nominated for Secretary of the Navy, had called on the President-elect only two days before his name was sent to the Senate, but he was allowed to leave Washington in ignorance of the fact that he was the coming man from Pennsylvania. He was a wealthy retired merchant, and had no disposition to surrender his ease for the responsibilities of office. He promptly declined, but was persuaded to remain for a few months, showing, during his brief term of service, excellent capabilities for the place. George M.

Robeson, who succeeded him on June 5, 1869, remained in office until the end of Grant's second term.

The appointments of John M. Schofield, Secretary of War, and E. B. Washburn, Secretary of State, were designed to be temporary, and were intended as personal compliments. General Schofield was succeeded within a week by John A. Rawlins, General Grant's former Chief of Staff, who continued in office until his death in September, 1869, and was followed, after an interregnum occupied by General Sherman, by William W. Belknap of Iowa, appointed October 25, 1869. When Mr. Washburn retired from the State Department after six weeks' service, he was succeeded by Hamilton Fish of New York, who took the portfolio with some reluctance. He held it with great acceptance for eight years; Madison, John Quincy Adams, and Seward being the only Secretaries of State having an equal term of service.

John A. J. Creswell, of Maryland, was appointed Postmaster-General, and held that office during the Presidential term. Mr. Cox was succeeded by Columbus Delano, of Ohio, November 1, 1870, and Mr. Hoar by Amos T. Ackerman, of Georgia, June 23, 1870. Mr. Ackerman remained in office only a few months, and was followed December 14, 1871, by George H. Williams, of Oregon.

These miscarriages and changes in the selection of the members of the Cabinet were an unfortunate beginning for the new Administration, though they gave great inward satisfaction to the gentlemen who believed in "playing politics." They were confident, and, as the result showed, with good reason, that their methods must in the end prevail; that no President could make himself independent of existing political conditions. As the Commanding Officer of the Army, and during his brief tenure of office as Secretary of War, Grant had learned something of the mysteries of political management, but he had not conceived a high idea of the politician as a type, and was disposed to make himself as independent of him as possible. At first, all the channels of influence between the White House and the party leaders were closed. The only access to the President was through the former members of his military staff, who continued on duty with him at the White House. They knew very little of politics or political managers, and to have borne a musket or carried a sword during the Civil War, established a higher claim upon their consideration than the ability to manage a political primary or to " work the machine."

The asserted domination of military influences at the White House gave offence to public men, who thought that their legislative experience and knowledge of civil affairs entitled them to be considered, or at least to be consulted with reference to appointments to office. The Administration of Mr. Johnson had been extremely unsatisfactory to the Republican party, now in complete control of the Government, and numerous changes were expected in the removal and appointment of Federal officers, but these were prevented by the Tenure of Office Act, passed for the special purpose of restraining Mr. Johnson's freedom of action. Grant would not consent to subject himself, or members of his Cabinet, to the disagreeable and undignified process of suspending, and formulating charges against, a public officer who was objectionable only because of his political opinions. The law was partially repealed, but the President insisted that this restraint upon his liberty should be entirely removed, contending that it was inconsistent with a faithful and efficient administration of the Government to compel the Executive to employ officials forced upon him, and those, too, whom he had suspended for reason.

No President has ever been able to secure universal approval of his selections for office; for where one is favoured, scores are disappointed. President Grant was no exception to the rule. As his determination with reference to various changes became known, opposition to the Administration increased, until he was subjected to the grossest abuse because " he would not yield to demands sometimes sordid and vile, touching patronage," and likewise to the unjust suspicion of abusing the appointing power for personal ends. He also suffered much from those described by him as being the most troublesome men in public life; "those over-righteous people, who see no motives in other people's action but evil motives, who believe all public life is corrupt, and nothing is well done unless they do it themselves. They are narrow-headed men, their two eyes so close together that they can look out of the same gimlet hole without winking."

After he had been long enough in office to learn something of the evils of the existing system for the selection of Government appointees, the President appealed to Congress to correct the " abuse of long-standing." " There is no duty," he said, " which so much embarrasses the heads of departments as that of appointments; nor is there any such arduous and thankless labour imposed on senators and representatives as that of finding places for constituents. The present system does not secure the best men, and often not even fit men for public place."

Receiving the necessary authority, in the act of March 3, 1871, a Board was convened to devise rules and regulations to effect a reform. The subject was referred to again at length in the next Annual Message, the President declaring that it had been his aim " to enforce honesty and efficiency in all public offices," holding to the rigour of the law every public servant violating his trust. " If," he said, " bad men have secured places, it has been the fault of the system established by law and custom for making appointments." Recommendations were made for appointment to office without a proper sense of the grave responsibility involved. In his Annual Message of 1872, and again in his Inaugural of March 4, 1873, the President pledged himself to maintain to the best of his judgment the spirit of the rules adopted by the Commission, but something more was needed; the direct and positive support of Congress. This was denied, and in his Annual Message of 1874, he said finally: " Under these circumstances, therefore, I announce that, if Congress adjourns without positive legislation on the subject of 'Civil-Service Reform' I will regard such action as the disapproval of the system, and will abandon it, except so far as to require examinations for certain appointees to determine their fitness."

Thus it appears from this record that the first earnest attempt by any President to reform our civil service originated with Grant. He was beset with difficulties within and without; he had to deal with an indifferent Congress; with professional politicians sneering at "snivel-service reform," and with unwise reformers who sought so to tie his hands with impracticable rules as to paralyse Executive action; complaining when necessary removals were made without formal charges, and insisting that other removals should be made on charges brought by irresponsible persons without good ground. To the writer of this biography Grant once explained his theory of civil-service reform. It was very simple, and was the fruit of a practical experience such as few men have had. He held that the President should be entirely free to make his own selection for office, the final appointment being held subject to a satisfactory examination for fitness for office. This is the system followed in the Army and Navy.

As to Grant's sincere desire to reform the civil service there can be no doubt, but he did not believe that Executive responsibility could be transferred to a board absolutely controlling selections to office. The question was not whether it was wise and right to purify every department of the Government, but what was the most effectual method of doing this.

"Has there been," asked Senator Morton, "an Administration within the memory of any man on this floor that has more promptly punished crime when it has been brought to light, or has more promptly removed the offender from office?" Senator Edmunds declared that with respect to the fidelity of its agents the Administration of Grant would "compare favourably with any Administration that ever preceded it from the days of George Washington to this day, when you take into consideration the number of persons necessarily employed in the Government now, compared with its early days, and the large amount of the transactions that they are obliged to perform." There were thefts and embezzlements, but the percentage was phenomenally small as compared with previous Administrations.

Charles Sumner, Senator from Massachusetts, gradually took a leading position among the critics of the President. His hostility grew so acrimonious that he finally said, in the language of Lord Durham to Henry Brougham: "Among the foremost purposes ought to be the downfall of this odious, insulting, degrading, aide-de-campish, incapable dictatorship. At such a crisis, is the country to be left at the mercy of barrack counsels and mess-room politics?" Mr. Sumner was a gentleman whose intellectual differences with others assumed to his mind the aspect of a contest between the forces of good and evil that admits of no compromise. Even his close political friend and ally, Mr. George William Curtis, in resenting a personal attack on one occasion said: " Sumner, you must learn that other men are as honest as you are."

Between Grant and Sumner there was an absolute and irreconcilable incompatibility of temper. To James Russell Lowell, General Grant confided the fact that he had never strained his own intellectual processes to bring himself into touch with another man, so much as in the case of Senator Sumner. It was of no avail. Grant was an eminently matter-of-fact man, who, when he had once grasped facts, had an unusually clear perception of them in their relation to practical action, and was less concerned with methods than with the end to be accomplished. Sumner was an idealist; disposed to quarrel with those who sought to accomplish like results by ways that did not seem to him to be abstractly perfect. Grant was free from vanity and self-consciousness; Sumner found himself so pleasantly reflected in his own intellectual processes that, like Narcissus, he was absorbed in the contemplation of his own perfections. How could men so different be in accord?

The President had given offence to Senator Sumner by his failure to consider him in the matter of personal appointments, and when the occasion offered he assumed the attitude of unyielding opposition. At various periods in our history, overtures had been made looking to the transfer of the territory of San Domingo to the United States. In 1845 President Polk sent Lieutenant, afterward Admiral, David D. Porter, U. S. N., as a commissioner to the island, and in 1854 Captain, afterward Major-General, George B. McClellan, U. S. A., was sent on the same errand by President Pierce, who made an unsuccessful attempt to negotiate a treaty with San Domingo. Again, in 1867, President Johnson sent the Assistant Secretary of State, Frederick W. Seward, on a prospecting tour to the island.

Soon after the inauguration of President Grant, Baez, the President of San Domingo, sent a commissioner to Washington to represent the advantage of a union of the two Republics. His overtures received but little favour, and a second commissioner was sent on the same errand in July, 1869. Meanwhile, it had been resolved to send some one to San Domingo to inquire into the matter, and Mr. Benjamin S. Hunt, of Philadelphia, a gentleman in every way well qualified for this mission, was appointed by the President. But he was taken ill just as he was about to sail, and never visited San Domingo. Various considerations affecting the interests of the Dominican Republic made it necessary to observe absolute secrecy, so that no evil results should follow in case the matter never went beyond the stage of preliminary discussion. Following the precedent in the cases of Lieutenant Porter and Captain McClellan, President Grant selected as his representative an officer of the Corps of Engineers of the Army, Gen. Orville E. Babcock, who had been in close relations with him as a member of his military staff. With the discretion and secrecy customary in his profession General Babcock proceeded to San Domingo, and returned with the basis of an important treaty without any one suspecting his mission. In concealing the purpose of Babcock's visit to San Domingo, Grant simply pursued his customary method in important matters. He had learned by much experience that if you wish to keep a matter confidential the only way to secure perfect secrecy is never to reveal your plans to any one.

Intent only on accomplishing the object in view, he had unwittingly given great offence to those who thought they had a right to participate in the secrets of the Administration, and especially to Mr. Sumner, who was full of questionings as to the cause of so much reserve, and did not hesitate to charge it to the most unworthy motive, and charges of a like nature were caught up and scattered over the country. So much opposition was excited in this way, that a formal treaty for the annexation of San Domingo was rejected by a tie vote of the Senate, 28 to 28, June 30, 1870, after a heated debate, Mr. Sumner leading the opposition.

In his annual message in December following, the President renewed his recommendation for the acquisition of San Domingo with great earnestness; but the opposition in the Senate was still so strong that no action was taken, beyond the appointment of a commission to visit San Domingo and report upon the facts. In spite of the obvious fairness of this measure, it encountered the most virulent opposition from Mr. Sumner, the occasion for which was revealed when the commission presented a report completely answering all of his false charges, and clearly convicting him of misrepresentation or misinformation. It was made apparent that the Senator's morbid self-esteem had disposed him to listen too eagerly to stories to the discredit of one who had unwittingly wounded his *amour propre*.

As the President said in a special message to Congress: " No man can hope to perform duties so delicate and responsible as appertain to the Presidential office without sometimes incurring the hostility of those who deem their opinions and wishes treated with insufficient consideration." Bearing this fact in mind, we can better understand the powerful influences combining to make it appear to many that Grant failed in the administration of the Executive office of President.

Grant never yielded his opinion on the subject of the importance of securing San Domingo by peaceable means. Six years after the controversy had been settled he returned to the subject in his last Annual Message, repeating his arguments for annexation in vindication of his previous action, and declaring his belief that if his views " had been concurred in, the country would be in a more prosperous condition, both politically and financially." In his Inaugural Address of March 4, 1873, he said:

" I do not share in the apprehension held by many, as to the danger of governments becoming weakened and destroyed by reason of their extension of territory. Commerce, education, and rapid transit of thought and matter by telegraph and steam have changed all this. Rather do I believe that our Great Maker is preparing the world in his own good time, to become one nation, speaking one language, and when armies and navies will be no longer required."

Such was the broad creed of the great soldier, and it explains his interest not only in the San Domingo purchase, but in other projects for extending American influence by peaceful methods. In his first Annual Message he called attention to the importance of building a canal across the Isthmus of Panama to turn westward the current of commercial interchanges between the Atlantic and Pacific, and to strengthen the country for defence by enabling our ships of war to maintain communication between the eastern and western slopes of the American continent. Incidental to this he proposed to secure, by proper means, a foot-hold among the islands of the Gulf of Mexico and the Carribbean Sea, which by a short-sighted policy had been permitted to pass under the control of foreign States that might at any moment become hostile States. He understood better than any one else the importance of securing our ocean frontier by the possession of the bulwarks that nature has planted for the defence or the assault of our Southern ports, and he knew how much we suffered during the Civil War because of the opportunity given to the vexatious blockade runners by the existence, immediately off our coast, of ports under the control of a government showing them hospitality. But he could not arouse a sluggish Congress, even one in political sympathy with his Administration, to an appreciation of his own enlightened views, and the attempt to do so subjected him to misapprehension and abuse that he keenly felt, knowing, as he did, not only that he was moved by patriotic purpose, but that he was much better informed on the subject than were his critics.

Another subject that greatly interested the President was the restoration of our mercantile marine to the position it held before Confederate cruisers drove our commerce from the seas, and British shipbuilders had learned how to substitute the ores of England for the forests of America in the construction of steamships. The attention of Congress was called to this matter in the Annual Message of December 6, 1869, presenting "an earnest plea for early action in a way to secure the desired increase of American commerce." This was followed by special messages of March 23, 1870, and July 15, 1870, and the discussion of the subject was renewed in the Annual Message of December 2, 1872.

As a practical remedy, it was suggested that "liberality should be shown in the payment for carrying mails to American-owned and American-built steamers," requiring them to be so built that they could be used in war, the Government reserving the right to take possession of them when necessity required. This has long been the European system, and it has been adopted by the United States, following this suggestion of President Grant. In line with the project for promoting the interests of our commercial marine, were the constant suggestions in the President's messages that the Navy should be strengthened. There was improvement in this department of the public service without great increase in expenditure, the appropriation for the Navy in the last year of Grant's Administration being nearly seven millions of dollars less than for the first year. The attempt to accomplish necessary results with insufficient appropriations was an occasion for criticism by those who did not realise how large an expenditure is required annually to save our floating defences from deterioration and destruction.

CHAPTER XXI.

FOREIGN RELATIONS—TREATY OF WASHINGTON—NEGRO ENFRANCHISEMENT—RE-ELECTION.

1870–1873.

F President Grant had been as eager for foreign conquest as his enemies would lead us to believe, no fairer opportunity could have offered itself than the one presented during our difficulties with Spain, which grew out of the insurrection in the island of Cuba, and extended over the whole of Grant's two terms, or from 1868 to 1880.

The sympathy with the Cuban struggle for independence was very strong in the United States, and found expression in resolutions passed by the House of Representatives in 1869. Several of the South American states had granted belligerent rights to the Cubans, and the pressure upon our Government to grant the same privilege was strong and persistent. The President was anxious to recognise the Cubans when he could do so properly, but at no time did the contest, according to his judgment, assume such proportions as to justify him in doing so. To this fact he repeatedly called the attention of Congress, while at the same time he expressed in the strongest terms his detestation of the methods which led to the devastation of the fairest of the Antilles.

So long as Spain confined herself to the summary execution of her own subjects, it was not in the power of our Government to interfere. But when, in 1873, she captured the *Virginius*, a vessel bearing the American flag, and summarily executed American citizens found on board of her, the whole country was up in arms. The President's action was prompt and vigorous, and the unwillingness of Spain to show equal promptitude in repairing the wrong led to peremptory demands upon her which would have resulted in war had she not yielded to them. War with Spain would have been popular, especially with the old soldiers North and South, and the grim veteran who sat in the White House had no occasion to fear it. With wise precaution he made every possible preparation to meet the emergency if it came, and he would have been quite at home in making use of the vast powers of the United States to secure recognition of their rights. No country in the world had at that time so many trained and experienced soldiers and so many competent leaders. The plan of action proposed, in the event of war, involved the invasion of Spain by a flying column commanded by Sheridan and ostensibly organised for an attack on Cuba.

In Grant's Message to Congress on the subject of

Cuba will be found an exceedingly clear and able expression of the statesmanship which bears and forbears that it may promote peace, while never shrinking from the forcible assertion of just demands. "It has been the endeavour of the Administration," Congress was told, "to execute the neutrality laws in good faith, no matter how unpleasant the task, made so by the sufferings we have endured from lack of like good faith towards us by other nations."

The good offices of the United States were tendered to Spain with a view to a settlement of her difficulties. This tender was received with politeness, but declined with an expression of thanks for the friendly offer. In the case of her disputes with Peru and Chili, however, a similar offer was accepted, and, as a result of it, an honourable peace was arranged between Spain and the South American Republics, in an International Congress which met at Washington. The President said:

"I have always felt that the most intimate relations should be cultivated between the Republic of the United States and all independent nations on this continent. It may be well worth considering whether new treaties between the United States and them may not be profitably entered into, to secure more intimate relations, friendly, commercial or otherwise."

This was the policy followed during Grant's Administration with undeviating fidelity.

A like disposition to promote good relations was shown in his dealings with the nations of Europe and Asia. A request from the French Republic to intervene in association with other powers to promote peace with Germany, was declined, as in contravention of our policy of avoiding entangling alliances with European Powers. But the establishment of a Republic by the French was followed by a prompt and hearty recognition by telegraph which deeply touched the sensibilities of that great people.

Crowds surrounded the American Legation, bearing the French and American flags, and repeating the cries "*Vive l'Amerique; Vive la France!*" An address was presented by a delegation, and in his letter of acknowledgment to Mr. Washburne, the French Minister for Foreign Affairs, Jules Favre, said, " I look upon it as a happy augury for the French Republic that it has received as its first diplomatic support the recognition of the Government of the United States."

In 1871, a treaty was concluded with Italy, containing an agreement that " private property at sea shall be exempt from capture in case of war between the two Powers." "The United States," said the President in his Message to Congress, " has spared no opportunity of incorporating this rule into the obligations of nations."

In 1873, arbitration settled disputes with Spain and Brazil, and our Minister to Berlin, Mr. Bancroft, secured from Germany, after much effort, a recognition of " the inalienable natural right of immigration, not limited by any duty to the original Government, except where the performance of that duty has been formally initiated." This was a definite abandonment of the European doctrine of " once a subject always a subject."

Constant attempts were made, under Grant's Administration, to cultivate good relations with the Orientals, and these were very successful with China and Japan. Corea was less willing to be wooed, and resented, with haughty insolence, the attempt to inquire into the circumstances of the murder of the crew of an American vessel cast upon her shores. A naval expedition, under Admiral Rodgers, sent to Corea, was attacked, but the forts committing this outrage were taken by a gallant assault and destroyed.

The crowning achievement of Grant's Administration in the department of diplomatic intercourse, and one that is in itself sufficient to make that administration memorable for all time, was the negotiation of the Treaty of Washington. It elevated international intercourse to a higher plane, and gave convincing proof to all the world of the sincerity of Grant's declaration in accepting the nomination for the Presidency: " Let us have peace !"—in striking contrast to the hollowness of a similar declaration by Napoleon III.: " *l'Empire c'est la Paix !* "

During our Civil War our Government had been compelled to steadily protest against the unfriendly course pursued by England which tended to promote the dissolution of the American Republic, and thus remove a powerful rival from the path of England's commercial progress. Against hostile opinion in England, however influential, we could take no action, galling as it was to American sensibilities to see England's profession of fellowship and kinship thrown to the winds in sympathy with a confederation whose declared purpose was the establishment of a slave empire. We were compelled, through force of circumstances, to submit to the hostile and insulting criticisms upon America and the American people found scattered so liberally through Hansard's reports of the parliamentary debates of that period.

These sentimental grievances were not the only ones of which complaint was made, and it was the determination of Government and people that England should at the first opportunity be called to account for the substantial injuries we had suffered by her defiance of international obligations. Her colonies had been the " arsenal, the Navy yard, and the Treasury of the Confederates." From the shelter of her ports, and encouraged by the partiality and gross negligence of her Government, the Confederate cruisers had destroyed our shipping and almost driven our commerce from the seas. England prolonged our war, and compelled us to pay in precious blood and treasure for her premature granting of belligerent rights to the Confederates, and her readiness in furnishing them with money and supplies to carry on the war against us. Finally, forced by the persistent remonstrances of our Government to admit that wrong had been done to the United States, Earl Russell, then Lord John Russell, fell back upon the position that the honour of England would not permit her to make any restitution.

While displeasing to Northern sentiment, the selfishness of the policy pursued by the English Government had been so apparent that they won no friends in the South. Thus, when the greatest conqueror of our day found himself wielding the resources of a mighty nation, the American public sentiment was substantially united in favour of any hostile policy he might pursue towards England. As said Caleb Cushing, in his *Treaty of Washington*:

"Never in the history of nations, has an occasion existed where a powerful people, smarting under the consciousness of injury, manifested greater magnanimity than was displayed in that emergency by the United States. We had on the sea hundreds of ships of war or of transport; we had on land hundreds of thousands of veteran soldiers under arms; we had officers on land and sea, the combatants in a hundred battles; all this vast force of war was in a condition to be launched as a thunderbolt at any enemy; and, in the present case, the possessions of that enemy, whether continental or insular, lay at our very door in tempting helplessness. But neither the Government and people of the United States, nay, nor their laurel-crowned Generals and Admirals, desired war as a choice, nor would accept it but as a necessity; and they elected to continue to negotiate with Great Britain, and to do what no great European State has ever done under like circumstances,—that is, to disarm absolutely, and make thorough trial of the experiment of generous forbearance, before having recourse to the dread extremity of vengeful hostilities against Great Britain."

In February, 1869, Reverdy Johnson, who was filling a brief term of office as Minister to England, negotiated a treaty with that country which was so offensive to American sentiment that it was promptly rejected by the United States Senate without ceremony, as surrendering the whole American case against Great Britain. The report on this treaty was made a few weeks after Grant entered upon his first term as President. He entirely approved of it, and in his succeeding Annual Message said:

"I regarded the action of the Senate in rejecting the treaty to have been wisely taken in the interest of peace, and as a necessary step in the direction of a perfect and cordial friendship between the two countries. A sensitive people, conscious of their power, are more at ease under a great wrong wholly unatoned than under the restraint of a settlement which satisfies neither their ideas of justice, nor their grave sense of the grievance they have sustained."

In his Annual Message of December, 1870, the President clearly presented the apparently irreconcilable difference in the points of view of the two nations. That a great international dispute might be lifted above the level of personal contention, he advised that the Government should secure the ownership of all private claims against Great Britain on the part of American citizens, and the responsible control of all the demands against that country. "Whenever," he said, "Her Majesty's Government shall entertain a desire for a full and friendly adjustment of these claims, the United States will enter upon their consideration with an earnest desire for a conclusion consistent with the honour and dignity of both nations." Secure from the pressure of over eager claimants, we could then afford to wait the result with patience.

It was Grant who spoke; the man whose patient but inflexible determination of purpose no one could question. The British Government clearly perceived that there was a larger question involved in the dispute than that of merely quieting a few hungry claimants, who would fain content themselves with half a loaf if they could not get the whole. England could not afford to leave the precedent she had established, for America to follow when the enemies of Britain should demand the shelter of America's ports and the help of her resources, that they might more surely prey upon British commerce. Germany and France were at war, and there was a prospect of trouble between England and Russia. The interests of England clearly demanded the settlement of the Alabama claims, so called from the Confederate cruiser which had done the most damage to our commerce. This vessel was built in British dockyards, armed by British guns, manned by British sailors, and was destroyed, June 19, 1864, in a fair fight with the *Kearsarge* in the English Channel, in the presence of British spectators who had gathered to witness the discomfiture of the hated Yankee. The *Alabama* was the very embodiment and expression of the case of the United States against England.

The negotiations between the two countries had been abruptly, not to say rudely, broken; the question now was how to reopen them without loss of dignity. Means were found, the overtures this time coming from England. An understanding was arrived at by the British Minister and the American Secretary of State; authority was obtained from London by cable, and Sir Edward Thornton and Mr. Fish signed an agreement binding the two countries to submit to a commission all questions in dispute between them.

The President and the Queen each named five commissioners. The British Commissioners sailed without their commissions, and these were forwarded to them by special messenger. In less than a month from the date of the first proposition by Sir Edward Thornton, they were in New York, having departed from London, as the gossips said, " so hurriedly that they came with portmanteaus, leaving their servants behind to pack their trunks and follow." " Thus," says Mr. Blaine,

"the question which for six years, had been treated with easy indifference, if not with contempt, by the British Foreign Office, had in a day become exigent and urgent, and the diplomatic details which ordinarily would have required months to adjust, were now settled by cable in an hour. . . . For this change of view in the British Cabinet, and this courier-like speed among British Diplomatists, there was a double cause,—the warning of the Franco-Prussian War, and President Grant's proposition to pay the Alabama claims from the Treasury of the United States—and wait. Assuredly the President did not wait long!"

The two Governments appointed commissioners whose high character indicated the importance given to their deliberations. The British Commissioners were the President of the Queen's Council, a late Chancellor of the Exchequer, the British Minister at Washington, the Premier of Canada, and the Oxford Professor of International Law. The American Commissioners were a Justice of the Supreme Court, the Secretary of State, a Senator, the Minister to Great Britain, and the late Attorney-General,

Mr. Hoar. These Commissioners met at Washington on February 27, 1871, and, on May 8th, following, they signed an agreement known as "The Treaty of Washington."

In this it was provided that all claims growing out of acts committed by certain vessels named, and generally known as the Alabama claims, should be referred to five arbitrators—one to be named by the President of the United States, one by the Queen of England, one by the King of Italy, one by the President of the Swiss Confederation, and one by the Emperor of Brazil. The arbitrators met, in December, 1871, at Geneva, Switzerland, and, on September 14, 1872, after a session of nine months, decreed that the sum of $15,500,000 in gold be paid by Great Britain to the United States for the satisfaction of all the claims referred to.

Three other important disputes were determined between the United States and Great Britain by this treaty. To one commission was referred the question of our fishing rights in British American waters; to another, the claims of British subjects against the United States, and of Americans against England, for losses incurred during our Civil War by illegal acts committed by the officials of either country. To the Emperor of Germany was given the decision of the long-standing dispute as to the North-western Boundary, known as the San Juan Question. On October 21, 1872, the Emperor rendered his decision in favour of the United States, and this was promptly accepted by England. The other two commissions made awards requiring payment by the United States of $7,426,819. The most important of these decisions was that concerning the North-western Boundary. Concerning it, President Grant said in his Annual Message:

" This award confirms the United States in their claim to the important archipelago of islands lying between the Continent and Vancouvers Island, which for more than twenty-six years Great Britain has contested, and leaves us, for the first time in the history of the United States as a nation, without a question of disputed boundary between our territory and the possessions of Great Britain on this Continent."

The settlement of the Fishery Question, five years later, under the terms of the Treaty of Washington, removed from the arena of international discussion the last subject in dispute at that time between England and America.

The Treaty of Washington did not give universal satisfaction on either side of the Atlantic. It was assailed in the United States Senate, and the Democratic members of the Senate, with two or three exceptions, voted against it, but it had six votes beyond the necessary two thirds. The presentation, in deference to the views of Senator Sumner, of a claim for damages indirectly arising from the action of Great Britain, created great excitement in England. The unanimous decision by the arbitrators, that such claims were not to be considered, quieted this excitement, but it was renewed when the final award was made, against the protest of the British arbitrator. For a time these disagreements threatened a rupture between the two countries.

Incidental to the negotiation with England was a

further rupture between Senator Sumner of Massachusetts and the President. After the rejection of the Clarendon-Johnson Treaty, Mr. John Lothrop Motley, who was then our Minister to the Court of St. James, was instructed by our State Department to make certain representations to the British Government concerning the rejection of the treaty. His conduct in the affair did not meet the approval of the President, and, as he refused to resign, he was removed.

Mr. Motley had been appointed by President Grant, but he was considered impracticable, as he shared certain extreme views held by Mr. Sumner, who had gone so far as to propose that Great Britain should be asked to withdraw her flag from this continent as a preliminary to the settlement of this international difficulty. Mr. Sumner was greatly lacking in tact, and ability to co-operate with others who did not accept his extreme opinions. His presence at the head of the Senate Committee on Foreign Affairs was a great embarrassment, not only for this reason, but also because he was hardly on speaking terms with either the President or the Secretary of State. He was accordingly removed from his position as head of the Committee. The removal of Mr. Motley had been decided upon before the occurrence of the difficulty with Mr. Sumner, but the two things were connected in the minds of the friends of the two men, and the President was informed by the Saturday Club of Boston that his conduct in sacrificing Mr. Motley to his disagreement with Mr. Sumner, which he did not do, was certain "to offend all educated men of New England." The statement was a significant one, and it goes far to explain many of the President's subsequent difficulties with public opinion. Though he was a highly educated man, in the sense of having a well-disciplined mind, and was an alumnus of an institution more exact in its training than any other in America, he bore no academic honours, and was apt to be at odds with the doctrinaires and theorists.

Other causes of complaint were equally ill founded, as in the case of Senator Sumner's objection to the Dominican treaty on the ground that it threatened the interests of the black race, which he was especially ordained to guard, as these interests were represented in the negro Republic of Hayti. That the negroes did not share his apprehensions concerning General Grant in this respect was shown by their action on several occasions. The representatives of a National Coloured Labour Convention, held at Washington, waited upon the President and thanked him for his recognition of their right to places of honour and trust in the several departments of the Government, and a National Convention of coloured men, assembled in New Orleans, April 19, 1872, under the Presidency of Frederic Douglass, passed a series of resolutions in which they joined the names of Sumner and Grant in the special recognition of their services to the coloured race.

On the ratification of the Fifteenth Amendment in 1870, President Grant sent a special message to Congress calling attention to the act enfranchising four millions of men, who had been declared by the highest tribunal of the land not to be citizens, and not eligible to become so. This, he declared, " was a measure of grander importance than any one act of the kind from the foundation of our free Government to the present day." He appealed to the newly enfranchised race to remember how important it was for them to strive in every way to make themselves worthy of their new privilege. He urged upon Congress the duty of encouraging popular education throughout the country, and called "upon the people everywhere to see to it that all who possess and exercise political rights shall have the opportunity to acquire the knowledge which will make their share in the Government a blessing and not a danger."

This Message, dated March 30, 1870, is an excellent example of the high moral elevation of all of President Grant's public documents. He never indulged in speculations, or propounded mere theories. He was always plain and practical, and, though he appealed to common sense and to national self-interest, he never sought to influence men by unworthy motives, nor to excite popular prejudice for the benefit of his party. It disconcerted, and at times perplexed him, to find that projects designed only for the public good were opposed on the theory that they were intended for personal aggrandisement.

As General Grant's term of office drew to a close it became more and more evident that he was destined to be his own successor. He could not be

expected to satisfy those of an opposing political
faith; and if he had not succeeded in satisfying all
the men of public influence in his own party, and all
of the newspapers, his Administration commended
itself as a whole to popular approval. The unjust
and violent attacks upon him had not weakened
public confidence in his ability, his patriotism, or
his devotion to the best interests of the country.
The turmoil of Johnson's Administration had been
followed upon Grant's inauguration by comparative
tranquillity. It is true that disturbances continued
at the South, but Washington was no longer a storm
centre, and political interest was in a measure transferred to State and local affairs, thus re-establishing
the normal relations of State and National authority. Prosperity was general, except at the South,
and even there conditions had gradually improved,
as was indicated by an increase of seventy per cent.
in the annual product of the chief Southern staple,
cotton. Under exceedingly difficult circumstances
good relations had been maintained with foreign
Governments, and the soldier's triumphs in diplomacy were as great as they had been in war. Our
finances had been managed with skill, and the public credit maintained in spite of the determined
attempts to fasten upon the nation the dishonour of
repudiation. Everywhere had been shown a sincere
purpose to place the administration of public affairs
upon a higher level. If the censorious complained
because no more had been accomplished, the just-
minded were disposed to applaud because the movement as a whole had been in the right direction.

The most striking testimony to the success of Grant's Administration was the effort of his opponents to follow his lead, and go even beyond him in the direction he had marked out. The opposition within the Republican party gradually organised into what was known as the Liberal Republican movement. This originated in a convention held at Jefferson City, Missouri, January 24, 1872, which demanded equal suffrage for all, complete amnesty for all, and " a genuine reform of the tariff," so as to relieve the people of the burden of taxation imposed for the benefit of favoured interests. Aside from these positive demands, the resolutions consisted of a series of declarations of superior virtue, such as the " Outs " are always able to make at the expense of the " Ins." They closed with a call for a National Convention to be held at Cincinnati on May 1st, following. This Convention met May 1, 1872, and passed a series of resolutions, all of which might have been subscribed to by Grant, or by any one of his supporters. As the Liberal Republicans were not agreed on the subject of protection and free trade, they remitted " the discussion of the subject to the people in their Congressional districts, and to the decision of Congress thereon."

The principal candidates for the Presidency before the Liberal Republican Convention were Charles Francis Adams and Horace Greeley. On the sixth ballot the choice fell to Mr. Greeley; and B. Gratz Brown of Missouri was nominated for Vice-President. To the astonishment of the country, the Democratic Convention which met at Baltimore,

July 9, 1872, ratified these nominations, in spite of the fact that Mr. Greeley had been through life the most vigorous and effective opponent of the Democracy, and was the embodied representation of everything that a Democrat did not believe. The cry was " anything to beat Grant," and Liberal Republicans and Democrats were equally confident of their inability to accomplish this result without help.

John B. Vance, the ex-Governor of North Carolina, said: " If *Old Grimes* is in the Democratic Hymn-book, we will sing it through if it kills us." All Democrats were not so complacent, and what were called the " Straight-out Democrats " held a convention and nominated Charles O'Conor of New York for President, and John Quincy Adams of Massachusetts for Vice-President. Though both these gentlemen declined, the ticket received a few votes. No more could the Liberal Republicans agree among themselves, and a meeting of the discontented was held at New York, June 20, 1872, pursuant to an invitation signed by Carl Schurz, Jacob D. Cox, William Cullen Bryant, Oswald Ottendorfer, David A. Wells, and Jacob Brinkerhoff. At this meeting resolutions were adopted, and William S. Groesbeck, of Ohio, was proposed for President, and Frederick Law Olmstead, of New York, for Vice-President.

The Republicans now had the grim satisfaction of seeing their opponents divided into four hostile camps, the Democrats joining in the effort to elect a man whose principles and record were abhorrent to them.

The regular Republican Convention assembled at Philadelphia, June 5, 1872, and renominated Grant by acclamation as their candidate for the Presidency. Henry Wilson of Massachusetts was nominated for Vice-President. The platform presented the " glorious record of the past " as " the party's best pledge for the future." Aside from this, the resolutions made no distinct issue with the declarations of other conventions, except the last, which was as follows:

" We believe that the modest patriotism, the earnest purpose, the sound judgment, the practical wisdom, the incorruptible integrity, and the illustrious services of Ulysses S. Grant, have commended him to the heart of the American people, and, with him at our head, we start to-day upon a new march to victory."

This was really the only issue before the country: Should or should not the Administration of Grant be approved? The nomination of his chief opponent was described by the New York *Nation* as " the first attempt of that large class of quacks, charlatans, ignoramuses, and sentimentalists who are engaged in every civilised country to-day in trying to substitute the heart for the head—or, in other words, to make singing, weeping, and wailing do in politics the work of memory and judgment— to get possession of the Government of the United States."

The issue was made up, and the decision was left to the people. That decision was emphatic. Grant and Wilson carried every Northern State in the November election, and received 286 votes in the Electoral College to 18 for Greeley and Brown. Grant's popular majority over Greeley was 763,007 votes. No victory had been so complete since James Monroe was re-elected President in 1820 by a nearly unanimous vote of the Electoral College. In 1868, Mr. Lincoln received an equally large percentage of the vote cast, but no Southern State took part in that election.

Those accustomed to the rough and tumble of politics could not appreciate Grant's sensitiveness to the criticisms impeaching his integrity, forgetting that to doubt a soldier's honour is as offensive as to question a woman's virtue. The "silent man" did not conceal the satisfaction he felt at receiving such proof that the plots of his enemies had not lessened public confidence in him.

There are few men who cannot recall some occasion in life where bitter feeling was aroused by wounded *amour propre*. This was the secret of the most active opposition to Grant. The selfish nature of that opposition had been made apparent by the complete sacrifice of principle and consistency shown by his opponents in their attempt to defeat him.

CHAPTER XXII.

SECOND TERM — FINANCIAL REFORM — RECONSTRUCTION COMPLETED—THIRD-TERM CONTROVERSY—ELECTION OF HAYES.

1873–1876.

N his Inaugural Address, delivered on March 4, 1873, at the Capitol in Washington, at the commencement of his second term as President of the United States, Grant gave expression to his keen sense of the injustice done to him by vindictive criticism. He referred to his conscientious performance of public duty, without rest or remission, for the twelve years succeeding the eventful firing on Fort Sumter, in April, 1861, saying, in conclusion:

" Notwithstanding this, throughout the war, and from my candidacy for my present office, in 1868, to the close of the last presidential campaign, I have been the subject of abuse and slander, scarcely ever equaled in political history, which to-day I feel that I can afford to disregard, in view of your verdict, which I gratefully accept as my vindication."

In making up the Cabinet for the second term, Fish was continued as Secretary of State, Belknap as Secretary of War, Williams as Attorney-General, Delano as Secretary of the Interior. William A. Richardson succeeded Boutwell as Secretary of the Treasury, and was followed in succession by Benj. F. Bristow, June 4, 1874, and Lot M. Morrill, July 7, 1876. Alphonso Taft succeeded Belknap in the War office, March 8, 1876, and was, on May 22, 1876, transferred to the office of Attorney-General, succeeding Edwards Pierrepont, who had followed Williams, April 26, 1875. J. Donald Cameron was appointed Secretary of War, May 22, 1876. Cresswell retired from the Post-Office Department, and was followed by James W. Marshall, July 7, 1874, Marshall Jewell, August 27, 1874, and James W. Tyner, July 12, 1876.

The selection of General Belknap for Secretary of War proved to be an unfortunate one. He was one of three ex-officers of Volunteers recommended for the place by Generals Sherman and Sheridan, at the request of the President; he was the son of an army officer who fought with Grant in Mexico, and as a Collector of Internal Revenue his record was exceptionally good; yet he fell, as Adam fell in Eden, and he had the same excuse for his fall. He was detected in dishonest transactions in connection with post-traderships in the Army, resigned, and was impeached, but escaped trial on the theory that being no longer a Cabinet officer, he was not subject to the jurisdiction of the Senate. He was in many respects an excellent Secretary of War, and the disgraceful closing of his career was a surprise to all who knew him.

In his Inaugural Address the President had said: "Let it be understood that no repudiator of one farthing of our public debt will be trusted in public place, and it will go far towards strengthening a credit which ought to be the best in the world, and will ultimately enable us to replace the debt with bonds bearing less interest than we now pay." His faithful adherence to the principle of national integrity, through evil report and good report, is shown in his various communications to Congress in annual and special Messages. The favourable condition of our national exchequer to-day is a direct result of the clear intelligence and high sense of national honour shown by President Grant in dealing with the problems of finance, concerning which he was supposed to be so ill-informed. The first bill he ever signed was an act to " strengthen public credit," approved March 18, 1869. It was a declaratory act, in answer to the resolution of the Democratic platform in the preceding Presidential election in favour of paying all public debts in paper except when coin was specifically named in the law. The Democrats in Congress united in opposition to it, a few Republicans, under the lead of General Butler, voting with them. The bill promised the payment of all Government obligations, notes and bonds, in coin or its equivalent, except where the agreement expressly provided for the payment in lawful money.

In his first Inaugural Address, Grant had urged that measures should be taken to secure a prompt return to specie payment, and a series of legislative acts having this object in view were passed during his Administration, culminating in the act of January 14, 1875, providing for the redemption after January 1, 1879, of United States legal-tender notes, in coin. The expected result followed, and the paper dollar, worth only seventy-six cents in coin when Grant assumed office, advanced in value over thirty per cent., or within two or three cents of par, before he retired to private life. The soundness of his views on the subjects of currency and finance is shown not only in his official documents, but in private letters which were unmistakably the work of his own hand.

The most marked illustration of the President's determination to maintain the national credit at a high level is found in his veto, April 22, 1874, of what is known as the Inflation Act, " a bill to fix the amount of the United States Notes, and the circulation of National Banks, and for other purposes." It proposed to add one hundred millions to the paper circulation, and was, as the President declared in his veto message, " a departure from the true principles of finance, national interest, national obligations to creditors, Congressional promises, party pledges on the part of both political parties—and of personal views and promises made by me in every Annual Message sent to Congress, and in each Inaugural Address." Grant had shown his habitual determination of purpose in constantly urging the withdrawal from circulation of a medium of exchange having a fluctuating value, and " only worth," as he said, " what it will purchase of gold and silver, metals having an intrinsic value just in proportion to the honest labour it takes to produce them."

The pressure upon the President to secure his signature to the inflation bill was very great, and he was always reluctant to interfere with the progress of legislation by a veto, believing that others were as competent as himself to decide what wisdom required. It was a period of financial distress, and from all directions came a demand for more money, and a persistent assertion of the pernicious principle that it was in the power of the Government to create money to any extent, by simply setting its paper mills and presses to work. The President so far yielded to this pressure at one time, as to decide upon signing the bill, and he sat down to write a statement of his reasons for doing so. In endeavouring to find satisfactory reasons for departing from the declared purpose of his Administration and his party, it became clear to him that he would have to manufacture excuses for doing what did not approve itself to his judgment and his conscience. This was impossible to a man of his integrity of mind. He tore up the message of approval which he was preparing, after struggling over it for many hours, and rapidly wrote the veto message he sent to Congress.

Nothing in Grant's career more clearly illustrates than does this veto the influences that determined his action in great matters. The question as to how a given decision might influence his own fortunes, the fortunes of his party, or even the fate of his country, was always dominated in his mind by the larger question as to what was right in itself. If he was clear in his opinion that the step immediately before him was the right one to take, he gave himself no concern as to whither it might lead. Thus he was as calmly confident in adversity as in victory; when criticism and complaint pursued him, as when the echo of public applause gave such assurance as it could that his course was in the right direction.

Again, when the bill to restore specie payments was sent to him for signature in January, 1875, the President showed how keenly he appreciated the importance of a sound financial policy, by following the unusual plan of accompanying his approval of the bill with a special message, in which he declared that it was a subject of congratulation that a measure had become a law which fixed a date when specie resumption should commence. He suggested further legislation to make the bill more effective.

Let it be remembered by those who oppose national extravagance that the appropriations for pensions, which amounted to one hundred and forty millions in the year 1896, were only twenty-eight millions in the last year of Grant's term, 1877, and showed a decrease that year of nearly seven millions, as compared with 1871. Of his few veto messages, one was that refusing his signature to a Bounty Bill.

President Grant also interested himself in matters of tariff legislation, his policy being to limit the tariff to luxuries that the country could dispense with, and articles called for in excess of our ability to produce them, admitting, free, articles not produced in the United States, including tea, coffee, and other articles in universal use. Incidental to the changes in Customs Law, was the passage of a bill, in 1874, making radical changes in Treasury methods which had prevailed since the foundation of the Government, and substituting specific salaries for the moieties and perquisites theretofore allowed the customs officers for the detection of fraud upon the revenue. Though these were sanctioned by precedent and law, they had become a source of oppression to merchants, and a public scandal, due to harsh and arbitrary interference with the transaction of mercantile business.

Improvements were also made in the administration of the law for the collection of internal revenue, but "where the carcass is, the eagles will be gathered together." The immense sums collected from the whiskey tax, amounting to over fifty millions of dollars a year, offered the temptation, and defects in the law the opportunity, for dishonest men. Early in the year 1875 an extensive conspiracy to defraud the Government was discovered in St. Louis, and on May 10th, sixty-one distilleries and rectifying houses were seized by officers of the Treasury Department. Numerous prosecutions of dishonest Government agents and others followed. When the matter was brought to his attention, General Grant issued an order that became famous: " Let no guilty man, however high, escape." But partisan malice and personal hostility, sought to fasten upon him the responsibility for the loss of several millions of revenue, due to defects in the law that were corrected as soon as discovered.

The law then in existence apparently assumed that the two thousand three hundred storekeepers and gaugers, scattered over the country, were too honest to be tempted by the bribes of distillers, and no proper system of surveillance over them was provided. The President's generous nature prompted him to sympathise, in a measure, with men who had been subjected to unusual and improper temptations, and who were, as he believed, selected for punishment, not because they were more guilty than others, but because their punishment promoted the selfish ambition of men in authority. He was anxious that the law should be enforced with impartiality and strict justice, but he did not approve of what he regarded as an attempt to make political and personal capital out of the misfortunes of others, even though they were unworthy.

During our Civil War the ordinary machinery of public administration was destroyed, or strained to the breaking point. Everything had to be readjusted, and adjusted in the greatest haste, to entirely new conditions. New laws were passed, involving the collection and expenditure of hundreds of millions of dollars, under the direction of officials untried in their new duties, if not unfitted for them. Unwonted temptations came to men who had not been proved. Taking these conditions, in connection with the vicious system of appointment to office, it was inevitable that there should be much looseness, and some dishonesty, revealed. It was President Grant's misfortune that he had fallen heir to the loose methods resulting from enormous expenditures made under conditions that weakened the official sense of public accountability. It was his effort to discover defects, and when he honestly revealed them unfair attempts were made to hold him responsible for them.

The war was followed by an immense development of mental activity, vast progress in mechanical improvement, and great industrial and financial changes. To this day the ablest political economists and publicists are discussing the meaning and the future results of these changes. Grant was held responsible by excited public sentiment, as have been those who succeeded him, for results originating in causes beyond political control. The fetich worshipper, who beats his idol when it will not give him rain, is as common in civilised society as in the jungles of Africa.

The Indian Bureau was one of the departments which required thorough reorganisation, for there was constant complaint of dishonesty or irregularity in the distribution of supplies for the Indians. Grant shared the sympathy that is felt by all Army officers for the aborigines, of whose ignorance advantage was taken by shifty contractors. As a lieutenant in the Army, he had been thrown much in contact with the Indians in early life; he had witnessed the unjust treatment they received, and had resolved that if he ever had any influence or power he would endeavour to ameliorate their condition.

When the opportunity offered, he was faithful to this promise of his youth. Believing that officers of the Army were honest as a class, and that they would treat the Indians with justice and consideration, he endeavoured, but without success, to persuade Congress to transfer the care of the Indians from the Department of the Interior to the War Department.

Failing in this, he called upon the various religious bodies of the country to assist him in the selection of Indian agents. In his first Annual Message he had declared that " a system which looks to the extinction of a race is too horrible for a nation to adopt without entailing upon itself the wrath of all Christendom, and engendering in the citizen a disregard for human life, and the rights of others, dangerous to society." To avoid this, he proposed to gather the Indians on reservations, under territorial Governments, and to induce them to take their land in severalty. This is the policy that has since been pursued, but the greatest factors in quieting the Indians have been the completion of transcontinental railroads, and the consequent destruction of the buffalo. Grant foresaw and predicted the result that would follow these causes, but he found it impossible to carry out, in freedom, the policy which would in time lessen Indian outrages.

In one of his conversations, reported by Mr. Young, General Grant said: " there is nothing more natural than that a President, new to his office, should enter upon a policy of conciliation. He wants to make everybody friendly, to have all the world happy, to be the central figure of a contented and prosperous commonwealth. This is what occurs to every President; it is an emotion natural to the office." One of his roseate expectations when he assumed office was that he would be able to reconcile the South to the new order; but in this he failed. There was never a moment, he declared, when he would not have gone half-way to meet the Southern people in a spirit of conciliation, but they never responded, believing that by an alliance with the party in opposition to the Administration they could control the Government. During the whole of his first term, and during much of his second term, the country was kept in a ferment of excitement by the disputes concerning the control of elections in the Southern States. The condition of affairs at that time is well described by the Supreme Court of Mississippi in a decision rendered in 1896. In this the learned judge said of Mississippi, which was a typical State:

"Our unhappy State had passed in rapid succession from civil war, through a period of military occupancy, followed by another in which the control of public affairs had passed to a recently enfranchised race unfitted by education or experience for the responsibility thrust upon it. This was succeeded by a semi-military, semi-civil uprising, under which the white race, inferior in number, but superior in spirit, in governmental instinct, and in intelligence, was restored to power. The anomaly was then presented of a government whose distinctive characteristic was that it rested upon the will of the majority, being controlled and administered by a minority of those entitled under its organic law to exercise the electoral franchise. Within the field of permissible action under the limitations imposed by the federal constitution the convention swept the circle of expedients to obstruct the exercise by the negro race of the franchise."

Immediately after his entrance upon his first term, Grant sent a special message to Congress, suggesting that to restore the remaining States to their proper relations to the Government, it was desirable to remove all causes of irritation as promptly as possible, that a more perfect union might be established, and the country restored to peace and prosperity. Early in the following year the work of reconstruction was completed; the military governments whose just and fair administration had secured the peace of the South, were now withdrawn, and race and class interests once more started into activity. The law still required the President to interfere with local affairs when this seemed necessary to preserve the public peace, and he had authority to suspend the habeas corpus on occasion. This led to calls upon him involving the whole question of determining which of two rival State governments had the best claim upon his recognition. Whatever his decision, he was certain to be damned if he did, and damned if he did n't; for each faction had the sympathies of one or the other of the two great parties dividing the country.

The President was resolved to do impartial justice, but it was not easy to determine what justice required. When he sought to ascertain the facts, he found himself perplexed by the problem that disturbed Pilate: "What is truth?" He endeavoured to carry out the laws with strict impartiality, and those who were opposed to these laws, criticised him, in effect, because he would not make the mistakes that had ruined Johnson, and set up his own will in opposition to the enactments of the Legislature. Even his critics were forced to admit, however, that he used the extraordinary powers conferred upon him with discretion and moderation. In his Annual Message, December, 1874, he said, " The whole subject of Executive interference with the affairs of the State is repugnant to public opinion. Unless most clearly on the side of law, such interference becomes a crime." He declined as often as was possible to interfere with the administration of affairs at the South, and in answer to a call for troops from Governor Ames of Mississippi, he said to him, what he said in effect to others under like circumstances, " The whole public are tired out with this annual autumnal outbreak in the South, and the great majority are ready now to condemn any interference on the part of the Government. I heartily wish that peace and good order may be restored without issuing the proclamation, but, if not, the proclamation must be issued." The Constitution required that the Federal Government should render its assistance to quell disturbances in the States under certain conditions, announcing by proclamation its intention to do so; and the Executive of the State was the sole judge as to the emergency, when the Legislature was not in session. Though his official duty sometimes compelled him to recognise what were known as " Carpet-bag " Governments at the South—that is, government by emigrants from the North and negroes under their influence—the President did not favour them. He perceived how essential it was to a successful government at the South to avoid excluding from office the leaders of public opinion " merely because they were, before the Rebellion, of standing and character sufficient to be elected to positions requiring them to take oaths to support the Constitution, while admitting to eligibility those entertaining precisely the same views, but of less standing in the community." This opinion was expressed as early as 1871 in his Annual Message to Congress.

It was Grant's habit while he was President to seek rest and recreation at the seaside, and this subjected him to ill-natured criticism which finally led to the adoption by the House on April 3, 1876, of a resolution demanding that the President should give an account of his performance of executive acts and duties while absent from " the seat of Government established by law." The reply to this was dignified and crushing. The President denied the right of the Legislature " to require of the Executive, an independent branch of the Government, co-ordinate with the Senate and House of Representatives, an account of the discharge of his appropriate and purely executive offices, acts, and duties, either as to when, where, or how performed." At the same time he made a frank statement of the facts of the case, and showed that his practice had accorded with that of his predecessors, none of whom had " entertained the idea that their executive offices could be performed only at the seat of Government," as " evidenced by the hundreds upon hundreds of such acts performed by my predecessors, in unbroken line, from Washington to

Lincoln." Jefferson was absent, for example, from the seat of Government seven hundred and ninety-six days, or more than one fourth of the period covered by his two terms of office.

The public business did not suffer under Grant because it was transacted during a part of the year by telegraph and post. In the various departments there was an increase in efficiency and economy from the moment he entered upon the Executive office. The yearly financial report showed a progressive decrease in public expenditures, a steady reduction in public debt and the interest account, and a corresponding lightening of the burdens of taxation. The reduction in customs and internal revenue taxes during his eight years of office amounted to $158,000,000; the amount being nearly equally divided between customs dues and internal revenue taxes; thirty millions of this was represented by reduction in the cost of administering the Government, and thirty-two millions by a decrease in the interest on the public debt. The principal of the debt was decreased, meanwhile, by over four hundred millions. What remained of it was partially refunded at lower rates of interest.

Among the recommendations contained in the various Messages of President Grant was one advising the taxation of church property, and he urged Congress to legislate with reference to Mormon polygamy, the enslavement of the Chinese as coolies, and the debasement of Chinese women, by importing them for immoral purposes. Under his Administration international relations with reference to the delivery of postal matter were extended, all cities having ten thousand inhabitants or more, were included in the free-delivery system, postal-cards were adopted, and our Government took an active part in establishing the Universal Postal Union which now covers the civilised world, represents one thousand million people, " brings the postal service of all countries to every man's neighbourhood, and has wrought marvels in cheapening postal rates and securing absolutely safe mail communication throughout the world."

Among the " scandals " of his Administration was the transformation of Washington from a mudhole, with provincial means of communication, into one of the handsomest capitals in the world, with an excellent system of intercommunication. Those who accomplished this great work learned something of the ingratitude of republics, and that they who seek the interest of posterity, as in this case, do not always find it easy to secure the favour of contemporaries.

It has never been found necessary to undo the work of Grant's two terms in the Presidency. Progress has been along the lines he laid down, and our difficulties since have largely resulted from a neglect of the principles of finance and public administration he so clearly recognised. In such matters as the taxation of religious property, amounting in 1875 to one thousand million dollars; in his arguments for the extension of our relations with South American States; his recommendations concerning the Isthmus Canal; the possession of territory in the Carribbean Sea; and the establishment of continuous land-locked navigation along our coasts from Maine to the Gulf of Mexico, he was in advance of his time. If he incurred the malignant criticism of his contemporaries, as all Presidents have done in greater or lesser measure, posterity will rise up and call him blessed.

As President Grant's second term of office drew near its close the question of his nomination for a third term became an important political issue. There was no constitutional prohibition against his re-election, but no President had ever been elected for a third term. This fact was assumed to establish a precedent, having the force of unwritten law, prohibiting a President from twice becoming his own successor. By a vote of 234 to 18, seventy Republicans voting in the affirmative, the House of Representatives passed a resolution declaring:

> "That in the opinion of this House the precedent established by Washington and other Presidents of the United States, in declining a re-election after their second term, has become by universal concurrence, a part of our Republican system of government, and that a departure from this time-honoured custom would be unwise, unpatriotic, and fraught with peril to our free institutions."

The opponents of the Republican party and the Administration were filling the air with their lusty cries of "Cæsarism," and calling on the President to define his position on the question of "the third term." These demands he treated with silent contempt, believing it to be beneath the dignity of his office to state his opinions "before the subject should be presented by authority competent to make a nomination, or by a body of such dignity and authority as not to make a reply a fair subject of ridicule." But when the question of his renomination was formally considered by the Pennsylvania State Convention, in May, 1875, Grant wrote a letter to the presiding officer of that Convention, in which he said:

"Now, for the 'third term.' I do not want it any more than I did the first. I would not write nor utter a word to change the will of the people in expressing and having their choice. The question of the number of terms allowed to any one Executive can only come up fairly in the shape of a proposition to amend the Constitution, a shape in which all political parties can participate, fixing the length of time or the number of terms for which any one person shall be eligible for the office of President. Until such amendment is adopted the people cannot be restricted in their choice by resolution further than they are now restricted as to age, nativity, etc. It may happen in the future history of the country that to change an Executive because he has been eight years in office will prove unfortunate, if not disastrous. The idea that any man should elect himself President, or even renominate himself is preposterous. It is a reflection upon the intelligence and patriotism of the people to suppose such a thing possible. Any man can destroy his chances for the office, but no one can force an election or even a nomination. To recapitulate: I am not, nor have I ever been a candidate for a renomination. I would not accept a nomination if it were tendered, unless it should come under such circumstances as to make it an imperative duty—circumstances not likely to arise."

This was accepted as a positive refusal to become a candidate before the Republican Convention, and it was so intended. But, while declining in his own person to become a candidate for a third term, the President refused to pass judgment on a question that was not within his province to determine.

When the Republican Convention met at Cincinnati a year later, on June 14, 1876, Grant was not mentioned as a candidate, and Rutherford B. Hayes of Ohio was nominated on the seventh ballot, over his chief opponent, James G. Blaine. The Democrats met at St. Louis, June 28, and nominated as their candidate Samuel J. Tilden of New York. The election followed in November. Mr. Tilden received a plurality in the popular vote of 250,970 over Mr. Hayes, and a majority over all of 157,394. The question of his majority in the Electoral College was long in doubt. The accuracy or honesty of the returns from the States of Louisiana, South Carolina, Florida, and Oregon was in dispute. The air was filled with charges and counter-charges of bribery and corruption. Public feeling was greatly excited, and there were partisan threats of interference with the inauguration of Mr. Hayes if he should be declared elected. These threats did not greatly disturb the old soldier in the White House, but he took all proper precaution. In a conversation with Mr. Young, he said:

"I never believed there would be a blow, but I had so many warnings that I made all preparations. I knew all about the rifle clubs of South Carolina, for instance, the extent of whose organization has never been made known. I was quite prepared for any contingency. Any outbreak would have been suddenly and summarily stopped. So far as that was concerned my course was clear, and my mind was made up. I did not intend to have two governments, nor any South American pronunciamentos. I did not intend to receive 'commissioners from sovereign States' as Buchanan did. If Tilden was declared elected, I intended to hand him over the reins, and see him peacefully installed. I should have treated him as cordially as I did Hayes, for the question of the Presidency was neither personal nor political, but national. I tried to act with the utmost impartiality between the two. I would not have raised my finger to have put Hayes in, if in so doing I did Tilden the slightest injustice. All I wanted was for the legal powers to declare a President, to keep the machine running, to allay the passions of the canvass, and allow the country peace."

At one time there was some idle talk of inaugurating Mr. Tilden in New York City, in the event of Mr. Hayes's inauguration at Washington, and establishing a rival capital. Even a contingency so remote was prepared for, by giving instructions to put New York in a state of siege, in such event, taking military possession of the narrow peninsula connecting it with the mainland, and, with the aid of the Navy, cutting off its supplies of food and water.

In a memorable despatch to General Sherman, who was then the Commander of the Army, dated November the 10th, the President said:

"Instruct General Augur in Louisania and General Ruger in Florida to be vigilant with the forces at their command to preserve peace and good order, and to see that the proper and legal boards of canvassers are unmolested in the performance of their duties. Should there be any grounds of suspicion of a fraudulent count on either side it should be reported and denounced at once. No man worthy of the office of President should be willing to hold it if counted in or placed there by fraud. Either party can afford to be disappointed in the result. The country cannot afford to have the result tainted by the suspicion of illegal or false returns."

Congress finally passed a bill organising a Commission to determine the question of the count in the doubtful States, and Mr. Hayes was declared elected by a majority of one vote in the Electoral

College. Thus, again, the firmness and good sense of Grant enabled the country to pass safely through a most serious crisis in its history. His mere presence in command of the resources of the Nation was in itself sufficient to dissuade the violent from any attempt at incendiary proceedings. On March 4, 1877, he transferred to Mr. Hayes the powers of the high office he had exercised for eight years with such ability, fidelity, and devotion to the public interests, and quietly retired to private life. The cynics in the London clubs who had offered bets at the close of our Civil War that General Grant would within a few years be Emperor of the United States were disappointed, but lovers of liberty the world over rejoiced that free institutions had given certain proof of their ability to meet a crisis that would severely test the strength of any form of government.

CHAPTER XXIII.

TWO YEARS OF TRAVEL—HONOURS RECEIVED ABROAD.

MARCH, 1877–SEPTEMBER, 1879.

T the close of his second term of office as President, General Grant found himself, for the first time in sixteen years, relieved from all official responsibility, and free to follow his own course as a private citizen. His eight years of service as Chief Magistrate had been the most perplexing and harassing of his public career, and he resolved to seek relaxation in foreign travel. As soon as he had ceased to be a political factor, his popularity revived, and men of all parties and all classes united in showing him honour. Dinners and banquets followed each other in rapid succession, and when, on May 17, 1877, the ex-President sailed from Philadelphia in the steamship *Indiana* for Liverpool he was accompanied down the Delaware by a distinguished party, and a fleet of vessels of every character followed the departing steamer for miles, making, as became a naval escort, all the noise they could.

The following twenty-eight months were spent in a journey around the world with a party consisting of two members of his family (Mrs. Grant and Jesse Grant), Mr. Borie, late Secretary of the Navy, and Mr. John Russell Young, who has recorded the experiences of the travellers in a volume entitled *Around the World with General Grant*. In most of the countries he visited, the General was received with the honours reserved for the rulers of kingdoms, and with testimonials of personal respect that appeared to be as sincere as they were cordial. Rulers and statesmen conferred with him on questions of government and public policy; savants and scholars flocked to the receptions and dinners given in his honour; workingmen in England presented him with addresses, and the common people gathered by the wayside by tens of thousands to greet him as he passed, with a heartiness and good-will testifying to some deeper sentiment than idle curiosity. If he was the peer and companion of kings, he was also in sympathy with the humblest of their subjects, and in the imagination of the lowly he bridged the gulf dividing them from the great and powerful. He visited, during his circuit of the globe, the principal cities of the British Islands and the Continent, Egypt, Palestine, Siam, Burmah, India, China, and Japan. In England he dined with the Queen and with the Prince of Wales, and was received with cordiality in the most exclusive society, but was treated with just sufficient reserve to make it apparent that he was not recognised as belonging to the purple. He was not accorded the precedence shown to him elsewhere, and a circular was sent by the English Foreign Office to its representatives abroad, directing that the attentions shown to him should be limited to those accorded to a distinguished citizen.

In Belgium, the etiquette governing the intercourse of sovereigns was observed by King Leopold II., who called in person and invited General and Mrs. Grant to a dinner at the Royal Palace, where they were given precedence over all others. Similar courtesy was shown to the ex-President in Holland, where, in addition to the attentions extended to him by the King, he was invited by the chief cities to accept their hospitality. His brevity in speech, his impassive manner, and his constant cigar, put him *en rapport* with the Dutchmen.

The Spanish Government settled the question of etiquette by receiving Grant with the highest military honours, those accorded to a Captain-General of the Spanish army, and the young King Alfonso, when he met him at Vittoria, entered into a very frank conversation concerning his own perplexities as a sovereign. "The General had seen something of them, and knew what they were." The King of Portugal invited him to a dinner and an audience at the Palace, consulted with him as to a translation he had made from English poets, and gave him a copy of his Portuguese rendering of *Hamlet*, with an autographic inscription.

As General Grant reached Berlin just after an attempt had been made upon the life of Emperor William, he was courteously informed that nothing but the imperative orders of the Emperor's physician prevented an audience. Prince Bismarck was especially cordial in his attentions, finding time in the midst of his constant duties as Chancellor of the German Empire, and President of the Berlin Congress then in session, to show many courtesies, and to enter upon an exchange of views upon public matters at the General's hotel, and at his own home in Berlin, the Radziwill Palace. In Austria, Grant dined with the Emperor, and in Russia and Italy he received marked attentions, but only such as are shown to distinguished commoners. Marshal McMahon, the President of the French Republic, met him in the spirit of army comradeship, and the two old soldiers walked arm in arm in the Champs Élysées, exchanging experiences, each speaking his own language which the other understood, but could not use fluently. On the whole, however, France was less cordial in her greetings than other countries, and Victor Hugo led in an attack upon the distinguished visitor, whose sympathy with Germany in the Franco-Prussian war was ascribed to hostility toward France, whereas it was merely an expression of one of his few antipathies—a dislike of Napoleon and Napoleonic methods. In Switzerland the General was entertained by the President with the simple but kindly etiquette becoming a republic.

Grant made two visits to the British Islands, taking a flying trip in the interval to Belgium, the Rhine Country, Switzerland, Northern Italy, Alsace and Lorraine. His progress through the United

Kingdom was a continuous ovation. He was the lion of the London season, and within three weeks, three thousand cards were left at his door. He was recognised in the British Islands not only as the great soldier and pacificator, but also as one who, in power, had successfully exerted himself to establish better relations between the English-speaking peoples. Scotland opened wide her arms to receive the most distinguished representative of her famous clan. He had ruled over more Irishmen than any sovereign save Victoria, and Irishmen by the thousands had marched to battle and victory under his standard. The Irish heart warmed toward him, and one little girl in an Irish crowd felt so near akin that she begged that he would carry her love home with him to her aunt in America. Various cities in England, Scotland, and Ireland bestowed their freedom on the great American, or made him at home among them as an adopted citizen. Through streets illuminated because of his presence, and under arches bearing inscriptions of welcome, he passed in triumphal procession to attend banquets given in his honour. Crowds gathered in-doors and out-of-doors to listen to his slightest word, and to greet what he said with the hearty British cheer; when he entered a theatre the performance was stopped, and the audience rose while the band played American airs, or some famous singer led the chorus; the horses were taken from his carriage, and he was drawn by sturdy arms through streets crowded with people eager to grasp his hand.

But his trial came when the silent soldier was forced to meet the ceaseless flow of British eloquence with speech. His responses to the greetings of some of the ablest representatives of English thought and English public sentiment were as felicitous in what was left unsaid as in what was said. The opportunities for striking jarring notes met the warrior, unaccustomed to speech, at every turn, but they were always skilfully avoided. The reserve proper to such occasions necessarily limited his range of thought, but in many a happy turn of expression Grant showed that he could not only think clearly but could express himself happily; as when at a dinner given to him by Thomas Hughes, the host, in proposing the health of his distinguished guest, relieved him of the " burden of a formal reply," and Grant instantly arose and said:

" Mr. Hughes, I must none the less tell you what gratification it gives me to hear my health proposed in such hearty words by Tom Brown of Rugby."

Again, as at Dublin, where, after receiving the freedom of the city, enclosed in an ancient carved bog oak casket, before proceeding to more serious matters, he said to his " fellow-citizens of Dublin, amid much cheering and laughter ": " I may return to Dublin one day, and run against Barrington for Mayor and Brett for Parliament, and I warn these gentlemen that I am a troublesome candidate."

And witness this expression of noble sentiment at Glasgow, where the cheering was so general and continuous that the ceremonies could only be followed with difficulty:

"Though I may not live to see the general settlement of National difficulties by arbitration, it will not be many years before that system of settlement will be adopted, and the immense standing armies that are depressing Europe by their great expense will be disbanded, and the arts of war almost forgotten in the general devotion of the people to the development of peaceful industries. I want to see, and I believe I shall see, Great Britain, the United States, and Canada joined with common purpose in the advance of civilization; an invincible community of English-speaking nations that all the world beside could not conquer."

Through experiences that called for a display not only of ability, but the highest qualities of the gentleman, the ex-President passed with credit to himself and honour to his countrymen. Even his propensity to "talk horse," and his affinity with "horsey" men commended him to the aristocracy of England, if they did bring upon him the disapproval of priggish Americans who have no appreciation of any knowledge that is not fished for in an ink-horn. Nor was Grant's intercourse on the Continent confined to royal and official circles. He was called upon by nearly every man of note in the various countries he visited. Richard Wagner, the composer, visited him at Heidelberg, but as neither gentleman could speak the other's language, the meeting was not prolific of social exchanges. This was not without its advantages, for Grant's knowledge of music was in inverse ratio to his mastery of the art of war. It is doubtful whether he could have distinguished between "Yankee Doodle" and Sigmund's "Love Song."

It was in the East, however, that Grant received the most distinguished honours. He carried with him there not only the prestige of a great reputation, but also wisdom that is the ripened fruit of experience and reflection, of a sound head and a good heart. Accustomed to a keen study of human nature, the rulers of the Orient, and especially those of China, Japan, and Siam, seemed to recognise as by instinct that here was a man worthy of their fullest confidence; one representing a great Nation, whose friendship for them was not subject to the suspicion of a desire for territorial aggrandisement at their expense. They had been long accustomed to the assertion of might against right in their intercourse with foreign nations, to interference with their national prerogatives, not in deference to some grave necessity of state, but as a mere display of the wantonness of power. Grant represented to them the idea of power restrained by right and justice in international intercourse. They consulted him freely about the most delicate matters of state, and the candour and fairness of judgment he showed deepened the impression, and established him in everlasting remembrance with those who profited by his wise advice.

At Bangkok, a royal palace, adjoining that of the King of Siam, was placed at the General's disposal, and the King bestowed upon him what was in Siam an honour almost unheard of in that Oriental country, namely, that of returning his visit. He was placed next to the King at a dinner attended by members of the royal family and other high functionaries. The King's brother, one of the "Celestial Princes," with a retinue of other princes and noblemen, was charged with the duty of looking after his comfort. The young King Chulalongkorn conceived the most sincere friendship for the General. He sent him two personal letters welcoming him to Siam, and full of cordial expressions of good-will, also other letters while he was in the East, and corresponded with him upon his return to America.

The progress through the Chinese Empire was a triumphal procession. The Emperor of China was at that time a boy of seven, and the ex-President was received at Pekin by Prince Kung, the Emperor's uncle and representative. Grant gave the Prince advice which greatly impressed him, especially as coming from a foreigner, and so won upon his confidence and respect that he bespoke his good offices to settle a dispute of long standing with Japan concerning the Loo Choo Islands. This dispute was brought to a conclusion satisfactory to both Governments by the interposition of General Grant. Between the American General and Li Hung Chang, the great Viceroy of China, there was a bond of sympathy, having its origin in a similarity of experience, and to some extent in a similarity of characters, developed though they were in such different schools of training. The barrier of suspicion which closes the Oriental mind to the modern ideas dominating the West was torn down in the intercourse between these two great men.

No man visiting China for a brief period has ever had the opportunity to impress himself upon the statesmen controlling the destinies of that great Empire which came freely to this simple citizen of the United States, holding no official position, bearing no message of peace or war, and powerful only in the ripeness of his experience, in the vigour of his thought, and in the homely honesty and simplicity of his character. Over the road the English armies had marched when they destroyed and entered the Summer Palace at Pekin, this plain American was conveyed with honours accorded only to the highest, and returned leaving behind him an impression, which, according to high authority, had done " more than anything else to break down the great wall between China and the outer world."

On his arrival in the harbour of Nagasaki, Prince Dati, the head of one of the oldest and most powerful of the Daimio families, came aboard the steamer to greet the General in the name of the Emperor of Japan, and at Tokio he was lodged in one of the palaces of the Tycoon. Pictures of him, in heroic attitudes, were to be seen in the shop windows of Japan, and wherever he went through the streets, the courteous Japanese lined up by the wayside and bowed a greeting.

His chief delight was to come in contact with the people, that he might form his own conclusions with regard to their customs and habits. He was a tireless traveller, and laid out his route with great exactness in advance, following it with military precision. Thus he was able to make the most of his time, and it was in spite of himself that he was obliged to see so much of the world through the veil of official ceremonies and court functions.

Circumstances favouring, the Emperor of Japan took pains to select the anniversary of America's Independence as the day for receiving the American ex-President. When they met, his Imperial Majesty advanced and shook hands, somewhat awkwardly, and as one performing an unaccustomed function, for it was the first time that such a courtesy had ever been shown by the Emperor, and it was the greatest innovation upon the unbroken traditions of exclusiveness and sanctity guarding the oldest royal line in the world, one having the prestige of twelve hundred years of descent through a continuous succession of royal ancestors.

Grant was even more burdened with official ceremony when travelling abroad than he was at Washington; but he was free from care and responsibility, the endless weariness of selfish importunity, and the oppression of constant criticism and complaint. This freedom refreshed his spirit so much that when he reached home, his friends noticed the absence of the anxious look they had observed during his last years in public office. On his return to America he was much surprised by a greeting that showed how little the people had been affected by the slanders circulated to his discredit by political rivals and censorious critics, whose tongues should have blistered before they uttered them.

Reaching San Francisco on the evening of Saturday, September 20, 1879, he was met at quarantine by a delegation of distinguished representatives of the city in which twenty-five years before he had landed with an empty pocket, and perplexed to know where he was to find a night's lodging and a supper. Receptions, speeches, and functions of various sorts occupied the succeeding two months during General Grant's visit to the Pacific coast, and his progress to his home in Galena, Illinois. Everywhere he went he was called upon to exercise his recently developed gifts as a public speaker, and he delivered some thirty speeches in response to a flood of eloquence from governors, senators, municipal authorities, and statesmen.

An interesting feature of his reception, and one that deeply touched Grant's heart, was the greeting he received from the children belonging to the public schools in the various cities through which he passed. They met him with songs and cheers, and deluged him with flowers. Those interested in public education remembered with gratitude the important services which he had rendered to their cause, and they recalled especially the speech he had made to his comrades of the Army of the Tennessee at their reunion at Des Moines, Iowa, September 29, 1875. It was one of the most elaborate speeches he ever made, and perhaps the most eloquent.

In it he said:

"Encourage free schools, and resolve that not one dollar appropriated for their support shall be appropriated to the support of any sectarian school. Resolve that neither the State nor Nation, not both combined, shall support institutions of learning other than those sufficient to afford to every child growing up in the land the opportunity for a good common-school education, unmixed with sectarian, pagan, or atheistical dogmas. Leave the matter of religion to the family altar, the church, and the private school, supported entirely by private contributions. Keep the Church and State forever separate.

In another speech made during this journey from San Francisco to his home, he said: "I think that if there ever is another war in this country it will be one of ignorance and superstition combined against education and intelligence."

The reception of the ex-President culminated at Chicago, where, on November 12, 1879, he was received and escorted from the station, through the rain and mud, by a procession of from ten to twelve thousand soldiers and civilians, under the command of General Sheridan. The city was elaborately decorated in his honour, some of the most imposing displays adorning the houses of those who were known as his political opponents. Grant's comrades of the Army of the Tennessee were holding their annual session in Chicago at the time, and added their plaudits to the general welcome. No one who has not experienced it can realize how the old soldier is moved to the very depths of his being by anything that recalls his days of danger and comradeship, and how completely he abandons himself to the intoxication of enthusiasm in the presence of a leader who represents his days of glory and honour.

"This, too, shall have an end." Grant's days of travel and excitement were over for the time being, and in his quiet home at Galena he settled down to dreams of leisure and domestic tranquility. But vast changes had occurred during the eighteen years since he left the leather store in Galena, to resume his sword in the service of his country. He was no longer in harmony with his surroundings; restlessness and a desire for new scenes succeeded content.

In the winter of 1879 he made a visit to Cuba and Mexico, returning to Galena in the early Spring. In the following Summer he visited Colorado, and made a thorough examination of its mineral resources. This visit resulted in his election as president of a mining company.

Meanwhile the Presidential election was approaching, and Senators Conkling, Cameron, and Logan, representing the great States of New York, Pennsylvania, and Illinois, were uniting their efforts to secure Grant's renomination for President. They were greatly dissatisfied with Mr. Hayes's Administration, and remembered how narrowly they had escaped defeat at the time of his candidacy, through the fortunate turn of events that gave them the majority in the Electoral Commission. They believed that under the banner of Grant they could once more march to victory, but they could not obtain from him any formal consent to their plans, though his acquiescence in the election of delegates to the Convention pledged to vote for him, was accepted as a tacit consent to the use of his name. Grant always felt that he was the creature of events, and, as he tells us, had a superstitious feeling about interfering with the order of Divine Providence by seeking his own advancement in any way. He showed the same apparent indifference to the movement in his behalf that he had shown when he was chosen President for a first and second time. In this case, however, his feelings were more warmly enlisted, and his unspoken desire for renomination was stimulated by the wish of his family that he should return to office.

Among intimate friends with whom he could talk freely, he carefully calculated the probabilities of his being invited to resume a career in which he had made such distinguished success, and in which he felt that he could add still further to his own renown, and to the glory of his country.

Foreign travel, and especially his travels in Oriental countries, had warmed his imagination with the idea of great results to follow the formulation of a broader international policy. His ambition was legitimate and honourable, and as experience has since shown in the case of President Cleveland, his enemies entirely exaggerated the popular hostility to the nomination of the same man for a third time as a candidate for the office of Chief Magistrate. As a Presidential term intervened between Grant's retirement from office, and the presentation of his name before the Republican Convention of 1880, the two cases were analogous.

When the Convention met at Chicago, in June, 1880, Grant led the ballot with 304 votes, to 284 for Mr. Blaine, and 167 scattered among three other candidates. He held his friends together during an exciting contest of 36 ballots extending over two days, his smallest vote being 302, and the largest 313. Finally, the opposition concentrated on James A. Garfield, of Ohio, and he was, on the 36th ballot, nominated by 399 votes, to 307 for Grant and 50 scattered votes. Previous to the Convention, earnest efforts had been made by some of Grant's friends to persuade him to withdraw from the contest, and they succeeded so far as to induce him to write a letter authorising his friends, if they saw fit, to withdraw his name from the Convention. He accepted his defeat with much better grace than did some of his supporters, and exerted himself to persuade Senator Conkling, who had led his forces before the Convention, to enter the field in behalf of the ticket nominated. He joined the Senator in a tour through the country, attending political meetings, making political speeches, and contributing very much to the result that followed in the election of General Garfield. The heart of Conkling was not in the canvass, and to John Russell Young he said, after his manner, "The battle of Waterloo put back progress in France at least six centuries. The defeat of Grant has put back the progress of this country just as much."

When Grant became satisfied that his political record was closed, the question of choosing some other career presented itself to him. He was too active-minded a man to be idle, and the necessities of income compelled him to seek occupation, if he was not to be condemned to vegetating in a little Illinois town, or to living on a farm. Life in Galena was too dull and monotonous for a man who had passed through such varied and thrilling experiences; and a man of his public reputation needed the freedom of a great capital, which furnishes as near an approach to the independence of the wilderness as modern life affords. So he resolved to move to the city of New York, where he had numerous friends and admirers, some of whom had raised a fund amounting to $250,000, and trusteed it for the benefit of Mrs. Grant. The great city also offered the opportunity for a career to his three sons, concerning whose future he had a father's tender solicitude.

The recollection of his early experiences in Mexico was one of the romances of Grant's life, and subsequent experiences had strengthened his early impressions. He had a high idea of the character of the Mexicans, decided opinions as to the resources of their great country, and the possibilities of its development, and statesmanlike views as to the cultivation of more intimate relations between the United States and Mexico. Though he was not, as a rule, fond of foreigners in personal relations, he had conceived an almost romantic attachment for Señor Romero, for many years the representative of the Mexican Republic at Washington, and his attachment was reciprocated. He talked over his various projects with Romero, and together they conceived the idea of organising a company, with American capital, to build a railroad from the City of Mexico to the frontier of Guatemala, with branches running north to the Gulf of Mexico and south to the Pacific Ocean. This company was organised as the " Mexican National Railway," and General Grant was elected president, his office being established in New York. Though an important concession was obtained from the Mexican Government, the enterprise did not prove successful.

General Grant made two visits to Mexico, one in 1880 and another in the Spring of 1881, with reference to this railroad enterprise. At a dinner given to him at the City of Mexico, April 22, 1881, he said:

"I am sure that even if it could be shown that all the people of Mexico were in favor of the annexation of a portion of their territory to the United States it would still be rejected (by the United States). We want no more land. We do want to improve what we have, and we want to see our neighbors improve and grow so strong that the design of any other country could not endanger them."

By resolution of the Senate, passed April 5, 1882, negotiations for a commercial treaty with Mexico were authorised, and President Arthur appointed General Grant and Mr. William Henry Trescot, Commissioners. They negotiated a treaty which was signed at Washington, January 20, 1883, and approved by the Senate after a long debate, but the laws necessary to carry it into effect were not passed. Though the treaty was a fair and just one, and would have resulted in great benefits to both countries, it interfered with selfish interests, and subjected its authors to the most unjust reflections upon the disinterestedness of their motives. No longer in a place of power, Grant was without influence to secure the adoption of his views.

The scheme for building a railroad in Mexico was one of international importance, though ill fortune attended it as it did other projects upon which General Grant was persuaded to enter at this time. The clouds of misfortune were gathering thick about the head of the old soldier. His superstitions, or premonitions, as to the result of any attempt to advance merely selfish interests of his own, were destined to a speedy and bitter fulfilment. Once more the world was to be taught by conspicuous example that the noblest characters must be refined as if by fire.

CHAPTER XXIV.

"FORTUNE'S SHARPE ADVERSITE"—THE END.

1880-1885.

URING General Grant's visit to Europe, although he was really a national representative, he travelled at his own expense, paying his own mess bills when transported in a national vessel, so that the courtesies of Government were as costly as the expenses of private conveyance. He took from his little capital a fund of $25,000 for the expenses of himself and his family, and the question of the length of his stay was to be determined by the amount of travel this sum would provide for. During his absence, one of his sons had made fortunate investments for him in California, and added somewhat to the sum available. He thus acquired confidence in his son's business ability which had more tangible foundation than mere parental fondness. In New York this son had entered into partnership with a Wall Street broker named Ferdinand Ward, who had the reputation of being a "Napoleon of finance," and who soon carried out the simile by his passage from power to a

prison. While the firm of "Grant & Ward" continued, Ward contrived, by arts familiar to the designing, to create a fictitious display of prosperity that completely deceived General Grant, whose own methods were so direct that he had great difficulty in following the tortuous ways of the dishonest. He was not a shrewd man in a worldly sense. In matters that he understood his judgment was clear, and he reached sound conclusions with a certainty akin to perception. But he was easily misled where he depended upon the conclusions of others; his mind moved in straight lines, and he had but little discernment concerning devious methods. Fulsome praise was distasteful to him, but he was not insensible to that subtle flattery which betrays a man by making him think that his weakness is his strength, and that his seeming incapacity is merely ignorance of his own untried powers.

It is often the case with great men that they undervalue the accomplishment which comes so naturally, through the orderly operation of their intellectual faculties, that it does not reveal to their self-consciousness their own superiority. What is difficult of attainment seems the most precious, and accomplishment is measured, not so much by results, as by the degree of labour attending it. No one could flatter Grant by calling him a great soldier, and he had a strong aversion to discuss his campaigns in any personal sense. But when a Wall Street sharper sought to persuade him that he and his sons were great financiers, or, at least, that his sons were, he found a listening ear.

In November, 1880, General Grant, supposing that he was assuming the position of a special partner, was persuaded to invest in the firm of Grant & Ward all that he had, including the property of his wife. He had been given a house in Philadelphia, another in Washington, one in New York, a cottage at Long Branch, and a house in Galena, Illinois. These, with the various odds and ends of a fortune accumulated during his lifetime, made up a total of some $190,000, all of which disappeared with the assets of Grant & Ward, who speedily became bankrupt. He was, moreover, indebted to Mr. William H. Vanderbilt for $150,000, borrowed on his personal responsibility to tide over what seemed to be only a temporary crisis in the affairs of his firm. When difficulties came, the attempt was made to hold him responsible, as a general partner, for the firm's liabilities. The revelation of Ward's transactions showed him, too, what he had not known before, that extensive use had been made of his reputation to mislead investors, by means of those whispered conferences behind closed doors, so common in business transactions, especially where they are not legitimate. By skilful appeals to cupidity, Ward had succeeded in deceiving men of far greater acumen than General Grant, who, as a special partner, found no occasion to inquire into the details of the business, even if he could have understood them.

When the crash came, General Grant felt that everything had gone down in a general wreck—fortune, fame, the confidence and good opinion of his fellow-men. He had passed through many humiliations, but this was the sorest trial of all. He could have parted with his fortune without complaint, but there was the bitterness of feeling, that while he had himself been deceived, others had been misled by his apparent participation, if not acquiescence, in schemes for gain which his soul abhorred. His personal obligation to Mr. Vanderbilt he endeavoured to meet by turning over to him the valuable collection of souvenirs accumulated in part during his official career, and especially during his travels in Europe. His creditor would have cheerfully and gladly cancelled the obligation, but General Grant would not listen to such a proposition. And when, in a generous spirit, Mr. Vanderbilt persisted in transferring the property to Mrs. Grant, subject to its final transfer to the Government, she insisted that this transfer should take effect at once. On February 3, 1885, President Arthur sent a message to the House of Representatives calling attention to Mrs. Grant's offer to transfer these historical relics to the Government " as set forth in the accompanying papers." In his message, the President said:

"The nature of this gift and the value of the relics which the generosity of a private citizen, joined to the highest sense of public regard which animates Mrs. Grant, have thus placed at the disposal of the Government, demand full and signal recognition on behalf of the Nation at the hands of its representatives. I therefore ask Congress to take suitable action to accept the trust, and to provide for its secure custody, at the same time recording the appreciative gratitude of the people of the United States to the donors.

"In this connection I may pertinently advert to the pending

legislation in the Senate and House of Representatives looking to a national recognition of General Grant's eminent services by providing the means for his restoration to the Army on the retired list. That Congress by taking such action will give expression to the almost universal desire of the people of this Nation is evident, and I earnestly urge the passage of an act similar to Senate bill No. 2,530 which, while not interfering with the constitutional prerogative of appointment, will enable the President in his discretion to nominate General Grant as General on the retired list."

The articles deeded included the swords, paintings, bronzes, commissions, formal written addresses, and objects of art, presented by various Governments to General Grant; his army and corps badges, his numerous military commissions; his badges of membership in the Military Order of the Loyal Legion, the Aztec Society, and seven civil societies; resolutions and addresses innumerable, including the thanks of Congress, and his certificates of election and re-election as President of the United States. Among the articles was a Coptic Bible, presented by Lord Napier, who captured it from King Theodore of Abyssinia, and a complete set of Japanese coins, presented by the Government of Japan, the only one in existence, except that in the Japanese Treasury. These relics now repose in the archives at Washington—a testimony not only to the fame of General Grant, but to the high sense of honour that actuated him when overtaken by business adversity.

In accordance with the suggestion of President Arthur in the letter quoted, the Senate, on February 23, 1882, by a vote of 35 to 17, passed, after a long debate, an act authorising the President to place Grant on the retired list, with the rank of General. The bill passed the House March 3d, and the first official act of President Cleveland, after the nomination of his Cabinet, was to affix his signature to the commission of U. S. Grant as an officer on the retired list of the Army, with the rank of General. This gave him as pay $13,500 a year. On the 8th of December, 1884, Senator Mitchell, Chairman of the Committee on Pensions, had introduced a bill, granting a pension to General Grant, but this bill was withdrawn, as General Grant wrote, saying: "I understand the motive which has prompted this action on your part, and appreciate it very highly. But I beg you to withdraw the bill. Under no circumstance could I accept a pension, even if the bill should pass both Houses and receive the approval of the President." It was proposed to raise a private subscription for General Grant, and Mr. Vanderbilt offered to contribute a liberal sum. This offer was also declined.

After the failure of Grant & Ward, the editors of the *Century Magazine* wrote to General Grant's secretary, offering a tempting pecuniary inducement for two articles by General Grant, and his necessities at this time determined him to accept the offer, though he was reluctant to engage in a field where he had not tried his powers. In a single day he had passed from the control of ample means to poverty, and but for a loan of one thousand dollars, which his friend Romero forced upon him, and another of five hundred dollars sent by a stranger, "on account," as he said, "of my share for services ending April 1, 1865," he would have been without the means of meeting his household expenditures. Even Mrs. Grant's income from the trust fund of $250,000 failed at this juncture—some technicality of law temporarily suspending the payment of interest. So the opportunity to add to his income by the work of his pen was gladly accepted. Fame as an author he did not seek for or expect. His success as such was, however, decided, as soon as he learned from editorial hints and suggestions what was required of him. It was a surprise only to those who did not know him, for he had always shown great facility as a writer, and he had a marvellous memory, seldom forgetting a date, a fact, or a face.

At the time he commenced his literary labours, General Grant was suffering from serious illness, and this was aggravated by the depression of spirits resulting from mental distress. His body was in pain, and his mind was disturbed, less, however, by the contemplation of his own misfortunes than by the mortification and chagrin he felt that he had unwittingly betrayed others into losses for which he was powerless to make restitution. For this condition, occupation with his literary labours, and the revival of the memory of happier days, gave some alleviation.

Encouraged by the favour with which his articles in the *Century* had been received, he was persuaded to prepare his two volumes of *Personal Memoirs* for the press, finding the work both profitable and congenial. These *Memoirs* remain as a testimony to General Grant's skill as a writer. They will compare favourably with any similar work, not excepting the *Commentaries* of Cæsar, and surprised his critics by their high literary merit and their mastery of graphic description. They were his own work, some names and dates being all that were supplied by others. Until disease had destroyed his power of speech, they were dictated to a stenographer, and the final chapters were written on pads held in his lap, as he sat propped up in his chair, his nerves quivering with the agonising pains that gave no promise of relief, until death should come with its welcome release from bodily sensation.

Written under such circumstances, and prompted as they were by a desire to leave some provision for his family, they are a noble evidence of the strength of Grant's affections, the clearness and force of his intellect, and his invincible determination of purpose triumphing over death. How eagerly they were received by the public is shown by the payment of copyright to the amount of $200,000 in a single check, and a subsequent payment of $240,000.

A letter written by Grant when a cadet at the Military Academy shows unusual power of description for a youth, and his public career later in life gave him great opportunities for cultivating his capacity for expression. He wrote his own orders and despatches in the field, his own Inaugurals and Messages as President, calling upon others only for the details of departmental administration. His style was easy and flowing; he was never at a loss for an expression, and seldom interlined a word or made a material correction. The evidence of this is found in the fact that most of his important papers are in his own handwriting, prompted by the suggestion of the moment," and sent off without emendation or change." The foundation of good writing is clear thinking, and Grant would neither write nor talk about subjects that he had not mastered. Bismarck said of him: " I saw at once that he knew his subject thoroughly, or else he avoided it completely." His official reports show a progressive advance in mastery of expression, and his report of the final campaign is a model of its kind, receiving just commendation at the time as " more compact than Cæsar, more lucid than Jomini, more pungent than Napier." Grant's conversations on his campaigns, during his trip around the world, though much less extended, rival in interest those of Napoleon at St. Helena.

Up to the end of the year 1883, General Grant was apparently a man of unusual physical vigour, and though he was sixty-one years of age, he gave few indications of advancing years, being as strong as ever, if not so active. Returning to his home from a visit on Christmas Eve, 1883, he slipped on the ice as he alighted from a cab, and injured himself so severely that he had to be carried into the house, having ruptured a muscle in the thigh, and suffering acute pain. For weeks, he was confined to his bed, an attack of pleurisy having followed a few days after the fall. As soon as he was able to move about on crutches, he went to Washington and Fortress Monroe, by the advice of his physicians, returning in April, with health sufficiently improved to enable him to attend the meeting of his old comrades of the Military Order of the Loyal Legion, though he was obliged to refrain from visiting.

But a more insidious enemy was threatening his life. During the summer of 1884 he began to experience unpleasant sensations in his throat. To these he paid no attention until October, when he was casually examined by a physician who was making a call, and advised to return at once and put himself under the charge of some well-known specialist. His disease developed into cancer of the throat, and by December the General began to suffer the excruciating pains accompanying his disorder. Even in partaking of the liquid food to which his physicians limited him, he was subject to torture.

"For a while," says Badeau, in his volume, *Grant in Peace*, " he seemed to lose, not courage, yet a little of his hope, almost of his grip on life. He did not care to write, nor even to talk; he made little physical effort, and often sat for hours propped up in his chair, with his hands clasped, looking at the blank wall before him, silent, contemplating the future; not alarmed, but solemn, at the prospect of pain and disease, and only death at the end. It was like a man gazing into his open grave. He was in no way dismayed, but the sight was to me the most appalling I had ever witnessed:—the conqueror looking at his own inevitable conqueror; the stern soldier to whom so many armies had surrendered, watching the approach of that enemy before whom even he must yield."

If General Grant could not conquer death, he did, with invincible determination, conquer despondency, accepting with resignation the fate that was inevitable. He resumed work upon his *Memoirs*, and continued it unto the end in spite of physical pain and weakness, and with the tiger-clutch of fell disease fastening upon his throat, and draining his life-blood. In spite of discomfort, he enjoyed his work, and it furnished such distraction as was possible to him in his condition of hourly agony. His domestic affections, which were always strong, were awakened to increased activity, and he rejoiced in the thought that he was able by his own labour to provide for the future of his family. The tender offices of his loved ones, the prattle of his grandchildren, and visits from old friends, furnished further distraction for his thoughts.

But there was a wider circle of sympathisers gathered around the bedside of the dying man. Not only among his personal friends, but wherever his fame was known, there were tender thoughts of him; and from all parts of the world came by telegraph and post earnest inquiries as to his condition and prospects. Badeau, who was with him at this time, tells us that:

"Whatever had been said or thought injurious to him was instantly ignored, revoked, stamped out of mind; under the black shadow of Death the memory of his great services became vivid once more, like writing in sympathetic ink before fire. All the admiration and love of the days immediately after the war returned. The house was thronged with visitors, old friends, army comrades, former cabinet ministers, senators, generals, diplomatists, on errands of inquiry or commiseration. A hundred letters and telegrams arrived each day, with pity and affection in every line. The soldiers all over the country were conspicuous in their manifestations of sympathy—Southerners as well as Northerners. Army clubs and loyal leagues sent messages incessantly. Meetings of former Confederates were held to signify their sorrow. The sons of Robert E. Lee and Albert Sidney Johnston were among the first to proffer good wishes to him whom their fathers had fought. Political opponents were as outspoken as partisan friends, and the bitterest enemies of General Grant in the daily press were generous and constant in the expression of their interest. Rivals in the Army like Buell and Rosecrans made known that the calamity which impended over the nation was a sorrow for them, because they were Americans. Mrs. Jefferson Davis more than once uttered kind words which were conveyed to the sufferer. The new Secretary of War of the Democratic Administration called in person; the new Secretary of State sent remedies and good wishes. The new President despatched the Marshal of the District of Columbia from Washington to make inquiries. Ex-President Hayes and ex-Secretary Lincoln had called long before. State legislatures voted their commiseration; the Queen of England telegraphed her condolences, and little children from all parts of the country sent constant messages of affection and tributes of flowers."

On July 16, 1885, the sufferer was removed from his residence in New York to the summer cottage of Mr. Joseph H. Drexel, situated on Mount MacGregor, an elevation near Saratoga Springs, where purer air was to be obtained, and the quiet which the great city could not afford. Here General Grant continued to occupy himself in writing his *Memoirs*, as he grew weaker day by day. Speech so distressed him that he communicated with those about him only by writing. In the night of July 21-22, his symptoms grew more alarming, and at 8.08 o'clock on the morning of July 23, 1885, he quietly breathed his last. His family, who had hastily been summoned to his bedside just before this, were gathered about him as he passed away after an illness which had first become pronounced nine months before.

Bishop Newman, who was with General Grant during his last days, describes the dying man as being in a state of spiritual exaltation, and exhibiting perfect mental serenity. The only murmur that escaped his lips in his hours of intensest agony was an occasional exclamation to himself, "Oh, how I suffer!" He was never interested in the contests of creeds or the subtleties of theology, yet he was in the highest sense a religious man. Throughout his life he had exhibited a trust in the Invisible Powers that was never shaken; and a confidence in the Overruling Providence that shapes good, and seeming evil, alike to His purposes of mercy. This was signally shown during his last illness.

The death of General Grant was followed by

numerous expressions of sympathy for his family from personal friends and from public officials, which truthfully expressed the National sentiment. President Cleveland issued a proclamation announcing the sad event. Similar proclamations were issued by the Governor of the State of New York, and by the Governors of other States.

Various towns claimed the honour of furnishing a resting-place for the remains of the Nation's dead hero. He was born in Ohio, and was an adopted son of Illinois; Washington City claimed him because of her representative character as the capital of the Nation, and New York because it was his home at the time of his death. In a memorandum handed to his son Frederick, a month before his death, he said:

> "There are three places from which I wish a choice of burial place to be made: West Point—I would prefer this above others, but for the fact that my wife could not be placed beside me there. Galena, or some place in Illinois—because from that State I received my first General's commission. New York—because the people of that city befriended me in my need."

After much public discussion, the question was finally determined by the decision of General Grant's family to accept an offer of a burial place in Riverside Park, New York, on high ground overlooking the Hudson River.

The body was embalmed, and on August 4, 1885, simple funeral services were held at Mount MacGregor, under the direction of the Reverend Dr. Newman. On the same day a memorial service was held in Westminster Abbey, London, the funeral address being delivered by Canon Farrar, before a congregation composed of England's most notable citizens. After the services at Mount MacGregor the body was transferred to the custody of General Hancock, who had been designated by the President to take charge of the military parade at the funeral. It was removed that day to the Capitol at Albany, where, during the long night, it was visited by nearly eighty thousand people, who were permitted to view the face of the dead hero.

From Albany the remains were transferred to the City Hall, New York, where a still larger number of people, estimated at over 300,000, viewed them as they lay in state. On Saturday, August 8, they were removed to their resting-place in Riverside Park, accompanied by an imposing funeral pageant, and interred with appropriate ceremony; part of this ceremony being the simple liturgy recited by Grant's comrades of the Grand Army of the Republic. After reposing for nearly twelve years in a temporary tomb, they were, on April 27, 1897, removed with impressive ceremonies to an imposing mausoleum built by private subscription, which is the shrine whither thousands will journey annually from all parts of the world.

When Grant was in China he expressed the hope that he might some day have the pleasure of a visit in the United States from the Viceroy Li Hung Chang. In 1896 the Viceroy came, but Grant was not here to meet him, and he sought the resting-place of all that was mortal of his friend. As the great Chinaman stood in reverent contemplation before the silent tomb of the dead warrior, and laid upon it his chaplet of flowers, the Americans present remembered how their hero had added to his achievements in battle the more blessed victories of peace, and how he had used his influence with the rulers of foreign peoples, and the leaders of foreign opinion, to hasten the time when the nations of the earth shall dwell together in accord. As they thought on these things, the most appropriate of all mottoes for his resting-place seemed to them to be the words he had himself uttered, and which are inscribed upon his tomb:

"LET US HAVE PEACE."

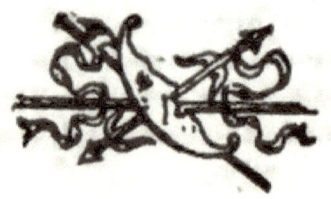

INDEX.

A

Abbot, Henry L., 277
Academy, Military, 15, 16, 229, 296, 322, 448
Ackerman, Amos T., 370
Acquia Creek, Va., 244
Action a necessity with raw troops, 140
Adams, C. F., 398; J. Q., 399; quoted, 363, 370
Aides, Grant's first, 77, 79
Alabama Claims, 389-92
Alabama, State of, 118, 120, 143, 190, 305
Alfonso, King of Spain, 425
Allatoona, Ga., 287
Allen, Robert, 148
Amelia C. H., Va., 312
American ignorance of war, 141
Ames, Adelbert, 414
Ammen, Dan'l., saves Grant's life, 11
Ammunition at Grand Gulf, 164
Anderson, Robert H., 93, 94, 260
Anecdotes, 10, 11, 12, 13, 16, 19, 20, 26, 29, 31, 32, 33, 38, 39, 47, 50, 51, 53, 57, 59, 61, 63, 66, 67, 69, 71, 73, 75, 78, 79, 82, 84, 135, 145, 169, 172, 178, 179, 181, 182, 183, 185, 198, 199, 203, 204, 205, 206, 213, 227, 231, 248, 258, 264, 285, 294, 296, 310, 312, 313, 315, 324, 325, 328, 343, 355, 363, 428
Annapolis, Md., 246
Appomattox River, Va., 310, 315
Appomattox, Va., 316, 318, 319, 322, 326, 330, 342
Arbitration with England, 392
Armies, Strength of, 241, 242, 246, 252
Army Corps: Second, 228, 262, 263, 274, 276, 302, 308; Fourth, 207; Fifth, 261, 275, 308, 309; Sixth, 261, 281, 308, 314; Ninth, 308; Eleventh, 196, 207; Twelfth, 196; Thirteenth, 190, 191; Fourteenth, 207; Nineteenth, 273
Army, effective, a vital organism, 138
Army in 1846, 27, 28, 29, 34
Army of Northern Virginia, 238, 243, 244, 245, 249, 259, 260, 261, 269, 270, 305, 306, 308, 314, 321, 329, 332
Army of the Cumberland, 80, 194, 198, 204, 205, 206, 215, 218
Army of the James, 80, 241, 269, 308
Army of the Mississippi, 80, 194; Confederate, 147
Army of the Ohio, 80, 133, 305
Army of the Potomac, 80, 181, 194, 196, 204, 236, 238, 239,

457

Army of the Potomac (*Con.*)
241, 242, 243, 245, 247, 250, 253, 255, 256, 259, 261, 262, 265, 267, 269, 271, 272, 273, 274, 275, 276, 279, 281, 288, 289, 304, 308, 314, 321, 329; Cliques of the, 239

Army of the Tennessee, 204, 434, 435; Confederate, 217

Army sociability, 25

Army traders, Grant's opinion of, 185

Army, Union, Cliques in, 240

Artillery, 251, 252, 266, 267

Art of War as written, 188

Arthur, Chester A., 440, 445; quoted, 444

Assaults, front, futility of, 276

Atlanta, Ga., 147, 165, 217, 241, 285, 288, 289, 290, 291, 292, 293, 294, 295

Augusta, Ga., 289, 301

Austria, Emperor of, 426

Averell, W. W., 272

Aztec society, 43, 445

B

Babcock, Orville E., 319, 377

Badeau, Adam, 351, 450, 451; describes Grant, 220

Baez, Buena Ventura, 377

Baker's Creek, Miss., 167

Baldwin, Miss., 146

Bancroft, George, 385

Banks, N. P., 153, 168, 171, 176, 187, 190, 191, 241, 273

Barboursville, Ky., 218

Barnard, J. G., 257, 300

Battles and battle-fields of the Civil War (see also Forts, page 462): Antietam, 149, 238; Averysboro, 302; Ball's Bluff, 92; Belmont, Mo., 86, 87, 90, 91, 93, 95, 228; Bentonville, 302; Big Black River, 156, 167, 168, 171, 187; Bull Run (First), 92, 129; (Second), 149, 238, 328; Cedar Creek, 281; Champion's Hill, 167, 170; Chancellorsville, 238, 249, 251, 259; Chattanooga, 120, 147, 191, 194-7, 199, 206, 208, 210, 212, 214-18, 221, 287-90; Chickamauga, 192, 196, 201, 205, 208, 209, 211, 213, 214, 270, 275; Cold Harbor, 271, 272; Ezra Church, 290; Fair Oaks, 149, 239; Five Forks, 308, 310; Franklin, 295, 296; Fredericksburg, 238, 243, 244, 245, 266; Gettysburg, 175, 189, 208, 239, 257, 324, 328; Helena, Arkansas, 176; Holly Springs, Miss., 152, 153, 184, 188, 228; Iuka, 150, 205; Lexington, Mo., 92; Lookout Mountain, 197, 200, 201, 202, 209, 210, 211, 214, 216, 259; Missionary Ridge, 200, 201, 204, 205, 208, 209, 210, 211; capture of, 212; casualties at, 214; North Anna, 268; Pea Ridge, 177; Petersburg, Va., 274, 275, 278, 280, 281, 301, 305, 307, 308, 310, 311, 312, 332; siege of, 277-283; Petersburg and Weldon R. R'd., 277; Port Gibson, Miss., 161, 163, 165, 187; Port Hudson, 152, 191; surrender, 176, 177; Raymond, Miss., 165; Seven Days' Retreat, Va., 149; Seven Pines, 149; Shiloh, (or Pittsburg Landing), 117, 120, 121, 122, 123, 124-140, 143, 144, 145, 149, 231; Spottsylvania Court-House, Va., 259, 260, 267, 268; Stone River, 154; Totopotomoy Creek, Va., 270; Vicksburg, Miss., 119, 147, 152, 153, 154, 155, 156, 157, 158, 159, 160, 161, 162, 163, 165, 167, 168, 169, 170, 171, 172, 173, 174, 175, 176, 178, 188, 189, 190, 191, 197, 198, 218, 235, 236,

Index. 459

Battles and battle fields (*Con.*) 251; siege and surrender of, 152–189; strength of the opposing armies at, 153, 155, 156, 162, 163, 165, 170, 171; Wilderness, 250, 251, 252, 253, 256, 257, 258, 260, 264, 272, 297, 328; Williamsburgh, 149; Wilson's Creek, Mo., 86, 92; Winchester, Va., 281, 305
"Battle in the Clouds," 209, 210
Battles, number of, during the war, 1, 157
Bayard, Chevalier, 323
Bayous surrounding, Vicksburg, 154, 159
Bazaine, Marshal, 340
Beauregard, P. G. T., 99, 102, 119, 122, 125, 126, 127 130, 132, 134, 140, 143, 145, 147, 209
Belknap, W. W., 370, 402, 403
Belligerent Rights for Cuba, 382
Benecia Barracks, Cal., 50
Bermuda Hundreds, Va., 269
Bethel, Tenn., 122
Big Hill, Ky., 218
Birthplace of Grant described, 8
Bismarck, Prince Von, 426
Blair, Frank P., 61, 364; Montgomery, 61
Blockade runners, 380
Bloody Angle, Va., the, 263
Blücher, Marshal, his obstinacy illustrated by Grant, 256
Booth, J. Wilkes, 335
Border States, neutrality, 85
Borie, Adolph E., 369
Boutwell, Geo. H., 369, 403
Bowen, John S., 174
Bowling Green, Ky., 96–8, 102, 111
Bragg, Braxton, 55, 127, 147, 148, 150, 154, 194, 195, 197, 199, 200, 202, 204, 206, 210, 212, 213, 215, 216
Branchville, S. C., 301
Brandy Station, Va., 246
Breckinridge, John C., 127, 131

Bridgeport, Ala., 143, 196, 201, 202, 203, 204, 205, 208
Brinkerhoff, Jacob, 399
Bristow, Benj. F., 403
British welcome to Grant, 424, 427
Brooks, Horace, 39
Brown, B. Gratz, 398, 401
Brown, Owen, 6
Brown's Ferry, Tenn., 201, 202, 203, 204, 208
Bruinsburg, Miss., 156, 161
Bryant, W. C., 399
Buchanan, James, 61; R. C., 52
Buckland, Ralph C., 125
Buckner, Simon B., 88, 94, 97, 103, 106, 107
Buell, Don Carlos, 51, 95, 96, 99, 102, 113, 114, 118, 119, 121, 124, 132, 133, 134, 140, 143, 144, 145, 147, 148, 150, 151, 240, 452
Burkesville Junction, Va., 306, 312
Burnside, Ambrose E., 198, 204, 206, 213, 240, 246, 252, 253, 254, 255, 279, 327; his testimony to Grant, 3
Burnsville, N. C., 150
Butler, B. F., 185, 241, 260, 264, 265, 269, 272, 274, 284, 285
Buzzard's Roost, Ga., 286

C

Cæsar, 235
Cæsar, Jomini, and Napier, compared with Grant as writers, 449
Cairo, Ill., 84, 87, 88, 89, 90, 91, 94, 104, 117, 120, 149, 164, 192, 193, 194, 197
Camargo, march from, to Monterey, 30; march from, to Saltillo, 35
Cameron, J. Donald, 403; Simon, 436
Campaign in Georgia, 285–294

Campaigns of Grant and others in Virginia compared, 327-9
Camp Salubrity, La., 28
Canals at Vicksburg, 158
Canby, E. R. S., 241, 305, 334
Cape Fear River, S. C., 302
Carpenter, Frank B., quoted, 232
Carpet-bag governments, 414
Casualties, 1, 329; in Army of the Potomac, 238, 247, 255, 264-8, 270, 271, 279, 281, 287, 289, 290, 292, 295, 298, 302, 308, 310, 314, 327, 328; in French and German battles, 328
Cavalry, 139, 144, 165, 245, 251, 252, 260, 261, 268-71, 278, 282, 291, 292, 306, 308, 310, 320, 333
Century Magazine, 446
Charleston, S. C., 301, 302
Chattahoochee, Ga., 288, 290; River, 285
Cheraw, S. C., 302
Chesapeake Bay, Va., 243
Chicago, Ill., 435
Children's tribute to Grant, 434
China, 424, 430, 431; and Japan, 386
Chinese, Grant's recommendations concerning, 416
Chulalongkorn, King, 431
Church, Congregational, oldest, 5
Cincinnati, O., 398
Citico Creek, Ga., 202, 206
City Point, Va., 260, 331
Civil administration deranged by war, 409-10
Civil-Service Reform, 403, 409; Inauguration of, by Grant, 373-4
Clarke's Mountain, Va., signal tower, 253
Clarksville, Tenn., surrender of, 149
Clarendon-Johnson, treaty, 394
Cleveland, Grover, 201, 437, 452, 454

Coffee and hard tack, soldiers' fondness for, 169
Coffee Point, La., 161
Cold Harbor, Va., 271, 272
Colfax, Schuyler, 363, 368
Coloured Labour Convention, 395
Columbia Barracks, Oregon, 50-52
Columbia, S. C., 301, 302
Columbus, Ky., 87, 88, 90, 91, 92, 93, 95, 96, 98, 102, 148, 152, 153, 193
Command, division of, during war, 235
Commissioners of Arbitration, 391
Comstock, C. B., 222
Concentration, policy of, 194
Conduct of War Committee, 279
Confederacy divided, 242; its forces at Shiloh described, 137; flight of its government, 331-333; prices in, during war, 178, 301
Confederate Cruisers, 380
Comte de Paris, his opinion of Grant, 216
Congress, 221, 230, 342, 343, 344, 346, 352, 373; Grant's relations to, 342, 344, 347, 349, 352, 360. and Johnson, 366, 383; votes medals to Grant, 216
Conkling, Roscoe, 436, 438
Coosawhatchie, S. C., 301
Coppée, Henry L., describes Grant, 17, 57
Cordon, military, surrounding Confederacy, 194
Corean difficulties, 386
Corinth, Miss., 118, 119, 120, 122, 124, 125, 127, 135, 143, 145, 146, 147, 148, 149, 150, 151
Corps, Army, consolidation of, 246 (see Army Corps)
Cotton bales for defence, 157
Council of War, Grant's nearest approach to, 174

Court of Inquiry on Burnside's mine, 279
Cowardice at Shiloh, 141
Cox, Jacob D., 369, 370, 399
Creswell, John A. J., 370, 403
Criticism on Grant, Origin of, 232
Crittenden, Thos. L., 150
Crook, George, 272
Crump's Landing, Tenn., 122
Crystal Springs, Miss., 167
Cuba, 382, 384, 436
Culpeper C. H., Va., 245, 246
Cumberland Gap, 93, 195, 213, 218; River, 80, 87, 95, 97, 99, 103, 112
Curtis, Geo. W., 375; S. R., 117
Cushing, Caleb, quoted, 388

D

Dahlgren, John A., 294
Dalton, Ga., 201, 286, 287
Dana, Charles A., 197
Danish War, 1866, 291
Danville, Va., 311, 312, 322, 331
Davies, Prof., testimony to Grant's ability, 18
Davis, Jefferson, 82, 88, 202, 204, 206, 299, 300, 302, 310, 311, 342, 452; flight and capture of, 331, 333
Decatur, Ga., 289
Defence, advantages of, 242, 265
Delano, Columbus, 370, 403
Democratic action and policies, 393, 399, 404
Democratic Senators oppose arbitration, 393
Dent, Fred'k T., 25, 26
Department of State, 340
De Shroon, La., 161
Dickens, Charles, describes Cairo, Ill., 89
Dinwiddie C. H., Va., 308, 309
Dispersion, policy of, 148
Dodge, G. M., 291
Dominican treaty, 395

Douglass, Fred'k, 395
Douglas, Stephen A., 359
Douthard's Landing, Va., 278
Drexel, Joseph H., 453
Drury's Bluff, Va., 265
Durham, Lord, remark to Brougham, 375

E

Early, Jubal A., 273, 274, 278, 281, 282
East Point, Ga., 290, 291
Edmunds, Geo. F., 375
Electoral Commission, 421, 436
England and America, 389-394
England's hostile course during our Civil War, 386-8
Epictetus quoted, 56
Etowah River, Ga., 269, 285, 288
Evansville, Ind., 94, 96
Ewell, Richard S., his opinion of Grant, 18, 267, 314
Executive acts performed away from Capital, 415-16
Expenses of the war, 334, 336

F

Fabian policy of Johnston, 289
Fairburn, Ga., 291
Farmville, Va., 314, 316
Farragut, D. G., 153, 157, 217
Fayetteville, S. C., 302; Tenn., 143
Fetich worshippers, civilized, 410
Field intrenching during the war, 123
Fifteenth Amendment ratified, 395
Fighting generals hard to find, 231
Fishery question, 392, 393
Fish, Hamilton, 370, 390, 402
Florence, Ala., 118, 293-295
Florida, State of, 333
Floyd, John B., 103, 105, 106, 107, 109

Fog of War, 141
Foote, Andrew H., 97, 98, 99, 100, 104, 105
Ford's theatre, 335
Forrest, Nathan B., 109, 125, 126, 133, 150, 153, 295
Fort Donelson, Tenn., capture of, 96, 110, 111, 112, 116, 123, 129, 141; results of, 177, 228
Fort Fisher, 6, 284, 302
Fort Harrison, capture of, 282
Fort Heiman, 97, 101
Fort Henry, Tenn., capture of, 96-116; results of, 119, 123, 228
Fort Hindman (Arkansas Post), captured, 155
Fort Howard, Va., 308
Fort Jessup, La., 26, 27
Fort McAllister, Ga., 294
Fort Monroe, Va., 214, 244, 449
Fort Pillow, Tenn., 90, 140, 146
Fort Stedman, Va., 307
Fort Sumter, S. C., 66, 83, 402
Fort Wood, Chattanooga, 206-207
Fourth Infantry, 35, 41, 47, 48; Grant joins, 24; at Fort Jessup, 26, 28
Franco-Prussian War, 141, 291, 328, 385, 390, 426
Fraternisation of Union and Confederate soldiers, 176, 206, 207, 324
Frederick the Great, 188, 228
Fremont, John C., 81, 82, 86, 91, 94
French ignorance of war, 141
French Republic, prompt recognition of, 385
Fry, Jas. B., story of Grant's horsemanship, 16

G

Galena, Ill., 434, 435, 438
Garfield, James A., 437
Garita, a, described, 37
Garland, John, 39, 45; testimony to Grant's ability, 45
Geary, J. W., 203
General-in-Chief, purpose of Grant's appointment as, 235, 236
Generals, complaining, described by Lincoln, 231
Georgetown, O., described, 8, 9
Georgia, State of, 191, 216, 269, 285, 297, 298, 343
Germany, treaty with, 385
Gibraltars of the West, 90, 156
Goldsboro, N. C., 302-305
Gordon, James B., 258, 294; quoted, 318
Gossip in the Army, 53
Grand Gulf, Miss., 156, 160-5, 168, 187, 235
Granger, Gordon, 207
Grant and Lee contrasted, 322, 323
Grant and Ward, 441-3, 446
Grant, Frederick D., 454
Grant, Jesse, 424
Grant, Jesse Root, 5, 8, 62
Grant, Lewis A., quoted, 263
Grant, Mrs. U. S., 25, 52, 424, 425, 430, 444
Grant, Noah, 4-5
Grant, Peter, 6
Grant, Scottish Clan, and its motto, 5
Grant's mother, 5, 6, 7
GRANT ULYSSES SIMPSON: ancestors, 4, 5, 7; birth, 5; named, 7; fever and ague, 9, 57; removes to Georgetown, 8; schooling, 9; family, 9; boyish sports, 10; joins debating society, 10; love of horses, 10, 11; escapes drowning, 11; rustic influences, 11; future prophesied, 13; change of name, 14; enters Military Academy and becomes Sam Grant, 15; at Academy, 15-22; testimonials to his ability, 18; romance, 19; artistic abil-

GRANT (*Con.*)
ity, 19; illness, 20; graduation, 21; classmates, 21; thorough education, 21; presentiment, 22; assigned to Fourth Infantry, 22; at Jefferson Barracks, 24; love and courtship, 25, 26; seeks a professorship, 26; salaries received, 26, 47, 56, 62; at Grand Ecore and New Orleans, 28; Corpus Christi, 28, 31; plays Desdemona, 31; first battle, 31; in Mexico, 31–33, 37–39; Adjutant Fourth Infantry, 32; quartermaster and commissary, 32, 41, 47–51; ride at Monterey, 33, 34; at Lobos Island, 35; marches from Vera Cruz to Mexico, 36; complimented by superiors, 39; dislike of staff duty, 41, 44, 45; loses public funds, 42; studiousness, 43; repugnance to bull fights, 43; joins Aztec Club, 43; remarkable and valuable young soldier, 44; at Pascagoula, Miss., 46; marriage, 46; at Sackett's Harbor, 46; difficulty with his superior, 47, 52; sails for California, 48; trying experiences, 48, 49; Benecia Barracks, 50; promoted captain, 51; Indian experiences, 51; farming ventures, 51; at Columbia Barracks and Fort Humboldt, Cal., 52, 53; confidence in future, 53; resigns, 53–55; experiences of poverty, 54–58; home in Missouri, 56; farming experience as a civilian, 57; real estate agent, 58; happy days of poverty, 59; seeks public office, 60; first vote, 61; custom house and tanner's clerk, 62, 63; deputy sheriff, 63; business man, 65; anticipates war, 65; presides at a war meeting, 66; reveals soldierly qualities, 67; declines appointment as captain, 67; helps organise volunteers, 67–69; clerk to adjutant-general, 69; visits St. Louis, 69; seeks position on McClellan's staff, 69, 70; offers services to Government, 71; appointed Colonel, 72; first duty, 74; commands sub-district, 75; skill in dealing with volunteers, 76; brigadier-general, 76; commands at Ironton and Jefferson City, Mo., 81; reports to Fremont, 82; commands district of S. W. Missouri, 84; prompt methods, 81, 84; seizes Paducah, 87; vigorous action at Cairo, 90; attacks Belmont, 92; nearly captured, 92; command enlarged, 95; eagerness for action, 95, 147, 148, 233; proposes to attack Columbus, 95; snubbed by Halleck, 99; captures Forts Henry and Donelson, 96–116; becomes "Unconditional Surrender" Grant, 111; difficulties with Halleck, 113–116, 141, 189, 192, 229, 280, 410; relieved of command, 114; restored, 118; battle ot Shiloh, 116–144; injured by a fall, 133; conduct at Shiloh, 141, 142; in disgrace, 141; change of views, 143; forbids pillage, 143; narrow escape, 144; second in command, 144; asks to be relieved, 144; commands district of West Tennessee, 144; department of Tennessee, 148; his methods, 148, 150; at Iuka, 150; Vicksburg, 152–189; unsuccessful movements, 158, 160; runs batteries, 161; takes Vicksburg in reverse, 162; abandons his

GRANT (*Con.*)
base, 163; Port Gibson, 165; takes Jackson, 166; Champion's Hill, 167; Big Black, 168; invests and captures Vicksburg, 169-176; courtesies shown to prisoners, 176; his removal demanded during siege, 180; opposition, to army traders, 184, 185; treatment of negroes, 186; difficulties with McClernand, 187; injured at New Orleans, 191-193; commands Military Division of Mississippi, 194; battle of Chattanooga, 194-216; first meeting with Stanton, 197; physical sufferings, 198-218; voted a gold medal, 221; Lieutenant-General, 221; visits Washington, 221; received by President, 222; assumes control as General-in-Chief, 223; development as a great commander, 226-235; joins Army of the Potomac, 236, 246; reorganises cavalry, 245; strengthens discipline, 247; crosses Rapidan, 251; Wilderness battle, 252-258; Spottsylvania, 260-265; North Anna, 268; Totopotomoy, 270; Cold Harbor, 271, 272; crosses James River, 274, 275; invests Petersburg, 277-283; interference of Stanton and Halleck, 280; extends his lines around Petersburg, 282; salutes Sherman's victories, 292; anxieties, 296, 297; result of Grant's command, 298; receives Peace Commissioners, 299; holds Lee's army in a vice, 305; strength and losses, 306; Five Forks, 309; assaults and captures Petersburg, 310; Richmond and Petersburg evacuated, 311; follows Lee's flight, 312; surrounds and destroys Lee, 313-14; corresponds with Lee, 315-19; surrender of Lee, 319-21; Lee and Grant contrasted, 322; magnanimity, 323; visits Washington, 325, 334; losses in Virginia, 327-28; results accomplished, 326-31; meets Lincoln at City Point, 332; visits Sherman, 332; final surrenders, 334; attends Cabinet Meeting, 335; narrowly escapes assassination, 335; chief citizen, 341, 349, 359; difficulties with President Johnson, 341, 343, 347-8, 351-7; protects Lee, 342; visits South, 343; visits North with President, 347; promoted General, 351; refuses to go to Mexico, 351-2; Secretary of War, 354-7, 371; termination of military career, 358; Presidential candidate, 359, 361; slandered, 362; nominated for President, 361; refuses to canvass, 363-4; elected, 365; inaugurated, 366; qualifications, 367-8; Cabinets, 368-370; distrusts politicians, 371; opposition, 371, 372, 375, 379; opinions on public policies, 379-84, 416-7; course toward Spain, 382-4; arbitration with England, 389-94; difficulties with Sumner, 394-5; relations to negroes, 395-6; success of first administration, 397, 398, 417, 418; financial administration, 416, 417; third term controversy, 418, 419, 436, 437; Hayes controversy, 421, 422; retires to civil life, 422; perplexities, 347, 423; travels abroad and honors received, 423-433; reception on Pacific coast, 434-5; visits Mexico and Cuba, 436, 439; moves to New York, 438;

GRANT (*Con.*),
elected Railway President, 439; negotiates treaty with Mexico, 440; misfortunes, 440-6; placed on army retired list, 446; declines a pension, 446; writes his Memoirs, 446-9, 451, 453; last illness, 447-53; death and burial, 453-6; monument in Riverside Park, 456

GRANT, ULYSSES S., personal characteristics, 3, 7, 9, 10, 13, 14, 16-20, 22, 23, 32, 33, 34, 38, 43, 47, 50, 52, 53, 55, 57, 59, 62, 63, 65, 69, 72, 75, 79, 83, 84, 95, 115, 133, 142, 164, 179-83, 198, 208, 219, 220, 226, 235, 256, 264, 299, 357, 358, 362, 365, 367, 376, 395, 396, 401, 407, 409, 428, 429, 434-6, 438, 440-43, 447, 448-9, 453, 456; personal appearance, 9, 180, 219; as a tactician, 256; skill as a writer, 448-9; as a public speaker, 16, 66, 365, 428-9, 434, 435; his worldly possessions, 438, 441, 447, 448

GRANT, ULYSSES S., quotations from his remarks, letters, and orders, 10, 17, 19, 22, 32, 38, 40, 41, 42, 44, 45, 46, 51, 53, 59, 60, 62, 66, 70, 71, 73, 75, 78, 97, 99, 100, 101, 102, 107, 109, 110, 115, 121, 127, 144, 157, 163, 169, 172, 173, 175, 176, 179, 181, 182, 183, 184, 185, 186, 188, 193, 200, 204, 205, 206, 210, 213, 223, 224, 227, 240, 244, 245, 252, 263, 264, 266, 269, 271, 292, 299, 300, 306, 309-22, 313, 315, 316, 317, 318, 319, 320, 322, 323, 333, 335, 343, 356, 358, 364, 365, 366, 368, 372, 373-4, 379, 381, 384, 385, 389, 393, 396, 402, 405, 408, 411, 414, 415, 419, 421, 428, 429, 434, 435, 440, 446, 453, 454; quotations from his inaugurals, annual and special messages, 368, 379, 380, 381, 383, 385, 389, 393, 402, 404, 405, 413, 414, 415, 416, 448

Graves at Vicksburg, 158-180
Greeley, Horace, 398, 399, 401
Green River, Ind., 96, 99
Greensboro, N. C., 331
Greysville, Ga., 213
Griffin, Ga., 318
Groesbeck, W. S., 399
Guadalupe, Hidalgo, treaty of, 46
Gunboats, use of, in military operations, 87, 91, 97-9, 100-105, 118, 132, 152, 156-8, 159, 169

H

Haines's Bluff, Miss., 156, 169, 170, 171
Halleck, Henry W., 55, 95, 96, 97, 98, 99, 100, 101, 102, 103, 108, 113, 114, 115, 116, 118, 120, 121, 126, 140, 141, 142, 144, 145, 146, 147, 148, 149, 151, 163, 168, 171, 187, 189, 190, 191, 200, 216, 229, 262, 266, 269, 272
Halsted, Murat, 232
Hamburgh Landing, Tenn., 121
Hamer, Thos. L., 14, 44
Hampton, Wade, 277, 278
Hancock, Winfield S., 254, 255, 262, 263, 268, 274, 305, 354.
Hanover, Va., 268, 269, 270
Hardee, W. J., 127, 128, 302
Harper's Ferry, Va., 231, 273
Harrisburg, Pa., 239
Haskins, Chas., 32
Hatcher's Run, Va., 308
Hayes, Rutherford B., 420-422, 436
Hayti, 395
Hazen, W. B., 203
Hoar, E. Rockwood, 369, 370, 392.

Hodges, Henry L., 55
Holland, King of, 425
Holmes, Theophilus H., 176
Hood, J. B., 289, 290, 291, 292, 293, 295, 297, 301
Hooker, Joseph, 142, 196, 198, 199, 202, 203, 204, 209, 210, 211, 212, 240, 259, 327
Hornet's nest at Shiloh, 129
Hovey, A. P., 148
Howard, O. O., 198, 207, 209
Hughes, Thomas, 428
Hugo, Victor, 426
Humours of the battlefield, 266
Humphreys, A. A., 308; quoted, 267
Hunt, Benj. S., 377; H. J., 324
Hunter, David, 266, 272, 280
Hunter's Point, Mo., 91
Huntsville, Ala., 143
Hurlbut, S. A., 120, 122, 129

I

Illinois, 436, 454
Indianapolis, Ind., 197
Indians, army feeling toward, 410
Indians, Grant's treatment of, 410, 411
Inflation bill vetoed, 405-6
Ingalls, Rufus, 325
Intrenchments around Petersburg, length of, 283
Ireland's welcome to Grant, 427
Iron-clads passage of Vicksburg batteries described by Sherman, 159
Irwinsville, Ga., 333
Island No. 10 captured, 117, 145
Isthmus canal, 417
Italy, treaty with, 385

J

Jackson, Miss., 162, 166, 167, 168
James River, Va., 80, 233, 241, 244, 274, 275, 278, 281, 282, 303, 308, 311, 312
Japan, 424, 430, 431, 432, 433, 445
Jasper, Tenn., 198
Jealousy, military, 232, 237
Jefferson Barracks, Mo., 24-26
Jefferson City, Mo., 398
Jefferson, Joseph, at Monterey, 34; Thomas, 416
Jewell, Marshall, 403
Jews, Grant's order against, 184
Johnson, Andrew, 335, 337, 341, 342, 343, 344, 345, 356, 371, 372, 377; impeachment, 357, 359, 360, 397, 413
Johnson, Reverdy, 388
Johnston, A. S., 100, 109, 111, 119, 123, 124, 125, 126, 128, 129, 130, 131, 133, 137, 140, 452
Johnston, Joseph E., 154, 162, 166, 168, 171, 217, 242, 265, 285, 286, 287, 288, 306, 307, 312, 313, 331, 333
Jonesboro, Ga., 291, 292
Jones, Sam, 334
Jordan, Thomas, 109, 125, 132

K

Kanawha River, Va., 80
Kansas-Missouri disturbances, 60
Kearny, Stephen W., 24
Kearsarge sinks *Alabama*, 390
Kelly's Ferry, Tenn., 202, 204
Kenesaw Mountain, Ga., 287, 288
Kentucky, 85, 86, 87, 88, 93, 97, 147, 233
Kilpatrick, Judson, 291
Knoxville, Tenn., 120, 198, 204, 213, 215, 218, 257
Königgrätz, casualties at, 328
Kung, Prince, 431

L

Lafayette, Marquis de, 4
Lake Providence, Miss., 158

Index. 467

Lee, Fitzhugh, 277, 278
Lee, Robert E., 43, 149, 175, 195, 238, 240, 249, 252, 254, 255, 259, 261, 262, 264, 265, 268, 271, 273, 275, 281, 282, 283, 285, 288, 295, 297, 299, 301, 303, 306, 307, 309, 312, 313, 323, 325, 326, 332; his opinion of Grant, 258; compared with Hood, 291; described, 322; surrender, 311, 322, 334, 336, 337, 342; quoted, 285, 310, 316, 317, 318, 319, 320, 321, 452
Legs of the soldiers, 253
Leopold II., 425
Leuthen, battle of, 228
Lexington, Ky., 218
Liberal Republicans, 398-9
Lick Creek, Tenn., 123, 126
Lieutenant-General, grade of, 221, 223.
Li Hung Chang, 431, 455
Loring, W. W., 167
Lost Mountain, Ga., 287
Louisiana, 162, 190
Louisville, Ky., 96, 197, 198
Lovell, Mansfield, 58
Lowell, James Russell, 376
Loyal Legion, Military Order of, 198, 445, 450
Lincoln, Abraham, 55, 95, 155, 210, 215, 221, 222, 230, 292, 297, 298, 332, 342; assassination, 335; calls for troops, 66; opinion of Grant, 181, 186, 231; quoted, 248, 249, 280, 292, 314, 368, 401
Locket, S. H., 169
Logan, John A., 86, 145, 163, 436
Longstreet, James, 195, 203, 204, 207, 215, 253, 254, 307, 318, 325; quoted, 309
Loo Choo Islands, 431
Lookout Valley, 201, 202, 204, 211
Luck in war, Grant's opinion of 189

Lynchburg, Va., 245, 272, 273, 304, 305, 311
Lyon, Nathaniel, 81

M

McCall, Geo. A., 29-31
McClellan, Geo. B., 38, 52, 55, 69, 70, 82, 94, 95, 98, 101, 113, 114, 115, 118, 142, 147, 148, 149, 238, 240, 248, 257, 271, 327, 329, 376, 377; opinion of Halleck, 118; orders arrest of Grant, 114
McClernand, J. A., 98, 100, 106, 109, 122, 155, 161, 187
McConnell, Thomas R., 50
McKinley, President U. S., 336
McKinstry, Justus, 82
McLean, Wilmer, 319
McMahon, Marshal, 426
McPherson, J. B., 123, 286, 289
Macon, Ga., 290; Railroad, 291
Madison, James, 370
Mahan, Prof., testimony to Grant's ability, 18
Mahone, William, quoted, 314, 315
March to the Sea, 165, 293, 294, 297, 298, 300
Marietta, Ga., 287
Marshall, Charles, 320, 321; James W., 403
Material of war taken by Grant, 92, 107, 110, 175
Mattapony River, Va., 262
Mayfield, Ky., 98
Maysville, Ky., Academy, 9
Maximilian, Archduke, 190, 339, 340
Meade, Geo. G., 219, 239, 240, 245, 246, 259, 261, 272, 275, 279, 308, 313, 327
Memphis and Charleston R. Rd., operations against, 119, 143, 147, 150, 205
Memphis, Tenn., 96, 118, 120, 144, 146, 147, 149, 152, 153, 155, 188, 189, 192, 204

Mexican battle-fields: Matamoras, 30; Palo Alto, 30; Resaca de la Palma, 30; Monterey, 30, 130, 227; Buena Vista, 35; Cerro Gordo, 36; Chapultepec, 37; Churubusco, 37; Contreras, 37; Molinos del Rey, 37; Siege and capture of Vera Cruz, 35
Mexico, 36, 38, 40, 41, 339, 439, 440; war with, 27-46, 403
Milford Station, Va., 268
Military Division of the Mississippi, 194, 241; of Missouri, 197
Military influence at the White House, 371
Military Order Loyal Legion, 198, 445, 450
Military reputations, factors of, 229
Milledgeville and Millen, Ga., 294
Milliken's Bend, La., 155, 158, 159, 163
Mine, Burnside's, 278, 279
Mine Run, Va., 259, 328
Mississippi & Ohio R. R., 122
Mississippi, 120; opinion of its Supreme Court, 120
Mississippi River, 80, 86, 90, 119, 122, 124, 143, 147, 152, 154, 155, 156, 157, 158, 160, 162, 165, 167, 182, 191, 195, 233, 241, 242, 333, 334, 365
Mississippi Valley, area of, 177; river system, 178; Cairo, key to, 89
Missouri, 69, 74, 75, 86, 233
Mitchell, O. M., 143, 147
Mobile, Ala., 146, 189, 217, 241, 305, 334
Moccason Point, 201
Monroe, James, 401
Montgomery, Ala., 290
Morgan, John H., 150
Mormon polygamy, 416
Morrill, Lot M., 403
Morris Island, S. C., 302

Mortars of wood at Vicksburg, 171
Morton, O. P., 375
Motley, John Lothrop, 394
Mound City, Ill., 94
Mount MacGregor, N. Y., 453, 455
Mulligan, James A., 81
Murfreesboro, Tenn, 112, 141, 154, 194
Murphy, R. C., 150, 153; surrenders Iuka, 150; and Holly Springs, 153
Music, Grant's dislike of, 47
Muskets, Confederate superior to Union arms, 175
Mustering out troops, 339, 340

N

Napier, Lord, 445
Napoleon I., 34, 188, 231, 233, 426, 449
Napoleon III., 190, 339, 386
Nashville, Tenn., 96, 112, 113, 119, 196, 198, 217, 218, 228, 293, 295, 296
Natchez, Miss., 190, 241
Natchitoches, La., 28
Nation, Weekly, quoted, 400
Navy, 35, 171, 241, 260, 275, 284, 285, 302, 312, 381, 421
Negroes, references to, 171, 172, 185, 186, 346, 356
Nelson, William, 113, 124
New Albany, Ind., 94
New Madrid, Mo., 88, 90, 91, 117, 145
Newman, Bishop, 454-455
New Market, Va., 266
New Orleans, La., 192, 217; capture of, 152
Newspaper attacks on Grant, 142
New York, State of, 259, 436, 454
Nickajack Creek, Ga., 288
Nicknames given to officers, 220
North Anna River, Va., 268
North Carolina, 284, 306, 339, 343, 399

North-western boundary dispute, 392-3

O

O'Conor, Charles, 399
Ogden, Richard L., 54
Oglesby, Richard, 84, 91
Ohio River, 8, 9, 10, 13, 80, 89, 94, 96, 150, 295, 297, 454
Ohio Valley, early settlers in, 4
Old Grimes, 399
Old Hundred at Vicksburg, 178
Olmstead, Fred'k, Law, 399
Oostenaula River, Ga., 285, 287
Orange & Alexandria, Va., Railroad, 244, 245
Orangeburg, S. C., 301
Orange C. H., Va., 246
Orange Plank Road, Va., 251
Orchard Knob, Tenn., 207, 208, 212
Ord, E. O. C., 308, 313, 318, 320
Ottendorfer, Oswald, 399
Outpost duty, ignorance of, 133, 138, 139

P

Paducah, Ky., 87, 88, 90, 94, 100, 120, 228
Pamunkey River, Va., 270
Parke, John G., 308
Parker, Ely S., 321
Peace negotiations, 298, 299
Pekin Summer Palace, 432
Pemberton, J. C., 155, 156, 162, 166, 167, 168, 171, 172, 173, 174, 175
Pensions, decrease of, during Grant's administration, 407
Peru and Chili, 384, 436
Phelps, S. Ledyard, 118
Phœnix, John, describes Cairo, 89
Pierce, Franklin, 377
Pierrepont, Edwards, 403
Pike, Corporal, bold adventure, 205

Pillow, Gideon J., 81, 88, 103, 106, 107, 109
Pine Mountain, Ga., 287
Pocotaligo, S. C., 301
Point Pleasant, O., 8
Polk, James K., 376
Polk, Leonidas, 86, 87, 94, 96, 126, 127, 285
Pope, John, 75, 117, 145, 147, 149, 238, 305, 327
Po River, Va., 259, 262, 268
Porter, D. D., 152, 156, 159, 161, 164, 169, 172, 284, 376, 377
Porter, Horace, 251, describes Grant, 219; quoted, 325
Port Holt, Ky., 94
Port Royal, S. C., 266
Portugal, King of, 425
Postal improvements under Grant, 417
"Potatoes and Onions" captured Vicksburg, 183
Potomac River, Va., 80, 244
Powder Boat, Experiment, 284
Prentiss, B. M., 81, 121, 128, 130, 131, 133, 135
Price, Sterling, 91, 150, 151, 305
Prince of Wales, 424
Prisoners captured by Grant, 107, 110, 175, 210, 214, 337
Provisions, price of, at Vicksburg during siege, 178
Pueblo de Los Angeles, Mexico, 36

R

Rabbits and squirrels announce a battle, 125
Railroad transportation, remarkable feat of, 196
Raleigh, N. C., 331, 332
Rapidan River, Va., 245, 246, 249, 253, 259, 275, 279, 327; passage of, 251
Rappahannock River, Va., 244, 245, 266
Rawlins, John A., 66, 77, 79, 84, 198, 222, 370

Reconstruction, 344, 350, 352, 367, 412, 413, 415
Red Oaks, Ga., 291
Red River Campaign, 190, 241, 273
Repeating rifles used by cavalry, 308
Republican Party, policies and action of, 363, 364, 400, 420, 437
Resaca, Ga., 287
Review of Union Armies, 337-9
Revolutionary settlers in Ohio Valley, 4
Reynolds, J. J., 55, 57, 60, 66
Richardson, Wm. A., 403
Richeson, Grant's school-master, 9
Richmond and Danville R. R., 306; Richmond and Fredericksburg, R. Road, 268, 272
Richmond, Va., 207, 218, 238, 239, 241, 243, 248, 252, 260, 265, 266, 268, 269, 270, 275, 278, 282, 285, 287, 289, 297, 299, 300, 303, 304, 305, 306, 310, 311, 329, 330, 332, 333, 334; scenes at evacuation of, 311, 312
Ringgold, Ga., 213
Rio Grande frontier, 339
Riverside Park, N. Y., 454, 455
Rivers, influence of, in our war, 80
Roads, bad, interference with military operations, 35, 36, 48, 49, 97, 98, 218, 232
Rocky Face Ridge, Ga., 286
Romero, Senor, 439
Rosecrans, W. S., 55, 145, 147, 150, 151, 154, 190, 192, 194, 195, 197, 198, 200, 202, 205, 208, 214, 450
Rothery, Mrs., friend of Grant's youth, 19
Rough and Ready, Ga., 292
Rules of war non-existent, 233
Russell, Earl, 387

S

Sadowa, Casualties at, 328
Sailor's Creek, Va., 314
St. Privat, Prussian Guards at, 253
San Domingo, 376, 377-9
San Francisco, Cal., 433, 435
San Juan Question, 392-3
Saturday Club, Boston, 394
Savannah, Ga., 119, 121, 122, 124, 130, 217, 293, 294, 300; Savannah River, 301
Saxe, Marshal, quoted, 253
Schofield, John M., 289, 296, 302, 303, 305, 370
Schurz, Carl, 399
Scott, Winfield, 34, 36, 37, 221; contrasted with Grant, 22
Scriptural names in Grant family, 5
Sedgwick, John, 261
Seward, Frederick W., 377; W. H., 223, 270
Seymour, Horatio, 364, 365
Sharpe, George H., 321
Shenandoah Valley, Va., 241, 244, 266, 268, 269, 273, 277, 280, 303
Sheridan, Philip H., 145, 195, 212, 214, 219, 245, 260, 263, 266, 269, 270, 272, 277, 278, 283, 300, 303, 306, 308, 313, 320, 326, 334, 340, 351, 354, 383, 403; success in Shenandoah Valley, 281, 283; quoted, 213, 281, 314
Sherman, William Tecumseh, 57, 82, 94, 101, 119, 120, 124, 125, 126, 128, 132, 133, 139, 140, 144, 145, 152, 153, 165, 169, 187, 188, 200, 204, 205, 206, 209, 210, 211, 212, 213, 215, 219, 236, 240, 244, 265, 269, 273, 285, 286, 288, 289, 290, 291, 292, 293, 295, 296, 297, 299, 300, 301, 302, 304, 305, 307, 326, 331, 332, 333, 337, 339, 349, 351, 370, 403,

Sherman, (*Con.*).
421; campaign in Georgia, 285, 294; first acquaintance with Grant, 15; Grant's correspondence with, when appointed Lieutenant-General, 224, 226; march from Savannah north, 300, 303; opposes Grant's plans at Vicksburg, 163; testimony to Grant's greatness, 2; quoted, 303, 352
Siam, 424, 430, 431
Sigel, Franz, 216, 241
Signal codes, deciphered by enemy, 174
Simpson, Hannah, Grant's mother, 6, 7
Slocum, H. W., 292
Smith, C. F., 91, 95, 99, 100, 106, 111, 113, 114, 115, 116, 119, 120, 121, 123
Smith, Gustavus W., 55
Smith, Kirby, 305, 334
Smith, William F., 55, 202, 203, 269, 274
Smithfield, N. C., 331
Smithland, Ky., 87
Snake Creek Gap, Ga., 123, 130, 286
Soldiers, average age of, 1
Soldiers, number in Civil War, 1
Soldiers' opinion of Grant, 247, 248, 257, 258
South Carolina, 301, 343
South, condition of, after the war, 344, 348, 349, 350, 352, 354
South Side Railroad, Va., 277, 282, 306
Spain and Brazil, 385
Spain, difficulties with, 382-4
Staff- and general officers in Mexican War obtain knowledge of topography from Grant, 43
Stanton, E. M., 197, 248, 299, 332, 354, 355, 356, 357, 363
Stephens, Alex. H., quoted, 298, 299

Stevens, Thaddeus, 344
Stewart, A. T., 369
Stone, Charles P., 55
Stoneman, George, 290, 305
Strength of Armies, 157, 285, 286, 291, 293, 295, 296, 301, 305, 306, 313, 326, 330, 334, 336, 339
Stuart, J. E. B., 260, 265
Sumner, Charles, 345, 375, 378, 393, 394
Supreme Court of U. S., 336
Surrender of Confederate Armies, 101, 107, 175, 319-22, 333, 334, 337
Swedenborg, Emanuel, 228
Sword presented to Grant, 216

T

Taft, Alphonso, 403
Tallahoma, Tenn., 194
Taylor, Richard, 305, 334
Taylor, Zachary, in Mexico, 27-31, 33, 34, 35, 43
Telegraphic despatches of Grant stolen by his operator, 113
Tennessee River, 80, 87, 95, 97, 98, 99, 102, 118, 119, 120, 130, 148, 194, 195, 196, 198, 200, 201, 202, 203, 204, 205, 208, 209, 215, 293, 295
Tennessee, State of, 85, 94, 97, 122, 124, 143, 147, 148, 190, 191, 214, 233, 305, 306, 343
Tenure of office acts, 354, 371, 372
Terrain in Virginia, peculiar character of, 242-244
Territorial extension, Grant's opinion of, 417
Territory held by Confederacy, 330
Terry, Alfred H., 285; 303
Texas, 190, 333, 334, 339, 350, 365; annexation of, 27
Thirty Years' War, 228
Thomas, George H., 99, 134, 145, 147, 148, 196, 197, 198, 199, 204, 206, 207, 208, 209

Thomas, George H., (*Con.*).
210, 211, 212, 213, 217, 219, 286, 288, 293, 295, 296, 305
Thomas, Lorenzo, 185, 186
Thompson, Jeff., 81, 91, 334
Thornton, Sir Edward, 390, 391
Tilden, Samuel J., 421
Tilghman, Lloyd, 101
T. I. O. Society, 22
Tod, Judge George, 6
Torbert, A. T., 268
Transports, army, run by Vicksburg batteries, 159, 160, 161
Treasury Department, army difficulties with, 184
Treasury methods, improvement in under Grant, 408
Treaty of Washington, 386-94
Trescot, Wm. Henry, 440
Tunnel Hill, Ga., 201
Tupelo, Miss., 146, 147
Tuscumbia, Ala., 143; River, 146
Tyner, James W., 403

U

Ulysses, Grant's prototype, 7
Universal Postal Union, 417

V

Vance, John B., 399
Vanderbilt, Wm. H., 443, 444, 446
Van Dorn, Earl, 150, 153
Venable, Charles S., quoted, 318
Veteran Reserves, 273
Veterans, admirable conduct of, 336-7; feeling toward Spain, 383; outrages upon, after war, 350
Victoria, Queen, 424, 452
Vining Station, Ga., 288
Vionville, casualties at, 328
Virginia Central Railroad, 268, 272
Virginia, State of, 93, 189, 233, 236, 238, 243, 291, 305, 306, 311, 328, 329, 331, 339, 343, 365

Virginius affair, 383
Vollum, E. P., 180, 181
Volunteers, American, characteristics of, 72-78, 104, 127, 128, 131, 132, 133, 135, 137, 138, 140, 180, 200

W

Wade, Benj. F., 360
Wagner, Richard, 429
Walker, F. A., quoted, 276
Wallace, Lew, 103, 104, 106, 125, 128, 132, 133, 134, 273
Wallace, W. H. L., 122, 129
Walnut Hills, Miss., 154
War, Civil, theory on which it was conducted, 345
War Department, 181, 263, 280
War officially ended, 350
Warren, G. K., 254, 261, 275, 282, 308
Warrenton, Miss., 155, 170
Washburn, C. C., 221
Washburne, E. B., 370
Washington City, 241, 243, 244, 245, 249, 266, 280, 285, 292, 295, 299, 326, 330, 333, 336, 338, 339, 345, 348, 397, 402, 417, 449, 454; Early's attack on, 273
Washington, George, 221, 416; opinion of Ohio Valley, 4
Waterloo, Battle of, 438
Weather conditions as affecting military operations, 30, 37, 97, 101, 102, 105, 119, 122, 154
Webster, J. D., 109
Weitzel, Godfrey, 308, 311, 312
Weldon R. R., Va., 282
Wells, David A., 399
Western Atlantic R. R., 286
Westminster Abbey, Service in honor of Grant, 455
West Point, N. Y., 228, 454
Wham, Joseph W., 72
Wheeler, Joseph, 196
Whiskey frauds of 1875, 408-9
White House Landing, Va., 270, 278, 304

White, John D., Grant's schoolmaster, 9
Wilcox, Cadmus M., 33, 55, 325
Wilhelm I. of Germany, 392, 425
Williams, Geo. H., 370, 403; Seth, 322
Wilmington, N. C., 302, 303
Wilson, Henry, 400; J. H., 305, 334
Winter of 1863-4, accounts of 217; of 1864-65, 283
Wood, Thomas J., 134
Worth, Wm., 35, 39
Wounded soldiers burnt in the woods, 255, 262
Wright, H. G., 261, 273, 307, 308

Y

Yates, Richard, 68, 90
Yazoo Pass Expedition, 187
Yazoo River, 154
York River, Va., 244
Yorktown Peninsula, 238 248, 329; evacuation of, 149
Young, John Russell, 227, 424, 438
Young's Point, Miss., 155, 158

Z

Zollicoffer, Felix K., 93, 94, 99

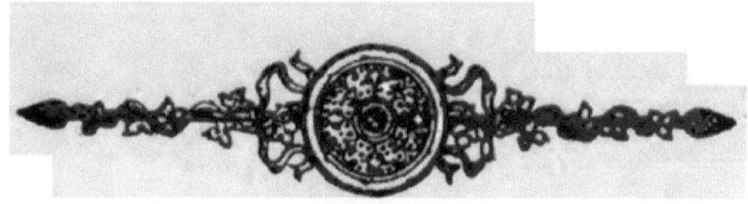

www.ingramcontent.com/pod-product-compliance
Lightning Source LLC
Chambersburg PA
CBHW051848300426
44117CB00006B/309